D0476155

The Enthusiastic
Employee

The Enthusiastic Employee

How Companies Profit by Giving Workers What They Want

Second Edition

David Sirota
Douglas A. Klein

Vice President, Publisher: Tim Moore
Associate Publisher and Director of Marketing: Amy Neidlinger
Development Editor: Russ Hall
Operations Specialist: Jodi Kemper
Marketing Manager: Megan Graue
Cover Designer: Alan Clements
Managing Editor: Kristy Hart
Project Editor: Andy Beaster
Copy Editor: Karen Gill
Proofreader: Sarah Kearns
Indexer: Lisa Stumpf
Compositor: Gloria Schurick
Manufacturing Buyer: Dan Uhrig

ISBN-10: 0-13-324902-6
ISBN-13: 978-0-13-324902-6

Pearson Education LTD.
Pearson Education Australia PTY, Limited.
Pearson Education Singapore, Pte. Ltd.
Pearson Education Asia, Ltd.
Pearson Education Canada, Ltd.
Pearson Educación de Mexico, S.A. de C.V.
Pearson Education—Japan
Pearson Education Malaysia, Pte. Ltd.

Library of Congress Control Number: 2013939241

This work is dedicated to our families:
Our wives: Barbara and Ilene
And our children: Rima and Abigail,
Brandon and Samantha

Our enthusiasm at its source.

Contents

Acknowledgments

As the saying goes, "it takes a village" ...to do any number of things. Well, in our case, it took the efforts of an entire company over many years to make this work possible. We refer, of course, to our colleagues, past and present, at Sirota Consulting, LLC. Over the years, the firm has been fortunate to have some of the best minds in the field of industrial and organizational psychology using attitude research methods to study human behavior in the workplace and assist in the improvement of organization effectiveness. As with the first edition, we had the support of a number of our colleagues.

In particular, this book would not have been written without the assistance of the firm's senior management, particularly the chairman and CEO, Michael Meltzer. Not only did Michael and his colleagues freely offer their own expertise, but they provided us with the full support of the company to undertake the work. Michael, who is also an attorney, was instrumental in identifying the permissions needed for the quotations used in this second edition and was supported in this by Pam Luciano and Melissa Maia. Others at Sirota played even more substantive roles. Michele Corman helped us select representative employee comments to include in the book from the nearly 200,000 "write-ins" collected during the past recession. Also, with Scott Gebhardt and Jason Guttaduria, Michele patiently reviewed our 170 citations for accuracy and completeness. Tiffany Ivory reviewed and then updated all the tables and commentary that referenced Sirota's normative database of employee attitudes. Dave Reeves offered his research and statistical skills to help us correlate company morale levels with stock market performance; those results are now part of the strong evidence we present regarding the business-relevance of an enthusiastic workforce. These were all tremendous undertakings, and we are grateful for their help.

Our work—this and the original edition—benefited greatly from the participation of many accomplished senior executives. In the course of writing this book, these leaders allowed us to test our observations and conclusions against their real-life experiences and, simply, to learn from them. They include Ed Finn (Barron's), Mary Dillon (U.S. Cellular), Jeff Elliott (Costco), John Goff (Crescent), Charles R. Larson (Admiral, U.S. Navy (Ret.)), Morton Meyerson (2M Companies), Bill Taylor (formerly of Mercedes), Tripp Welch (Mayo Clinic), Ewout Durieux (Shell Oil), and Tom Rauzi (Dell).

We also wish to express our appreciation to our publishers and the team that worked so hard to bring *The Enthusiastic Employee* to fruition, especially Russ Hall, our development editor, who supported the project early on and always provided reliable guidance and just the right dose of urgency and common sense; Karen Gill, who labored over the copy and patiently corrected our syntax and hyphens, and Andy Beaster.

On a more personal level, we would like to thank our wives, Barbara and Ilene, and our children for putting up with us for the months it took to get this second edition written. We are most appreciative for their patience and their help.

Finally, we express our gratitude for the insights and inspiration that Louis Mischkind, one of the co-authors of the first edition, provided to us over the years. Lou passed away in 2007, and we miss him greatly.

About the Authors

David Sirota has two abiding professional interests: organization behavior and survey research. Both of these interests took hold at the University of Michigan, where he received his doctorate, and where he worked at that university's Institute for Social Research, a leading center for applying survey methods to the study of organizations. Upon receiving his doctorate, David was recruited by International Business Machines (IBM) to help initiate behavioral science research there. He stayed at IBM for 12 years in a variety of research and executive positions, leaving in 1972 to set up his own firm, Sirota Consulting, now simply Sirota. The firm specializes in the diagnosis and improvement of the relationships of organizations with all of their key constituencies: employees, customers, suppliers, investors, and communities. In 1996, David became chairman emeritus of the firm, after completing his own succession plan with key employees. He continues to consult with selected clients, primarily on matters of leadership, and collaboration and conflict within and between organizations.

Parallel to his career as a consultant, David has had an academic career, having taught at the School of Industrial and Labor Relations of Cornell University, the School of Industrial Administration of Yale University, the Sloan School of the Massachusetts Institute of Technology, and the Wharton School of the University of Pennsylvania.

David is married with two children and lives in New York City.

Douglas Klein is, likewise, steeped in survey research, with 25 years of experience in the field. Prior to joining Sirota, he worked for AT&T, building leadership assessment centers and conducting employee research, and then at Time Warner, where he conducted employee and customer satisfaction research. Doug brought his insights into employee and customer research to Sirota and helped launch its "linkage" efforts, statistically relating employee attitudes, customer attitudes, and "hard" business metrics. He managed the normative database for the firm for more than a decade (on which so much in the book's first and second editions is based) and is seen by many as a real historian of employee attitudes. His current role as the firm's chief leadership advisor allows him to apply his strong analytical skills and decades of client experience to issues of organizational values and culture and to the day-to-day problems faced by senior executives in the management of their companies.

Doug is an active advisor, speaker, and writer. (See his blog on www.sirota.com and search for the many articles he has authored or to which he has contributed.) He holds a master's degree in industrial and organizational psychology from New York University.

Doug lives in Merrick, New York, with his wife Ilene and their two children.

About the Second Edition

The Enthusiastic Employee, published in 2005, was an action-oriented book about people at work: their goals, the way they were managed or mismanaged, and their resulting performance. Our objectives, simply stated, were to help companies obtain more from workers and workers more from their companies. Those are not contradictory objectives, because our basic premise is that, under the right kind of leadership, the more one side gains, the more the other side gains. The book was heavy on evidence (using extensive employee survey data) and, based on that, laid out two basic concepts: the "Three-Factor Theory" of human motivation at work, and the "Partnership" company culture that is based on the Three-Factor Theory and that, by far, brings out the best in people as they respond with enthusiasm about what they do and the company they do it for.

What's new about this second edition? Basically, two things. First, a lot has happened since the original book was published, most strikingly the Great Recession. In this second edition, we bring our updated survey data, collected since 2004, to bear on understanding these events and their impacts. Second, we received many inquiries asking for clarification and elaboration of key points, such as the desire for much greater detail on real-life companies with partnership cultures. We now provide these. We also received a few sharp challenges (our debunking of "new generations" theory was a particular target), and we address these squarely and with a lot of additional empirical evidence.

More specifically:

- **More Extensive and More Recent Data.** A hallmark of the first edition of *The Enthusiastic Employee* was the massive amount of data and data analysis on which our conclusions were based. The data were collected from survey questionnaires, administered to 2.5 million employees in 237 companies over a period of 10 years (1994 to 2003), that were correlated with "hard" performance measures. They were supplemented by numerous examples from the real world that added meaning to the raw numbers.

Well, for this revised edition, the database has become even more massive! It has grown since 2003 to include an additional 8.6 million employees in 412 companies, providing us with opportunities to test our conclusions on data that are both more recent and more extensive. The reader will learn from our data (the "norms") exactly how workers feel *today* about a wide variety of work-related issues, such as pay, benefits, and bosses, and how these attitudes relate to company performance.

Among the analyses that we updated is the one that showed a strong relationship between employee morale in a company and its stock market performance. We wanted to know whether this held up, especially through the tremendous turbulence in the market over the decade. The answer: it did, in spades!

- **The Great Recession.** The major economic event since the publication of our book, has, of course, been the Great Recession. Our surveys have continued throughout that time; therefore, we were able to trace the impact of the recession on the employees we surveyed. The results, in our new Chapter 5, may surprise you; they surprised us. Included in our analysis is the interplay between workers' attitudes toward job security, wages, and benefits as economic conditions change.

- **Organizational Culture.** Based on our research, the first edition of this book laid out the case for an organizational culture substantially different from that normally seen in American industry. It is a culture of "partnership"—partnership of a company with its employees and, indeed, with all its stakeholders. These partnership companies, we show, reap enormous long-term business benefits.

And, the evidence strongly suggests that they reap these benefits in good times and bad. A major theme throughout the book is that a culture of mutual obligations grounded in excellence, mutual trust and respect, openness, and shared rewards and sacrifices is the culture of choice for all conditions.

We were asked for more, and more detailed, examples of genuine partnership cultures. Among the ones we provide in this new edition is that of Mayo Clinic, an organization that has achieved the unusual distinction of providing world-renowned quality care at relatively low cost. We have studied Mayo extensively since 2005, and we include a description of its inspiring culture, the sources of that culture, and how it has been sustained for more than a century. Costco, also a high-performer and exemplar of partnership (and frequently criticized by Wall Street for its generous employee wages and benefits), is among the other companies that receive more extensive treatment in this new edition.

Also of interest to the reader will be those companies—such as Johnson & Johnson, Toyota, and Goldman Sachs—whose partnership cultures we and others have extolled but have since appeared to stray in serious ways from the path that brought them both admiration and profits. There is as much to be learned from the experience of these unfortunate examples as from those companies who have moved in a positive direction or, like Mayo and Costco, have stayed the course from the beginning.

- **Corporate Social Responsibility.** Quite a few of the communications from readers concerned "Corporate Social Responsibility" which, in the way we define and discuss it, is integral to a partnership culture. We were asked about the relationship between being a responsible corporate citizen—which means a lot more than contributing to local charities and not being a criminal—and business success. We strive to place corporate citizenship in a *business* context, showing how it is closely linked to *long-term* business success.

Indeed, in this new book we clarify that we have nothing much to say that will be of interest to those whose primary objective is quick profits. We don't make moral judgments about that goal; it is just that this book is about helping leaders and managers build organizations with *enduring* value.

- **Leadership.** Another set of questions from our readers was about leadership. We were just not as clear or comprehensive in the first edition as we should have been, either about leadership itself—what research has taught us about the characteristics of great leaders—or the implications of a partnership culture for leadership. Readers wanted to know, for example, whether a partnership culture makes obsolete the need for strong and decisive leaders. Our answer: absolutely not, and we discuss these and other apparent contradictions in the realm of "soft" versus "hard" management in our new chapter on leadership.

- **Telecommuting.** As this second edition was being written, Marissa Mayer, the newly installed CEO of Yahoo, had an edict issued requiring all Yahoo employees to work at the office rather than from home. This ban on "telecommuting" has been highly controversial and, armed with research evidence, we jump head-first into the fray, providing our conclusions as to the wisdom of the step Ms. Mayer took and recommending a course of action for Yahoo and for all organizations contemplating telecommuting.

- **Merit Pay for Teachers.** Over the past few years, there has been great public controversy and conflict about merit pay for teachers. Because we say quite a bit in both editions about merit pay in companies, we wanted to weigh in with our views of its application to America's schools. Our research forces us to conclude that it is, basically, a bad idea, and we have a different recommendation to make—one that will reward for performance without the harmful consequences of traditional merit pay.

- **Generational Differences.** We continue to read about big differences between generations (Gen Xers, Gen Yers, Millennials). We briefly discussed in the first edition our view of these differences and said, in effect, that it was largely nonsense. In response, we received vociferous objections, accompanied by numerous anecdotes "proving" that these differences both exist and are important. They don't and are not. We bring to bear in this revised edition more evidence—systematic evidence—that, we hope, completes the debunking of this harmful myth.

- **Women and Minorities.** A serious oversight in the original volume was our inattention to the situation of women and minorities in the workplace. While a full exposition of this matter awaits our future publications, we have mined our survey data to determine the satisfaction levels and viewpoints of women and minorities in today's corporations.

Our New Website

The advances of technology continue to be rapid, and we are poised to take greater advantage of them with this revised edition. A considerable portion of our data will be placed on a new website, and we plan to update it regularly both with new data and analyses and with commentary on workforce issues of the day. The website will also allow for interaction between readers and us. Our new website address is http://www.sirota.com/enthusiastic-employee.

Introduction

The impact shook everything for blocks. Fire, charged by thousands of gallons of jet fuel, sucked so much oxygen out of the air around the impact zone that windows in nearby buildings blew out as the towers of the World Trade Center began to wither and then collapse. On the 32nd floor of the World Financial Center, the offices of *Barron's Magazine* shook. Computers, office supplies, and equipment flew out the windows. Stunned workers held on for dear life. Then, they carefully made their way out of the building to safety. The editorial and business offices of *Barron's Magazine* had been almost instantaneously decimated. The damage was so great that it took more than a year to refurbish the offices.

Yet, on September 11, 2001, as people fled the building, *Barron's* employees had already turned their attention to the task of publishing the magazine on time. Months later, Ed Finn, *Barron's* Managing Editor recalled that the attack had not prevented his employees from publishing a full edition of the magazine three days after their offices were destroyed. In fact, the idea of not publishing never even came up; the only question any employee asked was how the team would accomplish it. None of us would want to face the challenges that *Barron's*—and many, many others—faced that day, but we can all appreciate what the *Barron's* employees did. We can all agree that most organizations would love to have employees who display that level of enthusiasm for their jobs, their companies, and their colleagues.

This is a book about enthusiastic workers.

Managers at all levels often spend an inordinate amount of time with "difficult" individual employees—employees who are angry, uncooperative, or perhaps neurotically demanding of attention. The task of dealing with such behavior problems is widely considered a significant human-resources cost. But the reality is even worse, because the bigger problem is the vast number of workers who are not openly troublesome, but who have become largely indifferent to the organization and its purposes. This is the greater problem because the troublemakers can be identified and dealt with; the "walking indifferent," however, are silent killers. They have learned to expect not too much and to give not too much. Yet, these workers are normal people with reasonable human wants. Somehow, their human needs are only marginally satisfied, if at all, by the companies for which they work. In return, they give to the companies a mere fraction of what they are capable of contributing. The economic cost of this underutilization to the affected businesses is enormous.

How does a company tackle this problem? One approach is to more closely supervise employees, pressuring them to do more. On a more positive note, other managers treat their workers to a procession of "motivational" speakers, rah-rah events, and programs. Neither approach will do much good—in fact, the former will likely exacerbate the problem. We need to get to the root of the matter—the source of employee indifference—and we need to address it. The real challenge is to turn indifferent workers into enthusiastic workers. The solution might surprise you.

First, we must understand what workers want. Then, we must give it to them!

This may sound absurd to some, a sure road to insolvency. On the contrary, it is a powerful path to business success. Why do we say this?

1. Many years of research have established that, surprisingly, little real conflict exists between the goals of the overwhelming majority of workers and those of their employers.

It is a common, but harmful, misconception that people and their organizations are in a natural state of conflict. This book starts by setting the record straight, examining the source of this confusion, and providing a fresh start to understanding what workers really want. We show that the key question is not how to motivate employees, but how to sustain—and prevent management from destroying—the motivation that the great majority of people naturally bring to their jobs.

2. Workers have basic human needs that management can and should work to address. Creating an environment in which these needs are met results not just in satisfied employees, but in enthusiastic employees. It is grossly inaccurate to think of these needs as insatiable, characterized by greed and self-indulgence. That's a traditional view of people at work: wanting to do as little work as possible for as much money as possible, and always complaining. We have a different view that we summarize in our Three Factor Theory of worker motivation.

3. Employee enthusiasm—a state of high employee morale that derives from satisfying the three key needs of workers—results in enormous competitive advantages for those companies with the strength of leadership to manage for real long-term results.

4. Basic to satisfying worker needs are specific policies and practices that, when taken as a whole, constitute a culture of "partnership," demonstrably the most powerful culture for elevated and enduring employee performance.

Our proof of these propositions lies in our over 40 years of survey research into the effect of employee perceptions and attitudes on organizational effectiveness. We explore what the data show, illustrating the results with verbatim comments from workers and many company examples, and we connect the data to business outcomes.

Asking the Questions

How do we claim to know what workers want? It is not by untested hypothesis, imagination, or philosophy. It is not by thinking "out of the box" as the vogue term goes, or by generalizing based on a series of anecdotes. The only real way to learn what's on workers' minds is to *ask them*! This involves asking simple and direct questions using survey methods that ensure that the results are representative and valid.

Real data are the best antidote against jumping to conclusions based only on personal biases, the latest fad, or anecdotes. By using real data, we know what workers want, why they want it, and what it means.

We have been asking workers questions for more than 40 years at Sirota, having collected since 1972 over 13.6 *million* survey responses from employees in over 840 companies around the world. The questions have been asked about various specific topics or dimensions of attitudes. Over the course of time, and based on statistical analyses, we organized those dimensions into a model that aligns employee attitudes with bottom-line business outcomes.

Asking the Right Questions

Although it is certainly a positive thing that we have collected extensive attitudinal data by actually asking workers about their opinions, we imagine that a few readers are now wondering how we know which questions to ask. The answer to that requires a little background.

In 1972, David Sirota organized a small business to pursue his mission of improving organization performance through the systematic assessment and analysis of the attitudes of all key corporate constituencies: employees, customers, communities, suppliers, investors, and the public at large. From 1959 through 1972, David was a director of Behavioral Science Research and Application for IBM. There, his activities included the establishment of IBM's worldwide employee-attitude survey program.

David has a broad industrial and academic background. With a doctorate from the University of Michigan, he was a study director at that University's Institute of Social Research. He has taught at the School of Industrial and Labor Relations of Cornell University, at Yale University, the Sloan School of Management of the Massachusetts Institute of Technology, and as associate professor of management at the Wharton School of the University of Pennsylvania. He is now Chairman Emeritus of Sirota.

Co-author Douglas Klein is, likewise, steeped in survey research, with 25 years of experience in the field. Prior to joining Sirota, he worked for AT&T and Time Warner where he conducted employee and customer satisfaction research. Doug brought his insights into employee and customer research to Sirota and helped launch its "linkage" efforts: statistically relating employee attitudes, customer attitudes, and "hard" business metrics. He has been a vital part of the firm's expansion into surveys focused on customers, organizational culture and values, and leadership. His current role as the firm's Chief Leadership Advisor allows him to apply his strong analytical skills and experience to the day-to-day problems faced by senior executives in the management of their companies. Doug holds a master's degree in industrial and organizational psychology from New York University.

As David's and his firm's reputations grew, both for superior research and for an ability to collect meaningful data that could be used for real business improvement, the small business expanded into an internationally known and respected consultancy. Sirota is now one of the larger independent privately owned companies in the United States that specializes in organizational survey research. Sirota consultants have conducted a variety of surveys for hundreds of organizations around the world. The company's mission remains much the same as it was when David first started it: to use survey data to help organizations build strong, productive relationships with all of its key constituencies.

Our experience, although extensive, is not the only basis for the statement that we know which questions to ask. The research done by Sirota consultants over the years has followed a widely accepted protocol for attitudinal research: individual interviews, focus groups, and reliability and validation testing. The topics we cover in our surveys emerge from our interviews, focus groups, and post-survey analyses and discussions, and from the work of other researchers. Our basic criterion is to ask questions that truly *count* for worker morale and organization performance. You can find more detailed information on our survey methodology in Chapter 2, "Employee Enthusiasm and Business Success," and in two appendices on our website at www.sirota.com/enthusiastic-employee: Appendix A, "Survey Administration and Population Composition," and Appendix B, "Reliability and Validity of the Data."

Our years of research, experience, and testing have resulted in an enormous pool of responses from which the data for this book have been drawn.

Questions Result in Data

What are our survey data made of? Regarding the kinds of questions we ask, our approach, as we said, is to ask simple and direct questions. You will see that we "psychologize" neither in the interpretation of the answers to our surveys nor in the way we ask our questions. If we want to know how employees feel about their pay, we ask them how they feel about their pay. We don't use "projective" techniques (such as asking them how they feel *others* would rate their pay) on the assumption that they would be hesitant to tell us how they feel but would "project" their views onto others. Although there is some debate among survey researchers about the use of direct versus indirect techniques, the evidence is clear: when administered correctly, such as with guarantees of confidentiality, almost all employees answer direct questions honestly. Furthermore, there is no confusion when the responses to such questions are reported to management: when employees say that they are happy or unhappy with their pay, that's exactly what they mean. You can find a detailed discussion of this matter and examples of the numerous reliability and validity tests we have applied to our data methods in Appendix B on our website at www.sirota.com/enthusiastic-employee.

How about the kinds of people we survey? This is an important question because we need to know just how representative and recent our evidence is. First, the analyses in this book are based on updated employee survey data: they were collected from 2004 to 2012, while the data in the first edition of the book were collected from 1994 to 2003. Second, although the data come from many organizations and are representative of them, we do not claim that they are representative of all workers everywhere over that period. That would be an over-generalization. Yes, a wide variety of industries is represented, but our evidence comes predominantly from the private sector, with just 5 percent of the organizations surveyed being from the government and not-for-profit sectors. Because survey efforts of this type are, for various reasons, not typically done in small organizations, large corporations predominate in our sample. Many participating companies are multinational corporations; most are headquartered in North America, and 75 percent of the employees surveyed work in the United States or Canada. The majority of the others work in Europe. See Appendix A on the website for further details on the composition of the surveyed populations.

Our data, obviously, come only from organizations that asked us to survey their employees. To the casual reader, it might seem that this fact might make the participating organizations unrepresentative because the sample would be made up of companies that are probably more interested in employee satisfaction than the average company. Although that's theoretically true, the reality is that the overwhelming majority of large organizations in all sectors have conducted employee surveys, so this is not significant.

Another issue concerns the types of organizations that would commission this particular firm, Sirota, to conduct the survey. To help ensure survey utilization, Sirota employs a rather intensive data-feed-back and action-planning process that requires more management time than is true of the typical employee poll. Agreeing to this process might mean that management is more serious about morale than is the average company and, therefore, possibly has higher morale than elsewhere. We have collected and reviewed the data from many surveys performed by others—both external and internal consultants—and we find a great similarity between their results and ours. This, therefore, is not an important problem, either. Appendix D on the website contains a comparison of our data with those from research done by others.

The main issue, then, is the skewed nature of our sample with respect to organization size and geography. However, while the company's clients as a whole may not be perfectly representative of the universe of all organizations, there still is considerable diversity among them: in size, type of industry, types of occupations, average ages of the workforce, and the like. We show in this book that the basic patterns of results we describe hold across all these differences. In statistical terms, therefore, having a sample more representative of all organizations—for example, with more small companies—would likely have little impact on our results and conclusions.

We can bring together the results from surveys of many different organizations because, although the surveys are geared toward the needs and conditions of individual clients, a core set of questions is appropriate and is asked just about everywhere. The core questions permit a broad, reliable depiction of worker attitudes across many varied organizations, and an analysis of those attitudes determines their causes and their business consequences. These data and analyses—amply supplemented by the systematic studies and thoughtful observations of others—form the research basis of this book. The data are also liberally supplemented throughout by "qualitative" and "anecdotal" information. The quantitative information and analyses—the "numbers"—provide *scientific rigor*; the qualitative information helps to give *meaning* to the numbers. One source of qualitative information is the open-ended questions in our surveys to which employees are asked to respond in their own words (in contrast to a fixed-response question). When, say, 73 percent of employees in a company respond negatively to a fixed-response question about their ability to get their jobs done, the answer to an open-ended question can tell us a lot about why they feel that way. For example, in answer to the open-ended question, "What do you like least about working here?" an employee in that company wrote:

> *The biggest problem here is the maze of bureaucracy and red tape. I frequently see long e-mail chains that show very clearly how often people have spent days, if not weeks, just trying to track down the proper person or department to contact for assistance or approval. Why do we need so many approval levels? I often feel this company cannot get out of its own way, not unlike the ill-fated Titanic.*

Many similar comments about "bureaucracy" appeared in that company's survey.

Our other major sources of qualitative information are:

- Focus groups, conducted before just about every survey with small groups of randomly selected employees from throughout the organization. We use these free-wheeling discussions to help determine the unique issues that need to be addressed in that organization's questionnaire and to help in the interpretation of the quantitative data that the questionnaire generates.

- In-depth interviews and case studies from clearly identified high-morale, high-performing client organizations to give greater insight into what those managements do. These are both total organizations and segments of them (such as *Barron's* Magazine, which is a division of Dow Jones).

- Our own informal observations and discussions over the many years we have been doing this work. For example, we have observed how managers struggle with a variety of pay-for-performance plans, seeking the one that will best reward and most motivate employees (or, at least, will result in the least dissatisfaction). As we move from company to company, we observe which plans seem to work best and which least well, and we share these observations with the reader. When sound research on these issues is available, we bring it to bear on our conclusions.

Therefore, the data in this book consist of a *combination* of quantitative and qualitative data.[1] Although disputes have raged in the social sciences between proponents of the two kinds of information, *both* are important; neither stands well by itself. One provides statistical reliability and proof, and the other provides meaning—it brings the dry statistics to life and can therefore also provide direction for dealing with the issues uncovered by the survey. Most of the underlying framework for our book, however, comes from the quantitative data—the percentages of employees that report satisfaction or dissatisfaction on our surveys and the way those numbers relate statistically to each other and to management practices and measures of performance. As will be seen in this book, our results, as well as the survey findings of others, repeat themselves in similar basic patterns in study after study. This is the great benefit of quantitative research: its results can be testedthrough replication using scientific methods. Qualitative information—such as anecdotes—doesn't have that power: one can "prove" or "disprove" anything through a selected anecdote or write-in comment. The power in qualitative information lies in its giving depth to the statistics.[2]

In conclusion, the Sirota firm has been studying the attitudes of people at work—and the business consequences of those attitudes—for more than three decades. Since 2004 alone, we have surveyed approximately 8.6 million employees in 412 private, public, and not-for-profit client organizations in over 160 countries. Sirota's database of responses is extensive and, supplemented by our sources of rich qualitative data, provides insight into what workers want and why smart managers give it to them.

After the Honeymoon

It is a well-known phenomenon that the overwhelming majority of people begin a new job with a sense of enthusiasm. As they enter a job, people are naturally excited about their work and their organizations, eager to be part of a productive team of co-workers, and reasonable in how they expect to be treated. This is true for about 95 percent of any worker population; the other 5 percent—largely those who might be described as "allergic" to work—should never have been hired and, while at work, can be managed only with continuing close supervision and credible threats of dismissal. A major problem is that, in many organizations, management generalizes the behavior of this small group to just about every worker, which makes the work environment oppressive for all and suppresses the natural enthusiasm that most people bring to their jobs.

For that reason and others, usually starting about six months after being hired, something happens to the great masses of employees who began work enthusiastically. We find declines in morale in 9 out of 10 companies after the "honeymoon" period. It is not just that the novelty wears off; the decline—and its deleterious impact on performance—is a consequence of management practice. Indeed, one can say that, often, it is *management* that kills or dampens enthusiasm!

Yet, we find that in about 14 percent of organizations, worker enthusiasm does not materially diminish. What accounts for this difference? And, does the difference affect business success? These are central questions that this book explores and answers.

A Quick Look at "Old-Fashioned" Theories

Some people might see this book as having an old-fashioned point of view because our thinking flies in the face of the currently vogue opinion that "loyalty is dead." The "loyalty is dead" advocates suggest that new economic conditions have made untenable the previous paternalistic pattern of lifetime careers in "caring" companies. In short, the new theorists argue that it's every person for himself in a highly competitive, often brutal, new environment where the employment relationship becomes no more than a business transaction.

We argue that loyalty between workers and management is, indeed, dead if it derives from the old parent-child model of paternalistic organizations. That's not what we talk about when we argue for satisfying workers' wants. We think of most workers as mature and independent adults, not children.

The paternalism of the past does not have to be replaced with a value-neutral transactional system where, in essence, employees "are owed nothing but a paycheck" and are removed from the payroll as soon as they are no longer needed. (In fact, if at all possible, they are not put on the payroll and are instead employed as "independent contractors.")

The gains from a transactional relationship are usually temporary, in part because such organizations receive from most of their workers little beyond what is required and monitored. For example, can a company expect its employees to treat customers with individual care and concern—the care and concern that create loyal customers—when the employees themselves are treated as invisible, interchangeable, and expendable parts? A transactional relationship is therefore often a prescription for short-term success (in terms of cost reduction) and long-term mediocrity.

We therefore maintain that neither a paternalistic nor a transactional relationship is the most effective way to achieve truly high levels of long-term organization performance. The policies and practices we describe in this book represent, in their sum, a third alternative, which we call *partnership*. (We will describe as well a fourth type of culture—adversarial—in which the workers are treated neither as children, transactions, nor partners, but as *enemies*. Those employees display the lowest—truly low—morale.)

The loyalty in a partnership relationship is not the kind that parents and children have toward each other, but rather the bonds that develop among adults *working collaboratively toward common, long-term goals and having a genuine concern for each other's interests and needs*. As we use the term, partnership is a business relationship *plus*—the plus being the human dimension, the trust and goodwill that allows people to perform above and beyond what is required by monetary calculations, formal contracts, and very short-term interests. Partnership has not been used often to describe the actual or even ideal employee-management relationship, but, in our view, it most accurately captures the spirit of the policies and practices we find repeatedly in enthusiastic, high-performing organizations.

This book is old-fashioned in other ways as well. For one, there is a strong tendency for modern authors in our field—the field of organization psychology—to focus almost exclusively on what they term higher-order employee needs, such as "self-actualization." There is less written about the fact that people also work for a living! Ignoring or downplaying matters such as pay, benefits, and job security is an error of monumental proportions. As we show in this book, management can do little to maintain high employee morale if workers harbor a fundamental sense of unfairness as to how they are treated on those basic issues.

A related error is made by "new economy" theorists who disparage what they consider characteristics of "old economy" companies and older workers, such as the need for work direction and structure. At the extreme, these theorists seem to advocate extraordinarily fluid organizations, almost chaos, as what today's workers want and what organizations need to survive in a rapidly changing business environment. Nonsense! Many classical dictums about leadership, direction, and structure are as applicable today as they were before the "information age." We wonder how much of the implosion of companies in the hi-tech sector at the start of the century was a consequence of their inattention to the basics (the "blocking and tackling") of management. And we will show that workers themselves have not changed that much. Although frustrated by micromanagement, they certainly don't want an absence of management, no matter what their industry or their age.

When, therefore, we speak of a partnership culture, we are not advocating "laissez-faire"—"do-whatever-you-want"—management with minimal performance goals and standards. Quite the contrary: the partnership organizations we have studied and cite in this book have clear, tough goals and standards and outstanding performance results. Take Mayo Clinic as an example, which is world-renowned for its performance and whose culture we describe in some detail in Chapter 12, "The Culture of Partnership." Nobody would accuse Mayo of having low performance standards, but among the ways it achieves excellence of care is by treating as genuine *partners* those who actually provide the care: its employees, at all levels and in all occupations. The enthusiasm of those Mayo employees for their work and for the institution is, as we shall demonstrate, exemplary.

Solid Theory, Research, and Management Practice to Which We Are in Debt

We find ourselves in sharp disagreement with those in our field whose views and pet nostrums are supported neither by research evidence nor business results, yet there has been a great deal of substantial and illuminating research that, while generating less publicity, has had a significant and steady impact on management practice and has been immeasurably important to our own work and to this book. We are indebted to the seminal work of five giants of our field: Douglas McGregor (his "Theory X—Theory Y" paradigm), David McClelland (the needs for "achievement" and "affiliation"), Abraham Maslow (the "hierarchy of needs"), Elton Mayo (the importance of social relationships at work), and Rensis Likert (management systems and styles).[3] A good deal of what we ask in our surveys is strongly influenced by the concepts of these five, as are our interpretations. For example, our repeated assertion of the desire of most workers to do their work and do it well is a direct descendent of McGregor's Theory X—Theory Y.

We are also greatly indebted to a number of contemporary researchers, and we reference their relevant studies throughout the book. Among the more important for us have been Jeffrey Pfeffer, Edward Lawler, James Collins and Jerry Poras, Fredrick Reichheld, and Wayne Cascio. Their work is distinguished by solid research and thoughtful interpretation. Although they cover somewhat different areas than we do, there is, where we overlap, considerable congruence between their findings and conclusions and ours.

How This Book Is Organized

This book's basic organization is straightforward. Chapters 1 and 2 discuss in detail employee enthusiasm and its consequences for performance. They also contain a description of, and evidence for, the Three Factor Theory, which is the three key needs of employees whose satisfaction is the basis for an enthusiastic workforce. Chapters

3 and 4 and Chapters 6 through 11 break the Three Factor Theory into specific practices that organizations can deploy to maintain employee enthusiasm. Understanding and applying these specific practices within an organization results in marked improvements in employee commitment and performance and in long-term business success. In Chapter 5, we examine the impact on employee goals and attitudes of the Great Recession. Chapter 12 provides a wrap-up, where we show how the various policies and practices add up to a "partnership" culture. That chapter includes an in-depth description of the internal culture of Mayo Clinic. Chapter 13 is a new chapter on leadership and the partnership culture; it includes a discussion of the basic attributes that research has taught us are universally vital for effective leadership. Finally, Chapter 14 provides practical guidance for achieving genuine cultural change, covering both the basic principles of change and specific recommended steps.

Appendices A through D on our website, www.sirota.com/enthusiastic-employee, describe our research methods and provide additional data and statistical analyses. Appendix E contains a Readiness Questionnaire to assist with cultural change.

The conclusions and recommendations throughout this book are at both the broad cultural and the policy level for senior management and for individual managers at all levels working day-to-day to achieve the highest possible performance from their own employees. Although at times it might appear so to the reader, our recommendations are not Utopian. Even the exemplars of partnership culture that we cite throughout the book are composed of human beings with all their frailties. Central to the philosophy of this book is that we do not seek to remake or perfect people (or even, as is commonly supposed, to "motivate" them). Frankly, we don't know how to do that. Rather, we seek to create and sustain an organization in which the good instincts that people already have can emerge and become dominant, to the benefit of their organizations and those whom the organizations serve.

Part I

Worker Motivation, Morale, and Performance

1

What Workers Want—The Big Picture

"Human capital will go where it is wanted, and it will stay where it is well treated. It cannot be driven; it can only be attracted."

—Walter Wriston, Former Chairman, Citicorp/Citibank

An accurate understanding of motivation in the workplace is more than an academic pursuit. The effectiveness of critical business policies depends on the extent to which our assumptions about human motivation are accurate. If they are not accurate, they either have no impact at all, or worse, they boomerang and damage the organization. Accuracy depends not only on wisdom and experience, but on *systematic research.* Research protects us from personal bias, seeing what we want to see instead of what is there. Research also protects us from the lure of fads and fashions.

The problem with many theories in this field is not that they have nothing to say, but rather that they:

- Focus on just *one* aspiration as *the central* motivator (and, therefore, the central explanation) of employee morale and performance
- Claim that most people are frustrated with the achievement of that aspiration (the "sky is falling" scenario) and that dealing with that single frustration will solve all problems
- Typically assert that what the theorist has uncovered characterizes a "new generation" of workers and is therefore novel

It is helpful to review a few of the more prevalent motivational myths and fads—those involving generational differences and those about people's attitudes toward work—before we review the results of systematic research.

Blame It on the Young

"Children today are tyrants. They contradict their parents, gobble their food, and tyrannize their teachers."

—Socrates (470–399 B.C.)

For reasons that we will soon show are misguided, popular theories of what employees want change continually, and the change is often couched in terms of "new generations" of workers whose needs and expectations differ sharply from those of their predecessors. We are told that there are important differences between the "Baby Boomers" and "Generation X." And, here come the "Millennials." It is theorized that they all need to be dealt with differently because they are all different.

These seemingly significant differences make for interesting reading, and the business media have surely accommodated us. Numerous stories have been published on generational change and its implications for management practice. Generation X, for example, is widely assumed to put maximum emphasis on individual freedom and minimum emphasis on company loyalty. A number of years ago, the author of a *Fortune* article on "GenX" advised that, "If your competitor lets employees keep a birdbath in the office, you will have no choice but to follow suit."[1] A *Time* columnist summed up the generation as one that, "...would rather hike in the Himalayas than climb a corporate ladder."[2]

These observations are seductive; managing people is a difficult and complicated job filled with many headaches, and most managers want to learn all they can about human motivation. Furthermore, the answers provided by the theories on generational change seem intuitively correct. When a certain age in life is reached, people almost inevitably begin to talk about "that new generation" in a way that means, "What's this world coming to?" The new generation is not only "not like us," but they are "not like we were at that age." This discussion has been going on forever. See the Socrates quote that opened this chapter.

The fact that young people are so often viewed with apprehension by their elders should make us think hard about the validity of assertions about genuine generational change. It may be just a matter of age, but even more important, it may be a confusion of what's apparent, such as the clothes and music preferences of young people, with what is real, such as their basic goals as they enter the workforce.

An early and dramatic example of this tendency to confuse youthful tastes with human needs in the workplace occurred in the early 1970s. As the tumultuous '60s ended, a deluge of books, television specials, and newspaper articles spotlighted a new generation of workers. These young people were (supposedly) severely discontented with work. Even worse, it was popularly suggested that the traditional sources of worker grievances (unhappiness with pay, benefits, hours, and working conditions) were no longer the primary causes of worker dissatisfaction. We were told that the very nature of the work itself drove the "new" worker to near distraction. This worker was depicted as a product of the '60s, when rebellion against "over 30" adult materialistic values appeared widespread, and freedom and self-actualization were the goals. These workers, it was claimed, would not settle for their fathers' routine and mind-numbing jobs.

The concern about workers and work at that time was perhaps best summarized in a 1973 study sponsored by the U.S. Department of Health, Education, and Welfare, titled *Work in America*. In describing the profoundly negative impact work seemed to have on so many young employees, the study's editors reported the following:

> *The discontent of trapped, dehumanized workers is creating low productivity, increasing absenteeism, high worker turnover rates, wildcat strikes, industrial sabotage, poor-quality products, and a reluctance of workers to give themselves to their tasks.*

> *Work-related problems are contributing to a decline in physical and mental health, decreased family stability and community cohesiveness, and less "balanced" political attitudes. Growing unhappiness with work is also producing increased drug abuse, alcohol addiction, aggression, and delinquency in the workplace and in the society at large.*[3]

That statement was quite an indictment, and one that the media repeated endlessly. Of course, when a single factor (in this case, "dehumanizing" work content) is presumed to be responsible for so many business, social, and personal ills, rest assured that a single cure would soon follow. In the case of the HEW report, the cure (or, more accurately, the cure-all) was seen as the magic of "job enrichment."

The Lordstown Strike and Job Enrichment "Solution"

Based on Frederick Herzberg's "motivator-hygiene" theory, job enrichment was seen as an attempt to reinvigorate work with the prospect for real achievement, thus creating genuine satisfaction and motivation. In brief, the motivator-hygiene theory states that the work itself—the challenge of doing a job from start to finish, and so on—is the true motivator of workers, while the work environment— "hygiene" factors such as pay, benefits, and human relations—cannot positively motivate workers but, when adequate, temporarily prevents them from feeling unhappy. Therefore, the key to true motivation and lasting satisfaction is job enrichment: structuring work so it provides workers with a sense of achievement and accomplishment.[4]

The motivator-hygiene theory and the job-enrichment solution were extraordinarily popular in management thinking and teaching for much of the 1970s but have since largely faded from view. That is not surprising because, for one thing, cure-all solutions for cause-all problems are seldom real. Despite its academic trappings, the hulla-baloo smacked of patent-medicine salesmanship. In fact, considering that so much of the expressed concern was about blue-collar workers on assembly lines, why had no labor unions placed demands for more meaningful work on their collective-bargaining agendas? Indeed, many labor leaders explicitly declined to join the rising chorus of voices concerned with job content.

The attention given to a 1972 workers' strike in the Lordstown, Ohio, assembly plant of General Motors reinforced the skepticism about job enrichment and its claims. This strike was initially and widely interpreted to be the result of the dehumanizing nature of assembly-line work. However, the reality of Lordstown differed almost entirely from the way the strike was generally portrayed in the media and aca-demia. In the 1960s, GM built a new factory at Lordstown that was specially designed to assemble Vega passenger cars that GM hoped would prevent foreign manufacturers from eroding GM's margins in the compact-car arena. By 1966, GM was hiring workers for the fac-tory, eventually employing about 7,000 people. This new plant, with advanced robotics, represented a $100-million investment by the company.

GM recruited younger, better-educated workers who, it was claimed, were products of the ethos of the 1960s. Many of the employ-ees even had long hair, so this was indeed a "new generation." Then, GM adopted a variety of efficiency rules designed to increase the pro-duction of the new Vega plant from 60 cars every hour (or 1 every minute) to 100 cars in the same time (or one every 39 seconds). The company did not increase the workforce or decrease the number of procedures each worker was responsible for. It just required its work-ers to increase their pace. The workers fell behind, not being able to keep up with the line's speed.

If the pace was maddening, the results were disastrous. Workers tried various self-help remedies, such as letting cars go by without the required procedure or part and "doubling up" (surreptitiously doing an additional procedure for a short period of time—usually very poorly—so that a friend could rest). Absenteeism increased, and harsher work rules were imposed that violated many traditional but unspoken shop-floor conventions.

The workers went on strike. The primary reason for the strike was the workers' view that the company was engaged in a speed-up, which is hardly a novel issue in the history of labor-management conflict. It was not a sense that the work itself had become dehumanizing, but that the company's demand for faster work was impossible to reasonably satisfy. As one writer put it, "The main principle of Lordstown technology is the speed-up as developed by Henry Ford."[5]

The Generation Gap Mythology Re-Emerges

The interpretation of workforce problems as due to new generations of workers has re-emerged in a more sophisticated form over the past two decades and blossomed into a virtual industry. Many consultants now advise managers on how to deal with new generations to obtain the most productivity from them and to assure harmonious inter-generational work relationships. Four generations are usually identified: Workers born before 1945, often termed Traditionalists; Baby Boomers, born 1946–1964; Generation Xers, born 1965–1980; and the newest members of the workforce, the Millennials, born 1981–1995.

The generations are presumed to have different characteristics. While the descriptions vary among authors, here is a pretty common set:[6]

- **Traditionalists.** Hardworking; loyal (to their country and employer); submissive (respect authority, don't ruffle feathers); resistant to change; tech challenged.

- **Baby boomers.** Work-centric (extremely hardworking, define themselves by their professional accomplishments);

independent (confident, self-reliant); achievement-oriented; competitive (want to win).

- **Generation X.** Individualistic (independent, resourceful, value freedom and responsibility, casual disdain for authority and structured work hours); technologically adept; flexible (adapt well to change, more willing to change employers, tolerant of alternative lifestyles); value work/life balance ("work to live rather than live to work").

- **Millennials.** Tech-savvy; family-centric (willing to trade high pay for fewer hours, flexible schedules, and a better work/life balance); achievement-oriented (ambitious, confident, high expectations of their employers, seek out new challenges); question authority; team-oriented (value teamwork, want to be involved, seek the input and affirmation of others, crave attention).

These descriptions and their variants have been widely accepted as accurate, as was the depiction in the 1970s of young workers as "alienated." But, as was also the case in the '70s, *there is not a shred of systematically collected evidence that any of these depictions of generations are true*. They are based entirely on anecdotes and have their source, in part, in a fundamental error: the confusion of the effects of age and, especially, tenure with "generation." After all, so-called Traditionalists were not only born and reared in an assumedly different era culturally—they also have had longer tenure in their companies and are older. Their resistance to change—if it even exists—may have nothing to do with their generation and everything to do with their tenure or age and their reluctance to trade what has worked for them for years for something untried. In other words, the Millennials, when they age and work longer for their companies, might be no different than the Traditionalists are today.

To our knowledge, there have been just two genuinely systematic studies specifically testing the theory of generational differences, one by the Conference Board of Canada,[7] and the other by Jennifer Deal of the Center for Creative Leadership.[8] Both studies were based on surveys, in the Conference Board case, of 900 Canadian employees, limited to three generations: Baby Boomers: born 1945–1965; X: born 1965–1979; and, Y: born 1980–2000. Deal, on the other hand, surveyed 3,200 U.S. workers and divides her population into five generations: Silents (born 1925–1945); Early Boomers (born 1946–1954); Late Boomers (born 1955–1963); Early Xers (born 1962–1976); and, Late Xers (born 1977–1986).[9]

Here, in brief, are the conclusions from these studies:

- The authors of the Conference Board report conclude that, "There are some sharp differences in how the generations see one another, many of which mirror popular (and often negative) generational stereotypes. Yet, workers from across all three generations want many of the same things from their work, their colleagues, and their employers. In short, many of the supposed differences between the Boomer, Gen X, and Gen Y workers are based on perception, not reality."[10] Companies therefore need to "...provide what all workers want: respect, flexibility, and fairness."[11] Only two differences in preferences of any significance were found: Boomers somewhat more than the other two generations prefer face-to-face communications rather than technological means, such as emails (are any readers surprised?) and they are less interested in after-hours socializing with co-workers (considering the Boomers' ages, there's no surprise in that).

  The Conference Board study explodes a number of specific myths about generational differences. Among them is the belief that "Gen Xers do not like to work in teams, whereas Boomers and Gen Yers are more collaborative and team-oriented." Their data: "In fact, 62 percent of Gen Xers said that they prefer to work alone, compared with 59 percent of Boomers and 64 percent of Gen Yers. As well, 57 percent of Gen Xers said that they like to work in teams, compared with 55 percent of Boomers and 61 percent of Gen Yers."[12] Another prevalent belief: "Boomers value work over life, Gen Xers value life over work, and Gen Yers only value life outside of work." But the data show that "all three generations seek work-life balance. They all work for the enjoyment of working and to have the means to enjoy a personal life." The report's authors caution that "...employers need to be wary of programs and practices that warn of vast gulfs between the generations, and promise to elevate organizational performance through what might be termed 'management by stereotype.' It does not work that way. The keys to success in managing a multigenerational workforce are not to be found in designing workplace policies to fit particular generations of workers; they come from developing a human resource management system that makes all workers feel equally valued and is based on respect, shared values, flexibility, and fairness."[13]

- Jennifer Deal presents similar data and comes to strikingly similar conclusions: "...the generation gap at work is one more of appearance than substance.... People want about the same things at work, no matter what generation they are from."[14] Deal's advice to management: "Remember, you don't have to tie yourself into knots (or worse!) trying to accommodate each generation's individual whims, and you don't have to worry about learning a new set of whims when the next generation comes along. People from different generations are largely alike in what they think, believe, and want from their work life. Once people accept this fact, and make their actions consistent with the principles that apply to working with people of all generations, the (generation) gap will be retired."[15]

Still, in the work setting, employees and managers resist these conclusions about the lack of differences between generations because the conclusions belie what they claim they actually see and experience every day. They *see* Boomers acting more conservatively, and more loyal to, and satisfied with, the company. They *see* Traditionalists being more positive than nearly everyone at work regarding the company as a whole. As The Conference Board emphasized, there *are* differences in the way the generations *see* each other. It is also true, however, that Boomers are older and more likely to have been at the company significantly longer than, say, Gen Xers and thus may be more invested than them in it. And, Traditionalists, the oldest cohort, are more likely to be in management, a population we know to be generally more positive. So, both tenure in the company and level confound what people are seeing with their own eyes—you can't "see" tenure, but you can "see" age, which they equate with "generation." A related data analysis that we performed shows the impact of the demographics on overall satisfaction. We found that when we statistically take out the effect of both tenure and level, the differences by age (that is, "generation") disappear—with the exception of a very small positive effect for Traditionalists. Our analysis thus teaches us that with regard to overall satisfaction, it is tenure—not age/generation—that has the real impact. People tend to join companies enthusiastically, hopeful that they have found an organization where their work-related goals, interests, and aspirations will be met. In most companies, however, initial expectations are not met and attitudes then decline, reaching their lowest points during their third to sixth years of employment, and begin to recover later on, as shown in Table 1-1. These effects have held up year after year since we started collecting data in 1972, and they hold up for both management and non-management. Here is the analysis between tenure and satisfaction, performed on our recent survey results.

Table 1-1 Overall Satisfaction by Job Tenure: 2011-2012 Data (% Favorable)

	< 6 mos.	6 mos. – 1 yr.	1 yr. – 3 yr.	3 yr. – 6 yr.	6 yr. – 11 yr.	11 yr. – 16 yr.	> 16 yrs.
Management	87	83	78	76	77	80	84
Non-Management	85	78	76	72	73	77	78

Further analysis shows that this effect of tenure occurs at all ages! Age itself, other than a slight positive bump for Traditionalists (those over 68 years of age), has no effect. When, say, a middle-age person joins a company, he shows over time the same tenure versus satisfaction results as do younger people. (For these analyses, see our website at www.sirota.com/enthusiastic-employee.)

The recovery in attitudes later in one's work career is likely a function of employee attrition (many unhappy employees have left), dissonance ("If I am still here, I must be satisfied!"), and habituation ("After all this time, the place has grown on me.") Other than being on guard against the generational differences stereotypes, the only practical conclusion for managers about the research on the topic is this: if you are searching for a way to add a few points to your workforce satisfaction scores, you might consider hiring only those 68 years of age or older (the Traditionalists)—and employing them for no more than one year!

Myths About the Work Itself

There has long been a widespread belief—quite deeply engrained in our culture—that most people, of whatever generation, simply don't like to work. This is an ancient point of view (after all, work was one of Adam's punishments for eating fruit in Eden: "In the sweat of thy brows shalt thou eat thy bread"), and for millennia a lot of work was, indeed, extremely hard and often performed under dangerous, even brutal, conditions. But much has changed, especially in today's developed economies. Backbreaking, endless labor has to a large extent disappeared, replaced by the tools of the industrial and information revolutions and constrained by societal norms and labor laws. And yet, the view persists that work is inherently distasteful to almost everybody.

In our employee surveys, we regularly ask people specifically how they feel about the work itself, as opposed to other aspects of their employment, such as their pay or their relationship with their supervisors. Our job satisfaction "norm" is 78 percent. This means that, on average, 78 percent of all workers across all the organizations surveyed generally enjoy the work they do. Although a 78 percent average satisfaction rate does not approach unanimity, it appears to belie the notion that work for most employees is somehow intrinsically unsatisfying.

Further, contrary to unsupported theories about worker attitudes, such as the generational-difference and job-enrichment fads, we find that the overall satisfaction of workers with the type of work they do is strong and constant over a wide variety of ages, industries, and occupations. For example, on the high end, the job-satisfaction figure for those working in the insurance industry is 83 percent. At the low end is the job satisfaction of retail workers, which is at 75 percent. That's not much of a difference. Management across all industries is somewhat more positive than non-management (84 percent versus 77 percent on the average), and the higher the management level, the more positive. Historically, non-management professionals (such as engineers, accountants, and salespeople) have a slightly higher satisfaction rate than other salaried employees (such as clerical workers) who, in turn, are higher than hourly (mostly blue-collar) employees. But, over the past eight years, hourly attitudes have improved and are now on a par with other salaried, nonprofessional employees. Therefore, the percentage of people satisfied with their work is high for every group; most of the remaining employees are neutral, and a small percentage express dissatisfaction. The differences among the various groups are small and, by and large, in line with what one might expect.

Also, there is no evidence that younger workers are more (or less) disenchanted than their elders. Racial and gender differences are also small or nonexistent, as are those by regions of the world. Appendix C, "Job Satisfaction: Demographic, Occupational, and Regional Breaks," details the job-satisfaction data for the various demographic, occupational, and regional groups and can be found on our website at www. sirota.com/enthusiastic-employee.

Our results on job satisfaction may seem counterintuitive to those unfamiliar with employee attitude survey findings. However, as noted in the Introduction (and summarized in Appendix D, "Comparisons with Other Norms," on the aforementioned website), our data are similar to those collected by other researchers. Furthermore, going back to 1972 when Sirota began its surveys, we find hardly any change at all. The average level of job satisfaction on our surveys in 1972–1982 was 73 percent and in 2002–2012 it was 77 percent.

If, contrary to popular social myth, people generally like the work they do, why is it that some workers nonetheless appear more highly motivated than others, that workforces in some companies routinely perform better than others, and that workers are often unmotivated to do their jobs well, despite apparently liking what they do? In other words, if people generally like the work they do, why are they often unhappy with their work situations? Are they being irrational? What accounts for this apparent disparity? We find out by going directly to the workers.

Let's Ask

What can you learn by asking workers about their goals and views in a simple and direct way? First, that identifying what *most* motivates employees is a waste of time. The vast majority of employees want a *lot* of things "most." Indeed, it is a psychological illness to want just one thing, such as money to the exclusion of everything else, or affection to the point that one is willing to sacrifice anything for it, including fair compensation for one's labor.

The Sirota Three-Factor Theory

Based on our survey research, we assert that there are three primary sets of goals of people at work: equity, achievement, and camaraderie. We call this our *Three-Factor Theory of Human Motivation in the Workplace*, and we maintain that:

1. The three sets of goals characterize what the overwhelming majority of workers want—whatever the generation.
2. For the overwhelming majority of workers, no other goals are nearly as important as these.
3. To our knowledge, these goals have not changed over time, and they cut across cultures, at least the cultures of the economically developed sectors of societies (the only sectors we have studied).
4. Understanding the three sets of goals, and establishing organizational policies and practices that are in tune with them, is the key to high workforce morale and firm performance. There is no conflict between the goals of most workers and the needs of their organizations.

Note

Keep in mind that our focus is on the goals of people *at work*. There is more to life than work, and our theory is not meant to cover all human motivation.

We have been highly critical of theories of human motivation that are unsubstantiated by systematic evidence—in fact, are *contradicted* by the evidence that does exist. What is the evidence for our assertions about human motivation? We have been in the business of observing and querying employees for more than four decades. After all this time and the literally tens of thousands of employees with whom we have had direct contact and the millions we have surveyed by questionnaire, we see certain themes repeating themselves time and again. They repeat themselves no matter what the occupation—from assembly-line workers to research scientists—no matter what the region of the world (North America, Europe, Latin America, or Asia), and no matter their sex, race, or age. The specifics vary, of course, but everywhere we have worked, people want to be proud of the work they do. They want to be paid a fair wage for their efforts and have job stability. Their co-workers—their cooperation and congeniality—are important to them. There is no escaping these fundamental needs of people at work and the enthusiasm they experience and express when the needs are satisfied—and the frustration when they are not.

More specifically, our evidence includes:

- Statistical analyses of the answers to the multiple-choice questions in our questionnaires that invariably show that the questions correlating most highly with employee morale and performance are those measuring the three factors (equity, achievement, and camaraderie).

- When we ask employees directly what they want from their jobs and their companies, they mention several goals, and the bulk of their answers fall into the three factors.

- When we ask employees, in focus groups and in the "write-in" questions at the end of the questionnaire, what they like and dislike most about working for their company, a careful, quantitative analysis reveals that their likes and dislikes almost always reflect the three factors.

- In our research on employee turnover, we learn that the major reasons people stay with or leave an organization—other than personal reasons, such as a spouse getting a job in a different geographical area—almost always reflect the three factors.

In short, the evidence is overwhelming, and we review a portion of it later in this chapter. But first, here are our descriptions of the three factors and the degree of satisfaction of employees with them as uncovered by our surveys.

Equity.   To be treated justly in relation to the basic conditions of employment.

Certain basic conditions are expected simply by virtue of the employment relationship. They are unrelated to position in the company or to performance. They are defined by generally accepted ethical and community standards and, while the basic goals do not change over time, a number of the standards that define what is acceptable do change. The basic conditions are as follows:

- Physiological, such as having a safe working environment, a workload that does not damage workers' physical or emotional health, and reasonably comfortable physical working conditions.
- Economic, such as having a reasonable degree of job security, satisfactory compensation, and satisfactory benefits.
- Psychological, such as being treated respectfully, having reasonable accommodation made for personal and family needs, having credible and consistent management, and being able to get a fair hearing for complaints.

Are those things surprising? Of course not. What is surprising is how little we hear of them in many modern theories of management. *But, enlisting the willing cooperation of a workforce in achieving the aims of an enterprise is impossible unless people have a sense of elemental fairness in the way they are treated.*

We use the term "reasonable" frequently in our definitions because employees do not expect a level of perfection unrelated to the realities of the business. For example, the desire for job security does not mean that employees expect a lifetime-employment guarantee. They are not naïve; they understand that such a guarantee is virtually impossible in a modern, capitalist economy. But they are angry when they (or their co-workers) are laid off without the company having a pressing need to let them go (when, for example, it is already highly profitable or when it has not exhausted other more obvious ways to reduce costs). Their anger is magnified by insensitive handling of layoffs, such as when layoffs are done without adequate notice or financial and job-placement assistance.

In other words, employees become angry when, in their view, elementary considerations of fairness are completely submerged by the company's single-minded pursuit of its short-term business interests, such as the anticipated immediate impact of an announced layoff on a company's stock price.

Similarly, consider compensation. Most people know that becoming extremely wealthy is more fantasy than reality. So, the common assumption that "employees will never be happy with their pay" is fallacious. Our norm on our satisfaction-with-pay survey question is 51 percent favorable and 25 percent unfavorable. (The rest are neutral about their pay.) Although pay satisfaction is among the lower-rated aspects of work, it is hardly very negative. Furthermore, those are the averages across many organizations, and the range of responses is large: the most positive company response is 78 percent favorable, and the least positive is 25 percent.

Contrary to "common sense," people *can* view their pay as fair. Our research shows that perceived fair compensation is a function of a number of variables, including perceptions of what other organizations pay for similar work, the relationship of pay to employee contribution, and the company's profitability. Chapter 4, "Compensation," elaborates on these variables. The underlying attitude that these results reflect is simply whether the organization tries to be fair with its salary policies or whether it tries to squeeze every last nickel from its employees. And "fair" does not mean wildly generous. Everything else being equal, and under most circumstances, we find employees pleased with "competitive" pay and very pleased with compensation that is even a few percentage points above other companies' pay.

Similar observations can be made about other elements of the equity factor, such as benefits. But there are elements where the ultimate is expected, such as the following:

- **Safety.** Where loss of life or limb is at stake, perfection has become the goal, and understandably so.

- **Respect.** People want to be treated like responsible adults, but many workers—primarily in factories but also in certain factory-like white-collar settings—are, as they see it, treated like children or criminals, subjected to strict monitoring of their work and other behavior to coerce performance and conformity to the "rules." The response to this kind of treatment is that anger builds up in workers over time, and this has always been a major element in the more severe industrial relations conflicts we have studied. Even when the reaction is not explosive, this mode of management is self-defeating for the company. It is based on false assumptions about the great majority of workers (for example, that they are irresponsible) and becomes a self-fulfilling prophecy: management that expects the worst from people typically gets it.

- **Management credibility.** A basic need of human beings from childhood through adulthood is to be able to trust the word of those whose actions have a significant impact on them. A major source of discontent among many workers is information about important matters that is incomplete, unclear, contradictory, or simply absent. When workers assume that the company is deliberately withholding information, the void is filled with paranoid thoughts about what is really going on. This is a sure way to poison the relationship between management and its workforce.

How do workers feel about the degree to which their needs for equity are being met? Our research indicates that the highest degree of average satisfaction concerns how people feel about safety at work, while the lowest is about pay. The range is 81 percent favorable for safety to 51 percent favorable for pay, demonstrating that employees make sharp differentiations among the various aspects of their work.

See Table 1-2 for a sample of the normative data relating to equity. We show in that table the average percentage satisfied across all our surveys (the "norm") for each question and its range: the lowest score we have ever obtained on the question (the "minimum") and the highest (the "maximum").

Table 1-2 2004–2012 Norms and Ranges for a Sample of Equity Questions

		Range	
Question	**Norm**	**Min**	**Max**
Safety	81	59	96
Treated with respect and dignity	74	43	93
Supervisor's human relations competence	73	57	87
Physical working conditions	70	38	91
Amount of work expected	70	52	87
Job security	67	50	89
Company interest in employee well-being	65	23	92
Sr. management's actions consistent with its words	64	29	88
Company communication on important matters	64	34	86
Benefits package	62	23	94
Favoritism (lack of)	54	41	71
Pay	51	25	78

The overall ranking of items is similar within most of the individual organizations that we survey. When we discover an exception to the pattern, it is cause for particular attention. Take safety, for example. In general, safety is highly rated in our surveys, but there are a few organizations, especially in heavy manufacturing, where it is among the lower-rated items. But, there are exceptions to that, too. As an example, see the discussion in Chapter 7, "Organization Purpose and Principles," about Paul O'Neill (the former Secretary of the Treasury) and his work on safety when he was chairman of Alcoa. These "exceptions to the exceptions" are particularly noteworthy and illuminating because we learn from them that in management practice, little is foreordained. Much can be done if there is a will to do it.

Although this pattern tends to hold up across organizations (with exceptions, as noted), the *levels* of satisfaction—within the same broad pattern—vary widely. Thus, for example, employees in companies A and B can rate safety among the highest and pay among the lowest of all the equity items, but company A employees can be much higher than those in company B on both of these (and on just about every other equity item).

The large variations between organizations can be seen in the ranges in Table 1-2, and they are extremely important. First, they lend the lie to the commonly held assumption that people, no matter where they work, are similar to each other in their disgruntlement with their employment conditions. What management does is critical, and the differences between organizations in management behavior—and, therefore, employee response—can be huge. Second, the variability allows us to answer the key "So what?" question about employee attitudes: does satisfaction matter for business success? In Chapter 2, "Employee Enthusiasm and Business Success," we show how business performance varies markedly between organizations with different degrees of employee satisfaction.[16] The variation in the degree of satisfaction, we must stress, is not usually between highly satisfied, or "enthusiastic," and highly dissatisfied, or "angry," employees. Much of the variation resides in the difference between highly and moderately satisfied employees. That is a basic point of this book:

the big difference in motivation and outcomes when employees say "This is a terrific place to work" vs. feeling that "It's pretty good" or "OK."

Achievement. *To take pride in one's accomplishments by doing things that matter and doing them well; to receive recognition for one's accomplishments; to take pride in the organization's accomplishments.*

A sense of basic equity in the employment relationship serves as the foundation on which high employee morale can be built; the powerful need to feel proud of one's accomplishments and the accomplishments of the organization is then freed to drive behavior toward high performance. Pride comes both from the employees' own perceptions of accomplishment and from the recognition received from others.

That is why the often-asked question, "How do you motivate employees?" is foolish. Most people enter a new organization and job with enthusiasm, eager to work, to contribute, to feel proud of their work and their organizations. Perversely, many managers appear to then do their best to *demotivate* employees!

You may reject that argument if you believe that people (other than a few saints, overachievers, or neurotic workaholics) are basically greedy and lazy when it comes to work. The reverse is true: most people are reasonable in what they expect in terms of treatment and are eager to perform in a way that makes them feel good about their performance. When we observe the opposite in an employee, it is either an atypical case (see the following discussion on individual differences) or, most commonly, because management has damaged that employee's motivation.

Our statistical analysis shows that a sense of achievement has six primary sources:

- **Challenge of the work itself.** The extent to which the job uses an employee's intelligence, abilities, and skills.

- **Acquisition of new skills**.
- **Ability to perform.** Having the training, direction, resources, authority, information, and cooperation needed to perform well.
- **Perceived importance of the employee's job.** To the organization, to the customer, and to society.
- **Recognition received for performance.** Both nonfinancial (such as a simple "thank you" from the boss or a customer) and financial (compensation and advancement that are based on performance).
- **Working for a company of which the employee can be proud.** Because of its purpose, its products (their quality and their impact on customers and society), its business success, its business ethics (treatment of customers, employees, investors, and community), and the quality of its leadership.

As with the equity items, the surveys reveal a mixed picture regarding achievement. A sample of the normative data relating to achievement is shown in Table 1-3. We ask many questions about this factor, and these are discussed in the relevant chapters. But for now, note that among the most positive ratings are those focused on two opposite organization poles: the macro and the micro. Employees, on the average, are most favorable toward the overall characteristics of the organization (such as the quality of the organization's products and services, its profitability, and its ethics) and, at the other pole, toward the immediate work environment (such as the job, the co-workers, and the technical ability of the immediate supervisor). The least positive ratings tend to be about efficiency at a "middle" level (such as bureaucracy, consistency of direction from management, and, as will be seen later, cooperation across units) and about reward. There are some apparent contradictions, such as the view of many employees that the amount of work expected of them hurts quality and yet the very positive feeling about the quality of the products and services the organization delivers to its customers. All these matters are discussed in detail in this book. Where we have comparisons with surveys conducted by others, the results are similar to ours. (See Appendix D, "Comparisons with Other Norms," at www.sirota.com/enthusiastic-employee.")

Table 1-3 2004–2012 Norms and Ranges for a Sample of Achievement Questions

		Range	
Question	**Norm**	**Min**	**Max**
Clear idea of results expected	86	63	95
High-quality products/services for customers	82	52	96
Supervisor's technical competence	82	67	95
Pride in organization	82	55	98
Corporate citizenship	79	43	95
The work itself	78	24	92
Skill and abilities used	76	53	89
Tools and equipment to do job	72	33	91
Information to do job	69	37	91
Company overall is effectively managed	67	32	93
Recognition for good job	64	38	86
Feedback on performance	63	45	82
Employees treated as important	62	38	81
Participative environment	61	24	74
Training	60	29	84
Not a lot of wasted time and effort	50	24	70
Decisions without undue delay	49	8	77
Don't receive conflicting instruction from management	44	33	56
Merit salary results from performance	40	5	91
Bureaucracy (lack of)	39	12	72

Camaraderie.   To have warm, interesting, and cooperative relations with others in the workplace.

Human beings are decidedly social animals. Positive interaction with others is not only gratifying, but essential for mental health. We often neglect the extent to which an organization—and parts of organizations—function not only as business entities but also as *communities* that satisfy the social and emotional needs of their members.

"What do you like most about working here?" is a typical write-in question we ask on our surveys. One of the most frequent and consistent responses to that question involves co-workers. That is because co-workers are important and because, by and large, people get along well with each other within their work units. We receive considerably fewer positive comments about relationships with other units in the organization; those comments are often in response to what employees like *least*. For example, note the following:

- From an employee in a real estate company (what employee likes "most"): "My team is full of intelligent people who are friendly and constantly want to do better and help each other. We work beautifully together."

- From an employee in a factory (likes "most"): "The people I work with." Simply this phrase, or variations of it (such as "the great people I work with"), appears repeatedly in almost every survey in response to the question about what respondents like most.

- From an employee in a hospital (likes "least"): "Cooperation and communication between physicians and nurses needs to be much better. Nurses truly know the patients. We are at the bedside dealing with families and the patient. Many times, we are ignored. It's like we're the physicians' servants and we should jump when they say so."

- From an employee in an information-technology group in a bank (likes "least"): "What gets me most upset is the way the departments we have to service are absolutely clueless about how busy we are and short-handed we are. We can't do everything just when they want it. They don't care, and when they complain to our V.P., he doesn't support us."

The quality of interaction in organizations is obviously greatly affected not just by friendliness and mutuality of interests but also by co-workers' competence and cooperation. In that environment, a friendly slacker is an oxymoron: being unhelpful to co-workers is, by definition, unfriendly. This is another example of the way employees' needs—in this case, for positive interpersonal relationships in the work setting—are congruent with the organization's needs for high performance. And, as we shall discuss in Chapter 8, "Job Enablement," innovativeness is often the result of positive interaction among colleagues.

The camaraderie concept issomewhat less complex than equity and achievement, and we came to an explicit realization of its importance somewhat later in our work. Therefore, in our surveys, fewer questions have been asked about camaraderie, and these are shown in Table 1-4. The most favorably rated aspect of camaraderie is simply the relationship between co-workers, followed by teamwork within the workers' unit, teamwork across departments in a given location, and finally, teamwork and cooperation across the entire company.

Table 1-4 2004–2012 Norms and Ranges for a Sample of Camaraderie Questions

Question	Norm	Range Min	Max
Relationship with co-workers	90	71	97
Teamwork within work unit	80	39	92
Teamwork across departments in location	66	26	88
Teamwork across company as a whole	62	23	87

Teamwork, as we mentioned, is not just a camaraderie issue. It also has a major effect on achievement. And, it is clear that teamwork is more positive at the *micro* level—within units—than at what we have termed the *middle* level—across units. The differences between companies, however, are large, which shows that familiarity and proximity do not always breed contentment or distance antagonism. For example, although the norm for teamwork within the unit is 80 percent, the range is from 39 to 92 percent! Also, the norm for teamwork across units is 66 percent, but the range extends from 26 to 88 percent.

Chapter 11, "Teamwork," discusses camaraderie, its impact on performance, and ways of enhancing it. That chapter also discusses how camaraderie can sometimes work against organization goals. For example, solidarity in a workgroup might develop in opposition to a management whose practices are considered unjust by employees. Management becomes the "enemy camp" and, in those situations, equity issues must be dealt with first.

That summarizes the key sets of goals of the overwhelming majority of employees. Other than extreme cases in which our theory does not apply (which will soon be discussed), we assert that a manager does not need to know much more about human motivation at work. That is quite an assertion, but we invite readers to suggest other motivators that are as powerful, relevant in the workplace, and widespread. We claim further that a genuinely high-morale, enthusiastic, and highly productive workforce is impossible if those needs go unsatisfied.

The three goals we propose are distinct needs that, unfortunately, cannot be substituted for each other. For example, enriching the content of a job does not increase satisfaction with pay or cause an employee to minimize the importance of his pay dissatisfaction. Discontent with pay can be ameliorated only by more pay! Similarly, unhappiness with a boring job can be solved only by restructuring the job or transferring the employee to work that is more interesting; paying the employee more won't solve the problem. Each goal—and most every subgoal—must be dealt with individually. There are no panaceas, no silver bullets that solve all issues.

The Specific Evidence for the Three-Factor Theory

We make rather strong claims—some might say startling and unbelievable—about the pervasiveness of the three sets of goals. We claim that the goals are nearly universal, applying to roughly 85 to 90 percent of a workforce. (That's just about any workforce.)

Our assertions might appear to go against common observation and common sense. After all, managers and employee-relations experts talk endlessly about differences: the differences between individual workers and between categories of workers (such as males and females, older and younger workers, professionals and nonprofessionals) and between workers in different countries. Are we saying that this is hogwash? Yes, in large measure.

Consider the following questions in relation to the three factors: do you believe that an entire category of workers—demographic (age, sex, race, and so on), occupational, or national—does not consider being treated fairly by their employer—say, in wages—to be of very high priority? Do you believe that a category of workers exists in which the overwhelming majority does not want to take pride in their work and in their organization? Do you believe that there is a category of workers for whom having congenial and cooperative co-workers is unimportant? Of course, there are *individuals* to whom these rules do not apply—even individuals who willingly allow themselves to be exploited economically by their employers—but never more than a very small minority in any category.

Are there no major demographic, occupational, or national differences in these needs? Not in the fundamentals we have described (the desire for equitable treatment, achievement, and camaraderie). The differences emerge largely in *what* will satisfy these needs, which vary because of differing objective conditions and expectations. Let's consider a few examples of this:

- **The work itself.** In Chapter 9, "Job Challenge," we discuss the satisfaction people seek from the kind of work they do, and we say that workers want to be proud of their work. Pride in work has numerous sources, among them the employees' feelings that their intelligence and skills are being used; that, in turn, is partly a function of the latitude they have to exercise judgment in doing their jobs. We know that the latitude given to, say, the average engineer is normally going to be much greater objectively than that given to a blue-collar machine operator. *Despite this difference, the machine operator may experience the same degree of satisfaction—which is subjective—with his job autonomy.* The machine operator doesn't expect—indeed, would consider it inappropriate—to have the engineer's latitude. But he doesn't want to be treated as an automaton; that is, he wants to exercise the judgment that makes sense *for that job and for his skills,* and that latitude can be considerable (as the reader will see in Chapter 9). People at work are not stupid and do not have outrageous expectations. Machine operators— no less than engineers—have a need to be treated on the job as intelligent human beings, but the standards by which this is judged are obviously somewhat different.

- **Job security.** Chapter 3 discusses job security. How an organization treats employees in this respect is a key source of employee morale, but what is considered fair has shifted greatly in the United States over the past few decades. Although employees in quite a few large corporations previously expected lifetime job security, today's workers rarely expect that. They understand that the business world has changed, but this does not mean that their desire for security has diminished. *The change has been in the criteria that employees use to judge the fairness with which the issue is handled by organizations.* Organizations differ greatly in this regard—for example, in whether layoffs are treated as a last resort instead of the first action taken—and these differences have a profound impact on the morale and performance of a workforce.

- **Vacations.** A concrete and visible example of a cultural difference is that between the vacations enjoyed by workers in the countries of Western Europe and those received in the United States. On average, Western European countries have much longer vacations, with even new employees receiving at least a full month. (Vacation time is five weeks in France, Sweden, Austria, Denmark, and Spain.) This certainly is a major difference, with profound cultural meaning and probably significant economic effect, but what are its implications for our argument regarding the commonality of the major needs? Are European workers lazy? Are they less interested in doing a good job? Do they find their jobs less interesting? *There is absolutely no evidence for any such assertion.* By virtue of broad historical and social trends, different countries evolved different patterns of employee relations, including different vacation time expectations. These differences result in different subjective standards of what is "fair," but in no way undercut our proposition regarding the fundamental goals of workers.

Similar comments could be made about the satisfaction of many other goals and subgoals: employee expectations in the United States regarding the benefits an organization provides, such as medical insurance, have changed greatly, and what might have been considered unfair a decade or so ago, such as a large corporation not paying full medical-insurance premiums, can be entirely satisfactory today. Operating in the opposite direction is equipment, where the tools people use on their jobs *improve* continually, so what was satisfactory before is rarely satisfactory today.

Our argument, then, is not that there are no demographic, occupational, or cultural differences or that the differences are unimportant. It comes down to this: when we say that workers want to feel pride in their work, we mean almost all workers, whoever they are, whatever they do, and whenever or wherever they do it. The fundamentals are constant, but knowing how to satisfy those fundamental needs often requires knowledge of the expectations of particular groups of workers. As an extreme example, suppose an American multinational corporation decided to halve the vacation time of its European workers based solely on the assumption that their fundamental needs to do a good job and to be treated fairly are the same as American workers. That organization is in for big trouble.

But don't make the opposite error—namely, to assume that the obvious cultural, occupational, and demographic differences in expectations and standards signify major differences in basic goals. For example, treat a blue-collar worker as if all that interests him is his wages—that exercise of his judgment on the job doesn't matter—and you wind up with an indifferent or hostile employee. At the other extreme, treat engineers and scientists as if wages don't matter—that all they want is an opportunity to be creative—and you wind up with hostile engineers and scientists (if they stay with the organization at all).

Table 1-5 summarizes a representative portion of the strong quantitative evidence on which we base these claims about the pervasiveness of employee goals. As we will explain, the table shows that employee morale relates strongly to the degree to which each of the three needs is satisfied, *and the relationships are extraordinarily similar across* all *demographic, occupational, and national groups*. There are no differences in the strengths of the goals to speak of; they are, indeed, nearly universal.

Table 1-5 Evidence for the Near-Universality of the Three Factors

	Correlations with Overall Satisfaction		
	Well-Being (Equity)	Use of Skills (Achievement)	Teamwork (Camaraderie)
Total	.59	.43	.36
Race/Ethnicity			
White	.60	.45	.34
Black	.57	.45	.34
Hispanic	.58	.47	.41
Asian	.63	.45	.41
Native American	.54	.44	.37
Tenure			
0–2 yrs	.60	.48	.35
2–5 yrs	.60	.45	.33
5–10 yrs	.58	.42	.33
10–20 yrs	.59	.44	.36
> 20 yrs	.56	.39	.36
Gender			
Women	.59	.42	.35
Men	.59	.45	.37
Level			
Management	.58	.44	.33
Non-management	.58	.43	.36
Position			
Professional	.60	.46	.36
Non-professional	.55	.39	.30
Regions			
North America	.60	.45	.37
Europe	.58	.40	.32

How do we know, in a systematic, quantitative way, whether a goal is important and how universal it is? One way is to correlate employees' satisfaction with it with their *overall* satisfaction with the organization. Table 1-5 shows these results. Overall satisfaction is a product of the degree to which employees feel their specific goals are being met, so the higher the correlation between satisfaction with a specific goal and overall satisfaction, the more important we can assume the goal to be. If an employee doesn't care much about something—say, the color of the walls where she works—liking or not liking it would have no impact on how she feels about the organization as a whole. Compare that to the importance of how she feels about her pay or her boss. This reasoning is identical to how the performance approval rating of the president of the United States— determined from political-opinion polls—is a function of how Americans feel about specific aspects of the president's performance, such as his handling of the economy, of national security, and his perceived interest in the well-being of the average American. The stronger the correlation between a specific aspect and the overall approval rating of the president's performance, the more important that aspect is.

The relationship between variables (such as between overall satisfaction and satisfaction with pay or the color of the walls) can be assessed in various ways. In our analysis, it is measured by a statistic called the *correlation coefficient*, whose symbol is "r." The higher r is, the stronger is the relationship. r can range from .00, which means no relationship, to 1.00, which means a perfect relationship. (r can also be negative, in which case, the relationship is inverse: the higher on one variable, the *lower* on the other.)

Our basic finding is that there are highly significant positive correlations between the questions on our surveys that tap the three needs and overall satisfaction. These correlations hold up in *all* demographic, occupational, and national groups *and at approximately the same level.* Illustrations of these correlations are shown in Table 1-5, where the following questions are used to tap the three needs:

- **For equity.** "How would you rate your organization on taking a genuine interest in the well-being of its employees?"

- **For achievement.** "Do you agree or disagree: my job makes good use of my skills and abilities."
- **For camaraderie.** "How would you rate the cooperation and teamwork within your work unit?"

The question measuring overall morale is "Considering everything, how would you rate your overall satisfaction in [organization] at this time?"

The correlations shown in Table 1-5 were calculated using data from the many thousands of employees we survey in organizations where the four questions were asked in identical ways.

This table contains the correlations for three demographic breaks: race/ethnicity, gender, and tenure, and for occupations and regions of the world. Those familiar with correlational data, will, we trust, be amazed at just how similar the patterns are. In *every* instance, the item measuring the equity goal correlates in the .50s or .60s with morale, that measuring achievement in or near the .40s, and that measuring teamwork in the .30s and .40s. The possible reasons for the differences in sizes of the correlations—why equity should be the highest and teamwork the lowest—are discussed later in this chapter. Suffice it to say for now that not only are all the correlations highly significant statistically, which verifies the importance of the goals, but, to all intents and purposes, they are the same for all categories of employees.

Which aspects of work do we find *not* correlated with overall employee morale? They tend to be what might be termed the "frills" of work. Although senior management often spends much time on them, they don't really touch on workers' basic goals and what goes on in important ways in their daily workplace activities. We refer to matters such as the aesthetics of the physical work environment, recreational activities (such as holiday parties), various formal "programs" (such as suggestions programs), and formal communication mechanisms (such as the company newsletter). It's not that employees don't care about these at all, but that they matter much less than other, more fundamental concerns. It matters much less to them, for example, that there be a well-designed company newsletter or a suggestions program than that their immediate supervisors communicate and listen to them. We are in no way suggesting that the frills be dropped—almost everyone likes a holiday party—but that they be seen as supplements to, not substitutes for, the more basic policies and practices that we discuss throughout this book.

Similar findings are obtained in analyses of answers to the open-ended questions, questions such as what workers "like most" and "like least" about their organizations. The things employees spontaneously write in about almost invariably involve the three factors. These findings are given as examples throughout this book. The frills are almost never mentioned in answer to these questions.

How the Three Factors Work in Combination

Our analyses show the three factors interacting with each other in a somewhat complex way. The Three Factor Theory asserts that employees seek to satisfy three needs—equity, achievement, and camaraderie—in any employment situation. It further asserts that when all three needs are met, it results in enthusiasm directed toward accomplishing organizational goals. As we have said and will more fully explain in Chapter 2, enthusiasm is not just about being happier or more content—it is employees feeling that they work for a *great* company, one to which they willingly devote time and energy beyond what they are being paid for or what is expected and monitored. A great company for employees is one that largely meets *all* of their needs for equity, achievement, and camaraderie. Until that happens, it is no more than a "pretty good" company, one with which they are "moderately satisfied."

Statistical support for this idea can be seen in the way individual satisfaction of the three needs interact to produce overall satisfaction.

They don't just add to one another in their impact, but *multiply* each other's impact. Figure 1-1 shows how employees respond to the question, "Considering everything, how would you rate your overall satisfaction in [organization] at this time?" The percentages shown are just those saying "very satisfied," the highest possible response to the question. The percentages are shown for four categories of employees: those whose satisfaction with all three needs is relatively low (labeled "None"), those who have just one need being satisfied, those who have two, and those for whom all three needs are being satisfied (labeled "All Three"). The questions used to assess satisfaction with the three needs are the same as in the correlational analysis shown in Table 1-5, namely, "How would you rate your organization on being concerned about the well-being of its employees?," "My job makes good use of my skills and abilities," and "How would you rate cooperation and teamwork within your immediate work unit?"

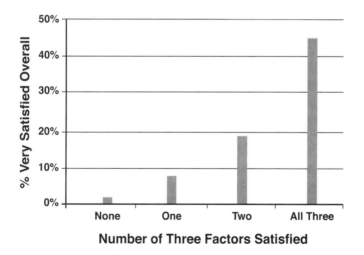

Figure 1-1 The exponential impact of the Three Factors.

It can be seen that as more satisfied needs are added, the percentage of very satisfied employees increases *exponentially*. When all three needs are being satisfied, the percentage is 45! What would you think of as a great company in which to work? It's probably not just having very good pay and benefits, or challenging and enjoyable work, or having terrific co-workers. It involves *all* of these needs, and when all of these needs are satisfied, something unique happens to many employees and their relationship with the organization... *It is what we call enthusiasm.* This finding is essential to keep in mind in reviewing our data and arguments. While, for example, 74 percent of employees say they are treated respectfully by the company—so aren't they therefore enthusiastic?—that, by itself, is insufficient to generate enthusiasm. Say, they are on a boring job and they want challenging work to do. Or, perhaps they are having difficulties with their co-workers, and that is aggravating to them. Enthusiasm requires satisfaction with all key areas of working life.

A second important complexity is the special effect of equity. More in-depth analysis suggests that although all the needs are important, equity has a certain *basic* importance. That is, if people are dissatisfied with the fairness with which they are treated, satisfaction of either of the other two needs has a relatively minor effect on morale. On the other hand, feeling fairly treated does have a fairly significant impact even when one or both of the other needs are not being satisfied. That is the reason the correlations of overall satisfaction with the equity need are consistently higher than the correlations with the other two factors.[17]

The moral of the story is that it can be difficult to get employees excited about a company that, say, gives them challenging work to do (part of the achievement need), when they have a basic sense of inequity as to how they are treated. But equity alone is not enough to create enthusiasm: the impact of fair treatment is greatly magnified when all three needs are being satisfied.

These analyses and conclusions hold up in an amazingly consistent way across demographic groups, occupations, and world regions. The finding about the exceptional importance of equity—especially job security—is fundamental to our understanding of the impact of the Great Recession, to be discussed in Chapter 5, "The Impact of the Great Recession: Flight to Preservation."

Racial/Ethnic and Gender Differences

In the first edition of this book, we said very little about differences between racial and ethnic groups and between women and men. Our readers communicated with us repeatedly about this, and we include this new section here to help remedy that oversight.

We showed (in Table 1-5) that the importance of the three factors varies hardly at all for subgroups: the correlations of the factors with overall satisfaction are virtually the same for the subgroups, including those defined by race and ethnicity and by gender. But, are there differences in the satisfaction *levels* of these subgroups?

First, here is some "objective" data. We know that a great deal of progress has been made integrating minorities and women into the workforce. For example, women make up 47 percent of the workforce today according to the Bureau of Labor Statistics, compared with 30 percent in 1950. But, using just one criterion of advancement, only 4.2 percent of the CEOs in Fortune 500 companies in 2012 were women. Minorities now constitute a growing 33 percent of the workforce, but less than 1 percent of them hold CEO positions in the Fortune 500 companies. Although many minority entrepreneurs are leading some of the nation's most successful small businesses,[18] it is clear that, with regard to both women and minorities, quite a bit remains to be done.

We turn now to the attitude data: the overall satisfaction scores on our surveys for minorities and women can be found in Table 1-6. Because there are disproportionately large numbers of men and whites in management, we have divided the data so that management and non-management can be seen separately.

Table 1-6 Overall Satisfaction with Company: 2004–2012 (% Favorable)

		Management	Non-Management
Men	**Asian**	81	79
	Black	84	80
	Hispanic	84	79
	White	82	76
Women	**Asian**	77	77
	Black	80	77
	Hispanic	86	80
	White	82	79

Table 1-6 reveals, first, that the differences between racial/ethnic and gender groups are quite small: all of the percentages are in the 70s and the 80s. Among the differences we do find, albeit not very large, are these:

- First, regarding management and non-management: not surprisingly, for every line of data except one, management is more satisfied than non-management.

- The differences between men and women are inconsistent: men are sometimes more positive, sometimes less so, and the two are sometimes equal.

- Asian managers—both males and females—show almost no difference from their Asian non-management counterparts. The reason, the data show, is that Asian managers' scores are somewhat depressed, the lowest of the management groups.

- The most favorable groups of all are Hispanic women—both managers (especially) and non-managers.

- The least favorable group of all is white males in non-management.

- Blacks show no particular pattern of differences in their levels of overall satisfaction.

Now, let's see how the different groups compare on a question dealing directly with diversity. The question is, "To what extent do you agree or disagree: the company has created an environment where people of diverse backgrounds can succeed," and the responses can be found in Table 1-7.

Table 1-7 The Company Has Created an Environment Where People of Diverse Backgrounds Can Succeed: 2004–2012 (% Favorable)

		Management	Non-Management
Men	**Asian**	79	77
	Black	69	72
	Hispanic	81	77
	White	86	79
Women	**Asian**	72	75
	Black	66	65
	Hispanic	76	76
	White	81	80

Here, as can be seen, some larger disparities emerge:

- Contrary to the overall satisfaction data, the differences between management and non-management are not consistent on this question on diversity: for some racial/ethnic and gender groups, managers are more favorable, for some the same, and for some less favorable than their non-management counterparts.

- Also contrary to the overall satisfaction data, women are, in just about every comparison, less favorable than men. By and large, the differences in attitudes between men and women—with women less favorable—are larger in management than in non-management.

- Blacks—whether in management or not and whether male or female—stand out as the least favorable group on this question. Although it would be inaccurate to call them negative, they do see the least progress toward diversity.

- The most positive groups are whites—that is, they report seeing the most progress. White men in management are especially favorable.

- Asians and Hispanics consistently score somewhere between blacks and whites on this question.

Considering both the overall satisfaction and the diversity attitudes, the data are both surprising and unsurprising. It may come as a shock that the overall satisfaction levels of the various groups show such small differences, considering the issues that women and minorities have faced in our society, including the workplace. But those issues *are* reflected in answer to the question directly about diversity where the results are, perhaps, more predictable: women are less favorable than men, and blacks are less favorable than whites and the other minorities.

How can workers be—as blacks and women are—less positive toward the progress their companies have made on diversity but not, on average, much different than others in their overall satisfaction with their companies? And, how can the reverse be true for white, non-management males who are more favorable regarding the amount the company has done for diversity but the *least* positive of all the groups on overall satisfaction?

As we have said, overall satisfaction is the resultant of a number of different, specific forces and these can balance each other. We therefore analyzed the attitudes of these groups on a host of other, and more specific, survey questions. (The full analysis can be found on our website at www.sirota.com/enthusiastic-employee.) The highlights of this analysis are as follows:

- In line with the diversity findings, blacks do tend to be less favorable than the others with regard to various equity or fairness issues, such as pay, benefits, and favoritism. But they turn out to be *more* favorable regarding *effectiveness* matters, whether on the immediate job (such as having the resources—tools, information, and so on—needed to do the job), or broad company performance (such as the company being effectively managed overall, effectively responding to change in its business environment, and satisfying customers). That is, blacks are more impressed than others with the company's business management but less with their own treatment on matters of equity—resulting in an about-average level of overall satisfaction.

- Hispanics are, by far, the most favorable racial or ethnic group. Among all the many specific questions we examined, they are consistently less favorable on just one: "My manager is sensitive to my work/life balance issues."

- A distinctive characteristic of the attitudes of Asian employees is the lack of difference between those in management and those not. Asian management employees are the least favorable of the racial and ethnic management groups on the great majority of specific questions we examined. In contrast, Asian employees holding non-management positions are, on average, among the *most* favorable of the non-management groups (three exceptions: benefits, fairness of pay, and training, where they are among the least favorable). Because the attitudes of management employees are, in general, more positive than those in non-management, the result is that Asian managers and non-managers are very similar to each other in their attitudes.

- The pattern for whites is also quite distinctive: white managers—whether male or female—are quite similar to the other ethnic and racial management groups, but white non-management males are consistently the least, or among the least, favorable cohort overall. It is not easy to discern the reason for their relative discontent; among the larger differences in a negative direction are those relating to the effectiveness of higher management, such as the overall effectiveness with which the company is managed, having a clear sense of direction, and responding to change in its business environment. That is in direct contrast to blacks, who tended to be more favorable in those respects. Also, in direct contrast to blacks is that white non-management males are among the most favorable on the progress the company has made toward diversity. Based on other research we have done, that attitude may be a two-edged sword, with some portion of these employees feeling that, in effect, too much progress has been made.

- Taken as a whole, women tend to be less favorable than men on a majority of the specific questions. The questions on which they are more favorable are those dealing with benefits, the training they have received, and a number of aspects of company effectiveness. Among our more interesting findings is that women are especially—and quite consistently—less favorable than men on "openness" in their companies, such as the company confronting and solving problems; employees' ability to express their opinions without fear of retribution; people accepting a variety of ideas and perspectives; top management encouraging employees to report information up the line even if it's bad news; and management acting on employee ideas and opinions. Perhaps these results about openness reflect women having higher standards than men about what open communications means. Or, they may feel that, as women, they are less a part of the communications network in their companies. Women are also less positive on being valued as an employee and knowing a career path they can follow.

Women *in management* show an interesting pattern: the differences between them and men in management are greater, and more unfavorable, than the differences between non-management women and non-management men. In addition to the attitudes mentioned earlier (where, on the whole, their differences with men are greater than those of women not in management), they show rather large differences with regard to the reasonableness of their workloads and their ability to maintain a reasonable balance between their personal and work lives; their authority; the degree to which high levels of performance where they work lead to greater advancement opportunity; the consistency with which policies are administered; and, favoritism. To be clear, we are not saying that women in management are less satisfied than women not in management. To the contrary, people in management—including women—are generally more satisfied than those not in management. It is that women, when promoted to management, do not appear to gain as much morale benefit from that advancement as do men. In fact, in certain respects, it might be a disadvantage, as in their ability to achieve a balance between their personal and work lives. On the "balance" question, not only are women less positive than men in management, *they are also less positive than their non-management female counterparts*. We surmise that moving into positions of greater responsibility, has not, for many women, resulted in an equivalent reduction of responsibilities outside of work.

To summarize, we can say that, in general, the progress of minorities and women in our surveyed companies has undoubtedly been quite substantial—otherwise, the attitudes of these two populations would have been quite negative—but the survey data, as well as what we know from other sources, also indicate that there is still a way to go. Women and minorities (especially blacks), while not necessarily negative, are less sanguine about progress toward diversity than are whites. The review we did of an array of more specific attitudes showed the following: less sense of fair treatment among blacks on many of the equity questions; relatively depressed attitudes of Asian managers; some possible backlash among whites, especially among male non-managers; and a number of concerns of women, such as work/personal life balance (especially among women in management jobs).

Individual Differences

We have repeatedly referred to the goals of "the overwhelming majority of the workforce," and argued that these characterized broad classes of workers. But, of course, there are individual differences in the strengths of needs. Some people are less socially oriented than others; some are more prone to see injustice in their treatment than are others; for some, work can be less important as a source of pride, perhaps because of fulfilling outside activities. The differences between individuals that are of most practical relevance to managers are the employees at the extremes, people who with regard to the equity need, for example, see injustice at every turn, or, at the other end, never see it. We estimate these extremes to constitute approximately 12 to 15 percent of a population of workers, 5 percent who are almost invariably negative and about 7 to 10 percent who are almost invariably positive. Our theory, and its practical implications for management practice, is much less relevant for these workers at the extremes.

Where do we get these estimated percentages of people at the extremes?

At the most general level, when employees are asked about their overall satisfaction with their organization, even the most positive companies in our database (over 85 percent satisfied) still have 6 to 8 percent of workers rating themselves as dissatisfied. (The rest are neutral.) Some portion of these people are not invariably unhappy but might be unsuited to their particular positions in that organization, to a particular manager, or even, perhaps, to an enthusiastic culture. But, we do know that, by nature, some people are cranky and won't be positive about their employment anywhere. Our rough estimate, based on largely informal assessments over the years, is that these constitute about 5 percent of virtually every workforce.

At the other end of the continuum, even in very low morale companies, 12 to 15 percent will express satisfaction. Some of this is no doubt due to a fortuitous fit, albeit unusual for those organizations, between themselves and their jobs, their managers, or the culture. (Some of them are likely to be the ones making everyone else unhappy!) But, we know also that there are people who, no matter how bad the environment is, come across as happy souls, the proverbial optimists who try to see the bright side and usually give management the benefit of the doubt. It takes an enormous amount to frustrate or anger these people and our rough estimate is that they constitute about 7 to 10 percent of an average workforce.

That's the general condition of the exceptionally and persistently dissatisfied or satisfied individuals. Our theory has less relevance for them because their satisfaction (or lack of it) will not be much affected by management's actions. At a more specific level relating to the three factors, consider the exceptions to what we said about the achievement goal. We asserted that most people want to work and be proud of their work. But we know that there are employees who are, in effect, "allergic" to work—they do just about anything to avoid it. For them, our question, "How do you keep management from demotivating employees?" is nonsense. They *are* unmotivated, and a disciplinary approach—including dismissal—is about the only way they can be managed.

At the opposite extreme are employees who are just about impossible to *de*motivate—namely, workaholics. They work through any and all obstacles that the organization puts in their path, perhaps even unconsciously relishing the obstacles because these provide an excuse for spending additional time at work. For them, too, the motivational issue that we are discussing is largely irrelevant:

In a workshop, one of the authors of this book conducted on recognition practices, managers were asked to describe their experience with "unintended effects" of recognition. One spoke of her experience with two employees who were, by far, the most productive people in her department and among the most productive she had come across at any time. She had already given them several large salary increases but wanted to do more. She called them into her office and announced that she was granting them two additional paid days off as a token of her appreciation. They frowned, so she asked them what was wrong. Were two days not enough? Their response was extraordinary: for them, days off from work were a punishment, not a reward. Such was the level of involvement in their work. She replaced the days off with dinner-for-two rewards, and they expressed their appreciation.

Similar extremes can be found on the equity and camaraderie dimensions. For example, some people feel unfairly treated no matter what ("collectors of injustices," as it were), and others never see injustice no matter what management does. Also, there are social isolates for whom social interaction appears to be unimportant (or even distasteful), and those for whom it is all-consuming.

Obviously, managers must be sensitive to these extremes and adjust their behavior accordingly. But a major problem is the tendency for many organizations and individual managers to mistake the extremes for the whole. This is especially obvious, and dysfunctional, with regard to the achievement goal. Many organizations and managers assume that the desire of an employee to do something that matters and do it well is the exception rather than the rule. So, when an isolated problem occurs, control systems and supervisory styles are applied to everyone, and that has the effect of demotivating the great majority who come to work eager to contribute.

In summary, this chapter presented what is essentially a positive view of the nature of people at work. That view is supported by the mountain of evidence we have gathered over many years of research, by the thinking and systematic research of others, and by the success of organizations whose policies and practices reflect such optimism.

We say that the essentials of human motivation have changed very little over time. If significant change is observed, it is not that workers' goals have changed, but that management is acting differently and is reaping the consequences of its actions.

For example, treat workers as disposable commodities, which began to happen with the downsizings of the late '80s and the '90s, and—surprise!—employees are no longer "loyal." Why would they be? Most people are eager to strongly identify with an organization of which they can be proud and that treats them well. But it would be irrational for people to be loyal to organizations that show no interest in them other than as, essentially, "hands"—temporary hands at that—to get the work done.

Nothing is very complicated about what we have proposed. Although the detailed implications for management practice are reserved for future chapters, those are not complicated either. Let's call them the "blocking and tackling" of an enlightened management, enlightened in its understanding that what the overwhelming majority of people seek from work doesn't conflict with management's objectives and, in fact, usually strongly supports them. Satisfying these goals—fairness of treatment, pride in work and company, and a sense of camaraderie with fellow employees—is to everyone's advantage. The results will be outstanding. Let's now look in more detail at the evidence for the business implications of employee enthusiasm.

2

Employee Enthusiasm and Business Success

"...there is one key to profitability and stability during either a boom or bust economy: employee morale."

—Herb Kelleher, Southwest Airlines Founder

"Only people who want to, work this hard."

—Jim Mittelhouser, Netscape Founding Engineer, commenting on the 70-hour workweek norm at Netscape

Having explored the question of what workers want in the previous chapter, we now address the obvious business question: so what? Simply put, what does employee enthusiasm have to do with business success? Because, from the organizations' perspective, unless there is a connection between what workers want and the business results that organizations need, there is little reason to pursue the subject.

Making the Connection

Over the years, many of our clients have been notable for their long-term success. These clients include companies such as Starbucks, Intuit, American Express, *Barron's* Magazine, US Cellular, and Mayo Clinic. These organizations have, on the surface, little in common; they vary by industry, geographical area, and business model. However, they do share one thing: the morale of their workers, as measured by our surveys, is much higher than most other companies. We posit that this is one of the key characteristics of virtually every company that has had long-term success and that the high morale of their workers is due to specific policies and practices that engender enthusiasm in their employees for their jobs and their companies.

What these organizations do specifically to achieve employee enthusiasm is detailed in future chapters. For now, let's closely examine what we mean by worker enthusiasm and show how it relates to business success.

Employee morale is measured on a continuum, but we make a rough distinction between four levels of morale: enthusiasm, satisfaction, neutrality, and anger. These levels are operationally defined simply by asking workers to consider everything that can affect how they feel about an organization and then to rate their overall satisfaction with it. This is the same question we used in Chapter 1, "What Workers Want—The Big Picture," to test the universality of the Three Factor Theory. It asks workers, in effect, to provide a summary measure of their morale. What goes into this mental calculus is left up to that individual (for example, how much weight an employee gives to pay, to her boss, to advancement opportunities, and so on). By not characterizing satisfaction or setting conditions or comparisons, we are most likely to get a clear and unbiased picture.

We have asked about overall satisfaction using that formula since 1972, and some striking differences emerge between organizations. Before we review the specifics, let's define organizations with enthusiastic employees: these are organizations that generally have more than 85 percent of their workers indicating overall satisfaction and less than 10 percent indicating dissatisfaction. Based on this criterion, we find that of all the many organizations we have surveyed, only about 14 percent can be categorized as having an enthusiastic workforce. The focus in much of this book is on the very important difference—a difference rarely commented on—between organizations with moderately satisfied employees, which make up the bulk of our surveyed employees, and those organizations with enthusiastic employees. (The small minority of companies with truly discontented and angry workforces is discussed later in this chapter.) That is, as we have said, there is a world of difference between working for a "pretty good" company and a "terrific" company.

Organizations, especially very large ones, are complex entities that, while having distinct cultures and practices and therefore morale levels significantly different from each other, nevertheless exhibit quite a bit of internal variability.

For example, in one of our companies with high morale—a very large corporation with hundreds of departments—the bulk of the departments show high overall satisfaction, but the range across departments is 100 to 41 percent. In one of our lowest scoring large corporations, the range across departments is 65 to 30 percent. These ranges are typical, and there are many reasons for them—the most important being differences in the styles of individual managers within those organizations.

Why do we call companies with superior overall satisfaction scores—whether total companies or units within them—enthusiastic? Why not simply call them "highly satisfied?" Because something going on at these elevated ranges is much different from what we find in organizations where employees are just moderately satisfied. And, as we show in the next section, organizations with enthusiastic employees are, on average, much *higher performing* organizations than the rest.

Telling Us in Their Own Words

Not only do these high-enthusiasm/high-performing organizations look different in the statistical data, but their people literally sound different when providing "write-in" comments. At the conclusion of most of our survey questionnaires, as we have mentioned, we ask employees to summarize their views in their own words instead of responding to a multiple-choice question. Employees are usually asked, "In your own words, what do you like most about working here?" and "What do you like least?" (or, occasionally, "What do you most want to see improved?"). We categorize the answers into various content categories.

Here's a sampling of the comments from workers in enthusiastic organizations:

> *We are totally committed to our customers. This is the passion of this company from the executive suite to my colleagues on the front line. I know from firsthand experience that customers believe they are the primary focus of our business and greatly appreciate the level of service and attention we provide them.*

> *We are a dynamic company with first-class leadership. Our boss is the best. Her word is her bond. It may sound corny, but I would go into battle with her as my leader. We, almost to a person, are always striving to be the best. We are...able to move quickly in a rapidly changing marketplace because we have business-savvy leaders. But, I feel our greatest strength is managers with high levels of integrity.*

> *The bottom line isn't everything here; employees count, too.*

> *We really work together like a team. Everyone listens with respect to your ideas. I've never worked at a place like this. It's almost never who you know or your background that matters but what you know. We can speak our minds and tell it like it is. Nobody points fingers— if there's a problem, we roll up our sleeves and fix it.*

> *I mean it, I feel like I've died and gone to heaven here. If things stay this way, I'd like to spend the rest of my working life for this company. You feel like a real person, not just a number.*

Employees in enthusiastic organizations have concerns as well. Here are some of their responses to the question, "What would you say are the organization's key areas for improvement either as an employer or as a business?"

> *Keep the improvements in communication with [a certain group] going! We do read those e-mails, and I have been surprised how*

much it means to my staff to feel like they are included in what is going on.

The company spends too much on legal bills. Why does the company have an internal legal staff, but high outside legal bills? The company could save a lot of money by changing how it does business in this aspect.

It would be helpful to help people understand "the big picture." What I mean by this is that sometimes corporate will ask something of the divisions and we do not understand "the big picture" on why it is needed. Maybe a flow chart to show how reporting is put together. It could make everyone see how they fit into the puzzle.

Eliminate redundancy and unnecessary paperwork to speed up the approval process in all aspects of their business. It's gotten better, but it's not good enough.

Develop better internal relationships between departments. I still feel there is a power struggle between certain areas of the [department name] management group and the [department name] group. Maybe it only involves the employees at my level. This area could benefit from improved personal relationships and communication.

My team knows what it's doing. We just have to get [a higher-level manager] off our backs. He means well, but he's too damn nervous.

Re-evaluate the pay scale from time to time. We might start losing people.

Most of the concerns are business-oriented rather than about personal grievances. And so even their frustrations demonstrate their commitment to the company in that they want to see it even more successful.

On the other hand, employees in companies we have labeled "moderately satisfied" tend to express a liking and appreciation for the organization, but with little sense of active enthusiasm or involvement. Take these comments, for example:

The pay is not bad and the benefits are competitive. I especially appreciate the tuition refund program.

This is a company that has been around for a long time. This gives me a comfortable feeling about my job security.

My manager is a considerate person, and I like her. She is flexible when a family problem arises.

They seem to understand that everyone makes an error now and then, and the world doesn't come crashing around you when you have a bad day.

I love the location.

Here is what employees in the moderately satisfied companies say about what they'd like to see improve. Now, many personal gripes are expressed, often accompanied by a lack of confidence in management:

The pay is not keeping up with the cost of living, and please explain why new hires doing the same job are making as much as the people who have been here for years, like me. Doesn't loyalty count?

At my location, there is a lack of structure, and the qualifications and experience of people with the same jobs are different and varied. Nobody will explain to me why this is so and why the pay should be so different from person to person.

The endless changes that happen at every moment without any rhyme or reason as far as I can tell. Doesn't management know what it's doing?

There is an undue emphasis on systems and procedures that interfere with the delivery of services.

There is little opportunity for people like me because I don't have the sheepskin. It's very discouraging since my evaluations are always very positive, my co-workers come to me for advice, but I can't get ahead because I don't have a degree.

I rarely ever see my manager. He stays in his office and only shows up when there is a crisis. Also, it wouldn't be a bad idea if the people at the top would visit now and then.

There's a lot of favoritism in who gets overtime.

Enthusiastic employees are caught up in the organization and identify with it, so its successes and failures become, in effect, the employees' successes and failures. This is above and beyond a pragmatic calculation, such as the impact of the company's performance on employees' income potential or job security. This is also a psychological phenomenon: psychologically, the company becomes part of an employee's self-image so that company performance is felt as if it were the individual's own performance. This is not too different from the avid sports fan's "living and dying" with the ups and downs of his team. This is my team; this is my company.

Employee enthusiasm is therefore not just a feeling or an attitude: it is a motivated state, impelling people to action. Unlike sports fans, employees can do a lot to *directly* affect the success of their team; in fact, if all they do is cheer from the sidelines, the company gets into trouble. Everyone who has worked knows the potential that can be tapped when people really care about their companies and their jobs. That potential is an employee's discretionary effort: the difference between the minimum an employee has to do on the job and what he is capable of doing.

Enthusiastic employees routinely produce significantly more than the job requires, often working all kinds of hours to get things done (and done right); search for ways to improve things rather than just react to management's requests; encourage co-workers to high levels of performance and find ways to help them; welcome, rather than resist, needed change; and conduct transactions with external constituencies—such as customers—in ways that bring great credit (and business) to the company.

Moderately satisfied employees, on the other hand, comprise a generally willing workforce, doing what the company wants and usually without complaint. However, it is more of a passive loyalty. Enthusiastic employees don't need to be asked.

Individual employees often come to mind when managers think of differences in enthusiasm. There are, of course, differences in proneness to enthusiasm among individuals (some people are by nature more "up" than others), and no company has policies, practices, and managers that suit everyone and evoke uniformly positive attitudes. But, as our data show, there are marked organizational and unit differences in the enthusiasm felt and displayed by workforces as groups. Let's examine a few specific organizations that have enthusiastic workforces.

A Few Leading Organizations

We will provide in this book numerous illustrations of how the principles we advocate have been applied—or violated—in the real world and the positive—or negative—consequences for those organizations. The most comprehensive example will be Mayo Clinic—one of the world's premier healthcare organizations (in Chapter 12, "The Culture of Partnership"). Here, early on, are some brief, real-life illustrations of the concepts we have discussed thus far.

Intuit

For about 30 years, Intuit has led a burgeoning industry of software development and sales in the important area of business and financial management of small organizations, the accounting professions and consumers, through its popular Quicken, QuickBooks, and TurboTax products. Intuit also surveys its workforce regularly, most recently through Sirota.

Consider their survey data. First, overall satisfaction measures at 88 percent. This, in and of itself, is a very high percentage—much higher than the Sirota norm of 74 percent. But the Intuit data are yet more instructive and impressive. The firm's survey includes questions that address the three factors. For example, the company asks its employees to rate management on its respectful and dignified treatment of workers (Equity), the extent to which employees are encouraged to find innovative ways to do things (Achievement), and their sense of belonging to a group that works well together (Camaraderie).

Table 2-1 shows that the Intuit results on those questions are well above external norms.

Table 2-1 Intuit Survey Results Versus the Norms

	% Favorable	
	Intuit	**Norm**
Equity	93%	65%
Achievement	85%	76%
Camaraderie	88%	80%

Intuit gives its employees something to achieve: "Our goal is to create new ways to manage finances and small businesses that are so profound and simple that our customers cannot imagine going back to the old way." And, the company has an "Employee Value Proposition" that it takes seriously and tracks continuously. The proposition states that Intuit will create a great place to work by fulfilling the following employee expectations:

- Help me be productive, do great things, and be the best I can be.
- Let me know where I stand and how I'm doing.
- Invest in me to help me grow fast.
- Pay me fairly and recognize my contributions.
- Make me an integral part of the team.
- Create a positive work environment.

Intuit's dedication to keeping its promises to employees is exemplified by the way it carefully tracks its performance: "The measurement system [employee surveys] at Intuit provides an ongoing check on how the company is living up to its values, values that reflect what managers know to be related to the firm's ultimate financial success."[1] The fact that survey results are taken seriously by the company is indicated not only by the high scores it achieves, but by the 90 percent plus response rates to its surveys year after year. Employees clearly trust that the surveys—and the Employee Value Proposition—are more than public-relations exercises.

Herman Miller

We said that a hallmark of enthusiastic employees is their taking initiative—they don't have to be asked. Consider this example from Herman Miller, an office-furniture company widely admired both for its business success and for its highly progressive employee relations practices:

> On learning that the American Airlines national office was about to become their neighbor, enterprising employees at a Dallas branch of Herman Miller, the office-furniture company, wrote a letter asking the airline to consider furnishing their new office with Herman Miller products.
>
> Their initiative paid off in a sizable order. But, the week before the airline office opened, the employees who went over to check that the order had been delivered properly found that the packing crates had crushed the plush on the fabric of hundreds of chairs. So, the employees formed teams to work around the clock and over the weekend to raise the plush with steam irons.[2]

Federal Express

The management literature is replete with anecdotes from companies such as Herman Miller that demonstrate the great lengths—sometimes, nothing short of heroic—to which highly motivated employees will go to serve their company and its customers. Frederick Smith, the founder of Federal Express, tells this story:

> ...a Rocky Mountain blizzard had knocked out a mountaintop radio relay, cutting off phone service at several Federal Express offices. The phone company would not be able to repair the connection for five days. So, Hal (a FedEx telecommunications expert) chartered a helicopter (using his personal credit card). When the pilot couldn't land, Hal jumped out, slogged through waist-deep snow, and reconnected the cables. He didn't go through layers of approval. He just acted. He knew what he had to do was right.[3]

Crescent Real Estate

Enthusiasm is actually one of the stated "values" of Crescent Real Estate, a well-known national real-estate company. The company values include "integrity, leadership, people, teamwork, innovation, service, communication, relationships, discipline, and performance." Detailing its "people" values, Crescent declares, "We will hire, develop, retain, and reward exceptional and *enthusiastic* (emphasis added) people." CEO John Goff pointedly commented to us, "I'd rather have enthusiasm than smarts." So, the following comments by Crescent workers should not come as a surprise:

> We never stop trying to outdo ourselves in regards to the services/ amenities that we provide. Our people bring pride, passion, and commitment to real estate. Everyone I talk to takes pride in their work, with a passion to see our company succeed.

> The people respect each other and believe there is value in the contribution they make individually and as a team to make the workplace environment "solution oriented."

> Coming to work does not feel like a chore but a joyful part of the day.

> No matter what the problem may be, they [the company] always seem to go the extra mile to try and solve the problem and make sure the person and/or persons are taken care of.

> Crescent really cares about its employees. That personalization, in my opinion, is what breeds loyalty by team members. (You feel like a real person—not just a number.)

Enthusiasm is not a recipe for perpetual bliss or automatic success, and it has little in common with "contentment." Avid sports fans want their team to win all the time, so frustrations are inevitable. Caring employees are therefore often frustrated employees. Not only does their company—their team—sometimes lose, but in a changing and competitive business world, the status quo is rarely good enough, so the drive for success translates into a continual striving for improvement. It is no wonder that people who strongly identify with an organization can often say, in response to praise about the organization's performance, that they are still unhappy with where things are. It's the curse of caring.

We said that employee enthusiasm decreases in most companies after the first 6 to 12 months of employment. This shift would be even larger if first-year attrition were taken into account, because most voluntary turnover occurs within the first year as people and their employers learn whether they've found the right fit. The employees who leave are, on the average, much less satisfied than those who stay and, if they were not able to leave, would depress the later satisfaction scores even more.

Yet, although the overall results show declines, there are major exceptions, companies where the decline is much less sharp. These are the "enthusiastic" organizations we have been discussing and from which we draw examples of the policies and practices that harness, rather than depress, the initial enthusiasm and excitement that people bring to their work.

Before concluding the discussion on enthusiasm, we need to consider the other end of the morale continuum—namely, severe discontent. Approximately 5 percent of the companies that Sirota surveys can be characterized as having highly discontented, often hostile, workforces. Hostility is obviously different from enthusiasm, but they are similar in one major respect: *they are both highly motivated states that impel people to action.* In that sense, they are different from both moderate satisfaction and neutrality. ("What the heck, it's a job," typifies the neutral employee's attitude.)

Anger is primarily a product of a sense of injustice. While the motivation of an enthusiastic employee is to go beyond the job requirements, the motivation of an angry employee is to do less and often to influence others, informally or formally, to restrict their work. In other words, the goal is to somehow harm the organization because this, in the minds of the aggrieved, at least partially redresses the felt inequities. This is not just an economic issue. People who feel unjustly treated also don't want to feel stupid by allowing themselves to be exploited. Other consequences of employee anger are poor treatment of the company's customers, poor treatment of "internal customers" (that is, a lack of cooperation with other units), absenteeism, tardiness, theft, and, in more extreme cases—when anger turns into rage, such as in explosive labor disputes—violence and acts of sabotage to the company's property.

A feeling of injustice, then, produces anger but, as we have shown, feeling equitably treated does not produce enthusiasm (for most people and by itself). It is a precondition for enthusiasm. That is, although it is nearly impossible to be enthusiastic about an organization that treats its employees poorly in terms of the basic conditions of employment (pay, for example), being treated well in those respects is just a part of the story. An assembly-line worker can be very well paid, have good benefits, and so on, but be terribly bored with the tedious routine. He is then likely to be "moderately satisfied." But, because the equity needs are being met, the employee doesn't feel much anger. Bored workers, figuratively or literally, go to sleep; they don't strike out at the company. However, add a sense of injustice to that, and anger is the likely result. (Remember the response to the speed-up at the Lordstown Plant that was discussed in Chapter 1.)

"Enthusiasm" Versus "Engagement"

Readers familiar with the recent literature in organizational psychology—especially since the original edition of this book was published—may be puzzled by our use of the term employee enthusiasm rather than the now-more-prevalent "employee engagement." The use of the latter arose largely in reaction to what some theorists saw as the inadequacy of "satisfaction" as a way to describe the employee sentiment in which companies should be interested. Employee engagement, as operationally defined, is usually some combination of employee satisfaction, pride, advocacy, loyalty, and discretionary effort. Satisfaction alone appeared to these theorists to smack of "contentment," as in a contented cow, arguing that "...a satisfied employee might show up for her daily 9-to-5... But that same 'satisfied' employee might not go the extra effort on her own..." and would probably leave for a small increase in pay. "Satisfied isn't enough."[4] The reader will quickly recognize the similarity—the near-identity—of engagement and what we have termed enthusiasm.

Although we can debate labels forever, the reality is that, for practical purposes, there is little difference between the use of satisfaction alone and its combination with other questions into an "engagement index." The Sirota firm asks all the engagement questions, and we are therefore able to correlate the scores on overall satisfaction with the engagement index. The correlation is .91! That high a correlation means that there is virtually no difference in the use of the two measures, and, to avoid confusing the many readers familiar with the first edition and its findings, we decided to continue to work with the overall satisfaction measure. Despite all the talk about the superiority of "engagement" over "satisfaction," there is just no practical difference.

On a more substantive level, we thought it wise to differentiate ourselves from others because the sources of enthusiasm discussed in this book are different in a major respect from what one finds in the engagement literature. Not only do the proponents of engagement show disdain for the traditional terms "satisfaction" and "contentment"—they are disdainful as well of what traditionally have been key determinants of sound employee relations, such as how and how well employees are paid, their job security, and their benefits. The focus in discussions of engagement is on the psychological aspects of work—such as communications, recognition, and teamwork—since, after all, engagement is a psychological state, a "heightened emotional connection." As you will learn, we in no way deny the importance of the non-material components of work and the work environment. Many of our chapters are devoted to precisely those topics. But you will also soon learn, in our Equity chapters (Chapters 3–6), that it is folly—indeed, nutty—to ignore the crucial role of the material dimensions of work if the goal is to build and sustain an enthusiastic, engaged workforce.

Enthusiasm and Performance: The Research Evidence

Thus far, our evidence for the relationship between morale and performance has consisted of anecdotes. As interesting as anecdotes are, we don't rely only on them to make our point since any argument—or its opposite—can be proven with a few stories. A large and impressive body of evidence, from solid, systematic research conducted across many companies, clearly demonstrates the strong statistical relationship between policies and practices that generate employee enthusiasm and business performance. Here is just some of the relevant research.

Jeffrey Pfeffer, in his comprehensive review of the research, concludes that gains of about 30 to 40 percent can be realized by companies implementing work practices that result in high employee commitment. The studies covered by his review are wide ranging; they include investigations of the survival rates of initial public offerings of companies with different work practices and detailed research on the impact of these practices on profitability and stock price in many different industries. For example, a study of steel mini-mills reveals that mills "...using commitment-oriented management practices required 34 percent fewer labor hours to produce a ton of steel and showed a 63 percent better scrap rate." A study of nearly 200 banks finds that differences in such practices are associated with an approximately 30 percent difference in financial performance.[5]

Russell Investments, the firm responsible for the Russell market indices, has tracked the 1998–2010 performance of the S&P 500 against the stock returns of the publically traded firms that made the list of the Fortune 100 Best Companies to Work For (see Table 2-2).

Table 2-2 How FORTUNE's 100 Best Companies to Work For Performed Against the S&P 500

	100 Best Companies to Work For	S&P 500
Annualized Return (1998–2010)	11%	4%
Cumulative Return (1998–2010)	291%	63%

Source: Russell Investments

The annualized return is the average annual return rate for the publically traded companies on each year's list of the "100 Best," starting in 1998. The cumulative return figure is the total return for each year continuously added from 1998 to 2010, and then expressed as the percentage gained.[6] Without question, investments in the "100 Best Companies to Work For" have greatly outperformed the S&P 500.

The results of our own research on the relationship between employee morale and stock market performance are equally striking. In the first edition of this book, we considered stock market performance in 2002, which was a bad year for the market. (The S&P Index declined 19 percent.) We analyzed the performance of the publicly traded companies we surveyed in 2000–2001. Using overall satisfaction as our measure, we divided the companies into high morale (75+ percent favorable), moderate morale (between 74 and 60 percent favorable), and low morale (less than 60 percent favorable). We chose those satisfaction criteria to provide sufficient numbers of companies at each level. The stock market performance in 2002 of each company was determined and the average performance for the three morale categories calculated. Because different industries perform differently on the stock market in the course of a year, and the companies in our morale categories differed considerably by industry, it was necessary to compare the performance of each of our companies with the performance over the year *of its own industry*. Table 2-3 shows the average changes in stock market price of the companies in each morale category, the average changes in the industries of those companies, and the difference between the two.

Table 2-3 Employee Morale and Stock Performance

Morale Category	Average 2002 Stock Market Performance		
	Of Companies in Each Category	Of Industry Comparison Companies	Difference
High	+1.8%	-18.2%	+20.0%
Moderate	-14.4%	-9.2%	-5.2%
Low	-24.9%	-19.9%	-5.0%

The companies with high morale performed considerably better than their industry comparison group—about 20 percentage points—actually showing a slight increase in stock market value in a bad year for the overall market. The moderate and lowest morale companies performed somewhat worse than their industry comparisons, about 5 percentage points.

For this second edition, we repeated our 2002 analysis (see Table 2-4), now using 2011–2012 stock market results. With overall satisfaction data collected in 2011 as our measure, we again divided the companies into high morale, moderate morale, and low morale. Although there are some differences from 2002 (for one, the market as a whole is more positive in this round), our conclusion remains unchanged: the higher the morale, the stronger the stock market performance. Thus, the high morale group outperformed its industry counterparts by 11 percentage points, the moderate morale companies outperformed its counterparts by just .8 percentage points, and the low morale companies were 13 percentage points *lower* than their counterparts. The relationship therefore holds up—and strongly—even after years of extraordinary turbulence in the stock market.

Similar findings are found for other standard measures of company performance, such as return on investment and return on assets.

Table 2-4 Employee Morale and Stock Performance

	Average 2012 Stock Market Performance		
Morale Category	Of Companies in Each Category	Of Industry Comparison Companies	Difference
High	+15.1%	+4.1%	+11.0%
Moderate	+3.2%	+2.5%	+0.8%
Low	−5.2%	+7.9%	−13.1%

The broad measures of business success are heavily influenced by how people perform day-to-day on the job. Our own research shows, for example, that enthusiastic workers often increase the quality of work by huge percentages—up to a 75 percent reduction in defect rates.[7] We and others find high positive correlations between employee satisfaction and customer satisfaction and sales.[8] In a fascinating study for the National Oceanic and Atmospheric Administration, our firm found strong positive relationships between the "organization culture" index of its various national weather service offices (as measured by an employee satisfaction survey) and a "critical success index," which is an objective measure of tornado warning performance that takes into account positive forecasts followed by an occurrence, occurrences that were not predicted, and false alarms.[9]

Over the past few decades, extensive research has been done around the world on human "happiness," including its meaning, causes, and consequences. As applied to the work situation (often within the context of "Positive Psychology" programs), two of the most prominent researchers in the field conclude: "Happy people are more satisfied with their jobs. They perform better on assigned tasks than less happy peers and are more likely to take on extra role tasks such as helping others. Happy people are less likely to exhibit withdrawal behaviors such as absenteeism. Overall, happy people enjoy greater workplace success than less happy people."[10]

To return to the stock market, there is even what might be called a happiness stock market fund—the Parnassus Workplace Fund—that was founded and has been run since 2005 by Jerome Dodson, founder of Parnassus Mutual Funds. The fund invests exclusively in large American firms demonstrated to have outstanding workplaces. Dodson started the fund when he learned of the previously-mentioned investment analysis of Fortune's "100 Best Companies to Work For," which showed their returns to be much superior to the S&P Index. Mark Crowley reports on the success of the fund in Fast Company, noting that since its beginning (April 2005–January 2013), it has enjoyed a 9.63 percent annualized return, outperforming the S&P by 6.84 percent. In the article, Dodson is quoted as saying that when the workforce is "contented," people are "willing to put out more effort [and] this consistently more engaged performance inevitably reveals itself in the firm's bottom line."[11] The reported period includes the Great Recession, and Crowley argues that in down times, people in these companies are more willing to "pull together to get through the crisis."

In short, the evidence for the positive impact of very high levels of employee morale on business success is strong.

Or is it? A statistician might object to the suggestion that we have provided "proof" that morale has a positive impact on performance. We know that our kind of research—as opposed to a pure experiment—never permits firm proof of causality or its direction. We can speak of a "statistically significant relationship," but the relationship may be from performance to morale rather than the reverse; that is, it is business success that breeds happiness, not happiness that breeds business success. As one executive commented to us regarding the rather mediocre survey results for his company, "Look, what we've got to do is get the profits up and the stock price up—that'll take care of morale. The morale problem is that our performance has been lousy." With this comment, the executive minimized the importance both of employee morale and the management practices that affect morale, such as treating employees respectfully. The only practices that matter, in his view, are those that have a direct impact on profits, such as the company's business strategy and economic and marketplace conditions.

There is no question that business performance has a major impact on employee morale, because an organization that performs well generates employee pride and optimism about job security and advancement opportunities. Furthermore, such organizations can afford to do concrete things, such as increase pay, that elevate morale.

But, does morale also have an independent effect on performance?

Building the People Performance Model

It is extremely difficult to disentangle statistically the various elements of the management-morale-performance equation. There are many variables to deal with, and the statistical methods for determining causality provide rough approximations at best. In a laboratory experiment, all the variables are held constant except the one of interest: the one that is being manipulated. However, in addition to the fact that many of the variables with which we deal cannot easily be manipulated in a laboratory (such as job security), the applicability of the findings in such an artificial environment to the real world is often questionable.

However, a great deal of research has been done that bears, at least indirectly, on this matter. We integrated the best research and thinking in this area and developed a model called the People Performance Model, which encompasses all the key variables (leadership and management practice, morale, and performance) and the way these variables relate to each other. This section shows how the model was built, piece by piece.

The model is not substantive: it does not depict *what* a company should be doing. Rather, it provides a picture of how the various broad categories of variables interact to produce organization performance. The substance for these categories—the specifics of what leaders and managers should actually do—are the subject matter of all the succeeding chapters of this book.

To start, the research we and others have done, plus simple logic, suggests that the relationship between morale and performance is *reciprocal*: each is both a cause and an effect of the other. Some research shows the causality mostly in one direction, some in the other, but most indicate that it likely goes both ways.[12]

As we build the model, the reader will see that we are dealing with a *system* of relationships with numerous feedback loops. As regards employee morale and performance, the morale that business success generates enhances employee performance, which enhances and sustains business success, which enhances and sustains morale, and so on. It is a system of interlocking, mutually reinforcing factors— a virtuous circle, or a vicious circle if the direction is negative.

A good example of how this works is the relationship that's quite consistently found between customer satisfaction and the satisfaction of employees who deal with customers. What causes what? Logic and experience tell us that happy employees make for satisfied customers (that is, morale results in performance), but it goes both ways: having satisfied customers boosts employee morale because it is a key source of pride for them (and generates improved business performance, which we discuss later). Figure 2-1, then, is the first component of the People Performance Model.

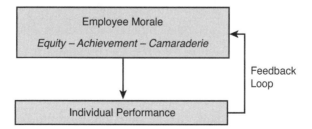

Figure 2-1 The People Performance Model—employee morale and individual performance.

As we develop the model, we will see that it includes a number of reciprocal relationships (or feedback loops). Because we said that employee performance positively affects business performance, Figure 2-2 adds business performance to the People Performance Model, taking into account that business performance also has a positive effect on employee morale.

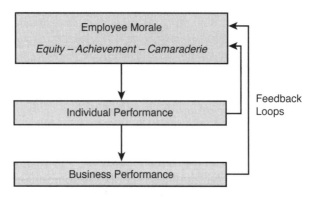

Figure 2-2 The People Performance Model—adding business performance.

Now bring management into the equation. Throughout this book, we discuss how management practices affect performance by their impact on employee morale. But management's actions also directly affect performance. As an example, consider teamwork. A management that encourages teamwork achieves higher performance because of the teamwork itself (collaboration improves performance for the great majority of tasks) and because teamwork elevates the "spirit"—the motivation, the enthusiasm—of employees (by satisfying the camaraderie need). This causes employees to perform at an even higher level. Because the morale-performance relationship is reciprocal, the higher level of performance raises morale further, which leads to even higher performance. Figure 2-3 adds the practices of management into the People Performance Model.

The management practices that are of the most significance in this model—the ones that have the greatest effect on employee morale and performance—are those that fulfill the equity, achievement, and camaraderie needs.

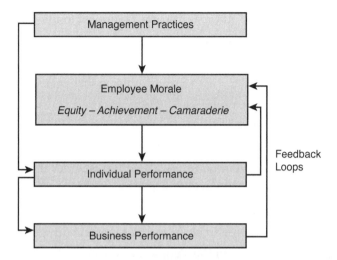

Figure 2-3 The People Performance Model—adding management practices.

Let's get a little more complicated. It is helpful to distinguish management (those whose practices have a direct impact on employees on a daily basis) from leadership (senior management, which sets the organization's overall direction and culture). This distinction is important for understanding how organizations function and also to target leverage points for action. Little of lasting significance changes in an organization without the concurrence and involvement of the leadership.

Similar to management, leadership has both direct and indirect effects on performance. Leadership determines the business strategy. Although this book focuses largely on employee morale and performance, they are obviously not the only determinants of business success. Aside from noncontrollable aspects of the business environment, the other major variable in business success is the sheer competence of senior management, especially the CEO, and the soundness of its business strategy. The soundness of the business strategy, as measured by business success, then loops back to affect employee morale and performance and has a multiple effect on the performance of the business: directly and through the impact of success on employee morale.

The effect of leadership is further magnified by the fact that it sets the organization's culture; therefore, to a large extent, leadership determines the daily management practices that have an impact on employees. Although there are differences between managers in their practices (for example, some are more respectful of employees than others), there is a broad conformity to what senior management wants and stresses. The proportion of disrespectful managers is much greater in organizations where the leadership is either indifferent to, or disdainful of, the importance of treating employees respectfully. These broad cultural differences are true of all the management practices that affect employee morale and performance. Figure 2-4 adds the effect of leadership to the People Performance Model. (Leadership is discussed in considerable detail in Chapter 13, "Leadership and the Partnership Culture.")

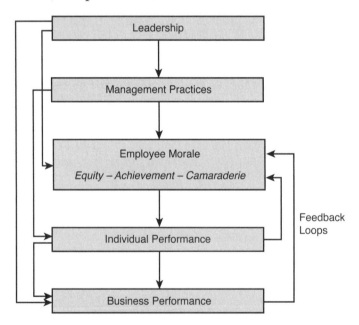

Figure 2-4 The People Performance Model—adding leadership.

No organization exists without customers, and numerous studies have been performed that link the satisfaction and purchasing behavior of customers to the attitudes and performance of employees. This link allows us to include customer satisfaction and behavior in the model (see Figure 2-5). Customer satisfaction with a company has quite consistently been found to relate to a company's profitability.[13] We find that customer satisfaction is a function of the products or services purchased from a company, the business processes with which the company interacts with its customers, and the way customers are treated by the company's employees. The treatment employees give customers, in turn, largely depends on how an organization treats and manages its employees (for example, how organizations pay, show respect for, and assign goals for its employees). As previously noted, customer satisfaction is also part of a feedback loop: it is both a cause and an effect of employee morale.

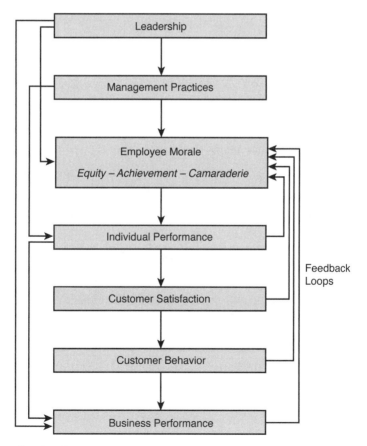

Figure 2-5 The People Performance Model.

Although it might seem complicated, the People Performance Model we show is actually a pared-down version of our full model. For example, we have omitted the other factors that obviously affect customer purchasing behavior, such as price and competitive alternatives. Also, we have not discussed a few arrows in the model, such as the way individual performance (especially employee efficiency) directly affects business performance. No matter. The key points are as follows:

- People and their morale matter tremendously for business success, including customer satisfaction.
- Employee morale is a function of the way an organization is led and the way that leadership is translated into daily management practices.
- Success breeds success (the feedback loops). The better the individual and organization perform, the greater the employee morale, which, in turn, improves and sustains performance.
- The management practices that matter most boost an employee's sense of equity, achievement, and camaraderie.

As we have said, what leadership does—the sheer competence of it, such as setting business strategy—obviously has major and direct effects on employee performance and business success. That is the focus of business scholars and journalists who study and write about the strategic effectiveness (or lack of it) of organizations: products, markets, pricing, mergers, acquisitions, and so on. But, as any true leader knows, having the correct strategy is just part of the story. To be fully realized, especially in the long term, the workforce at all levels needs to be mobilized in its execution.

The remainder of this book discusses the ways in which to win the battle for the minds and hearts of workers. The next chapter begins with justice: basic fairness in the way workers feel their company treats them.

Part II

Enthusiastic Workforces, Motivated by Fair Treatment

We begin our exploration of the policies and practices that facilitate employee enthusiasm with the concept of equity: the degree to which people believe they are treated by their employer with fundamental fairness. This can be addressed either from the point of view of individual employees (such as perceptions of their treatment relative to others in the company) or the treatment of large segments of a workforce. This chapter's focus is on the treatment of large groups, usually entire companies. For this purpose, equity refers to the collective treatment of workers relative to fundamental and generally accepted societal standards. Examples of such societal standards are a "living wage," adequate nonwage benefits (especially, in current times, medical insurance), sensitivity in handling layoffs, safe working conditions, a reasonable workload, and equality of employment opportunity.

These standards are usually seen as defining the fundamental relationship of employers and their workers, and the extent to which groups collectively conclude that they are decently treated.

Traditionally, unions have been concerned about these issues, but the matter is somewhat more complex.

Perceptions of equity are not limited to the obvious physiological and economic factors that are the focus of collective bargaining. So, for example, a key psychological essential in most workers' view of fairness is the need to be treated respectfully. In the workplace, respect means, simply, to be treated as a responsible adult, rather than as a child, criminal, or enemy. Respect might not feed families, but it is vital for employee self-esteem and the extent to which that need is satisfied has profound implications for worker-management relations.

Our discussion of fairness begins, in Chapter 3, "Job Security," with the most basic of workers' economic needs: job security. Chapter 4, "Compensation," is devoted to compensation. Those two chapters were published in the first edition of the book, before the onset, in 2008, of the Great Recession. The recession would, of course, be expected to have a huge impact on employees' attitudes toward their security especially and also their pay. We left Chapters 3 and 4—written in "normal" times—essentially the same for this edition while the specific impact of the Great Recession is the subject of a new Chapter 5, "The Impact of the Great Recession: Flight to Preservation." Hopefully, our economy will soon return to a more normal, less problematic state. Chapter 6, "Respect," is devoted to respectful treatment of workers.

3

Job Security

First, a caveat: the fact that we treat job security as basic for employee morale and performance does not mean that we advocate lifetime employment guarantees. That's impossible for just about any organization. We do urge, however, that if an organization seeks to have enthusiastic workers, it must understand that those employees cannot be treated as fungible objects.

How do workers, in general, view their job security? The "norm" (or average) is 67 percent, which is not too bad, but the range across companies is enormous: 39 percent to 89 percent.

To be sure, the lowest scores are, in part, explainable by reality. For the most part, organizations with scores at the lower end of the range are, in fact, those that recently experienced employee layoffs, had announced plans to do so, or were rumored to have a downsizing soon. For example, in one such company, a very large downsizing had just been completed. In another case, the company had sharply cyclical sales, more than most, so it was repeatedly laying off and staffing up by large numbers. It, too, had a low score for this item.

Another similar company went through a series of layoffs (three waves in only three and a half years), even though the company had promised that there would be no more layoffs after the first wave. Surveyed employees expressed a belief that the layoffs were merely short-term measures to please the investment community and were driven by broad percentage quotas (paying no attention to the critical skills the company lost), had destroyed morale, and had a devastating impact on one small community.

One conclusion might be simply that when workers express anxiety about their job security, it is because their jobs are insecure! But that is only part of the answer. It does not, for example, explain why some companies report much more positive scores on attitudes toward job security despite the fact that they, too, have experienced layoffs caused by economic downturns. Nor does it address the rather straightforward notion that if job loss is the result of financial necessity, why don't workers simply understand that and "suck it up" (emotionally speaking)? Why, in so many cases, is there anger? Why don't "these people" simply understand that job loss is one of the most commonly used and necessary organizational responses to the ups and downs of the economy and that business conditions are often unpredictable?

The fact is that workers often experience layoffs not as prudent business stewardship but as base inequitable treatment. Where does this attitude come from? The answer has two parts: the sense of "substantive equity" (whether the thing itself is fair), and the sense of "procedural equity" (whether what is done is done fairly). First, consider substantive equity.

Alan Sloan captured the spirit of a new era in a 1996 *Newsweek* article:

> *Firing people has gotten to be trendy in corporate America, in the same way that building new plants and being considered a good corporate citizen gave you bragging rights 25 years ago. Now you fire workers—especially white-collar workers—to make your corporate bones... Wall Street and Big Business have been in perfect harmony about how in-your-face capitalism is making America great.*[1]

This new management attitude includes ordering layoffs when a company is doing *well*. In the early 1990s, several large corporations downsized despite being profitable. In 1993, *The New York Times* reported that "...despite being consistently profitable, the Xerox Corporation... (stated)...that it would cut...nearly 10 percent of its workforce over... three years to improve productivity." In so doing, Xerox became another big company trying to improve the efficiency of its operations by dismissing large numbers of people. The day it announced these layoffs, its stock went up about 7 percent.

What message does management convey by these and similar actions? It might be an encouraging message to the investment community (although later we argue that it should not necessarily be), but to workers it is simply this: "Forget all that talk about you being an *asset* to the company; you are really a cost and a disposable commodity. And we will keep our costs down!"

How do workers react to the type of corporate conduct described by Sloan or displayed by Xerox? Consider these comments made to open-ended questions in our surveys:

> *...the greatest detriment to morale in this company...(is) the frequent layoffs. Layoffs have become a lifestyle. You may feel such action is necessary so that a real profit can be made even in bad years, but you are paying a huge cost in disloyalty of employees, stress-related illnesses, etc. I understand you feel you have no choice, but I can't help but wonder if there wasn't another way.*

> *There is no job security. Skills and training do not provide job security. Employees are commodities, not assets. No one gets credit for past performance; now it is passed performance.*

> *How can an employee feel any loyalty to a company whose top management keeps reaping benefits in the millions of dollars and keeps laying off employees to better their position? The golden umbrella is another example of upper-management benefits.*

People react strongly to a loss of security and the lost sense of fair treatment that comes with it in circumstances such as these. We already noted that the need for people to feel that they are being treated fairly is basic, and nothing is more basic for most employees than job security. The impact of employees feeling that they are not treated equitably in this respect can be strongly negative on the organization. Again, look at a few more real-life comments:

> *How can people be expected to grow and better themselves when faced with constant layoffs? As a young person, I know there is little opportunity here for me. That is why I have recently accepted an offer with another company and will be leaving soon. (The result: "brain drain.")*

> *This company's plans for the future are easy to state—layoffs. Isn't that what they keep saying? I am a contributor...(but) now they say they may consider outsourcing! The moods and attitudes are worse than they have ever been, except for the execs! (The result: polarization.)*

> *There is absolutely no loyalty to people here—it's here today, gone tomorrow. What's the point of working hard? Whatever you do, you're just as likely as not to be out on the street tomorrow. (The result: lessened effort and performance.)*

> *These continual layoffs lead me to believe it's time we got union representation. We hear they'll be outsourcing jobs while they're laying off domestic employees. Unions have the power to protect against that. We need that power. (The result: industrial conflict.)*

Although companies can preach forever that "our people are our most important asset," that means little when dismissing workers in times of economic difficulty is the first thing a company does instead of the last. What's even worse is laying off people despite the business being successful. The impact is equally negative when standards of "procedural" justice are violated, such as when employees who are laid off are provided with minimal financial and other assistance or where the layoffs occur with little or no notice. No magic potion exists, and no one would rationally suggest that companies should not lay off workers when there is no other choice. However, even where workers understand the financial necessity, the manner and methods used by the company may be seen as unfair.

Again, look at some real-life comments:

I feel the layoff policy is unfair. I am leaving the company soon and told my manager so because we know that layoffs are coming in our group.... He told me I would probably save someone's job by telling him and creating a vacancy. However when I asked for the package, I was denied. He did not even try to see if it was possible. My feeling is this: if they are going to let a certain number of people go and my job will be considered as one of those, why should I not be entitled to the same treatment (the layoff package)? Management has consistently said it's not voluntary, but this case is different. They're counting my vacancy as one of their "numbers" to lay off.

We are treated as stepchildren compared to other companies! I come to work, do my job, and go home at night wondering... I really don't think the company realizes what its employees go through with all these layoffs. If you are going to lay off, "do it all at once." Get it over with and stop the phony promises that "this is the last one." These people who don't get laid off this time are not survivors because you'll do it again! Please do what you have to and get it over with.

A major issue is the amount of notice that employees get before being laid off. Here are some horror stories from dot-com companies as they downsized during the implosion of the industry in 2001:

- In one company, emails were sent to 20 percent of the workforce telling them to be at a meeting at a local hotel in 15 minutes. There, they were told that they were being laid off; they were locked out of the building and had to make appointments to clean out their desks.

- In another company, 60 employees met in a large conference room where the names of the 40 who were being laid off were announced.

- Employees in a company went to a meeting where they were told that some of them would be laid off; they were instructed to return to their desks and check their emails. Forty of them received emails that communicated their dismissal.

- An employee in a company returned from his vacation to find his work-team's desks occupied by an entirely new group of people. Half an hour later, management told him that he had also been laid off.

How companies deal with job security is one of its defining characteristics in its employees' eyes. It is a defining characteristic because, in addition to its economic effects, a decision to lay off people sends a message of fundamental importance to the workforce about the way the company views its people: not as assets but merely costs (necessary evils).

We argue that the way many American companies now seem to operate, by essentially using downsizing as a strategic maneuver rather than as a last resort compelled by economic necessity, is largely misguided and self-defeating. It violates a fundamental need of workers and, in doing so, severely damages the sense of equity that's necessary for effective organizations.

Some people urge that this argument is old-fashioned and that today's workers have different attitudes about job security. Their view goes something like this: starting in the mid 1990s, a "new generation" of workers entered the American workforce—young people who readily move from company to company and for whom job security is a low priority. These thinkers posit that the "new workers" want an environment where they feel "empowered" and "self-actualized" and, above all, in which they can develop the necessary skills to find a job in another company when they decide to leave.

Suppose, however, that employment elsewhere is difficult to find. How uninterested in job security are these young people then? It was not security in general that became unimportant for many young people in the 1990s—instead, it was security in *one* company. The late 1990s were boom times with plentiful job choices; why be concerned about continued employment in any one company if employment elsewhere is so easy to obtain? But, times changed in late 2000. The high technology sector imploded, and the country experienced its first economic downturn in a decade. Hundreds of thousands of workers were laid off and, once again, the media were filled with tales of high anxiety in the workplace. Surveys clearly showed that job security rose to its usual high position on the list of worker concerns. For example, workers in the telecom industry, whether currently employed or not, ranked job security as the number-one attribute they looked for in employers.

The impact of the Great Recession on workers will be discussed in Chapter 5, "The Impact of the Great Recession: Flight to Preservation." We just note here its recent, enormous impact in the political arena. The predominant theme of the 2012 presidential campaign was "Jobs! Jobs! Jobs!" Does anyone still believe that job security is unimportant for American workers and their families, "new generation" or not?

Don't believe for a moment that stable employment—the predictability, not just the size, of a paycheck—is ever a trivial issue for workers. An environment in which many jobs are available is, by definition, a secure environment. The late 1990s-type boom is uncommon in the career experiences of the great majority of workers, so for most people most of the time, the employment stability that a company offers is critical.

Equally momentous is a company's decision *not* to downsize when other companies in the industry take that path. Such companies do exist. The in-your-face capitalism described by Sloan and others, while increasingly prevalent, is not a universally accepted model; if it were, our survey data would be nearly all negative! The alternative philosophy is exemplified by these comments from two highly successful CEOs:

"Sure, we could take out a lot of our people. But we could give up our future. One, we'd demotivate the people who remained. Two, they surely wouldn't have the loyalty they have now. Three, if there were any good people left, they wouldn't be here long. They'd be looking around. And uncertainty reduces risk taking."[2]

—Wolfgang Schmitt, Rubbermaid CEO, when growth of his company slowed

"I had always figured out how to maintain full employment, because I totally believe that when you bring people into your workforce, they're taking on debt, they're building families. They're trying to go forward in terms of their lives. To pull that from under them is probably one of the biggest disgraces I could ever imagine."[3]

—Jack Stack, CEO of Springfield Remanufacturing Corporation

The policies represented in these views are not just humanitarian—*they are the best for the business.* How do we know that? Let's examine the heart of the claim, which is that layoffs are good for a company in the ordinary course (the implication being, of course, that the financial benefit trumps the human issues). To some readers, Xerox's actions (described earlier) will no doubt sound like good business. These are the kinds of actions that, we are told, have finally dispensed with old-fashioned and inefficient paternalistic management.

Sure, a layoff often results in a short-term spike in a company's stock price. However, the impact on the long term can be quite different. *There is now a mountain of evidence that casts doubt on the efficacy of downsizing for many companies as a cost-reduction strategy.* At the least, the projected savings are greatly overestimated. Basically, the studies show that only about one-third of companies that downsize gain increased productivity and profits over the subsequent 3- to 5-year period. Further, these companies *underperform* the stock market over that time. Research done in the mid 1990s found that downsizing companies outperformed the S&P only slightly during the 6 months following news of a restructuring, then lagged badly, netting a negative 24 percent by the end of 3 years.[4]

The theory of keeping a company "lean and mean," then, may really be only "mean." One study found that, on average, a 10 percent reduction in workers resulted in only a 1.5 percent reduction in costs.

Why the surprisingly poor results for downsizing companies? Lester Thurow of MIT argues that, "Layoffs are painful and costly. There are innumerable reasons they should be avoided if possible." Among the reasons he cites are the cost of severance payments, the loss of skilled workers who will have taken other jobs and not be available when the company rehires, the retraining of new hires, and, when the layoffs are made, the lower morale and reduced loyalty among the surviving workers.[5]

Contrast the in-your-face-capitalism approach with the approach of *highly successful* enterprises that have made it company policy to avoid or minimize layoffs:

- Southwest Airlines has never laid off any workers, not even after September 11, 2001. CEO James F. Parker said at that time, "We are willing to suffer some damage, even to our stock price, to protect the jobs of our people."

- Federal Express is dedicated to the principle that its people are its most important asset, as evidenced by its "People, Service, Profit" corporate philosophy. People are deliberately placed first because, in the company's view, putting people first makes good business sense. These are not just words: FedEx has an explicit commitment not to lay off employees except under the most extreme circumstances as determined by the CEO.

- Lincoln Electric is a Cleveland manufacturer, famous in the management literature both for its extraordinary business success over more than a century and for its innovative management practices, which include guaranteed job security for its employees. The former chairman, James F. Lincoln, wrote, "The greatest fear of the worker...is lack of income. The industrial manager is very conscious of his company's need of uninterrupted income. He is completely oblivious, evidently, of the fact that the worker has the same need."[6]

- Nucor, a successful steel company—by far the most profitable in its industry—has never had a single layoff. Ken Iverson, Nucor's former CEO and the creator of its culture, writes, "'Painsharing' has helped us get through the tough times without ever laying off a single employee or closing a single facility for lack of work, even when the industry overall was shedding thousands of jobs. But, our history of no layoffs is not noble, altruistic, or paternalistic. It's not even a company policy. We've told our employees time and again, 'Nothing's written in stone. We'll lay people off if it is a matter of survival.' The question is, when is laying people off the practical and sensible thing to do? To compete over the long term, a company needs loyal, motivated employees. Can management expect employees to be loyal and motivated if we lay them off at every dip of the economy, while we go on padding our own pockets?"[7]

- The well-being of employees is a "central value" and layoffs "a last resort" in world-renowned Mayo Clinic. Chief Administrative Officer Shirley Weis says that, "It is our physicians, our scientists, our allied health staff, our nurses that really make a difference.... We are very committed to job security. We'll do everything we possibly can to preserve jobs. Of course, we can't guarantee anything."[8]

Our point, obviously, is not that companies should never lay off employees. For some, that would be suicidal. The real issue is whether employees see the company's decisions as balancing its immediate business interests with a consideration of how those decisions affect employees. Or, is it all just this quarter's earnings and stock price, and everything else be damned?

Few people would expect employee well-being to be the sole, or even the paramount, consideration in business conduct. Certain actions had better be taken in the short term because, otherwise, there might not be a long term! However, things are rarely that black and white. Many factors affect a decision, and the problem, from the point of view of employees in so many companies, is that employees' interests are a distant last—if they count at all—in top management's calculations.

As we have seen in most companies, downsizing the workforce is frequently a short-term solution with little or no long-term benefit.

A short-term business orientation is decidedly not characteristic of highly successful organizations such as Southwest Airlines, Federal Express, Lincoln Electric, Nucor, and Mayo Clinic. A significant part of their longer-term perspective is a respect for employees as assets that are not lightly disposed of. Another example: *Fortune*, in its 2002 "100 Best Companies to Work For"[9] report, describes the philosophy of Edward Jones, a stock brokerage that is now Number 1 on the list. The sinking stock market had a major negative impact on the company, and it cut bonuses but fired none of its 25,000 employees. John Bachman, Jones's CEO explained: "We want...the kind of relationship with workers that make them willing to go the extra mile. You can't do that if you get rid of them whenever times are rocky.'"

The *Fortune* report explains that steps such as hiring freezes and reduced pay may not be sufficient, making layoffs necessary; but it gave the companies credit in its "Best Companies" ranking for handling these layoffs with generosity and compassion. Cisco (Number 15) is an interesting example. Among the steps Cisco took was to provide laid-off employees with their full benefits and one-third of their Cisco salaries if they volunteered to work for a social service agency. They also had preference if rehiring commenced.

The *Fortune* report also contains a description of how Agilent Technologies responded to suddenly plummeting sales and a large workforce surplus. Agilent is a Silicon Valley company whose major products are chips, electronic components, and testing and measurement devices, mostly for telecommunications companies. The story describing what Agilent did in this time of distress is titled, "How to Cut Pay, Lay Off 8,000 People, and Still Have Workers Who Love You." The title is not facetious. Agilent management worked long and hard—indeed heroically—to, first, avoid layoffs, and when that was no longer possible, to cushion the blow. This company exemplifies the kinds of steps that demonstrate a genuine concern for people and their interests. The Agilent story starts with a description of Cheryl Ways, an employee who was told she would be laid off. Ways, responding to the news, worked harder and longer than ever and was typical, *Fortune* reports, of thousands of other Agilent employees faced with the prospect of a layoff. Three months after being laid off, Ways said of Agilent management: "I felt horrible they had to do this. This was my gift to them: To leave my job in the best way possible."[10]

Can a better example be offered of employee dedication to a company? Can anyone doubt the enormous value to a company of such dedication—a value in both good times and bad? Cheryl Ways is not that unusual as a personality—she is what many people are like under the right conditions. It is the policies and practices of companies such as Agilent that are unusual.

An implicit theme of our argument and the evidence we have marshaled is that companies should unhesitatingly scrap the notions that "loyalty is dead" and that displaying a genuine concern for the interests of employees is a sign of inefficient, outmoded, paternalistic management. "You get what you give" should be emblazoned on the office walls of all executives wondering why their employees are indifferent to the goals of the company. Perhaps this motto should be placed on their mirrors because the problem stems from the executives themselves. For, ultimately, workers will not reward the indifference of managers to their employees' basic interests with high levels of enthusiasm and performance. Practices relating to job security are central to employees' basic interests.

Specific Job Security Policies and Practices

So far, we have provided glimpses of how companies that are genuinely committed to providing their employees with stable employment treat those employees. This section provides a more systematic review of these practices, organized under the following five basic principles:

1. They are dedicated to exhausting all possible alternatives before laying off people.
2. When layoffs are impossible to avoid, they use voluntary methods if at all possible.
3. When layoffs are impossible to avoid and voluntary methods are not feasible, too costly, or do not achieve the required numbers, these companies handle involuntary layoffs with generosity and care.
4. They communicate honestly, fully, and regularly with their employees throughout the entire process.
5. They are cognizant of the impact of the layoff on the survivors and take steps to minimize that impact.

The specific practices are as follows.

Principle 1: Exhaust All Possible Alternatives Before Laying Off People

The alternatives to layoffs are most usefully thought of as "rings of defense"—that is, defenses against involuntary layoffs. They fall into three categories:

- Providing meaningful work for surplus employees through measures such as the following:
  - Freezing hiring that, because of normal attrition, opens up jobs that surplus employees might fill, or be trained to fill.
  - Eliminating or severely restricting the use of temporary employees, which again results in jobs that surplus em-ployees might fill.
  - Bringing in work that had been subcontracted.
  - Accepting lower-profit work the company would normally reject.
  - Having people perform other useful tasks, such as deferred maintenance.
  - Providing the training that had been postponed because of the prior heavy workload.
  - Putting people into sales to increase demand.
  - Building inventory.

  The solutions for dealing with surplus employees are, of course, easier to implement when the surplus exists in only one segment of a company that has other growing segments that seek workers. In that case, the company's own people have preference over outside hires, assuming that they have the required skills or can be trained in those skills.

- Reduction of nonlabor expenses through measures such as the following:
  - More efficient purchasing and use of resources (materials, and so on).
  - Deferring capital expenditures.
  - Travel reduction.
  - Cutback in minor expenses, such as newspaper subscriptions and holiday parties.
  - Reduction in dividends to stockholders.

- Reduction of labor costs through measures such as the following:
  - Major work-process restructurings that enhance labor productivity.
  - Reduction or elimination of overtime.
  - Deferring or reducing salary increases.
  - Salary freezes.
  - Across-the-board pay cuts.
  - Elimination of bonuses.
  - Shortened workweeks.
  - Unpaid vacations.
  - Unpaid leaves of absence.
  - Reduction in company contributions to employee benefits.
  - Temporary loan of employees to other companies, such as customers and suppliers.

Taking these steps before considering layoffs has a major positive impact on employee morale, but there are significant ancillary benefits as well. For example, a policy that seeks to avoid layoffs imposes a planning discipline on the organization: workload and staffing projections must be made carefully. When a company is clearly committed to avoiding layoffs, recruiting and hiring are likely to be more purposeful and far more carefully carried out. We are not aware of research on the matter, but it is our impression that, by and large, companies that engage in these policies are more selective in their hiring practices and wind up with significantly more capable workforces. Because these companies typically gain reputations as good places to work, the pool of prospective workers from which they can draw is larger than for an average company. Such organizations also do more training and retraining than the average because a premium is placed on workforce flexibility. They will also more likely promote from within the company. These mutually reinforcing policies and practices help make a reality the company's orientation toward the workforce as a genuinely valued asset.

A particularly impressive demonstration of the impact of a lay-off-avoidance policy on planning can be found in Reflexite, which is a small U.S. manufacturer of reflective materials. As described in a publication of Business for Social Responsibility,

> *"[Reflexite] has a Business Decline Contingency Plan (BDCP), designed to take the uncertainty out of the situation when faced with a downturn or flat sales. The BDCP outlines four levels of severity, the symptoms of each situation, the actions to be taken at each level, and the expected results of that action. So, for example, at Stage I, with 'sales below budgeted sales but ahead of the same period in prior year,' the plan dictates that the company 'defer some budgeted hires,' 'defer some budgeted activities,' 'heighten awareness of current situation,' 'discuss at staff meetings,' and 'monitor overall economic conditions.' In the middle stages, the plan calls for, among other things, soliciting ideas to cut costs and improve productivity and efficiency; cutting overtime; accelerating new product introductions; voluntary leaves and furloughs; deferring lower-priority capital items; deferring raises; and reducing hours. At Stage IV, the most severe condition, where Reflexite 'generates losses for a period of two quarters or more,' the plan calls for 'salary deferments or reductions for balance of exempt employees,' 'trim benefits,' 'early retirements,' 'voluntary resignation offering,' and—finally—layoffs."*[11]

Principle 2: When Layoffs Cannot Be Avoided, First Ask for Volunteers

After all the options are exhausted and before resorting to involuntary layoffs, these companies seek volunteers to leave the company, through either voluntary separations or early retirement. This is accomplished by offering financial incentives, such as cash bonuses coupled with an extension of health insurance coverage and other benefits. Invariably, outplacement assistance is provided. Such programs are typically successful in producing the number of volunteers the company needs.

The major reason the programs succeed is that, for many employees, the offers are simply too good to refuse. They make it financially possible for people nearing retirement to retire early and for others to begin new careers that might otherwise not have been feasible. Also, employees who do not accept the packages leave themselves open to the possibility of involuntary layoffs if the company cannot achieve a sufficient number of volunteers from their efforts.

For many companies and employees, therefore, voluntary downsizing is, to a large extent, a win-win situation. The downsides of these programs for the company are that, in the short term, they're more costly and time consuming than involuntary layoffs. Also, by offering voluntary separation, a company might lose some employees with the most-needed skills because of opportunities that, prior to the offer, the employees could only dream of. Companies that have successfully downsized often make a special point of telling these employees how much they are valued and encouraging them to stay.

Principle 3: When Layoffs Cannot Be Avoided and There Are No More Volunteers, Act Generously and Decently. From a Business Standpoint, You're Doing It Not Just for Those Who Are Let Go, But for Those Who Will Stay

When a company must resort to involuntary layoffs, the best companies—best in our terms—do so in ways that are most supportive to the people being laid off and least damaging to the morale of those who remain. As we saw in the case of Agilent Technologies, doing it right can actually strengthen the bond between the company and its employees.

Doing it right has three components: financial assistance, outplacement assistance, and communications. With regard to financial and outplacement assistance, the best companies tend to be uncommonly generous and helpful in what they do for employees. Thus, while a fairly typical severance for lower-paid employees is one or two weeks for each year of service, these organizations might offer a month's pay for every year of service, plus assistance with medical insurance coverage. Although it has become the norm to provide outplacement assistance to help find a new position, these companies might provide supplements such as financial consultation (including preparation for the tax implications of their severance packages) and an allowance for education and retraining costs or a small-business startup. They often actively help employees find other jobs. Also, they usually guarantee laid-off employees priority consideration for rehire when business conditions improve.

Whatever the specifics, the basic principle is simple: Provide the assistance to employees that makes it clear that the company is doing a great deal to buffer the impact of the layoff. This is a company putting its money where its mouth is and, when preceded by visible and genuine attempts to do whatever possible to avoid layoffs, has a large positive impact on the morale of those laid off and those who remain with the company.

Principle 4: Communicate Honestly, Fully, and Regularly Throughout the Entire Process

These companies do not adhere to the usual communications criterion, which is to communicate to employees only what they need to know. The "need-to-know" rule is precisely the wrong one at this time for this population. That rule says, basically, "Tell them as little as possible," and is appropriate for adversaries from whom a company wants to keep information. But employees whose jobs are—or might be—in jeopardy are not adversaries. The criterion in this situation should instead be, "Tell them everything they will find useful and that is not clearly confidential." And tell them that information as early as possible.

We showed previously how insensitively some dot-coms acted in laying off employees. Although those actions are not necessarily typical of American companies—they might not even be typical of dot-coms—most organizations are not particularly adept at communicating in ways that promote an appreciation on the employees' part that the company genuinely cares about their circumstances. We are referring not just to communications at the time of involuntary layoffs but also to communications from the time that it begins to appear that there is a reasonable possibility the company will have surplus employees. What have we learned from companies that do it well?

For one, these companies communicate to employees as early as possible—even when the need for downsizing is just a possibility. In addition to the "need to know" criterion that causes little information to be communicated, a common management assumption is that it is important to shield employees from upsetting information. Although it's ostensibly an attempt to be helpful to people, this attitude is profoundly unhelpful. If a company is truly interested in assisting its people, it would supply as much information as possible as early as possible so that employees could make important decisions on a more informed basis, such as whether contemplated major expenditures should be postponed.

The credibility of management is one of the factors that most affect employees' sense of being treated justly. This is nowhere truer than in relation to job security. Being seen as hiding known information in this respect—or providing it only when it is absolutely necessary to do so, such as at the last minute—is extraordinarily corrosive to employee morale and to the performance the company receives from its workers. The converse is equally true: leveling with employees, when combined with clearly genuine efforts to maintain security to the extent possible and to buffer the impact of job loss, is a precondition for workforce enthusiasm as we have defined it.

Are we serious? Can we speak of employee enthusiasm when there is a serious prospect of being laid off? Isn't that a contradiction? Of course, no one is enthusiastic about being laid off. Here, we refer to how employees—those who have been laid off and those who remain—view the company. People are realistic. They know about business cycles and the ups and downs of individual companies. As we have said, the basic question for them is, "Is the well-being of employees given serious thought in management's decisions?" If so, employees can be enormously appreciative of their organizations, even in times of pain. We saw this in the case of Agilent, and Continental Airlines is another example. The airline laid off thousands of its employees—about one-fifth of its workforce—in the wake of September 11. In its story on the event, KPRC, a Houston radio station, reported how the employees seemed to bear little resentment toward the company, repeatedly expressing their appreciation for the Continental "family." Said a former employee, "I'm being laid off, but I'll be back. It's the best company I ever worked for, and I'll be back. They're going to rebuild, they're going to need people back."[12] See our discussion of Continental's culture in Chapter 14, "Translating Partnership Theory into Partnership Practice."

Continental's problems, of course, came on suddenly. More typically, the problems emerge over a period of months. The following should be continually communicated to employees from the time that a labor surplus becomes a possibility:

- The company's business environment, both current conditions and, to the extent discernable, future prospects.
- The company's vision and strategy to deal with the business environment, such as new product development, sales initiatives, and the restructuring of work processes to make them more efficient.
- How the company seeks to enlist employees' help to deal with the business conditions, such as getting ideas for cost reduction.
- How the business environment can affect employees and what the company will do to buffer that impact.
- What, to the best of the company's knowledge, employees can expect—in general and as individuals.

Here are some additional communications guidelines:

- The communicators should include various levels of management, especially top management and the immediate supervisor. Employees greatly appreciate the involvement of the top person. Lower levels of management can handle more specific questions and concerns, and managers must receive training to learn how to conduct these meetings.

- Formal media, such as the house organ, should supplement—not be a substitute for—face-to-face meetings.

- The meetings should be designed to give employees the opportunity to register their concerns, ask questions, and make suggestions.

Principle 5: Recognize the Impact of What You Are Doing on the Survivors, and Take Steps to Minimize Negative Impact

A major purpose of everything we've suggested is to ensure that those who are not laid off maintain their commitment to the company and their jobs. What we have described will, in fact, enhance that commitment because a company's basic attitudes toward its people are most convincingly displayed when times are tough—when being generous does not come easy.

Although business operational and strategic issues are beyond the scope of this book, note that an additional key variable in determining the impact on the survivors is the degree to which downsizing takes place in the context of a serious business improvement plan. That is, the impact is a consequence of the way people are treated and the way the company is, in effect, treating itself by effective business management.

We previously mentioned that layoffs may yield little in terms of long-term cost reduction and profitability. In addition to the harmful consequences of lower employee morale, a major factor in these failures is that the efforts are often undertaken as short-term fixes rather than as part of a plan that involves rethinking a company's culture, structures, systems, and processes for lasting improvement. When not part of this broader plan, the likelihood is high that, over time, costs will again inflate as the company seeks to complete its work in the original, inefficient ways.

Survivors' morale is both a cause and an effect of business inefficiency. A downsizing that's handled poorly in terms of employee treatment has a negative impact on employee morale and, therefore, business performance, but morale is also markedly influenced by whether employees view the downsizing as just a short-term fix. In those times, it is especially important that the survivors have a vision of where the company is heading and their role in it. They want to know how the downsizing will serve to not only cope with the company's immediate business difficulties, but also provide it with competitive advantage and a more secure future. Laying off individuals without basic changes in the company's operations and strategies doesn't provide much ground for optimism. We previously noted that the company's approach to coping with current business difficulties and its vision for building a successful future are key elements of what needs to be communicated to the workforce.

In conclusion, another caveat: do not confuse providing employment stability with tolerance for unsatisfactory employee performance. We must distinguish between conditions over which employees have no control—such as a market downturn or the introduction of labor-saving technology—from those where an individual simply chooses not to perform. The latter—whom we estimate to consist of about 5 percent of the average workforce—should, after appropriate counseling and warnings, be terminated. Let's face it: some people would rather not work, at least not hard. This chapter is not about them.

4

Compensation

The reader is reminded that this chapter was written originally in "normal" times—that is, before the Great Recession. The chapter's data and cases have been updated as needed, but a number of its arguments require considerable elaboration for periods of severe economic downturn, and these will be provided in Chapter 5, "The Impact of the Great Recession: Flight to Preservation." In that chapter, for example, we discuss in considerably greater detail how the importance of pay—especially pay *increases*—declined as the importance of job security increased in the recession. But pay is trivial to no one, and for quite a few workers in quite a few companies (especially those doing well), it remained central. Further, be assured that pay's prominence will grow very rapidly once the economy recovers and job insecurity lessens.

We have also added a note to this chapter on how our arguments and recommendations apply to merit pay for teachers—a highly publicized and controversial element of the nation's efforts to improve student performance.

Money as Seen by Workers

Workers see money as:

- Providing for their basic material needs and, ideally, to live in a manner that satisfies them.

- Providing a sense of equity—that is, receiving a fair return for their labors.

- Providing a measure—one of the major measures—of their personal achievement.

- A potent symbol of the value that the organization places on the contribution of both the workforce as a whole and of the individual employee.

Money as Seen by Employers

Employers utilize money to:

- Attract and keep the number and kinds of employees they need.

- Define the organization's objectives, because what the organization pays for—not necessarily what it says—is what it truly wants.

- Motivate employee performance.

- Avoid labor conflict.

Although executives generally (and incorrectly) assume that "employees will never be satisfied with their pay," they are aware that extreme dissatisfaction—a sense of great inequity—hampers the achievement of their attraction, retention, motivation, and industrial peace objectives. To avoid this, companies install pay systems that they hope prevent inordinate discontent and that can be held up as fair but ones that, at the same time, meet the organization's desire to obtain services at the lowest overall cost. What does our research (and the research of others) show about attitudes toward pay, its determinants, and its consequences? Here are the basic findings:

- The level of compensation and the system by which it is determined and distributed are generally equal in their importance to workers.

- People want to earn as much as they can, and it is rare for workers to express that they feel overpaid. In fact, because most employees (about 80 percent) rate their performance as "above average" in their organizations, it logically follows that people would not feel overpaid.

- However, although it is the rare employee who feels overpaid, only about 26 percent (which is our "norm") express dissatisfaction with their pay—that is, feel underpaid. Fifty-one percent of workers say they are satisfied with their pay.

- The higher the level of an employee in an organization, the greater the satisfaction with his pay. In our surveys, senior executives are usually ecstatic with their pay.

- The greater the satisfaction with pay, the higher the overall satisfaction with the organization, trust in management, and a sense that management treats the workforce as an important part of the company.

- We have shown that there is tremendous variability across companies in the percentages of employees satisfied and dissatisfied with their pay. The range is 25 percent to 78 percent satisfied and 10 percent to 58 percent dissatisfied.

- At the extremes—very low or very high actual pay—pay attitudes are determined primarily and simply by the amount of compensation. It's difficult to be satisfied at barely subsistence levels of pay, or for one's complaints to be taken seriously, even by one's self, about pay when earning millions. Between those extremes, the degree of satisfaction with pay is very much a result of comparison—with others, with one's history, with one's perceived performance, with the cost of living, and so on. In roughly the order of their importance, here are what we find to be the major determinants of pay satisfaction:

- How well the organization pays relative to what employees believe other organizations pay for similar work.

- Whether pay increases over time and how increases in one year compare to increases in past years. Tenure, whether explicitly acknowledged or not, is therefore a major criterion people use to judge the fairness of their pay.

- The extent to which pay increases are believed to reflect the employee's actual contribution (performance) and potential contribution (what the employee is able to do because of his training and skills and expanding experience over time).

- The extent to which pay increases reflect increases in the cost of living. During times of high inflation, the cost of living becomes an all-consuming issue.

- The perceived generosity of nonwage benefits, especially medical insurance. As healthcare and medical-insurance costs have skyrocketed, employees have increasingly come to see pay and their benefits costs as offsetting one another. In the minds of many, the increase in medical costs and premiums offset pay increases; therefore, they may see the latter as little or no increase at all ("just barely breaking even, if that"). In general, then, the more generous the medical benefit, the greater the satisfaction with pay.

- How well the employee is paid compared to what other employees in the company, especially those at similar skill levels, are believed to earn.

- Company profitability, or how much the company is believed to be able to pay.

- The discrepancy between the compensation of the general workforce and that of senior management. A large discrepancy is not an issue when the organization is doing well and the workers feel that they are also benefiting from that success: "Let him earn as much as he wants—he deserves it and it's been good for me."

We describe in this book the conditions that distinguish enthusiastic from unenthusiastic employees. Pay is vital in that respect, both substantively—it provides the material wherewithal for life—and symbolically—it is a measure of respect, achievement, and the equitable distribution of the financial returns of the enterprise. As shown in the previous chapter, a sense of equity—of which pay is a key component—acts something like a "gate" to the functioning of achievement and camaraderie. Without a feeling of being treated fairly, the impact of the latter two is greatly diminished. The power of pay is further amplified by the fact that, in and of itself, it is a satisfier of both the equity and achievement needs.

Pay also affects the fundamental credibility of an organization in the eyes of its workers: is it putting its money where its mouth is? For example, is an organization that does well and that claims that its employees are "its most important asset" seen as nickel-and-diming the workforce when it comes to pay? Is a stated emphasis on product quality and customer service made real with rewards for those who produce high quality and provide good customer service? Our surveys frequently reveal large gaps between words and deeds, with employees often defining "deeds" in terms of how an organization pays.

Typically, management bases its evaluation of its pay-system effectiveness on "objective" data, such as labor cost percentages and trends, salary surveys, and formal job evaluations. Aside from the question of the validity of such data, they beg the fundamental question, "How do *workers* see things?" For example, if they see no pay for performance, *there is no pay for performance.* To reward and motivate, pay for performance must be seen *by workers* to exist. As we now explore pay attitudes and their effects in detail, keep in mind the basic proposition that management's views of its policies—pay fairness, its relationship to performance, and so on—are irrelevant (except for management's views of *its own* pay).

In thinking about pay and formulating recommendations for effective compensation policies, it is useful to distinguish the level of pay from the way it is distributed, especially in relation to performance.

Levels of Pay

We mentioned previously that it is virtually impossible for companies to inspire loyalty and commitment in workers who are treated as disposable commodities. Similarly, it is difficult for a company to be able to achieve loyalty and commitment from its workers when it's seen as one of the lower-paying companies (especially in relation to its competition and its profitability). Still, for many workers, job security comes first; when a choice has to be made, workers will usually moderate their pay demands to preserve their jobs. But pay is a close second.

Contrary to popular belief, employees don't expect wildly generous pay for their labors. In fact, they would likely question the motives or competence of management if pay were astonishingly high. Therefore, we must differentiate between the wish for a lot of money and workers' views of what is reasonable and fair. They are capable of separating wishes and fantasies from realistic expectations. Most workers express satisfaction with pay that they consider to be "competitive" and *great* satisfaction with pay they consider to be even a few percentage points above the competition. A few percentage points can mean hundreds of dollars, and that's both materially and psychologically significant to the average employee.

A few examples of individual comments might help give meaning to our argument. These comments are responses to the question, "What do you like most about working here?" We will soon show how employees dissatisfied with their pay express their views.

What I like most about the company is that the pay is decent.
The medical benefits are good, and the pay is comparable to other companies.

I like the pay that I receive here. It is the highest, although by a slim margin, among other companies in the same field. The company shows it values its employees.

The opportunity to contribute to a high-class business such as this one and make a pretty decent paycheck in the process.

The pay is above average for the type of work we do.

I think that the benefits are outstanding and the pay is very reasonable in today's workplace. I also appreciate that the company reimburses my tuition costs.

Unfortunately, the same principle of differentiation holds when pay is below that of the competition: just a few percentage points can count greatly. This principle also comes into play in how workers react to pay increases. An increase that's even slightly below the rise in the cost of living—when that rise has been significant—is generally considered a pay *decrease*. Most workers know the rate of inflation, especially in times of high inflation, down to the last decimal point.

Furthermore, workers are not happy when a pay increase they have just received is less than increases they previously received. This can also be viewed as a decrease or, at least, a disappointment.

To workers, it is critical that their standard of living not fall (as is the case when pay does not keep up with inflation), and it's important that the *rate* at which they move ahead does not decline. These might appear to be small, and even trivial, concerns to highly paid executives, but they are important to the masses of workers who count every dollar. Of course, it is not just a material issue because pay has great symbolic value to workers; it signifies respect, achievement, and equity. Therefore, attitudes toward pay and pay increases have major consequences for pay-for-performance systems. For example, if a "merit" increase is not felt to be an increase because it does not keep up with inflation (in fact, if it is viewed as a decrease), how credible, satisfying, and motivating will the merit pay system be for that employee? We discuss merit pay in detail later in this chapter.

The opinions workers have of their pay are also greatly affected by how they see their organization's financial condition. We have repeatedly asserted that the overwhelming majority of workers are realistic and reasonable. Therefore, they expect more generous pay and pay increases when times are good and less when times are bad. When times are truly bad, they may even be willing to accept pay cuts, especially if those seem necessary to avoid or reduce layoffs.

But, acceptance of pay cuts—or reduced increases or no increases—as *legitimate* depends on whether employees trust their management. Trust, which is often lacking, is in this case a function of:

- The overall views that workers have, based on the totality of their experiences in an organization, of management's credibility and its interest in the well-being of the workforce
- The degree to which sacrifice in bad times is seen as shared from the top to the bottom of the organization

When trust is present, the kind of support an organization can receive from its workers is absolutely amazing.

Here are some additional open-ended comments that demonstrate the various points we have made about pay. They are responses to the question, "Now, what do you like *least* about working here?" We have included an abundance of comments about pay so that the reader gets a full appreciation of what is on employees' minds when they are unhappy on this subject of such importance to them:

> *I have no trust at all in the brass and what they tell us. This company is doing well now. Why is so little trickling down?*

> *Additional workloads that are constantly placed on you and really no compensation in pay. We could be equal in pay to other companies, but we do about 12 times the amount of work.*

> *I don't like the fact the pay in my area is not adjusted according to cost of living at all. We've fallen behind.*

Other employers are offering somewhat higher pay. I can't continue to work here when I know there are better opportunities.

The worst thing is working and doing so many tasks at work and not getting compensated for it. The pay here really sucks in that regard. It's at least 5 percent below what other companies pay.

Medical and dental plans increase much more each year than the pay does. Therefore, we are not increasing our pay but decreasing it.

We work for a multibillion dollar company and still cannot pay for rent, utilities, and food. With overtime, I cannot support my family of three. Shame on you!

The pay scale and raises are also disgusting. I have been here for 4 years and barely get paid $9.00 an hour. New employees here are currently hired here at $10.00 (on the average) an hour.

Being able to make ends meet. Salary needs to be more competitive. I don't feel that we are paid enough to do the job that we do. Stop with the balloons and silly games and pay us instead. Most people today do not have the luxury of two incomes.

The pay rate for employees is below industry average. No wonder the turnover rate is so high here.

The fact that my benefits are going up, my co-pays are increasing, and my prescriptions cost more yet we cannot get a decent percentage in our merit raises. A cost of living increase would be appropriate, even a couple percent.

This company does not even keep up with the cost of living index; thus, any annual raise is no raise at all. In essence, the longer you are at this company, you are actually staying the same or going backwards pay wise. I feel this is one of the main reasons good, qualified people leave the company.

Our take-home pay should be much better. This company makes billions. Give us a bigger slice of the pie; there is no you without us.

I agree with the changes to incentive pay plan. It makes sense that if profits are down that we make adjustments to curb the monthly take by sales associates... So why is this information presented to us with the conviction of a parent trying to convince their kid that

Santa's still real? "These changes are a good thing." "These benefit you." Really? All that said, I agree with the need for the changes, but what's with the lying? In fact, that still remains my biggest issue: the dishonesty.

I feel that I have been lied to on a few occasions, one regarding raises being offered. I was told "absolutely, you will be eligible for a raise on the same schedule as the rest of [the company]." When I voiced my concern, I was told, "I don't think there is anything we can do." I was never asked what I would consider an acceptable raise; I was just flat out told no, even though my pay was less than the other managers of my level.

I quite honestly don't believe anything my senior leaders tell me regarding pay or bonuses. Their words conflict with what my immediate manager tells me. They also conflict with common sense. And finally, their words have often later proven to conflict with their actions.

The last two years I received a 3% raise, which does not even keep pace with inflation. I have never worked harder and given more and received so little in return, and yes my reviews have all been highly positive. Additionally, I do not trust the leaders of this company because they are managing for quarterly results for Wall Street and care very little for the associates or the customers.

What does motivate really mean? To me, it means that I would get something in return for going above and beyond, either material or immaterial. If I do go beyond, not only do I get nothing, but my manager takes credit for whatever was accomplished.

With perks being slowly taken away one by one from the employees, you can't help but wonder where it is going to stop, if ever. It would be one thing if things were taken away from us as employees equally, across the board, but it is not. The announcement of no bonuses or raises was also, quite frankly, a piss off. Why should the employees have to suffer for the mistakes and bad decisions made by the top executives who have little or no knowledge of the way the company works from a customer point of view?

Now, what is the impact of pay level on organization performance, such as profitability? One would think that, everything else being equal, the higher the pay, the greater the cost to a company and therefore the smaller the profits. We have already commented on the relationship between pay and enthusiasm, so there is some reason to believe that the relationship between pay and cost would by no means be perfect—the positive effect on employee morale and performance should offset to some extent the impact of labor costs on profits. But it goes further than that.

In economics, there is a body of theory, termed "efficiency wage theory," that deals with this issue. Based on observations such as the fact that higher pay rates are found in more profitable industries, the theory states that compensation above what a firm has to pay (that is, above the "competitive market-clearing wage") drives up labor costs but also produces benefits, such as greater work effort, that increase output and revenue for the firm. In his article "Can Wage Increases Pay for Themselves?," David I. Levine concludes that "...business units that increase their relative wages for workers of similar human capital [skill level, training, etc.] have productivity gains approximately large enough to pay for themselves." He found that, in units where wages declined over a three-year period (factoring in inflation), worker output increased 2 percent. Where wages increased, worker output grew by 12 percent.[1]

The research evidence points to four explanations for the relationship between wages and productivity:

- **Worker reciprocity and morale.** The "gift" of higher wages from the employer is reciprocated by a "gift" from workers of higher productivity. This is in line with what we have said about the impact of morale on performance. Employee performance over the long term, of course, is not just a matter of productivity, but also the cost savings and profits generated by higher quality, better customer service, and so on.

- **Lower turnover.** Higher paying companies lose fewer people, so they have lower turnover-related costs, especially for recruitment and training.

- **Decrease in "shirking."** For those employees not inclined to work hard, higher pay means that dismissal is a greater penalty than if the job paid less.

- **A superior pool of job applicants.** Higher pay attracts a larger number of better job applicants from which to choose.

All four factors appear to play a role.

Obviously, there's a limit to the relationship between high wages and productivity. Levine found that the relationship holds less strongly in firms with large percentages of unionized workers. In those companies, he suggests, wages have gone beyond what could be made up by increased productivity.

An important practical lesson of the research on wages is the error of confusing labor *rates* with labor *costs*. Labor costs are a function not just of how much is paid to workers—that's the rate—but also how much workers produce. The correct measure of the labor cost to organizations is the ratio of wages to productivity, what economists call unit labor costs (ULCs). Low wages and low productivity can offset each other in terms of their effects on ULCs, potentially making labor expensive when wages are low. In this connection, it has long been observed that the nations with the highest wage rates tend to be the most productive. Although low-wage countries still have a competitive advantage, that advantage is cut in half, on the average, when comparing ULCs.

The analysis also applies to individual companies within a country where there are large differences in productivity. For example, Japanese automobile manufacturers in the United States long had a huge labor-cost advantage over their American-owned counterparts, despite similar wage rates, because they were much more productive. Table 4-1 shows the historic difference, measured in 1996 (the data available for the first edition) and again in 2006, between the labor hours that North American automobile manufacturers require to produce a vehicle.[2] As we can see, although an advantage remains ten years later, it has diminished significantly.

Table 4-1 Labor Hours per Vehicle Produced by Manufacturer[3]

Automobile Manufacturer	1996	2006
Nissan	27.36	28.46
Toyota	29.44	29.40
Honda	30.96	32.51
Ford	37.92	35.82
Chrysler	43.04	33.71
General Motors	46.00	33.19

Differences in labor cost say little about quality and other key aspects of company success. Few systematic studies specifically correlate wage rates with product quality, but the research available suggests a positive correlation.[4] High wage rates should affect quality in much the same way they affect productivity (for example, by allowing the organization to attract and retain more highly skilled workers that will do higher quality work). That was the reasoning of the president of Wendy's, who was confronted with soaring costs and declining sales in 1986:

> "[I] found we had lost our focus on—people. We had such fear in our hearts about numbers, about the power of computer printouts and going by the book, we'd managed to lose sight of our customers and employees.... A number of basic changes were made, including significant improvements in compensation...and benefits.... Our turnover rate for [general managers] fell to 20 percent in 1991 from 39 percent in 1989, and turnover among co- and assistant managers dropped to 37 percent from 60 percent—among the lowest in the business. With a stable—and able—workforce, sales began to pick up as well."[5]

The Costco Wholesale Corporation is a warehouse-retailer that, despite its fame and popularity, has frequently been criticized by Wall

Street analysts for the generosity of its employee pay and benefits policies. "From the perspective of investors, Costco's benefits are overly generous," says Bill Dreher, retailing analyst with Deutsche Bank Securities Inc. "Public companies need to care for shareholders first. Costco runs its business like it is a private company."[6] "Whatever goes to employees comes out of the pockets of shareholders," claims Sanford C. Bernstein & Co. analyst Ian Gordon.[7]

In a recent personal communication, Jeff Elliott, Costco's Assistant Vice President of Financial Planning and Investor Relations, informed us that the average wage of U.S.-based Costco employees is $21.50 per hour (not including medical and other benefits), and that employees receive, in addition, twice-a-year bonuses, ranging from $2,500 to $4,000 each period. The average annual U.S.-based Costco employee's wage, therefore, is approximately $45,000 for full-time employees. 90 percent of U.S. employees are eligible for medical benefits, and the company pays about 92 percent of all employee medical costs, including dental and vision. The company also contributes to a 401(k) plan for each employee and does so whether or not the employee makes a contribution. The annual contribution, based on years of service, ranges from 3 percent to 9 percent of employees' annual compensation. "We recruit heavily from college campuses, and younger associates may not value their retirement savings as they should, so we make a contribution for them regardless," Mr. Elliott said.

How does this contrast with the wages and benefits provided by other retailers? The Bureau of Labor Statistics (BLS) reported the average hourly wage for retail workers in Q1–Q3 of 2012 to be $13.29, whereas the National Retail Federation reported on its website that in 2010 the average hourly wage in the industry was $12.97. These are substantially lower than the rate for Costco ($21.50), but the best comparison would be a similar retail company, such as Sam's Club, a division of Walmart. Unfortunately, Walmart does not break out Sam's Club wage data, and we have not been able to locate reliable wage information for Walmart as a whole after 2006. (There are a number of more recent figures published, but these tend to be from Walmart's many and vociferous critics, and we have no idea how reliable those data are.) Coleman-Lochner reported that in 2006 a Walmart employee's average hourly wage was $10.11.[8] The BLS, in the same year, reported hourly wages and salaries in the retail sector to be $11.85. The Costco average hourly wage that year was $17.00.

With regard to benefits, BLS reports that 63 percent of all retail workers had access to healthcare benefits in 2012, and a leading payroll processing company found that 70 percent of the premiums were being paid by the employer.[9] Greenhouse of the *New York Times* reported that fewer than half of Walmart's workers had benefits coverage in 2005, and Walmart paid just 33 percent of those premiums.[10]

So who is Costco being run for anyhow? The employees? One good way of determining who profits from Costco, besides employees, is the company's stock market performance. We see in Table 4-2 that Costco outperforms the major indices, and Walmart, by substantial margins.

Table 4-2 Cumulative Stock Market Returns from May 1, 2001 Through May 1, 2012

	11-Year Cumulative Return
Costco	122%
S&P 500 Retail Index	86%
Walmart	27%
DJIA	14%
S&P 500	4%

It does not appear that the Costco stockholders have suffered, at least not comparatively.

We make no claim that Costco's—or any company's—performance is a result solely of how employees are treated. Senior management's business competence and business strategy are crucial for success, and Costco's strategy—such as its membership model and limiting the number of items it stocks—has been lauded by many students of business.

But from the point of view of Jim Sinegal, the company's cofounder and former CEO, how employees are treated *is* critical and, indeed, is considered a central element of its business strategy. "Imagine," he said in 2006, "that you have 120,000 loyal ambassadors out there who are constantly saying good things about Costco. It has to be a significant advantage for you.... Paying good wages and keeping your people working with you is very good business.... Why shouldn't employees have the right to good wages and good careers?"[11] And, says Mr. Sinegal, "It absolutely makes good business sense.... Most people agree that we're the lowest cost producer. Yet we pay the highest wages. So it must mean we get better productivity. It's axiomatic in our business—you get what you pay for."[12] In 2012, operating income per full-time equivalent employee was $28,800 at Costco versus $17,400 for Sam's Club.

Costco's current CEO, Craig Jelinek, succeeded Sinegal in 2012 and, in a recent statement, expressed a similar perspective: "Most good CEOs serve their people; their people don't serve them. That's what it's all about. If you work with your people and give opportunities for your people to grow and help them succeed in what they want to accomplish, only good things happen for you. At Costco, we know that paying employees good wages makes good sense for business. Instead of minimizing wages, we know it's a lot more profitable in the long term to minimize employee turnover and maximize employee productivity, commitment, and loyalty."[13]

Yes, Costco executives are crazy—like foxes. Here are some additional data: BLS reported that in 2011, the annual quit rate for retail nationwide was about 26.5 percent. It is currently less than 11 percent at Costco. "Shrinkage" (essentially, theft) is less than ¼ of 1 percent at Costco, six times lower than the national average, which is approximately 1.5 percent.

And Wall Street complains!

The evidence clearly suggests that the normal inclination of many executives to pay as little as possible is often misguided. Organizations need to strive to compensate their workers *well*—even *above* the competition to the extent affordable. The edge over the competition, however, does not have to be in base pay. We discuss variable pay later in this chapter, such as gainsharing bonuses, which has the advantage of providing an organization with a mechanism that adjusts compensation to the performance of the workforce and the fortunes of the business.

Paying for Performance

We come now to the system by which pay is distributed, especially as it relates to performance.

In our preceding discussion, employee performance was treated as a "dependent variable"—that is, as an effect of the level of pay. In Costco, for example, we—and its senior management—argue that higher pay can mean higher performance. Let's turn that around and think of it in the more customary way—that is, as an "independent variable": the way employees' performance affects their pay.

Most organizations have a pay-for-performance system of one kind or the other. The organizations that don't—or have it for just a segment of the workforce—tend to be in unionized environments and government agencies. In those cases, pay increases are negotiated or are simply the consequence of tenure and "in-grade" promotions (promotions where compensation increases, but job responsibilities basically do not).

First, let's consider systems meant to pay employees for their individual performance. The two most common are piecework and merit pay. Both sound terrific—they certainly fit the American ideology of individual effort and reward—but they have been found to be seriously wanting in practice.

Piecework

As the name says, employees working under this system are paid by the piece. The occupations to which this system is most typically applied are production workers and salespersons. For the latter, the "piece" is the amount of the sale, and the system is a commission plan. We first discuss piecework as applied to production workers.

Piecework in a production environment appears to be eminently sensible and fair because it aims to tie compensation directly to performance, and the measure of performance is objective (pieces produced that can be counted). The reality, however, is that disputes about these systems are extremely common. In many unionized environments using piecework, the system is the largest single source of employee grievances. For this and other reasons, the percentage of organizations that employ piecework has been declining.[14]

What are the issues? In factories, the key problems concern the way productivity standards are developed on which the piece pay rates are based. The standards define what is expected of the workers: the number of pieces per unit of time (hour, day, and so on). Typically, industrial engineers who rely on time study or some form of predetermined (synthetic) data develop the standards. The organization decides—or, in negotiation with the union agrees—on what a fair wage would be for a job if the employee meets the standards. The piece rate, then, is the standard number of pieces per time period divided into the agreed-upon fair pay for that time period. For example, if the standard is 100 pieces per day and the fair pay is $100 per day, the piece rate would be $1. Workers could earn more than $100 per day if they produced more than 100 pieces.

This measurement approach generates two serious problems. First, there is the question of the fairness or the accuracy of the standards. Typically, workers complain that they are unreasonably high. In union shops, these often become the subject of an endless stream of grievances and negotiations. The "objectivity" of the standards—a key assumption of the system—is, obviously, a matter of considerable dispute.

The second issue is equally important, although it's less commented on. The standard is production expected *using a particular method.* If a worker were to think of a better method for doing the job—which would increase her production, say, by 25 percent—the production expected from her (the "standard") would be increased by 25 percent, and she would have to produce 25 percent more to earn the same income as before. Otherwise, she might be earning "too much." In effect, the company has cut how much she is paid per piece and has pocketed the savings. The term "piecework," therefore, is in part a misnomer. The employee is not being paid for pieces produced per se, no matter what the method; she is being paid for pieces produced *with a particular work method.* This has two consequences:

1. There is little or no motivation for employees to make method improvements that increase the overall output of their jobs. It is true that workers, after some time on the job, usually discover how to improve methods, but these improvements are typically kept to themselves because revealing them brings no reward; in fact, it is seen as punishing. This represents an enormous waste of an extremely important resource—the talent, the initiative, and the creativity of the workforce—and is antithetical to improvement goals. Although the system is designed to get workers *up to* the standards, it discourages them from *beating* the standards. The losses in productivity that are engendered are large.

2. By treating workers as if the only thing that matters is their physical exertion, we remove from them a major source of achievement and self-esteem—namely, the opportunity to demonstrate their ability to think. We set up systems in which we have specialists in thinking: the methods engineers. Their job is to develop "best methods" by which the workers should

get their jobs done. All we ask of workers is that they follow orders and work hard. But anyone familiar with such factories knows that workers can be mighty creative as they go about making life difficult for line management and its staff representatives: fooling the time-study man when being studied, submitting formal grievances whenever possible, and hiding new methods.

The theory of piecework—that a straight-line relationship exists between the wages a worker can earn and the effort he is willing to expend on the job—is therefore seriously flawed. An additional important problem for such systems is the effect that they have on group cohesiveness. It has often been observed that individual incentives discourage teamwork because each employee is out for himself. Although this is true in many white-collar occupations, the opposite is often the case on the factory floor. The systems often *increase* cohesiveness among workers, but only in *opposition to management*. Workgroups set their own production norms and expect their members to adhere to them. The worker exceeding the norm is the *rate buster* (that's one of the more polite terms), and he does not have an easy life on the factory floor.

Most production workers are not like most salespeople for whom individual competition on the job is normal and a pathway to a sense of achievement. We elaborate on that difference later in this chapter.

In factories, the piecework system results in a continual tug-of-war between labor and management: workers and workgroups pressuring to hold down production and management pressuring to increase it. This seems to contradict our earlier optimistic view of workers and worker motivation, but keep in mind that workers' attitudes and behavior are a function of not just who they are, but how they are treated. In the situations we have described, workers see deceiving management, submitting grievances, and restricting production as means to survive in the face of a management that's bent on turning its workplace into a sweatshop and limiting its pay opportunities. That's usually not the way management sees it, but that's the way *workers* see it.

We have focused on the employee relations and productivity consequences of piecework. There is another issue, one that afflicts many pay-for-performance systems. A company that seeks to pay for performance must define what performance means. Part of the attractiveness of piecework (whether on the production floor or in sales) is that it relies on objective measures. (Things get counted.) So, the definition of performance is often narrowly limited to what is countable. Because people focus on what is measured and rewarded, we often find workers cutting corners to produce what is expected. Workers might run machines at higher speeds than instructed, the quality of the output might be sacrificed, and so on. This is not only an attempt to reach the expected production levels, it is also part of the game, the tug-of-war, between a workforce and management. "Okay, you want x number of pieces, we'll give it to you and wait until the junk comes back!" Management has to then introduce additional controls and penalties to help ensure quality and protect the equipment. It's all expensive and, as we will show, needless.

Is piecework ever appropriate? Yes, if it's applied in the right conditions and to the right people. The problems and costs of piecework tend to be least when the tasks are simple, repetitive, can be done independently, and when management genuinely responds to workers' concerns about wages and the accuracy of the standards. Complex, nonrepetitive jobs generate the most disputes about standards, and the impact of individual incentives on teamwork is largely irrelevant if teamwork is rarely needed. Coupling those conditions with a management that has a genuine concern for its employees' well-being can make individual piecework the most effective system. A good example of this is Levi Strauss, a progressive management that switched from individual piecework to group-based incentives and suffered a decline in production.

And some workers *prefer* an individual piecework system. Research done in the 1950s by William F. Whyte[15] found that these workers tend to be socially isolated from their co-workers, owners of their own homes, and Republicans. Making money has a moral dimension for them, providing proof that they work hard. They are the rate busters—disliked, but uninfluenced, by their fellow workers, and beloved by management.

Salespeople are similar to the rate busters in their compensation preferences. There are differences between the two groups in their personality traits and abilities—on the average, salespeople have much stronger social and communications needs and skills—but great similarity on traits such as independence, assertiveness, confidence in their ability to achieve high earnings, and high earnings serving as a major source of self-esteem. The salesperson personality profile fits the sales job perfectly and is, of course, why those people gravitate to that type of work. It is also why a compensation plan that is oriented to individual rewards attracts them (the sales commission plan). For most of them, it would be frustrating to work in any other environment and, with few exceptions—such as when teamwork is absolutely essential for high performance—that is the incentive plan recommended for them.

This is not to say that individual incentives in sales do not present problems, some of them similar to what we find in factories. Sharp disagreements can occur about the fairness of quotas and commissions, the amount of differential payment for different products, and the handling of charge-backs. A frequent and major concern is the way high productivity and earnings are dealt with. As with factory workers, salespeople are often faced with disincentives to high performance because, if they produce and earn a lot, their quota is raised or their territory reduced. Therefore, salespeople seem to be continually negotiating with management about the terms of their commission plans.

Despite the problems, our survey data show that professional salespeople are significantly more positive toward their compensation than nonmanagement employees in general. This is so because, for one, an incentive compensation system fits their personalities and objectives. Second, they tend to be among the more highly paid employee populations. They are paid well because their performance is seen as among the most essential to the success of business: they bring in the money! Finally, because salespeople are so vital, they have a lot of bargaining power—especially the more successful salespeople—and management usually makes arrangements to keep them at least reasonably happy.

Besides matters of equity, sales-compensation plans can generate *organizational* issues, such as the deleterious effect individual commissions might have on needed teamwork and the tenuousness of the ties of salespeople to their organizations when a large proportion of their compensation is commission (rather than salary). Over the years, these problems have been recognized and, increasingly, when teamwork is essential, group incentives have become the norm. Today, most salespeople are paid a base salary with commission averaging about 10–35 percent of their total compensation.

Merit Pay

The great majority of salaried (as opposed to hourly) workers in the United States work under some form of "merit pay" plan. One of the major differences between merit pay and piecework is that in the former, pay adjustments are made not directly and immediately on the basis of production; instead, they are made on the basis of the boss's subjective evaluation of the employee's performance over a period of time (usually a year).

Among the less positively rated areas in surveys is the degree to which organizations that profess to pay for individual performance are seen as actually doing so. Our norm on perceived pay for performance is 40 percent favorable and 40 percent unfavorable. In other words, despite the theoretical attractiveness of paying for "merit," the pay-for-performance systems in place are not particularly credible for quite large numbers of workers. Part of the problem stems from the boss's evaluation of the employee's performance. It is not that employees disagree with the evaluations; in fact, our research shows that there is considerable agreement.[16] Instead, it is that the evaluations are biased upward. That's why so many employees agree with them! It is only slightly facetious to say that, in effect, merit increases determine the performance evaluations rather than the other way around. That is, to avoid unpleasantness in their performance-evaluation sessions, many managers tend to rate just about everyone highly (at least "satisfactory" or its equivalent). The tendency would be less pronounced if pay increases were not tied to the evaluations but, because the latter mean money, the positive bias is strong indeed.

The problem of biased evaluations is magnified by the systems through which pay increases are supposed to be related to performance. A common approach is to use a "grid." Figure 4-1 shows an example of this grid.

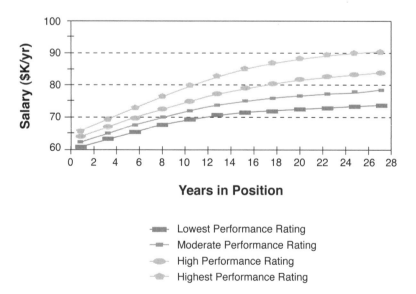

Figure 4-1 Example of a performance-based salary grid.

The vertical axis of the grid defines the pay range of the job (from minimum to maximum). The line graphs represent employees at different levels of evaluated performance. The major objectives of the grid are to differentiate the increases of employees with different levels of performance, while containing salary increase costs. These objectives are, in practice, somewhat contradictory. For example, newer employees are typically at the low end of the range *no matter what their performance*. Also, the salary increases of employees at the upper end of the range level off *no matter what their performance*. Both outcomes help contain costs but greatly dilute the relationship between salary increases and performance. Technically, the organization *is* paying for performance with this system, but *taking into account position in range*. Unfortunately, employees don't perform the mental gymnastics required to allow them to feel that they have indeed been rewarded for their performance. An employee doesn't say, "It's okay that I received a smaller increase this year than last year, even though my performance was the same. After all, my pay is now higher in the range." It would take a saint to accept that reasoning—and a clairvoyant one because in many companies employees are told little about what's going on concerning ranges, grids, and so on.

The following further compound the problem:

- **Budgets.** In recent years, organizations' salary increase budgets have been approximately 2–3 percent. These budgets are especially important to control because they are not one-time costs: a salary increase becomes part of an employee's base salary and is therefore an expenditure as long as the employee stays with the company. But managers with very small salary increase budgets cannot make a lot of differentiation among employees without angering those who are not outstanding, but still satisfactory, performers.

- **Change.** Salary increase budgets change year to year depending on how much the organization believes it can afford to pay. The amount of increase for a given level of performance will therefore change with the budget, adding to the ambiguity and perceived arbitrariness of the relationship between an employee's performance and the size of her salary increase.

- **Inflation.** We have said that when an increase does not exceed the rate of inflation, it is usually not viewed as an increase; if it is less than inflation, it can be felt as a decrease. If, say, inflation is 3 percent and managers with a 3 percent increase budget are asked to differentiate increases on the basis of performance, some—maybe half—of their employees will feel that their pay has been cut. Most of these employees are likely to be wholly satisfactory performers. Furthermore, companies almost never distinguish for employees the amount of the increase that is due to the rise in the cost of living, which makes the performance-pay relationship even more ambiguous. Market-based increases to meet the competition—again, rarely distinguished from merit increases—add to the problem.

We can now understand why it is so difficult for many employees to see a relationship between their pay and their performance. It comes down to this: most managers very much want to pay for performance, but to get their day-to-day management jobs done, they tend also to be concerned with minimizing employee discontent. The merit pay system, coupled with their own discomfort at delivering unpleasant news, makes it difficult to reward as they truly believe they should. Therefore, many managers focus on figuring out the size of the increase for each employee that results in the fewest problems for them. They know, for example, who is likely to complain and who is likely to accept their word that, "This is really a tough year for the company. I don't have much money to spread around; I'm doing the best I can." They try to make sure that all—or almost all—of their employees receive as much of an increase as their budgets allow and then give some more to those who are likely to give them a particularly hard time. This minimizes differentiation among employees, with the exception of the "squeaky wheels" and, sometimes, those whose performance is truly and visibly inadequate.

Managers also seek ways around the system: for employees who are likely to leave the organization (and whose leaving would be a loss), or who might raise hell, or who are, indeed, truly outstanding performers, they might seek "exceptions" (a larger increase than the grid suggests), or in-grade promotions, or position re-evaluations to move the jobs to higher levels. It depends on what is possible and what will least frustrate other employees and those in a position of power.

The result is a half-baked version of pay for performance with which not many are satisfied, but one that normally doesn't have serious repercussions: people "live with it." Our statistical studies of organizations' merit pay systems show that *tenure*, not performance, is by far the highest correlate of employee pay within a job grade. That is, the net effect of the system, and the machinations that surround it, is not that much different from approaches that base pay exclusively on seniority. Only, it is less clear.

Recommendations

We have been hard on individual pay-for-performance systems. It is difficult to argue with approaches that are designed to pay individuals for their performance—it's almost un-American to do so—but the fact is that they tend to have numerous and severe problems. For many companies, they become bureaucratic and administrative nightmares without doing much to further their basic goal: rewarding people for their performance.

Is there anything better? Yes.

The better alternative is not to junk pay for performance and simply pay all employees in a particular job grade wherever they work the same or compensate by seniority. Those should be avoided because, when implemented properly, pay for performance can indeed be very positive and powerful in that it does the following:

- Gives financial reward to employees for reasons of both equity (sharing in the organization's financial returns) and recognition.
- Gives direction to employees by aligning rewards with the organization's goals and objectives. Pay is probably the most salient communicator of organizational goals.
- Can provide a mechanism for adjusting compensation costs to the ability of the organization to pay.

It should therefore be clear that we are in no way opposed to rewards based on performance. The question is, *how*? We know that organizations—and segments of organizations—differ, so no one approach will be appropriate for all. Here are the basic principles we believe should guide the design of pay-for-performance plans and concrete illustrations of how these have been put into practice. The principles are:

- Employee compensation should include both base pay and variable pay.
- Base pay should be competitive and should keep up with inflation.
- Variable pay is on top of base pay and should, for the large majority of employees, be based on the performance of groups rather than individuals.
- Variable pay should be distributed as a percentage of the employee's base salary.
- Individual performance should be rewarded by "honors."

Let's elaborate on these:

- **Variable pay versus merit salary increases.** The basic structure we recommend is one in which employees receive base salary or wages *plus* variable pay that is geared to performance. This is similar to piecework systems where employees receive base pay plus an amount per piece; the difference, as we shall see, resides in the way we recommend performance be measured (as a group rather than on an individual basis).

  Using a base-plus-variable-pay approach is different from merit pay. A merit pay increase becomes part of the employee's salary—it is, in effect, an annuity cost for the organization. Variable compensation, on the other hand, is tied to the organization's ability to pay, such as to its profitability or to cost savings that have been achieved. This is an enormous advantage because it makes payroll costs much easier to control. It might not seem like a plus for employees because the extra compensation does not become part of their salaries. But employees' base pay will increase anyway to compensate for inflation, and most people are pleased to know that. *The recognition and reward portion of their pay is clear*, which eliminates the ambiguity of the merit pay system where performance-, cost-of-living-, and market-based increases are confounded.

- **Group versus individual performance.** For the great majority of the workforce, we recommend that variable pay be based on group, rather than individual, performance. We have two reasons for this preference. First, performance of a group is usually easier to measure; it's more objective and credible than that of an individual. At the total company level, for example, contrast the relatively objective measurement of company profit with the highly subjective judgments about the contributions of individual senior executives to that profit. In a cost center, such as a manufacturing plant, contrast measuring the cost performance of a plant as a whole with measuring the efficiency of individual workers. We saw how individual production standards can generate a flood of grievances about their accuracy. If the goal is to distribute financial rewards among workers according to their individual performance, workers must be *compared* to each other. How is the performance of a maintenance person to be compared with a production worker? Not easily.

The second reason for preferring group measurement is that performance almost always depends not just on individual capabilities and effort but also on teamwork. The profound power of pay should be used to encourage, not discourage, teamwork and individually-based plans do little, at best, to stimulate cooperation and they can produce dysfunctional competition and conflict. The teamwork that group pay plans encourage has two positive effects: it boosts performance in and of itself, and it satisfies workers' camaraderie needs, which adds to their enthusiasm and performance.

How about the "shirkers"—those who prefer not to work hard? Doesn't a group approach give them an out, a way to be rewarded for not much effort? Research shows exactly the opposite: under a well-administered group pay plan, the responsibility for dealing with workers who won't work is shouldered in part by the work group. Shirkers hurt group performance and, therefore, workers' pay, and a group norm develops that puts pressure on low producers to produce. This is almost invariably more effective than management dealing with the problem alone. Aside from shirkers are those employees who are motivated to perform but who need performance coaching or other kinds of assistance. Group-based plans strongly reinforce the natural desire of employees to provide such help to their co-workers.

How about the truly outstanding performers? Isn't a group payment approach unfair to them? Our experience with employees working under these plans reveals few problems in this respect. The reason is that these outstanding performers are contributing significantly to the well-being of the entire group and receive a great deal of recognition from their co-workers. This contrasts with the reactions of workers to "rate busters" working under piecework. In those cases, high individual performance is seen as detrimental to the group's interests. We will suggest later, however, that the informal recognition that high performers receive under group plans be supplemented with individual formal awards.

What are the group compensation plans that are available to organizations? Countless plans exist, but almost all can be grouped into three major categories: stock ownership, profit sharing, and gainsharing. Which one(s) to choose? Here are the criteria that should govern the selection of a plan. A plan is more effective to the extent that:

- It steers employee performance to the achievement of important organizational goals.
- It allows employees to see the impact of their performance and to see that impact in a timely way.
- The optimal achievement of the goals requires teamwork as well as individual effort.
- The performance measures are clear and credible.
- The financial return to employees is, in their eyes, substantial.
- The plan serves to satisfy employees' equity, achievement, and camaraderie needs.
- The plan enhances employees' identification with the organization.

Of all the plans, gainsharing meets the above goals to the greatest extent by far. But it, too, has gaps; therefore, for most organizations, a combination of the plans is preferable. The following are descriptions of the plans and the key research findings on their effects.

Employee Stock Ownership

The ownership by employees of stock takes three basic forms: employee stock ownership plans (ESOPs), pension assets invested in employer stock, and stock owned directly in the company through stock option and stock purchase plans. Combining the three forms of owning stock, it is estimated that about one-fifth of American workers hold stock in the company in which they work.

Employee stock ownership has strong proponents, some almost evangelical in their advocacy. Their arguments are based on both financial and motivational considerations. Stock ownership is touted as a good way for employees to increase their assets through participation in the growth of the American economy. This certainly was a credible theme in the late 1990s, but sudden and severe declines in the stock market since then have made that argument somewhat shaky. On the motivational side, two claims are made. First, by creating a "capitalist working class," stock ownership increases the identification of workers with the free-enterprise system. Second, and of particular relevance to this book, is the argument that ownership of an employer's stock increases employees' identification with their companies and their motivation to perform.

What is the research evidence concerning the impact of stock ownership on employee attitudes, behavior, and company performance? Overall, the findings are modestly positive, the largest impact tending to be on employees' identification with the company. A smaller percentage of studies—but still most—show a positive effect on more specific employee attitudes, such as job satisfaction; on employee behavior, such as absenteeism; and on company performance, such as overall labor productivity. Regarding labor productivity, the average productivity improvement that appears to result from employee stock ownership is on the order of 2–6 percent. To our knowledge, there has been no instance (at least none published) where the effect on performance has been demonstrably negative. (The studies in which the results were not positive simply showed no significant impact one way or the other.)

Why is the impact on firm performance not greater, especially because stock ownership seems to increase employees' overall identification with the company? Part of the answer lies in the indirect relationship between how employees perform on the job and how their company's stock performs. Numerous market forces affect stock price—forces well beyond employees' control (and even a company's control). Even if there weren't such broad market forces, there are few individual employees (or groups of employees) in most corporations whose performance can realistically be said to have an impact on stock price. Workers can feel proud of their company's stock performance and feel good about the financial benefits to them—those are important—but what is almost entirely missing is the personal sense and pride of *direct impact and achievement.* Recall that one of our criteria for the selection of a variable pay plan is that it should allow employees to see the impact of their performance. Theorists in the field refer to this as "line of sight," and, of all the variable group pay plans, stock ownership is the weakest on this criterion.

Employee identification with the company in relation to stock ownership needs some elaboration. Although we lack systematic research on this, anecdotal and indirect evidence point to the company culture—especially employee participation in decision making—as affecting the impact of stock ownership on performance. Think about it: suppose a company with a broad-based stock ownership plan has a top-down management style (a "do as you're told" style). The problems of line of sight are then compounded because employees have no mechanism—other than sheer physical effort—to influence even their own performance, much less the firm's overall performance. For most employees, ownership is both a psychological and a financial matter. To obtain the full power of ownership, owning shares and "owning" psychologically the product of one's job (because of involvement in decisions about it) should reinforce, not negate, each other. The strength of gainsharing, which is discussed later in this chapter, comes in significant measure from this reinforcement.

With regard to financial and psychological ownership, consider the condition opposite to what we have just described—namely, employees having much decision-making involvement but no financial return that is a direct result of that involvement. The theory behind many participative approaches (such as "quality circles") seems to be that virtue—such as employee ideas that cut costs—is its own reward. Not quite. In the United States, the history of these techniques suggests that, when successful, employees at some point begin to question why they are not sharing directly in the financial gains. This is more than employees seeing an opportunity for additional income. At least equal in importance is their sense of equity: the desire not to feel manipulated and exploited. Also, the impact of money on an employee's sense of achievement is lost when participation is not accompanied by financial return.

Another important issue regarding stock ownership is, of course, the impact on employees of a drop in stock value. Things are terrific when the stock appreciates, but a decline not only can be disappointing but can threaten to severely decimate an employee's life's savings. This can happen when the stock price drops simply due to economic or market conditions, but it can also be the result of unethical or blatantly illegal financial manipulations by corporate executives. The risks inherent in stock ownership therefore militate against this vehicle being selected as the primary—not to speak of the sole—means of variable compensation for a workforce.

Profit Sharing

About one-fifth of U.S. firms have some form of profit sharing, with the percentage among publicly held firms being close to two-fifths. The bulk of profit sharing is deferred, where the share is put into an employee retirement account. The plans are cash-only in one-fifth of the cases and, in one-tenth of the cases, employees can choose whether to defer or receive their share as cash. There is great variability in the profit-sharing formulas that are used—both in the amount distributed and in the threshold before distribution—and, in many companies, the formula is discretionary and can change each year.

As with employee stock ownership, profit sharing has its strong advocates. They argue that it is not only a way of sharing with employees the financial fruits of their labors but also a mechanism to increase employees' understanding of the financial condition of their firms and their identification with their firms.

What does the research show about the effects of profit sharing on employee attitudes, behavior, and firm performance? Surprisingly, there is little research evidence concerning employee attitudes and behavior. About the most that can be said reliably on the basis of the research is that employees generally like the plans, which should come as no surprise. The exceptions, of course, are the times there is little or no profit to share, especially after years of significant profit sharing when it has become an expected part of one's earnings or retirement savings.

Although research is lacking on the impact of profit sharing on attitudes such as identification with the firm, we would be surprised if they were much different from stock ownership. Profit sharing should promote a feeling that "we're all in this together," especially if there are not large discrepancies between the profit-sharing bonuses of top management and those of the rest of the workforce.

Quite a bit of work has been done on the effect of profit sharing on company performance. The findings are similar to employee stock ownership: the results range from positive to neutral, with the average improvement in labor productivity also in the 2–6 percent range. The proportion of studies with positive results is actually somewhat greater than is the case with stock ownership.

Profit sharing is similar to employee stock ownership in its relatively weak "line of sight" between employee performance and end-results. The flaw might be less severe than with stock ownership because profitability is not as affected by uncontrollable events as is stock price. Nevertheless, the contribution that most employees and employee groups can make to overall firm profitability is indistinct, so there is little impact on one's personal sense of achievement. Some companies have sought to deal with this issue by instituting unit—such as divisional—profit-sharing plans. But, these units have also tended to be rather large entities, and it is doubtful that much improvement in line of sight was realized. In truly small organizations, such as small business units or independent businesses, the problem should be less severe.

In both stock ownership and profit sharing, the lack of timeliness of the reward magnifies the line-of-sight problem. It is well established that a reward has more impact if it is given close in time to the behavior being rewarded, since it better reinforces the desired behavior. This is a major problem in merit increase programs (where the employee's performance is typically appraised and the salary increase given annually) and in stock ownership and profit-sharing plans.

As with employee stock ownership, there is some evidence that profit sharing has a greater impact when it's part of a generally compatible culture, such as a high level of employee involvement in decisionmaking.

Gainsharing

Although it's not as well known to the general public as are stock ownership and profit sharing, research shows that gainsharing has the largest positive impact on employee attitudes and performance. As the name says, it is a method for sharing gains with employees—the gains that employees themselves, as a group, achieve for the organization. Although a number of gainsharing plans exist—the most common being the Scanlon Plan, the Rucker Plan, and Improshare—they have the following characteristics in common:

- They are used in relatively small organizations (most successfully when the number of employees is less than 500).

- The performance is an operational measure, such as productivity or costs, rather than a financial measure such as profitability; only employee-controllable performance is used.

- The organization establishes a historical base period of performance for a group.

- Performance improvement over the base creates a bonus pool, which is the savings that the improvement has generated. Typically, about one-half of the pool is paid to employees, usually as a percentage of their base pay, with all participating employees receiving the same percentage. If there has been no gain, there is no pool; the bonuses are usually paid on a monthly or quarterly basis, the idea being that they should be paid as closely as possible to the performance that is being rewarded.

- Almost all gainsharing plans include heavy involvement by employees in developing and implementing ideas for improving performance.

Although gainsharing was employed until recently mostly in small manufacturing organizations, it has spread to service organizations, such as hotels, restaurants, insurance companies, hospitals, and banks. Estimates vary, but a good guess is that about 20 percent of American companies have gainsharing plans. In most cases, however, gainsharing is applied to just a minority of the workforce, such as those in a corporation's manufacturing facility. The popularity of the approach appears to have increased over the last two to three decades.

A review of the research on gainsharing shows significant improvement in productivity in the large majority of organizations using the plan. The range of improvement, however, varies widely—it has been as low as 5 percent and as high as 78 percent, with the average at about 25 percent. The results, therefore, can be substantial. "The most important thing we know about gainsharing plans is that they work," says Edward Lawler, probably the most prominent organization psychologist studying compensation systems and their effects.[17]

Here is an example of how a simple gainsharing plan might work:

- The average monthly sales in a base period, usually the previous year or 18 months, are calculated; say this is $1 million.

- The average monthly wage costs over the same base period are calculated; say this is $200,000.

- The ratio of wage costs to sales in the base period is therefore 20 percent.

- If sales in the first month of the gainsharing period is $1.2 million, the application of the ratio produces wage costs of $240,000.

- If the actual wage costs are $210,000, there is a $30,000 savings, which is to be split 50/50 between the employees and the company.

This is a "simple" gainsharing plan because it focuses on just one performance measure: the ratio of wage costs to sales. Other plans include a number of additional factors, such as quality and delivery performance, with each factor given a weight in the calculation of the "gain."

The reasons gainsharing so often works well should be clear from our previous discussion. Of all the plans but individual piecework, gainsharing provides the clearest link between what employees do and the performance measure that determines the payment. Gainsharing has advantages in this respect even compared to individual piecework. In the latter, the "standard" developed by an engineer is often disputed and is likely to be increased if exceeded by the worker (through greater effort or a change in work method). Therefore, doing more (especially by being smarter) is usually the path to a heavier workload, not greater earnings. In gainsharing, the "standard" is the past—workers know it can be met because it *has* been met, and rewards are distributed based on improvement over it. The link is clear—do more to get more—and the system encourages, rather than discourages, improvement.

It is naïve to think that gainsharing, despite its obvious advantages, can be introduced simply as a formula mechanically relating productivity improvement to compensation. Its organizational context is critical: by far, the most successful applications are paralleled by a highly participative and team-enhancing process because the primary way gains are realized is by employees working collaboratively and innovatively to improve performance. We made this same point about "ownership" in our discussions of employee stock ownership and profit sharing, but it is even more obvious and important here. Gainsharing ties the bonuses of a group of employees to their ability to improve performance—the performance that they largely control—over the past year. Because gainsharing focuses on a specific group, it would be self-defeating and ludicrous for the organization not to encourage the group members to work together to generate and try out improvement ideas. The very structure of gainsharing calls for a process that achieves results greater than the sum of the efforts of individual employees. This is not nearly so much the case with employee stock ownership and profit sharing where, because of the broad compass of the measure (usually an entire company), the emphasis can still be on individuals' performances.

Given its proven effectiveness, why is gainsharing not more widespread? Among the most important of the conditions that make gainsharing difficult to implement are the following:

- When it is difficult to measure quantitatively the output of the organization, such as that of a research laboratory.

- When performance measures fluctuate widely because of factors well beyond the employees' control, and the employees' impact can't therefore be reliably assessed.

- When it is difficult to differentiate relatively autonomous, properly sized entities in an organization to which the plan can be applied.

- When little or no interdependence exists among the members of the group, or the group members are strongly disposed to working on an individual incentive basis.

- When the organization is not culturally ready for gainsharing, such as when management fundamentally does not believe in the value of employee participation, or when there is great distrust and conflict between management and workers.

A few words about trust: although gainsharing can reinforce and strengthen trust, it should not be expected to turn a hostile environment into one of sweetness and light. To be successful, gainsharing *depends* on mutual trust and confidence. Especially important, obviously, is that workers trust that higher performance leads to better pay. Even though a performance formula—such as the ratio of labor costs to sales—looks simple, it can be subject to considerable dispute and will almost certainly be disputed if fundamental trust is lacking. Therefore, when there is a history of conflict and distrust, it is important to make significant progress on those issues before introducing a gainsharing plan.

Employees must also feel they won't be punished for higher performance. How can a reward program be punishing? Ask workers what "higher productivity" means to them, and you often discover that it means "fewer workers needed." Another term for "rate buster," in fact, is "job killer." Workers won't voluntarily participate in the arrangements for their own funerals, so guarantees need to be given to them that any gains from gainsharing won't result in job losses for them. The most successful gainsharing programs do that.

Even when all the conditions we have described have been met, gainsharing still has two major gaps. For one, because it lacks a total corporation focus, it does little to enhance organization-wide identification or increase employees' understanding of the broad financial condition of a business. Lawler suggests that "the ideal combination for many large corporations would seem to be corporate-wide profit sharing and stock ownership plans, with gainsharing plans in major operating plants or units."[18] In other words, the three types of variable group pay plans we have discussed should be viewed as having somewhat different objectives and are often best used in combination.

The second gap is the lack of individual financial reward. We believe that in most situations—covering the great majority of workers—this should be handled not by differentiating bonuses by individual performance, but by giving special awards to group members who make a particularly outstanding contribution. Although these awards should have a monetary value, their basic function is to *honor* individuals. We discuss such outstanding contribution awards in Chapter 10, "Feedback, Recognition, and Reward." Suffice it to say for now that these awards should be truly special—given infrequently, given publicly, and signifying appreciation from both management and peers.

A Note on Merit Pay for Teachers

Among the most contentious issues in education today—and receiving great publicity since the publication of our first edition—is the compensation system for teachers. By and large, teachers get paid by their level of education and the number of years they've worked. The worrisome state of academic achievement of students in the United

States has resulted in numerous proposals for improvement, with the quality of teaching receiving outsized attention. Taking a page from the private sector, critics have homed in on teacher pay. The basic proposal is that the pay system be changed so that, emulating what is assumed to be the case in the private sector, high-performing individual teachers are rewarded with larger salary increases or other kinds of financial rewards.

We know of no reason to believe that merit pay will work any better for teachers than it has in companies. Indeed, over the past two decades or so, experimental merit pay plans for teachers have been introduced and studied, and the evidence for their effectiveness is, to say the least, not impressive. One scholar reviewing the research on merit pay concludes that, although these plans were expected to increase accountability among teachers and performance in the classroom, they "not only failed to improve student achievement, but also destroyed teachers' collaboration with each other and teachers' trust in the administrators...evaluating their performance."[19]

The National Center on Performance Incentives at Vanderbilt University published in 2010 a description of its research on merit pay for teachers in the Nashville public schools. Teachers were offered bonuses of up to $15,000 a year for improved student test scores on standardized tests. Their conclusion: merit pay "did not do much of anything." Teachers on the merit pay system showed no greater gains than teachers who were not offered merit pay.[20] Allan Odden concluded from his review of the experience and research in the field that "merit pay is at odds with the team-based, collegial character of well-functioning schools, and thus have limited potential to support school improvement."[21]

Our view is that some form of gainsharing, where both the performance measurement and the financial reward are school-wide, makes the most sense for teachers. Such programs have been tried (usually called "school-based performance awards" or "cooperative performance incentives") but, unfortunately, we know of no research that has been done to test their efficacy in direct comparison to individual merit pay or no merit pay at all. Everything we do know suggests that gainsharing—if introduced and managed properly—would stand a very good chance of succeeding. The performance measurement—on a school rather than an individual basis—would be more credible. Further, cooperation and mutual help among teachers—so important for their performance—would be supported rather than discouraged.

We say that gainsharing would work in schools "if introduced and managed properly." As in companies, gainsharing should not be viewed as a mechanical program whose effects are predictable in isolation from its cultural context, such as the degree of mutual trust between workers and management and the degree of participation by workers in decisions about their jobs. An effective gainsharing installation would require close cooperation between teachers, teachers' unions, and school management, not merely to negotiate a contractual compensation arrangement but also to develop a genuine atmosphere of mutual trust in the school and the mechanisms for involving all teachers in improving school performance. The "partnership" culture described in Chapter 12, "The Culture of Partnership"—and the way it can be introduced and sustained, as described in Chapter 14, "Translating Partnership Theory into Partnership Practice"—is what we have in mind when applied to a school setting.

The drive for teacher merit pay is closely related to another highly publicized and controversial issue, this one at the other end of the performance continuum: dealing with unsatisfactory teacher performance. As we said earlier, a collaborative group, trusting of management, will usually act, however informally, to help members who are having difficulty improve their performance and also bring the few "shirkers" into line or, when that's not possible, not stand in the way when management acts to dismiss them. This is especially true when unsatisfactory performance by one or a few means a smaller gainsharing bonus for all. Gainsharing, then, in combination with a participative, respectful work environment, can greatly reduce the protectiveness that employees often feel obligated to display to even the least deserving among them—and that unions are in considerable measure designed to provide—and replace it with a group discipline that will act in concert with management for the benefit of all.

5

The Impact of the Great Recession: Flight to Preservation

We have argued that three factors are characteristic of the goals of the great majority of workers: to be treated fairly (Equity), to have a sense of achievement (Achievement), and to have satisfying relationships with one's co-workers (Camaraderie). But we have also argued that although this has been true of all populations we have studied and at all times, the importance of the subgoals of these major three categories can vary greatly, depending on social, economic, and personal circumstances. For example, advancement opportunity—part of the Achievement factor—obviously becomes less important for those close to retirement. And, we pointed out how the desire for a secure job rose markedly for IT employees during the IT implosion of 2000.

Was the IT implosion and its effect on workers' goals and attitudes a small precursor of the impact of the Great Recession that began in 2008? Let's first review, in brief, what the recession has meant for workers in America:

- All told, 8.8 million people lost their jobs as a result of the recession, with the unemployment rate reaching 9.9 percent in early 2010. The average amount of time an unemployed person spent on unemployment rose to 33 weeks in 2010 from a prerecession level of 8 weeks.

- The Dow Jones Industrial Average dropped 53 percent from a high of 14,100 at the end of 2007 to a low of 6,600 during March of 2009. Because 401(k) holdings are mostly in equities,

161

the decline had a major impact on participants' retirement savings. The stock market, of this writing, has recovered to new all-time highs, but the negative impact on workers at its low point was potentially devastating, especially for those nearing retirement age.

- Home prices fell precipitously during the recession, a reported 29 percent from 2006 to 2009, and had failed to recover as of the third quarter 2012.[1]

- The employment, stock market, and, especially, housing declines resulted in the median net worth of U.S. families falling 39 percent to $77,300 in 2010 from $126,400 in 2007, adjusting for inflation.

The impacts of the recession were big in and of themselves but came on top of some recent historical trends that had not been encouraging for American workers. Real wages today are only slightly higher than they were in 1979, according to the Bureau of Labor Statistics. From 1979 to 2012, inflation-adjusted wages grew less than 5 percent—truly astounding!

To add to workers' burdens, the cost of health insurance has been skyrocketing, and some of those increases in costs have been passed on to them in the form of increased premiums, deductibles, copays, and coinsurance, For example, since 2002, premiums that employees pay have gone up 102 percent! And, in just two years—2008 to 2010—the percentage of employees with a deductible of $400 or more increased from 20 to 43 percent.[2]

Finally, job stability has been on the decline since the 1980s. Although unemployment returned to a low level after the 1981–1982 recession—from a high in 1982 of more than 10 percent to 5 percent in 1989—greatly increased foreign competition, restructurings, outsourcing to lower-wage countries, and the employment of temporary workers and independent contractors resulted in considerable and continuing job insecurity for many workers. This was greatly magnified, of course, by the Great Recession with its massive layoffs in both the private and the public sectors.

Integral to our understanding of the survey data we are about to show is the way the balance for workers between job security, wages, and benefits has changed over the past few decades. As to wages and job security, the change in the balance has been most visible in union contract negotiations where, starting in the 1980s, a pattern emerged in which job security replaced wage increases as the top contract goal of many American labor unions. Thus, for example, the United Auto Workers has had a laser-sharp focus, over the past few decades, on job security for its members, including pressuring the automobile companies in negotiations for the "in-sourcing" of jobs through the expansion of production in their U.S. plants. Among the major wage concessions the union has made to the companies is a two-tier wage system wherein new employees receive substantially less pay than those already on board. This has, indeed, been a dramatic change. For example, for workers supporting a family of six, the starting wage at GM assembly plants is actually at the federal poverty level. In a 2011 interview with Bob King, the president of the UAW, Jeffrey Brown of PBS went directly at these concerns:

> *JEFFREY BROWN: So when you came to the threshold issue in these negotiations, the thing you had to have to reach an agreement, is holding on to jobs more important now than negotiating higher wages?*
>
> *BOB KING: Absolutely. No worker is secure unless you have got new product and new investments coming into their facilities. That was our highest priority and the priority that we made the most gains and the most success.*
>
> *JEFFREY BROWN: And after so many members—losing so many members in the last decades and after what happened a couple years ago—do you go into negotiations like this inevitably from a position of weakness? Or how do you feel going in?*
>
> *BOB KING: No, I think that we...still have considerable leverage and power in the industry. I think that our view has changed, that*

we understand the people who have the most at stake in the long-term success of these companies is our membership.

CEOs change, shareholders change, management changes, but our members are there. And their long-term security, their pensions, their healthcare, their economic security is tied into [the] long-term success of the company.

So we're focused on making sure that there's new product, new investment, good technology, highest possible quality for the consumers. So our role has kind of shifted because we have gotten into more of a global economy and global competition.[3]

Negotiations in a number of states with public sector unions illustrate the same point about the balance between job security and wages. In the 2011 negotiations between New York State Governor Andrew Cuomo and the Civil Service Employees Association, the governor, because of declines in tax revenues, bargained hard with state employees. The *New York Times* reported that to help close the state budget gap, Governor Cuomo was relying on a "...bet that state employees would be willing to stomach a freeze on wages and an increase in the cost of health benefits in return for safeguarding their jobs." And it worked, as union leaders focused their message to members mostly around the promise of job security during difficult financial times. The union members voted 60 percent in favor to approve the contract.[4]

For many workers and their unions, therefore, job security has become the paramount objective. We see a similar pattern with regard to medical insurance: some sacrifice by workers in wage growth to preserve their insurance, or, at least, its essentials. Once considered a "fringe," the medical insurance benefit now looms large because of its rapidly escalating cost and because it is a key component of security—the security that insurance in general provides against unplanned and large expenditures. For most workers, no amount of pay increase they can realistically expect would cover such expenditures. Workers—unionized or not, reluctantly or not, and even consciously or not—have accepted some sacrifice in their wages to have employer-provided medical insurance.

The Survey Results

With that background, let's now review our attitude survey data. We ask: what has been the impact of the Great Recession on employee morale and commitment to their organizations? Because we know that the recession has had major and severe consequences for American workers, we would expect surveys of workers to reflect this, showing serious downturns in their morale. If you expect that, you're wrong! As were we.

We have selected from our database only those companies whose employees we have surveyed not just once, but multiple times—from before to during, and from during to after, the recession—so that we are comparing "apples to apples." This contrasts with the usual approach of employee survey research firms who, to detect trends over time, compare the results of all the companies they have surveyed in different years. The problem with that method is that the companies surveyed in one year may not be the same—in small or large measure—as those surveyed in other years. Companies drop in and out as survey clients, survey at different intervals, and so on. We have thus eliminated a source of potentially serious error.

What we have *not* eliminated, however, are other possible sources of error or bias:

- These are our clients and not necessarily representative of companies as a whole. Our companies tend to be larger than the average U.S. company, many are quite well known, and, we believe, will have fared somewhat better than the average company during the recession and be more "progressive' in their employee relations policies and practices. We say that because, first, although almost all the participating companies have laid off workers, just a few of them suffered a really serious decline in business, and that only temporarily.

Also, which companies would conduct employee attitude surveys during a recession? For one, they are unlikely to have been in severe and prolonged economic distress because employee surveys would normally be among the items to be cut in major cost-reduction drives that almost invariably follow downturns. Second, companies that conduct surveys, especially during a recession (whether seriously in trouble or not), and especially repeatedly, are likely to be run by executives who believe that employees and employee attitudes count. In that sense, too, these companies may be different from the average U.S. company and in ways that are important for our basic theses about the importance of how people are managed.

Because of these possible biases, we will be drawing liberally on the results of other surveys during this period to test the representativeness of our data and the validity of our conclusions.

- Not only are these companies our clients, but the workers being surveyed are, obviously, *employed*—that is, these are not, by and large, the workers who suffered the most because of the recession. This does not mean they are not anxious about their jobs—almost all of these companies have had layoffs and some of our surveyed workers may have been laid off in the recent past and been rehired—but the impact overall will certainly not be nearly as large as for those on the street at that time looking for work.

Keep in mind as well that these data reflect the impact of the Great Recession during which millions of workers were laid off. Layoffs then, for this period of time became the "new normal," something that was expected to happen in many companies throughout the country. From 2008–2010, 72 percent of U.S. companies reduced their workforces.[5] This is quite different than before the recession, when many layoffs were deeply resented by workers, reflecting as they often did in the minds of workers an avaricious management bent on wringing the last ounce of profits from the enterprise, whatever the impact on workers. At that time, however, jobs were much more plentiful so that the actual economic impact on most people, although real, was of shorter duration. Being laid off during the Great Recession could mean economic hardship for many months, even years.

Here, now, are our survey results from the Sirota client companies whose employees were surveyed multiple times over the course of the recession. First, overall satisfaction.

Table 5-1 Overall Satisfaction: Before ('06/'07), During ('08/'09), and After ('10/'11) the Recession

	% Favorable		
	Before	**During**	**After**
Considering everything, how would you rate your overall satisfaction in XYZ at the present time?	75	78	75

We can see that, on average, overall satisfaction actually *improved* by 3 percentage points over the course of the recession and then returned to its previous level. This was not a big change, but morale even holding its own in a recessionary period will come as a major surprise to many readers, as it did for us. Although we are working with a limited number of companies in these analyses, the number of employees involved is still in the tens of thousands, and the changes are highly significant statistically. (The "p" value for differences of this magnitude is less than .001.) They were, therefore, real—not chance—changes. Further, these were *average* changes, calculated across many companies. Viewed company by company, we find that 63 percent of the companies studied improved during the recession, 16 percent remained the same, and 21 percent declined.

A review of surveys by other researchers during this period reveals that our findings are not at all atypical:

- We referred in Chapter 1, to "Private Sector Norms" (to be found in Appendix D, on our website) to demonstrate that our normative data are quite close to those found in a large group of companies elsewhere. And we now find that *changes* in those norms for those companies over the years of the Great Recession were directionally similar to ours. For example, during the course of the recession, average overall satisfaction in those companies improved by 7 percentage points. Of all the survey results to which we compare our data, we have, on the basis of our knowledge of how the surveys were done, the greatest faith in these.

- Gallup, in its surveys, did find a slight decline, from 30 percent of employees were "engaged" in '06/'07 compared to 28.5 percent in '08/'09.[6] But, the Gallup researchers conclude, "Despite the...most severe recession in decades, employees' level of emotional engagement did not drop significantly..."

- Aon Hewitt uncovered improved employee attitudes in the United States throughout the recession, the largest increases found by any of the survey firms. The company also used an employee "engagement" index and found that, while engagement scores had increased 4 percent in 2007 (from 2006), they increased an additional 11 percent by the end of 2009—only to then drop 5 percent through 2010.[7]

- The Center for Creative Leadership found that engagement rose as much as 2.5 "standard score" units during the recession. (Standard scores, a statistical technique, enabled the researchers to combine a number of different measures into a single "ruler.")[8]

- Robert Half found that 31 percent of U.S. employees felt more engaged over the recession versus 18 percent who reported feeling less engaged.[9]

No other studies of comparable worker populations found downturns during the recession in overall employee satisfaction or "engagement."[10] We can therefore conclude with considerable confidence that, over the course of the recession, the average level of satisfaction of employed workers with their companies did not decline and likely improved.

Let's turn now to attitudes toward job security.

Table 5-2 Job Security: Before ('06/'07), During ('08/'09), and After ('10/'11) the Recession

	% Favorable		
	Before	**During**	**After**
How would you rate your job security (not being concerned about being laid off)?	68	66	68

The direction of the change—a decline, on average, of a couple of percentage points—is in line with expectations, although the decline is considerably smaller than what might be expected. On an individual company basis, however, we find that 13 percent of the companies showed an improvement in feelings of job security, 38 percent showed no change, and 50 percent showed a decline. This is in marked contrast to the percentages of companies we saw improved (63 percent), staying the same (16 percent), or declining (21 percent) in overall satisfaction.

We have argued that job security is a key determinant of employee morale. How, then, could 50 percent of the companies decline on that factor but only 16 percent decline on overall satisfaction? A good part of the answer is provided by the responses to the write-in questions in these surveys. Here is a sample of the relevant write-ins in response to, "What do you like best about working here?"

With the economy the way it is, I'm just grateful for my job.

I have a great job and thankful I have a job in today's market!

I am thankful for the opportunity to work.

I cannot think of one bad thing to say about this great company that I work for. In today's economy, we should all be thankful to work for a company that is so dedicated to its employees and contractors.

When I see what happened to the (company) plant on the other side of town, I thank my lucky stars I work for (writer's company). 30% of the people in that plant were fired. But (writer's company) does everything it can not to lay people off.

Total Rewards and Recognition [a compensation program] was changed drastically this year. Some felt that it was unfair. But some of us are very thankful that we have jobs in this economy and will remain working faithfully and loyally.

I am very grateful to have a job—especially a job that I am very happy with. It would be nice if the pay was higher because it's hard to survive out here when you are struggling financially. I know I have security and stability here. I do not want to leave this job because of pay; having a job now is more important than pay. But more money would help.

Pay/compensation is actually reasonable considering the economy at this time. With other online companies and call centers closing across the U.S., we're still here and running. Although raises and bonuses may be put on hold, I feel those are good actions to keep our business running and in positive numbers. I commend our upper management for that smart economic decision.

I am thankful that with today's economy, I still received a raise and quarterly bonuses.

I am grateful to have a job in today's economic climate at a company that I believe in and that I hope believes in me, the employee. I enjoy doing a good job for a company that takes care of its employees. It makes working hard a pleasure.

There is great difficulty in getting excited about my job when there is no incentive to do well. However, I am thankful to have a job. Incentives motivate people.

There have been several lay-offs, and I am grateful for the way they have been handled. We have known some of these folks for several years, and it's nice that everyone was given a warning and time to find new employment. It made me feel more comfortable and have more confidence in the company knowing they were not going to just throw us out after years of dedication.

Despite the economic downturn, (company) has worked to not have layoffs or take away significant benefits or compensation. That provided a sense of security so that we stayed focused on our job and didn't worry about what might happen.

Our benefits have been cut slightly. They were great and now they're just very good!

I am amazed that with all the trouble in the economy we actually got a small pay increase last year. Sure helps, because it kept us up with inflation.

The picture, for many employees, is quite simple and clear: *In this economy, I'm grateful to have a job!* Whether or not layoffs have recently occurred in their own companies—and they have in most of these companies—people are aware of what has been happening in their communities and nationally, and, despite understandably greater insecurity, they are thankful they haven't lost their own jobs. Let's call it "relative gratification" (as opposed to the more common "relative deprivation")—that is, workers are pleased relative to what they see or have heard happening elsewhere and relative to their fears as to what might have happened to them.

Although the predominant comment in these companies about job security was positive—grateful in these times to have a job—it was not universally so, especially with regard to how the managements of some of the companies handled layoffs. Here is a sample of those comments that were given in response to the questions: "What do you like least about working here?" and "What one suggestion for improvement would you make to management?"

The only barriers I see to being completely satisfied is the seeming atmosphere of job insecurity after last year's poor handling of reorganization [i.e., layoffs]. It seems every time there is a divisional conference call, everyone fears for their jobs.

Outsourcing jobs out of this country is shameful. Thousands of lives have been impacted by this process, leaving us too insecure about any future in the financial industry.

What I like least is the insecurity of being laid off.

We seem to have lost our edge. We are losing a lot of good people. The layoffs were poorly handled and demoralizing. It is difficult to get the resources my team needs. There is so much bureaucracy.

One thing that bothers me greatly is how [the company] handled the layoffs. A lot of people were rehired, so why weren't they given the opportunity to find another job prior to layoffs? Why put someone through the hardship and stress of being laid off only to hire them back. Some of the people let go were very talented and great contributors. The message [the company] sent to these people was that they don't care about what you have done for the company. You are just a number. It almost seems that the people who picked positions to layoff did so without any consideration for the people who filled them. Even if [the company] was restricted by the law on how to handle this, I still think there could have been communication to those who performed well that they did well and have other opportunities. The managers should have worked hard for these people to find them other jobs. The services that were provided were through an external company. I would much rather have had HR call me for jobs that matched my skill set.

The layoffs and reorganization were not well handled. After the initial layoffs, employees could figure out the remaining numbers and worked under the shadow of threat for weeks. After the reorganization, there was confusion regarding the roles of individuals and departments that were moved. There is still not a feeling of adequate integration of the reassembled departments.

After numerous rounds of layoffs during the last 5–7 years (pre- and post-merger), I believe that a considerable amount of company loyalty and teamwork has been eroded. Way too many very qualified people have been let go, which results in a callous attitude by those who are left behind. Additionally, teamwork is significantly reduced as people are quick to think that the guy they might be helping today could be the one they are competing with tomorrow to keep their job. I understand that reorganization and sometimes downsizing is part of the reality of business, but it has become a yearly (if not more frequent) occurrence over quite an extended period of time.

In a number of our surveyed companies, layoffs were seen to be handled incompetently or insensitively.

We come now to the data on satisfaction with pay and benefits.

Table 5-3 Pay and Benefits: Before ('06/'07), During ('08/'09), and After ('10/'11) the Recession

	% Favorable		
	Before	**During**	**After**
How would you rate the amount of pay you get on your job?	52	55	53
I am satisfied with my benefits package.	66	69	67

Attitudes toward both pay and benefits—especially pay—improved during the recession and then began a return to previous levels. Why would we find an improvement in these attitudes, considering the stagnant pay and some cuts in benefits that most workers have experienced? It is because attitudes toward pay, benefits, and job security cannot be considered in isolation from each other.

We saw in the write-in comments some evidence of workers' satisfaction with—or, at least, reluctant acceptance of—their pay and benefits compensation *in these times*. As we have said repeatedly in this book, security is, for most people, the most basic of needs. Its importance may not be evident when workers feel little insecurity—either in their own company or because there are plentiful job opportunities elsewhere. At those times—let's call them "normal" times—other needs, such as advancement in pay and position, predominate. But when security is threatened—as we observed in our reference to union negotiations—job preservation is of enormous consequence, and people are willing to make sacrifices to keep their jobs. Job security, after all, does mean getting a paycheck—however stagnant the amount—and having medical insurance—even though not as generous as before. Ross Douthat describes the new attitudes brought on by the recession.

> *Over the last two years, then, what still felt like an economic crisis during the 2010 midterms has become a grim-but-bearable status quo. In this new normal, Ronald Brownstein reports [from a nation-wide survey] in the National Journal, "a slim majority of Americans now say they define getting ahead as not falling behind—not losing ground or falling into debt—rather than the more traditional defini-tion of enjoying steady increases in pay and income.*[11]

> *Brownstein reports from the survey that "...a resounding 56 percent said they would prefer a job that 'offers a great deal of job security but only modest pay and little opportunity for advancement' over one that offered more opportunity 'and the possibility of high pay but little job security.' Patience, a young homemaker in Hesperia, Mich., who is looking for work, reflected that majority when she said that her priority 'is not so much promotions; it's job security. I want my job to be there no matter what.'"*[12]

That is the story of this recession for many Americans: a "flight to preservation." Perhaps it is not just Americans. In a survey conducted around the world, Towers-Watson found that the "...desire for secu-rity and stability trumps everything else right now, in part because employees see security as a fast-disappearing part of the deal."[13]

It is important, of course, not to exaggerate the degree to which workers willingly accept sacrifices in their pay and medical plans. Serious cuts in either are detrimental to the goal of preservation and security. As regards pay, workers find a reduction in the size or fre-quency of pay *increases* to be understandable when a company is in financial difficulty. Most acceptable of all, of course, is an increase that accounts for the cost of living but no more. That's actually quite a *plus* in a recessionary period: the employee hasn't taken a cut in real terms and still has a job. We should not try to calibrate the reactions too finely: they will vary by factors such as an individual's personal circumstances, the perceived financial condition of the company, and the amount of trust in management. The basic point is that the goal is preservation, and sacrifices to that end will be made and sometimes with a measure of relief when jobs are on the line. When business distress is clear and severe, actual pay cuts—while extremely unpleasant—are understood. But when that happens, it is especially important that those taking the cuts see all levels making significant sacrifices. Otherwise, those actions can generate resentment and anger.

Medical benefits have a similar dynamic. As we said, that benefit is no longer a fringe: it is really big money to the average worker. In that sense, medical benefits *are* pay, and cuts in them—such as increased premiums, copays, and deductibles—are felt as cuts in pay. Many workers are aware of the impact of this trade-off on company compensation policy: a 2011 nationwide survey of private sector employees reported that 49 percent agreed with the statement that "Rising costs of health care at my firm have reduced my annual pay increase."[14]

If a medical benefit has been very generous—and many companies once provided terrific benefits (often totally paid for by the company)—some reductions in them, we have found, are not only accepted, but are *welcomed*: "We still have great benefits," they say. "Thank goodness the changes weren't greater, as in other companies." As the economy has deteriorated and the cost of medical insurance has skyrocketed, more and more employees have been willing to accept less generosity on the part of their employers and assume more of the financial burden themselves. In June 2008 (before the onset of the recession), 19 percent of workers agreed that "I would be willing to pay a higher amount out of my paycheck each month in order to keep lower, predictable costs when using health care services." In June 2010, the percentage had risen to 42, and in June 2011, to 45.[15]

Cutbacks in benefits are, therefore, a bit different from those in wages: it appears now widely accepted that reductions in medical insurance plans are inevitable, but if not too onerous the importance of the security that the benefit provides outweighs for most what is, in effect, a cut in pay. And, as with wages, the reactions are very much conditioned by the context in which the reductions take place, such as the financial condition of the company and trust in management.

In this time of scarcity and insecurity, in sum, some sacrifice in pay is preferable to large cuts in medical benefits (insurance provides security) or job cuts, and some reduction in benefits is preferable to losing the benefit altogether or to job cuts. Broadly speaking, that is the current hierarchy of economic goals; it is a matter of balance in the workers' minds among their goals *in the service of the preservation of assets*.

The Role of Management

In addition to the economics of the matter—the balance between job security, pay, and benefits—the context within which this occurs must be taken into consideration. We mentioned that "trust in management" is a key variable determining how people will react to the company's response to recessionary conditions. We also said that the managements of companies in our sample may be somewhat different from others in the very fact that they are doing employee surveys in the midst of a recession—and are doing so repeatedly. This conjecture is supported by the employee evaluations of management revealed by these surveys, in two senses: management's effectiveness in responding to tough economic times, and their perceived concern for the workforce during those times. Over the course of the recession, the percentage of employees answering that the business is effectively managed and well run improved by 10 percentage points, and the perception of management's concern for employee well-being rose by 7 points. (We do not have good comparative data on this from other surveys, so we cannot say how representative in these respects our data are.)

It appears, then, that in our surveyed companies, trust in management—its competence and its concern for employees—grew significantly during the recession. At the very least, we can say that blame for the workers' employment woes—actual and potential—was not directed by them at their companies. A great deal of the blame for the recession was, we know, aimed at big banks and at the government. This condition is quite different from "normal" times (at least since the 1980s), when job losses were often seen as a consequence of either management greed or ineptitude. The recession was a great wave that swept over many companies and whole industries, leaving many with greatly reduced demand for their products and services. We saw in the write-in comments how gratified many of these surveyed workers were that they still had a job, and some expressed appreciation to management for their good fortune. Here are more direct comments on leadership "in these times."

> I think leadership of our organization does a very good job of communicating goals, mission, and strategy. The way our leaders have framed the message for change and set goals for the company has, I think, energized employees, even in the face of a tough economy and some downsizing that happened last summer. I think people really believe that [the company] can change and establish itself as an innovative growth company once again.

> Wow—when I look at all the bad news in the economy, I'm sometimes inclined to think that people like [our CEO and CFO] should run for president (of the U.S., that is!). While we can't fix the economy, our leaders have smartly focused us on what we can do for our customers, to genuinely help them, AND ensure a long future for the company and its employees. Maybe [our CEO] can run for governor someday.

> [Our company] cares about its employees and puts them first. Because of the leadership, the way the company as a whole is going is in the right direction and doing very well considering the current state of the economy. That leadership within the company also encourages employees to be innovative and to try new things.

> Executive leadership does a reasonably good job of challenging traditional paradigms and pushing this company forward with a good

vision given the current and future economy and market. Still room for improvement, but I wouldn't consider this a weakness.

The company is very successful even in this economy, and generally a very fulfilling place to work. Our company has a strong, passionate, and innovative culture.

I would say the way we are treated as a family; we are somewhat always kept in the loop as to what is going [on] in other financial institutions as well as [in] the economy, which currently is imperative. It is important to get the "Small Company" feel in a large corporation like [us].

I really feel like XYZ takes care of their employees through all its benefits, and I am really grateful that they are sticking to their values despite the failing economy. It's easy to like working for a company that likes you.

So much depends on executive skill and so much depends on their values, and it is in tough times that these qualities are truly tested and appreciated.

What are the implications for the future of our findings on employee goals—the "economics"—and on management practice? Regarding employee goals, all we can say is: it depends. It depends primarily on the major forces that affect the availability of jobs: how quickly and strongly the nation recovers from the recession; the degree to which outsourcing of jobs—especially overseas—continues; and the impact—greatly accelerating, it appears—of technology and automation on the need for human labor. The failure of so many experts to forecast economic events constrains us, as rank amateurs in economics, from making any such predictions.

However, based on our many years of research on people at work—including their reactions to economic ups and downs—we don't feel the same constraint in forecasting how workers will react to changes in the economy. We believe that if jobs soon become much more available, approaching a near-normal unemployment rate, we will see a startlingly quick reversal in goals with, for example, increased wages becoming a much more prominent driver of employee attitudes and behavior, and security less so. It is our understanding that the psychological effects of the Great Depression of the 1930s lasted a long time (the effects seen both in workers and their children), but the economic distress then was much worse than now. If current economic conditions continue to improve and accelerate, the Horatio Alger get-ahead model, so deeply ingrained in the American culture and the American psyche, should start to reassert itself and the "bad times" fade for most into a bad memory.

But the principles of effective management practice—such as not treating workers as fungible objects—are relevant for good times and bad equally. The principles are easier to implement when a company is large and growing—for example, finding jobs for surplus workers elsewhere in the organization is less problematic then—but even in those times, as we have shown, some companies choose to lay off workers to obtain a short-term boost on Wall Street. In tough times, avoiding layoffs for many companies is impossible, but the fundamental principles hold that that action should be taken as a last resort, and those laid off should be treated with care and sensitivity. Further, it is especially tempting during a recession to treat the survivors "as lucky to have a job," and, "if you don't like it, leave." It is precisely when management's power vis-á-vis its employees is greatest—when other jobs aren't readily available—that wise executives don't trumpet that enhanced power in word or exert it in deed. In times of economic distress—when management doesn't "have to"—workers' appreciation for the efforts made on their behalf are the greatest, significantly enhancing their long-term commitment to the organization and its goals over the long term. Loyalty begets loyalty.

6 ———————————————————————

Respect

"The best index to a person's character is (a) how he treats people who can't do him any good, and (b) how he treats people who can't fight back."

—Abigail Van Buren, Advice Columnist

"The real judges of your character aren't your neighbors, your relatives, or even the people you play bridge with. The folks who really know you are waiters, waitresses, and clerks."

—Katherine Piper, Author

"Nearly all men can stand adversity, but if you want to test a man's character, give him power."

—Abraham Lincoln

It's not particularly noteworthy that people in organizations are "respectful" of their bosses and that the higher in the hierarchy a person is, the more deference she receives. Whether or not appreciation is genuinely felt by their subordinates, bosses receive lots of thank-yous, and they rarely receive any verbal abuse or even sharp disagreement. We put this type of respect in quotes because this is not the kind of respect we address in this chapter.

The respect we have in mind—and that has such profound implications for worker morale—does not come from deference to power or the expectation of reward, but from a sense of the intrinsic worth of workers as human beings. We define the equity need as the desire to be treated justly in relation to the basic conditions of employment.

These conditions are expected simply by virtue of being employed and derive from generally accepted ethical and community standards. The major financial components of equity are job security, pay, and benefits. The major nonfinancial component is respect.

A few "write-ins" from our surveys vividly illustrate what we mean by respectful and disrespectful treatment of workers.

First, here are some comments from workers subject to disrespectful treatment at work (in response to the question, "What do you like least about working here?"):

> *My boss acts like a prison guard...and we're the chain gang! The way he barks orders feels like a threat. And he expects obedience. I've never felt this lack of basic human respect before.*

> *The most frustrating aspect of this company is the low degree of respect our management portrays toward employees here. I believe that all employees on my team are responsible adults who constantly make decisions based on what is needed for the client. Our team leader...has no respect for us. She is always passing nasty, sarcastic comments on to me and everyone in my team. She herself doesn't have respect for our so-called corporate values.*

> *Working with...leaders who...are mean spirited and tear individuals down instead of building them up. Senior leaders do not get after them for their behavior.*

> *The same commitment and respect given to customers is not given to employees who are the building blocks of the company.*

> *The total lack of respect and general condescending attitude of our management and supervisors' attitudes shows as a daily and constant reminder of incompetence and the lack of direction in which this establishment is headed. What is preached is blatantly not practiced, there is discrimination and favoritism—so many undesirable traits which our leaders all possess. I challenge top management to do a thorough clean up, or can they?*

> *[The manager] is the most unprofessional "manager" I have ever met. He intimidates and humiliates many of my peers. He seems to lack respect for anyone. He is extremely controlling and hot headed.*

I feel this could be a great place to work if he would not treat people so poorly.

The hourly workers here are like peons. If you're not one of the suits, you're nothing, a moron. It's from the union that we get self-respect.

We're always being watched like children who can't be trusted. The supervisor sneaks around to make sure we are not playing games on the computer or making personal phone calls or talking to each other. It's amazing we don't have to ask her for permission to go to the bathroom. That's probably next.

Now, here are some write-ins from workers who are more positive on this point (in response to "What do you like most about working here?"):

The people I work with are the best thing about this company. From my senior director and immediate supervisor and all of my fellow reps, I feel everyone respects each other and works very hard for one another.

My leader shows integrity and supports me when it may not be the popular thing to do. I have a lot of respect for her and value her input.

It is also wonderful to know that my leader treats me individually and considers whatever challenges I face with respect and consideration.

My supervisor...is honest and forthright and has had to make and deliver difficult decisions but has done so with sensitivity and respect.

My immediate supervisor has terrific people skills, and for that he is well respected and highly regarded as a role model. His open door policy is the best I have experienced at work.

I enjoy working here because of what my leader has created. He... understands people's needs and pays attention to every employee request. He is well respected for his honesty, dedication, and people skills that is a God-given talent. He is caring about employees and spends the time to solve employee issues. Every employee that reports to him enjoys working for him and the job. He is the best.

Treating people with respect and dignity and providing the generous severance packages during the reduction in force was extremely positive. During 9/11/01 and beyond, every level of the company demonstrated great care for our employees and customers, which is a positive reflection on the people that make up the leadership.

The best thing about working for [company] is the environment that surrounds you. You have the right to give ideas and improve work procedures that concern the front lines with our clients. Our leaders are open to new ideas and feedback at all times and are always there when you need them. You receive the respect expected in a work environment and even more.

This company has made a deliberate attempt to treat all employees as human beings. Their policies are wonderful, like being able to take time off when there's an emergency at home without being questioned to death. They trust the workers, and the workers want to give their all for the company.

The Heart of Respect

Equality is at the heart of respect—the treatment of each individual as important and unique without regard to any other characteristics, such as gender, race, income, or even perceived performance or contribution to the organization. Does equality mean that it is inherently disrespectful for some people to earn more than others or for some to have more power than others? That is the view only in extreme forms of egalitarian ideology, such as communism. The rest of us *expect* differentiation in income according to responsibilities and would find an organization with no differentiation in power ludicrous and dysfunctional.

The core issue is how people at legitimately higher income or power levels *treat* those at lower levels—that is, how they use their power.

To take a simple-minded example, do passengers on a plane see it as illegitimate for a pilot and crew to be in command and give orders? Of course not. But, in manner and attitude, how are passengers treated by the crew? Do they feel themselves treated as welcome guests of the airline, or rudely as necessary evils, or, perhaps most commonly, indifferently, as "seats?"

How customers are treated has a large impact on their willingness to continue doing business with a company; the impact is no smaller on employees and their willingness to perform at high levels. Here, we are dealing with a fundamental human need that, although it might sound trivial and corny—such as wanting to work for a boss with a friendly manner—has large consequences for human behavior and the effectiveness of organizations.

Lest we be misunderstood, we reiterate that although respectful treatment is terribly important to people, it is not a substitute for money. Both needs are *independently* important. In fact, respectful treatment and other aspects of good "human relations" are viewed as a sham if employees feel that they are at the same time being economically exploited. "Human relations" should not be treated as "public relations" in the sense of a friendly facade masking basic inequities.

What do our data show with regard to respectful treatment of employees? The question we generally use to measure respect is, "Rate the extent to which management treats you with respect and dignity—that is, as a responsible adult."

On the whole, the answers to this question are not negative. On average, 74 percent respond positively, but the range is large: the most positive organization has 93 percent of workers responding favorably, whereas the lowest has only 43 percent of workers answering this way.

Three broad levels of respectful treatment in organizations can be distinguished: positive, indifferent, and humiliating. Let's begin at the negative end of the scale.

Humiliating Treatment

According to our survey results, humiliation is a relatively rare condition, at least in most organizations and at least at the present time. But when it does occur—and it can occur in the treatment an employee gets from a particular boss in an otherwise respectful organization—it has a devastating impact on people and their performance.

Humiliation means being treated blatantly as a lesser being: as inherently incompetent or untrustworthy, or as a member of what is, in effect, a servant class. It comes in two forms: interpersonal, such as an employee's work being ridiculed by his immediate boss; and structural, such as formal organization controls that allow workers absolutely no decision-making authority in the performance of their jobs. Also on the structural side are practices that sharply differentiate status in a way that is particularly demeaning to those at lower levels (for example, separate entrances for hourly workers, separate and thoroughly unappetizing eating facilities, and separate parking areas that are long distances from the plant).

The major point of these managerial behaviors and status distinctions is to clearly delineate in the workplace higher from lower orders of humanity. They have no other goal because they have little to do with actual function—that is, with getting the job done. In more traditional societies, they are a way of saying (both on and off the job), "I was born right and you weren't." In America, their meaning usually is, "I have achieved and you haven't."

The civil rights, women's rights, and gay rights movements demonstrate the degree to which American society can be "traditional": being born with the "wrong" race, sex, ethnicity, or sexual orientation causes people to be classified as "less than" those in the more favored strata of American society. These social movements are all about equity, certainly economic equity, but also psychological equity in terms of respectful treatment. We don't need to repeat the innumerable humiliations to which various disfavored groups have been subjected. Suffice it to say that they have not been just petty annoyances and frustrations, but often sources of rage and powerful drivers for change.

In organizations, the consequences of humiliation show up most dramatically in labor conflict. The humiliation felt by workers has been significantly present in *all* the serious industrial disputes we have studied. These disputes have also been about economic issues— we make no claim that economic demands are less important than, or somehow a displacement for, psychological deprivation. But we have not seen genuine *rage* by large numbers of workers unless they have also felt seriously demeaned by management in their daily jobs. Labor and management can disagree about money but still respect each other and work toward a settlement in a business-like way. That's collective bargaining. But how does one bargain about assaults on workers' dignity?

The incidence of the more severe forms of humiliation—both interpersonal and structural—has almost certainly lessened considerably over the years in the American workplace. There are numerous reasons for the change, including the reduction in manufacturing employment as a proportion of the U.S. workforce (by and large, factory workers have been treated less respectfully than office workers), the influence of modern management theories being taught in U.S. business schools, the demonstrated effectiveness of "softer" management styles as antidotes to unionization, and the influence that Japanese industry has had on American management practices. The last reason has over the years been especially profound because Japanese companies have been remarkably successful in competition with American businesses, so what they have espoused cannot easily be relegated to "egghead" theory or a "soft-headed" management style.

The Japanese approach to workforce management emphasizes employee participation in decision making, teamwork, the minimization of status distinctions within a firm, and job security. Although few U.S. companies have embraced the Japanese philosophy fully (especially the importance of job security), its influence has neverthe-less been significant.

Indifferent Treatment

More common than blatant humiliation is simple indifference. Indif-ference covers a wide range of management practices. Sometimes it appears to overlap with outright disrespect, but it is often better termed benign neglect. As an example of the former, consider Ameri-can Airlines, which is a company with a long history of contentious labor relations. In 1993, P.T. Kilborn wrote in the *New York Times* about the causes of strikes at the airline:

> It is not so much the pay or benefits or sometimes grinding four- and five-city, one-day trips or the interminable, unpaid delays between some flights. It is the little things that striking flight attendants at American Airlines say grate on them and amount to a lack of re-spect. "They treat us like we're disposable, a number," said Helen Neuhoff, a 33-year-old flight attendant. Another attendant said, "I'd rather be on the planes. But I've got to stand up for what I believe. My self-respect is more important than my job." Nor did the issue go away. Four years later, when troubles at American Airlines brewed again, the theme remained the same. A disgruntled pilot complained, "As long as you treat your employees as merely 'unit costs,' like the Styrofoam coffee cups we throw out after every flight, morale will remain at rock bottom."[1]

The felt indifference of the company to its workers was aggravated over the years by the in-your-face style of the then-chairman, Robert Crandall. He was seen as being interested only in the bottom line and as being extraordinarily aggressive in his methods—with competi-tors, the community, the industry's regulators, and the workers and their unions. Crandall was given nicknames such as "Darth Vader" by his employees who feared his wrath.[2] In other words, he was an extremely tough and outspoken businessman who did not suffer fools (as he saw them) gladly or silently. However, employees believed him to be smart and, although insensitive to employees and their needs (as they defined them), dedicated 100 percent to the airline and its success. But his adversarial and brusque style magnified otherwise manageable problems into frequent and serious labor conflicts.[3]

Crandall's style puts him at one end of the indifference continuum. Most managements that are seen as indifferent to workers don't experience the labor conflict that he suffered. Here are some typical comments from that other environment, the one we term benign neglect:

> *Here, you're pretty much a number. They don't care whether you stay or leave. I stay because the pay is pretty good and I like the people I work with. And I think most companies are pretty much the same.*

> *What can I say; it's a job. Management doesn't bother you too much—just do your work and follow the rules and they pretty much leave you alone. You will hardly ever see them. Most important for me, it's a very convenient location.*

> *I've seen better and worse. The wages are OK and the medical benefit is good. Medical insurance is very important to me because of my son's medical problems. On the other hand, I don't get much feeling here that your work is really valued, I almost never hear from my boss—just see him from a distance except when he has to appraise me.*

> *Employee comments, suggestions, and concerns get ignored. Management lets me know that I am just a number and the company does not really care about my ideas.*

> *Management does not seem to care about you or your ideas. Their attitude is you are replaceable.*

> *I don't feel management cares what or how the lower-level employees think or feel about their jobs. Some employees have more knowledge and know-how than management gives them credit for. They should start listening instead of always telling. If you don't have a college education it doesn't mean you are stupid.*

They're businessmen—they're not mean, but when it comes down to it, all they care about is profits.

I have a negative feeling about the lack of leader presence. He does not make his presence known to staff and if in the work area, he is on a cell phone. It would be nice if the leader of the department could take a few moments to extend common courtesies, i.e., hello, good morning.

My supervisor arrives at work several hours after I start and never ever comes over to say hello or even let you know that she has arrived. Some days, you never even see her, even though you hear her.

Why do we say that an indifferent management, even one that's relatively benign, is inherently disrespectful? It is disrespectful in its implication that workers are not worthy of management's time and attention; therefore, workers feel insignificant. Indifference is a sin of omission—involving what management does *not* do—rather than a sin of commission, such as humiliation. Indifferent managers are not cruel or abusive; they are simply unconcerned with workers other than as replaceable economic entities. It is the essence of the previously described "transactional" worker-management relationship, epitomized by the view that, "We paid you; now we're even."

We defined respect as the treatment of workers as important and unique. Indifference conveys the message to people that they don't matter, at least not much. Being made to feel insignificant by being ignored is more difficult to deal with than being humiliated. Is the worker expected to shout, "Pay attention to me!"? In fact, other than in opinion surveys and among themselves, workers are unlikely to voice their need for attention. The desire for attention might be a profound human need, but in the business environment, it is not thought of as acceptable to come out and say it.

Unless aggravated by the behavior of someone such as Robert Crandall at American Airlines, the workers' response to indifference is less anger than disappointment and withdrawal and is usually accompanied by a sort of free-floating anxiety because workers get little feedback from management on their performance and often assume the worst. Although they might receive annual performance reviews, the reviews are usually formalities and not too informative. On a daily basis, they hear about their performance mostly when management is unhappy with it:

> *I feel like the most challenging aspect of the job for me is always having to pat myself on the back for the things that I do over and above for the client. You always hear the things you do wrong and the consequences for those, but people tend to grow when they are praised. I feel like my work ethic alone should speak for itself.*

A situation largely devoid of positive feedback gives rise to a feeling that management doesn't care whether an employee stays or leaves. The company, it is felt, will probably fire the employee at the first sign of a business downturn, or if he can be replaced with someone less expensive or who is judged to be a better performer or who is otherwise more favored (such as being a friend of a manager). Therefore, job insecurity can be pervasive in an indifferent environment:

> *It seems like we are easily replaced if we make a mistake or two.*

> *We are all tired of hearing about outsourcing. At every meeting, my team leader threatens us that we are going to be replaced because outsourcing would be cheaper for the company.*

> *They seem to make some of the metrics unattainable and harder to meet. It really doesn't motivate me into coming to work or making it a happy place to be when you feel you are being weeded out because there is always someone to replace you, or at least that is what they tell you if you're not happy.*

> *I see people around me being let go without good reasons, which makes me feel like we are not worth much to the company and are easily replaceable.*

> *I feel as though I am not truly valued by the company—that at any given moment I could be replaced and no one [in management] would care.*

Of course, the reality is that rarely is any one person indispensable. But, that's irrelevant to our argument. Although feeling indispensable to an organization is usually an immature wish, a worker wants to believe that she *counts*, that she is not invisible. This is not a childish wish at all. It is an important need throughout life. When workers do feel they count, it pays off in incalculable ways for the organization.

Indifferent managements are usually exclusively focused on the bottom line; for them, it's all business, and usually short-term business results at that. Because of this, one group of employees does receive a lot of favorable attention: those who, at any point in time, are clearly the top producers. This small fraction of a workforce— perhaps 10 percent—often receives lavish praise and rewards. But we don't call that type of attention respectful treatment, because what those employees receive is strictly a function of their current performance, and it can quickly evaporate.

Although there is some overlap, we distinguish between respect and recognition for performance. The key difference is that respect is unconditional; it does not derive from what the employee *does* but what he *is*—a human being. Recognition, on the other hand, is given to workers who have earned it by virtue of their contribution to the organization. Both are important, and Chapter 10, "Feedback, Recognition, and Reward," explores the importance and methods of recognition.

Is unconditional respect—is unconditional anything—realistic in an organization? It sounds more like advice for a sound parent-child relationship (the admonition for unconditional love) than one between management and workers. Our argument is not about love and it is not about children; it is about adults, and it is about decency in the way they deal with each other.

Whether it's financial or nonfinancial, the point of basic equity is that *everyone* is entitled to it. Not everyone is entitled to the same degree and kind of recognition. The distinction is seen most clearly in the way recognition and respect might conflict with each other. For example, not everyone can be promoted, and not everyone will be a boss. Promotion is an important form of recognition for most people and no organization can function without bosses. Is not being promoted to a managerial position disrespectful? Only when it serves not just to get the right person in the right job but in addition comes to signify, by the way the promotion is handled, the essential inferiority of those who didn't get the promotion. In other words, although it is rarely possible to promote someone without disappointing others, it is possible to do so without demeaning others. Demeaning others does not have to be consciously humiliating; it can simply be the result of indifference to the needs of those others (for example, to understand why they were not selected for the promotion, and what they might do to increase their chances for future promotions).

In a similar vein, we know that people don't want to be laid off. But, as we tried to show in Chapter 3, "Job Security," there are respectful, indifferent, and downright disrespectful ways to handle layoffs.

The Specifics of Respectful Treatment

Having discussed humiliation and indifference, let's now be more systematic and specific about just what respectful treatment is. An important sign that a worker feels treated respectfully is her belief, simply, that *management is pleased that she's there.* She is not just being tolerated (as in a "necessary cost"), but she is made to feel welcome and genuinely included. In that sense, it is the opposite not just of being humiliated, but also of being ignored. *Feeling welcome is a tremendous morale booster for every person.* We know that from our lives outside of work, and it is no less true at work.

What causes a worker to feel welcome, or not welcome, in an organization? Let's begin with what is one of the first introductions many new workers get to an organization: the employee handbook. Most handbooks are a lengthy recitation of rules, regulations, and warnings. The inherent message, then, is that employees are necessary evils: the company has to have somebody to do the work, but workers are troublesome and must be controlled through monitoring and discipline.

The focus on rules and their enforcement is the essence of the bureaucratic mentality that is so aggravating to those who deal with it. As customers, we have all encountered service personnel who seem set not on helping us, but, rather, enforcing a company policy that blocks or makes it difficult to resolve a complaint. We're frequently made to feel in these interchanges that we are a source of problems for the company instead of the source of its livelihood. The story comes to mind of the librarian so intent on having books returned that, when he finally gets them all, locks the doors so that no one will ever be able to take out a book again! No customers, no problems. And every book is in its place.

The bureaucrat might be defined as one so obsessed with her organization's rules that she forgets its purpose.

Now, consider this one-page employee handbook for Nordstrom, the hugely successful Seattle-based retailer:

WELCOME TO NORDSTROM
We're glad to have you with our company.

Our number-one goal is to provide outstanding customer service.

Set both your personal and professional goals high.
We have great confidence in your ability to achieve them.

Nordstrom Rules:
Rule #1: Use your good judgment in all situations.
There will be no additional rules.
Please feel free to ask your department manager, store manager, or division
general manager any question at any time.

This one-page handbook speaks volumes about the company. It highlights Nordstrom's focus on customer satisfaction, its deliberately nonbureaucratic culture, and the trust it places in the capabilities and character of its employees. The statement is the epitome, in words, of a welcoming and respectful organization.[4]

Words must, of course, be translated into deeds. The following is a categorization of the specific deeds that cause employees to feel welcome and respected by their organizations. Much of it is neither surprising nor complicated; with some exceptions, it comes down to matters of common courtesy and decency that are familiar to us all. As we previously mentioned, it is not particularly noteworthy to see someone showing courtesy and decency to someone in a position of power. *The major criterion here, therefore, is whether people of less power and importance are treated similarly.*

Physical Conditions of Work

We begin with a basic: physical working conditions.

> *"If the washroom isn't good enough for the people in charge [of the corporation], then it's not good enough for the people in the store."*
> —From a speech by Marcus Sieff, former chairman of Marks & Spencer, describing why the washroom is his first stop whenever he visits a Marks & Spencer store[5]

It is impossible to feel welcome in an organization whose work environment is unnecessarily dirty, congested, poorly lit, poorly ventilated, or ugly. Not taking care of oneself physically—in dress, cleanliness, and so on—may be a sign of self-disrespect. Not taking care of the environment in which employees work is a sign of disrespect for them. Workers don't normally expect lush surroundings; many would consider that a waste of money. However, they do expect an environment that, as the saying goes, is "fit for a human being."

Here are some comments from our surveys:

Physical office conditions are cramped and shabby compared to most companies. Getting away with least possible expense on employees in this area is clearly the priority. The company generally does a good job in many ways, but working conditions is not one of them.

Deteriorating working conditions reflect how little the "leaders of the company" value us. We walk past rows of vacant full-sized cubicles on our way to the shoeboxes we share for 8 to 10 hours a day. And remember casual Fridays? The morale-boosting tool which didn't cost a red penny? Gone. I guess that's progress.

The physical working conditions are horrible. We have shared cubes, and it is very difficult to get daily work done. No one has any room to spread out their paperwork. I'm very disappointed that we were not asked for any input. Everyone now knows exactly what grade you are by what kind of desk you have.

The restrooms are horrible. It's an insult to us.

One of the great things about this factory is the working conditions. You could eat your lunch off the floor! John [the plant manager] insists that we keep our work areas orderly and clean and that the clean-up crew doesn't slack off. What a difference from [company] where I used to work. It was dirty, greasy, messy, no air conditioning. They treated us like pigs. And because of it, tools and materials were always getting lost.

Not only do good physical working conditions make getting the work done easier; it boosts worker morale and productivity because of the respect for workers that it conveys.

Status Distinctions

The discussion of physical working conditions brings us to a consideration of status distinctions within companies. The reader unfamiliar with organizations can rest assured that few senior managers have filthy restrooms or offices. Even when these conditions for the bulk of workers are decent, they are likely to be significantly better for those in senior management. When the food in the employees' cafeteria is quite acceptable, there is often an executive dining room with superb food and probably waiter service. The list goes on.

Here is the question: if conditions for the masses of workers are decent, isn't it acceptable—indeed, appropriate—for those of higher rank to be treated still better, to have privileges not accorded to ordinary workers? After all, in addition to pay and power, isn't that what "rank" means?

Yes, that is what higher rank normally means—but no, these distinctions are mostly unwise.

It's not that employees who are generally well treated complain much about status distinctions. These differences are criticized in focus groups primarily when employees feel truly badly treated (not just comparatively so) or when senior management is viewed as incompetent (so why the perks for them?). Otherwise, employees tend to see the status distinctions as normal—the way things are.

We are not in this book interested in "normality." In the previous chapter, we saw that it is normal for most workers to believe that management has little loyalty to them, so their jobs can be cut with barely a second thought in the service of short-term profits. But we also saw that certain organizations stand out as exceptions to the rule: they have a genuine commitment to their employees' well-being, including job security, and that builds a foundation for high levels of employee commitment and outstanding performance over the long term.

Similarly, numerous companies deliberately and successfully seek to remove needless boundaries and distinctions among the levels of an organization. The operative word is "needless." Almost everyone concurs that an organization needs differential power and that compensation should be correlated with responsibility. But what is the function of distinctions based purely on status? *Their major function is to feed the vanity of those at higher echelons.*

Don't get us wrong: nearly everyone, ourselves included, gets a kick out of being treated royally. It feels good. The issue, however, is whether it is good *for the organization* that only certain individuals and strata receive that treatment.

Status symbols are decidedly not good for organizations because, at the most obvious level, they act to physically limit interaction among the organization's members. Executive floors, separate eating facilities, separate entrances, and so on, isolate higher from lower echelons and severely reduce the exchange of information and ideas among employees.

Status symbols also inhibit interaction by reinforcing differentiations in importance and authority. In organizations, the problem with "respect for authority," as commonly used, is that there is generally too much, not too little, of it: most people feel a lot of inhibition about communicating candidly with those of greater power. The free exchange of information and views is critical for performance, and organizations should encourage this exchange by making people less, not more, deferential to power in the way decisions are arrived at. Eliminating or minimizing overt symbols of power helps greatly in this respect because it makes power and position less "awesome."

For the sake of open communication and to demonstrate an egalitarian philosophy, an increasing number of companies have removed many common status symbols. For example, author Shari Caudron writes that "...the new Alcoa Inc. corporate headquarters in Pittsburgh was designed so that workspaces, all of which share the same dimensions, are nonhierarchical. As Agus Rusli, architect for the project explains, 'Cloistered spaces for the privileged few are replaced by open, flexible arrangements of workstations.'"[6]

Here is a simple rule for determining which status distinctions should be eliminated: consider eliminating all distinctions that serve no clear business purpose. A business purpose refers to what is needed for effective on-the-job performance. What is the business purpose served by separate dining rooms, parking spaces, restrooms, and entrances; or differentiations by colors of badges, uniforms, and hard hats, type of coffee service, and quality of office decoration? Most often, none!

When he was on the Board of General Motors, Ross Perot observed, "In Pontiac [Michigan], GM executive parking garages are heated, while the poor guys who work in the plant freeze their tails off walking to work in the snow. It costs $140,000 a year to heat one parking garage. I'd shut that thing down. It has nothing to do with cars."[7]

Should executives have private offices? That sounds like a heretical question, but a number of organizations have eliminated private offices entirely. Meeting rooms are set aside for the times privacy is needed for any employee that needs it.

In the 1970s, one of the authors of this book had an appointment with the CEO of Tektronix, located in Beaverton, Oregon, to discuss the company's state-of-the-art personnel practices.

At the time, the firm employed 20,000 people and was noted worldwide for the development and manufacturing of test, measurement, and monitoring technology. Tektronix is said to have been the pivotal influence in the development of Oregon's Silicon Forest (home of Intel and hundreds of other high-tech firms).

He entered the building and asked to be directed to the CEO's office. Eventually, he found himself sitting next to the desk of a young man finishing some paperwork. After a few minutes, he inquired where the CEO's office was located and when he would be available. The young man said he was the CEO, and he would be free in a few moments.

Marveling at this arrangement, the author asked what he did when he required complete privacy. He pointed to a small, fully enclosed, but glass-windowed office in the corner. He said that everyone had access to that office when they needed it.

New York City's Mayor Michael Bloomberg had an open-office arrangement at the company he founded and led, Bloomberg LP, and brought this idea to City Hall. Top officials of his administration, including the mayor, work in cubicles within a giant, open bullpen. Deputy Mayor Patty Harris says that the style extends to a first-floor conference room that is visible through glass doors from the City Hall rotunda. "The emphasis," Ms. Harris said, "is on keeping things open and transparent."

Compensation Status Is a Fundamental Distinction

One of the most fundamental status distinctions in industry is that between hourly and salaried workers; the former are paid for the number of hours worked, whereas the latter's compensation is based on a longer time period, be it a week, a month, or a year. In practical terms, it comes down to this: hourly workers lose pay if they are absent from, or late to, work, and they are required to be compensated for overtime work; typically, salaried workers receive the same amount each pay day, regardless of the number of hours worked during the period.[8]

The distinction between the two categories of workers is based on the different kinds of work they do. Hourly people typically perform physical tasks with physical outputs, such as assembling widgets or processing papers. When they are absent or late to work, things don't get produced, and a company is not obligated to pay for work not done. On the other hand, the jobs of salaried employees more typically involve complex mental activities, such as managing, administering, and planning—in a phrase, using judgment. These nonmanual activities are much less bound by time, so their effective performance is only roughly correlated with hours spent at work. For example, being an hour late to work rarely means an hour's less output from a salaried employee and, as managerial and professional people, they are not expected to "turn off the job" immediately upon leaving work or to be paid for the time they spend on evenings and weekends thinking about and actually doing work.

In workers' minds, however, this is what the distinction really comes down to: there are two classes (almost castes) of workers: those who are "part of the company" and can be trusted, and those who come to work simply for the wages to be made and have no particular loyalty to the company. In many unionized companies, in fact, hourly workers are considered almost as employees of the union, which is similar to the way temporary workers are considered employees of their agency rather than the company.

Another way of putting the distinction is that salaried employees are seen to be "professionals," and that means more than having an advanced education. A professional cares about the quality of her work and the organization for which she does it. Close supervision of her work is not needed because, well, she's a "professional." The others—the "workers" or "hands"—are simply there to earn a living and, with a few exceptions, are believed to perform well only when carefully monitored.

Time clocks are usually used to monitor the time that hourly employees spend at work; they are rarely used for professionals, and time clocks are greatly resented by them when required. The president of the New York union of professional employees, the Public Employees Federation, put it this way in response to a contract proposal by the state:

> *The state wants to remove our contract's prohibition against punching a time clock, to allow the use of ID "swipe cards" for time keeping.*

> *We will not let the state erode our professionalism and attack our dignity by using ID swipe cards as a means to track our time and location at the worksite.*

> *The governor and his staff don't punch time clocks. And doctors, lawyers, computer programmers, engineers, and other professionals in the private sector do not punch time clocks. To ask us to do so is insulting and demeaning....*[9]

Isn't it "insulting and demeaning" for hourly workers to use time clocks? Interestingly, although hourly workers sometimes complain about the way time recording is administered (especially the often draconian punishments for falsifying time records), they rarely express resentment at having to use time clocks. More basically, hourly workers almost never complain about the system that differentiates employees by hourly and salaried. As with the status distinctions previously discussed, these systems are so deeply engrained in organizations and in the psyches of the workforce that they are almost like laws of nature. They will therefore not show up in our surveys as denoting a lack of respect.

Frequent layoffs represent for many workers another "law of nature"—except in those organizations that do everything possible to avoid layoffs and do so only as a last resort. Indeed, many of those organizations have abolished, or never have had, a distinction between hourly and salaried employees.

An all-salaried workforce bolsters at its most basic level management's efforts to create a respectful work environment. It is a way of saying that the company hires and compensates workers at *all* levels for the use of their minds, not just their hands. It is a way to express trust in their integrity and commitment. For example, an all-salaried workforce results, in effect, in a "no-fault" approach to absenteeism. The motivation to come to work every day is left in the hands of the employees. We don't know of systematic research on the matter, but the anecdotal evidence is that companies changing to an all-salaried approach initially experience an increase in absenteeism that then declines to levels at or below industry averages. Of course, those few employees who take unfair advantage of the system—and it becomes quickly obvious who those employees are—need to be warned and, if they don't change, dismissed. Those are the 5 percent—at *all* levels of the workforce, not just hourly employees—for whom the assumption of trust is not warranted.

Job Autonomy

The discussion of trust brings us to the matter of job autonomy for workers. The issue is covered in detail later when we show that giving trained workers latitude in the way they do their jobs has a major positive impact on their performance. This is because workers usually best know how to do their jobs most efficiently and because, whether their ideas are objectively good or not, they are motivated to make ideas work that are *theirs*.

Providing job autonomy to workers obviously has profound implications for the respect they believe management has for them. A company mandating every step to be taken by trained and experienced workers in the performance of a job, and then closely supervising them to make sure that the steps are followed exactly, is treating workers as untrustworthy or incompetent.

The following comments illustrate this point:

> *My manager is a nitpicker. He doesn't seem to make sound business decisions. He tends to challenge when unnecessary and challenge less relevant things. He has yet to think/act strategically. He doesn't respect us, isn't a leader, and he isn't respected.*

> *Currently, the biggest challenge I am facing is working for a leader that micromanages to a point where we all have a tough time doing our jobs to the best of our abilities.*

> *I feel excessive micromanagement by our leadership group. It is one thing to monitor day-to-day activity but yet another when someone has to sit with you and watch over your shoulder, audit your work, and listen in to phone calls that you are making to advisors and clients.*

> *The most frustrating aspect here is the low degree of respect or sense of competency our management portrays toward employees. I believe that all employees on my team are responsible adults who constantly make decisions based on what is needed for the client, but they are not treated that way.*

> *The bureaucracy is stifling. Upward feedback can get you fired. People aren't treated with respect. They are treated like children.*

The view that people at work can't be trusted to carry out their jobs without close supervision is one of the hallmarks of bureaucracy. As we have said, a primary focus of bureaucracies is rules, especially what employees at all levels are not permitted to do or can do only if others approve. These rules affect a wide range of positions: from the plant manager who, even though she might be leading an organization that annually produces millions of dollars' worth of goods, can't purchase anything on her own that costs over $10,000, to the office worker who has to fill out a 15-line form and get it approved to buy postage stamps.

The rules, especially for employees at the factory and shop-floor levels, extend beyond the performance of the work itself to issues of "behavior" or "conduct." We refer to edicts about dress, tardiness and absenteeism, length of rest breaks, personal use of company equipment, freedom to leave work stations, conversing with co-workers, and, as one rulebook we saw put it, "loafing during working hours." Violating these rules is almost invariably accompanied by disciplinary procedures, up to and including dismissal.

In the discussion of employee manuals, we saw how in both substance and tone, the rules as typically written send a message to employees that they cannot be trusted. We contrasted that with Nordstrom's startlingly simple and respectful message to its employees: "Rule #1: use your good judgment in all situations. There will be no additional rules."

Unlike their reactions to time clocks, most employees resent the myriad, detailed rules organizations write to govern their conduct; they see these as appropriate for children, not adults:

> *I hate being micromanaged (time off, phone breaks, lunches) and being watched like children.*

> *This job is demeaning. Having every moment micromanaged, being accountable for going to the restroom, being reprimanded for 2- to 3-minute variances is degrading. It's easy to dread coming here.*

> *Dealing with my leader every day is a challenge. He treats every-one here like grade-school children and has no respect for what you think. What we do at work is less important to him than that we get here on time and don't leave a minute early.*

> *We are on the front line taking care of people, problems, mess-ups, questions, concerns, and we are the lowest paid and treated the worst. We are treated like we are in grade school, not adults. God forbid if we have to take a trip to the restroom; everybody knows about it, and supervisors make a big issue out of it.*

> *You are always being watched. It's very Big Brother here. They are always listening to your calls, always monitoring, always coming around your desk, don't want you to talk to each other on the job. Treat us like responsible adults!*

Does an organization need standards of conduct? Of course, it does. Even Nordstrom, through its training and daily communications, makes its standards clear. But such organizations are different from others in two respects. First, they would never even consider rules such as prohibiting employees from conversing on the job. What could be more demeaning or ludicrous when applied to adults? Enormous costs result from trying to enforce a restriction of this kind (in supervisory time and employee resentment). Second, when rules are needed, they are expressed in a positive tone and mostly as general guidelines or expectations rather than as rigid requirements. For example, consider the following "paid time off" guideline:

> *[Company] is a dynamic organization of skilled professionals. Our clients often retain our services in no small part because of our ability to perform complicated and large projects on a timely basis. The scheduling of these services is often done by our clients on the senior management level and affects thousands of people throughout the clients' organization. Our ability to meet deadlines and delivery goals is of paramount import.*

> *This high level of responsiveness requires that we all, in turn, be as flexible as possible in scheduling time off, whether for vacation, personal days, sick days, family emergencies, or religious observance.*

As fellow employees, we acknowledge that we need to support and contribute to the company's efforts; as individuals, we know that each of our personal needs for time off work will be unique and changing.

Please note that paid time off does not normally carry over into the next calendar if unused. However, we recognize that there may be unusual circumstances related to workload or other intervening factors, and your department head is authorized to make special arrangements to carry over some or all of the paid time off days for a period of time that they will determine, not to exceed one additional year.

We recognize that there may be times when emergencies or other unanticipated occurrences will cause someone to be unavoidably absent or late. Please notify your department head as early as possible if this occurs and, if at all possible, in advance. However, please note that simply notifying your supervisor that you will be absent or late does not mean that it is appropriate. In fact, absences and lateness are elements that will be taken into consideration during performance reviews. Your supervisor is expected to monitor excessive absences or lateness and take the appropriate remedial steps.[10]

The moral is that most employees are responsible and reasonable adults who understand reasonable rules and don't have to be threatened into compliance. The few employees who are, indeed, irresponsible need to be handled individually and firmly.

Constrained Communication

In our discussion of status symbols, we put forward a basic proposition: if a distinction between employees is simply puffery for those in higher echelons—that is, is not being made because of a business need—consider junking it. The same holds for rules about communications—that is, who is told what when. Knowledge might be power, as the saying goes, but it is also *status*: "I know something you don't, so I must be more important."

In business, one of the most counterproductive guidelines is to distribute information on the basis of "need to know." It sounds right—we, too, stress business need as a criterion for designing policies—but as interpreted in practice, it is usually a way of severely, unnecessarily, and destructively restricting the flow of information in an organization. The spirit of the guideline is rarely inclusiveness: "communicate this to *all* who have a need to know," but rather exclusiveness: "communicate this *only* to those who have a need to know."

The constraint is meant to keep confidential information confidential. Every organization, of course, has information that requires restricted distribution, but three problems undercut management's intentions. First, much less information needs to be confidential than management typically believes; second, plenty of information that management thinks is confidential is widely communicated anyway through the grapevine or other means; finally, employees fill in information gaps with surmises and, in these, they usually assume the worst.

Constraints on communication are often irrational and counterproductive, and they act to reinforce many employees' sense of second-class citizenship. Employees' frustration with a lack of communication is one of the most frequent comments we encounter in focus groups and in write-in comments. The following comments are responses to the question asking what employees like least in their organization:

> *My three biggest concerns: communication, communication, communication. When new policies are implemented, not all associates are informed. Don't we need to know?*

> *The extreme lack of communication between the various offices as well as within each office.*

> *Everything here is held so close to the vest. It's ridiculous; we are not the CIA.*

I find it difficult to do my job when I am not informed of changes that affect me or have an easy way of getting the information.

No communication between departments and what the function of our department is and what we handle. A lot of misdirected calls, causing frustration for the customer who has been bounced around. If the communication was clear, there would be less frustration for the customer and myself.

The lack of communication has been a big challenge. We're given information on a "need to know" basis only and several times, the information has been too little, too late. Why do they hold back information we must have? It makes no sense.

Lack of communication from management [about our] business practices. Overall, there is a high level of confusion, uncertainty, and fear of being displaced within the organization.

The challenge in my department is keeping up with changes due to the lack of communication when changes are made.

Organizations need to hold back very little information from employees. Consider financial information. Perhaps the most well-known proponent of sharing such information with all workers is Jack Stack, the CEO of SRC Holdings Corp. He has formalized his approach and termed it "open-book management." His view that financial information should be open for everyone to know, talk about, and focus on, stands in direct contrast to the use of information for status or power. He says that the biggest lie in business is "information is power": "This wrongheaded cliché...encourages people to hoard information. Information isn't power. It's a burden. Share information, and you share the burdens of leadership."[11] He has instituted "open-book management" through which everyone in the company has access to all operating and financial "metrics," believing that the more people know, the more willing they will be to pitch in to solve problems.

Stack's open-book management approach is part of his broader management philosophy that includes sharing the financial gains of improvement with employees and the company doing its utmost to preserve employee job security. His business results, which are largely attributed to this integrated philosophy, have been impressive.[12]

Both function (what employees need for their jobs) and psychology (what makes employees feel respected, included, and confident in the honesty of management) dictate that few restrictions be placed on the flow of information to the workforce. Providing assurance that the company is run honestly is a particularly important matter for all of a company's key stakeholders who rely on accurate business information for their own decisions. This is what is meant by "transparency" and the lack of it has become a major issue of our times in corporate America.

There are only two limitations to our admonition to be fully communicative to employees. First, obviously, a few items are indeed confidential or need to remain confidential for a specific period of time. Second, the injunction to communicate fully does not mean flooding the workforce with unorganized, unprioritized, and irrelevant information; that is another way of *not* communicating.

Day-to-Day Courtesies

In thinking about business and respect for people, it is easy to overlook the critical role of basic civility and courtesy. How a boss talks to employees is important. It might sound trivial and even corny, but common courtesy reflects an egalitarianism at the most basic human level: it is the boss saying, "My authority and power in no way diminish your worth to me as a human being." This is illustrated vividly by the way workers react to an informal visit to their work area by the head of the company, especially if during the visit he refers to them by name. They are pleased, even ecstatic; they'll talk about it for days and tell family and friends about it.

Interestingly, workers often feel that the friendliness is somewhat staged, that the boss has probably been briefed on their names and perhaps something about them individually. But it doesn't seem to bother them; they'll say, "He's a smart leader; he knows how to win over people." In other words, they admire his understanding that winning over the workers is important to the effective functioning of a business. That, in itself, is a sign of respect for workers. How different it is from the way they see managers who don't even make the effort to stage it and who, therefore, come across as indifferent to, or even contemptuous of, workers. The boss's friendliness boomerangs only when it is inconsistent with other practices. It's difficult to take a cheerful "good morning" seriously when it's given by someone who refuses to spend the money needed to correct bad working conditions.

One of Tom Peters' and Bob Waterman's major contributions in their influential book *In Search of Excellence* is their emphasis on "management by wandering around," best known by its acronym MBWA. They suggest that supervisors should be out of their offices 75 percent of the time. Doing what? Mostly "wandering" to provide an opportunity for informal two-way communication with their people. The major functions of MBWA are "listening, teaching, and facilitating," and through this method—in contrast to the traditional and formal bureaucratic channels—managers can learn the most and help their employees the most.[13]

MBWA can, however, backfire if it is a method for micromanaging employees. It needs to be a *conversation* through which the parties can exchange information and learn from each other. It can backfire as well if it is only a "state visit," with retinues, a rigid time schedule, and predetermined "canned" questions (and, likely, the company photographer to record the executive's visit with "the folks"). To be successful, the visit must be genuinely person-to-person. This brings us to a critical, usually unspoken, purpose of MBWA: to express respect for the value of workers as human beings. Status differences are reinforced when an executive sits in his office and "receives" his subordinates. An executive that comes out on the shop or office floor—informally, without the trappings of position—provides the opposite kind of symbol: people *as colleagues* working toward the achievement of common goals. A workforce appreciates an executive who lacks pretense and pomposity.

Of the executives with whom we have worked, few exemplify our point better than Don Graham, the CEO of The Washington Post Company. The son of the late Katherine Graham, the former CEO of the company, Don Graham moved into a high-level management position at *The Washington Post* newspaper following a bitter strike by the pressmen in 1975. He played a key role in bringing peace to the pressroom after the strike, in large measure because of his unassuming personality, informal manner, and continual visits and conversations with the workers. It is not, of course, just blue-collar workers who are appreciative of that kind of treatment. Here is Roger Wilkins' observation of what happened when he went to work for *The Post* in 1972:

> *[Wilkins] was the first black editorial writer on the staff, and he would go on to write most of the Post's editorials on Watergate. "One day," Wilkins said recently, "this guy shows up at my door. He's a big friendly guy with a big smile and he says—Wilkins's voice rises to a perfect imitation of Grah181am's all-American cadence— 'Hi, I'm Don Graham, and I just want to welcome you to the paper, and I just hope that you have the best time here.' Later, I figured out who he was. But, that was really nice, you know? Nice things like that do not normally happen in newspapers."[14]*

Hard-boiled, cynical newspaper employees are not supposed to care about "niceness." That's part of the mythology that they have created and try to foist on others (and perhaps themselves), but it's baloney.

Here's another example of the importance of courtesy and decency at all levels. In 1985, we worked with a railroad that needed help to establish a more positive relationship with its unions. The project was successful: among its achievements were highly productive joint efforts to improve performance and the quality of work life for the company's workers. Cooperative undertakings of that kind between labor and management would have been unthinkable on that railroad a year earlier. To a person, both company and union officials were pleased, and a dinner was arranged to celebrate the project's success. At the beginning of the evening, while awaiting the arrival of the company's CEO, one of the authors was chatting with the president of the railroad's largest union. The union official commented on how amazed he was at the success of the undertaking, considering how rancorous relationships had been until then. He was happy with that, but then the company president arrived and the official commented to the author: "Watch now, you'll see how he won't even say 'Hello' to me. That hurts."

The company president didn't say "Hello" until he was reminded by the consultant to do so. The union official is a tough guy—known over the years as being particularly belligerent toward management—for whom small gestures of common courtesy would seem to be irrelevant. They're not. Underscored once again is the danger of oversimplifying human needs, trying to figure out what *one* thing matters to an individual. Many things are important to this union official. Some are obvious, such as achieving results for his members, and some are not so obvious, such as being treated with basic respect by people in positions of authority.

Part III

Enthusiastic Workforces, Motivated by Achievement

The sources of a sense of employee achievement or pride range from the very broad—the very purpose of the organization they work for—to what happens to them day-to-day, such as the conditions that affect their ability to get their jobs done and done well. Taking pride in how one earns a living is normally thought of as the defining characteristic of "professionals," but we find it to be a strong need of workers at all levels of the organization. People want to feel good about what they do and for whom they do it, and, assuming the equity needs are reasonably satisfied, pride is a major driver of performance and commitment.

7 ⎯⎯⎯⎯⎯⎯⎯⎯⎯⎯⎯⎯⎯⎯⎯⎯⎯⎯⎯⎯⎯⎯⎯⎯⎯⎯

Organization Purpose and Principles

"Make no small plans...for they have not the power to stir men's blood."
—Niccolo Machiavelli, 1514

"The way I see it, leadership does not begin with power but rather with a compelling vision or goal of excellence."
—Frederick W. Smith, CEO, Federal Express

A critical condition for employee enthusiasm is a clear, credible, and inspiring organizational *purpose*; in effect, it's a "reason for being" that translates for workers into a "reason for being there." This might seem odd when talking about for-profit enterprises—isn't the idea simply to make a buck, and don't employees, in turn, understand that and simply want to be paid well? Well, in fact, no. We humans are not that simple. Not in what we want and not in what we expect from the organizations to which we belong and to which we are asked to give our talent and loyalty.

Elements of Pride in One's Company

It is difficult to exaggerate the importance to most people of being part of something they can be proud of and care about. We see this clearly in the way people identify with a nation, an ethnic or racial or religious group, a city, a school, or even a sports team. Workers start their employment caring a lot about the company. When their caring diminishes, it is largely because of the characteristics of management and the company, not those of the individual. For example, people find it difficult to be loyal to, or feel pride in, organizations that treat employees as little more than costs to be tolerated or reduced, rather than as genuine assets to the business.

It is also difficult to be loyal to an organization that stands for nothing but making money. Obviously, making money is far from trivial; in fact, the financial achievements of a company can be an important source of pride for its employees. But just as an individual employee derives pride from more than his income (from doing high-quality work, for example), so does pride in an organization depend on more than its profitability.

Our research reveals a strong correlation between pride in the organization and the overall satisfaction of workers with that organization.[1] We find four main sources of pride, all of which reflect different facets of a single attribute—*excellence*:

- Excellence in the organization's financial performance
- Excellence in the efficiency with which the work of the organization gets done
- Excellence in the characteristics of the organization's products, such as their usefulness, distinctiveness, and quality
- Excellence in the organization's moral character

People want to work for an organization that does well but also does good. Roughly speaking, the first two of the factors listed relate to doing well (working for a business that is profitable and well run), and the latter two relate to doing good (providing something of real value to its customers and conducting its business ethically). These four aspects of excellence are, of course, interrelated. As we shall show, it is difficult to produce excellent long-term financial results without providing value to customers, or to succeed for long with unethical business practices. But, as determinants of pride, each of the four is distinct and important. Thus, the desires of employees that their company act ethically and produce high-quality products are important in and of themselves, not only because ethical behavior and quality are, in the long run, good for business.

You might be surprised by our assertions about the importance to most people of working for a "good" organization. Our evidence comes from both the statistical analysis of our survey data and from our qualitative material (the write-in questions and the focus groups, where both doing well and doing good receive significant mention). Indeed, employees want their companies to do *very* well and *a lot* of good. Here are a few typical write-in comments from employees in a number of companies. First, positive comments. (These are responses to the question, "What do you like best about working here?")

> *The commitment to be the best. The folks who run [company] have the money to be the best, and they spend it.*

> *Keep up the good work of making [company] successful. I enjoy working for [company] and want to continue working for the company long term.*

> *Great product, great strategy, great leadership, great concern for employees, great care for customers, great honesty. Senior management is terrific. We are very lucky.*

> *It is a pleasure working with an executive leadership team that is willing to put actions to their words...gets it done for customers and shareholders. Thanks. It is great to part of the [company].*

> *I am insanely proud of my work as a [job] for [company] and insanely proud to be here. It is universally recognized as a great company with very high standards and integrity. Most importantly, I grow and learn every day, have a chance to show what I can do and feel I'm contributing to a common good... In fact, I still feel, after several years here, that I would almost pay for the privilege of working for [company]. I couldn't afford that, really, but you get the idea.*

> *It's the top of the game, like being on the roster of an organization like the New York Yankees.*

Now, some negative comments. (These are responses to the question, "What do you like least about working here?")

> As a company, we are not "leaders" in any areas anymore. We no longer strive for innovation or excellence. We do...what "everyone else is doing" yet we say we wish to be "best in class." You can't have it that way. The man who leads must break the wind...we sure are becoming mediocre.

> We seem to be going out of business with a knee-jerk approach to everything. We talk growth but that's all it is—talk and no growth. We are throwing out everything that's not tied down and that includes loyal workers. What happened to the great company that we were?

> Top performance is desired and is needed, but top management has done almost everything possible to make it a non-performer. The smallest detail must go to the top for approvals. Having the president determine the transfers within the lower levels of a technical function is incredibly inefficient and it takes forever to get a decision made. Where is the leadership?!

> They put up Quality posters all over the walls but the foreman tells you just get the pieces out the door. Nobody believes anything the company says; it's all baloney. They lie to customers.

> All they want to do is cut costs and people and the work today is sloppier than it has ever been. It's getting embarrassing to tell people where I work.

The desire for highly competent management—a real "winner"—will not come as a surprise to most readers, and most agree that employees don't want to work for clearly unethical management. But *outstanding* regarding ethical standards? *Outstanding* regarding product quality? You bet! Again, read the positive comments to sense the worker pride that comes from corporate excellence and ethics. Keep in mind that, here, we discuss the determinants of employee *enthusiasm*, not "contentment" and certainly not just the absence of anger. It is difficult to be enthusiastic about a company whose financial performance is mediocre, but of comparable importance are the questions: how is the business being conducted, and to what ends? Without good answers to these questions, one's job and organization tend to become mere means to the achievement of other goals, especially financial. They have no value in themselves and won't arouse or sustain enthusiasm except in those few people who are motivated by nothing but financial gain.

If you doubt what we say about workers, ask what, in addition to your pay and benefits, *you* want from your employment. For example, what does it mean to say, "I have done a good day's work"? Is it not a feeling that you did quality work that day, that your work showed skill, that your work was having a significant, positive impact on the organization or a customer? Furthermore, except for gangsters and other sociopaths, people usually don't feel good about a day's work that requires lying, cheating, or stealing.

And people don't want to work for *companies* that act that way. People don't want to produce products of mediocre quality. In early survey work for U.S. automobile companies, in the late 1970s, workers complained bitterly about the poor quality of the cars produced by their factories. In that period, the workers and their union were often blamed for shoddy U.S. products. However, most workers felt terrible about what they said they were being forced to produce.

Enthusiasm about one's company requires a company with purpose, especially in relation to its customers. And it requires principles.

The Impact on Performance of "Doing Good"

"I want to...express the principles which we in our company have endeavored to live up to... Here is how it sums up: we try to remember that medicine is for the patient. We try never to forget that medicine is for the people. It is not for the profits. The profits follow, and if we have remembered that, they have never failed to appear. The better we have remembered that, the larger they have been."

—George Merck II, Former CEO, Merck and Company, 1950

Why isn't it enough for an organization to focus just on doing well (as if that weren't difficult enough to achieve)? After all, pride in one's organization is certainly fostered by operational success in the sense of financial performance and excellence of process. Aside from purely moral considerations, is there truly that much more to be gained *as a business* by pursuing a higher good? Moreover, can most companies find a higher good to seek?

In fact, there is considerable evidence that, on average, organizations that "do good" have superior long-term performance. One of the most impressive studies in this area is the research of Collins and Porras, summarized in their highly regarded 1994 book *Built to Last*.[2] They compared companies that were the "best of the best" in their industries (and, importantly, had been considered so for decades) with companies that were just satisfactory. This was a comparison, as they put it, between the "gold medalists" and the "silver or bronze medalists." For example, General Electric ("gold") was compared to Westinghouse, Johnson & Johnson to Bristol-Myers Squibb, Procter & Gamble to Colgate, IBM to Burroughs, and so on. In 18 such paired comparisons, the best companies far outperformed the comparison companies, on average, as well as the market as a whole, over the long term. For example, $1 invested in the best companies on January 1, 1926 would have been worth $6,356 on December 31, 1990. The worth of the stock of comparison companies would have been $955 and that of the general market $415.[3] It is important to keep in mind that the research covers companies as they were *up to the time of the research*. As we shall see later in this chapter, companies can change radically, oftenwith the advent of a new CEO.

The Collins and Porras researchers sought to determine the factors that distinguished the best companies from the merely satisfactory. They referred to the former as "visionary" because among the key distinguishing features of those companies was emphasis on a vision that was "more than profits":

> *Contrary to business school doctrine, we did not find "maximizing shareholder wealth" or "profit maximization" as the dominant driving force or primary objective through the history of most of the visionary companies. They have tended to pursue a cluster of objectives, of which making money is only one—and not necessarily the primary one. Indeed, for many of the visionary companies, business has historically been more than an economic activity, more than just a way to make money.*[4]

Many examples are cited of the "more than profits" visions, such as the earlier quote from George Merck II and this one from an interview with John Young, who was the Hewlett-Packard CEO from 1976 to 1992:

> *Maximizing shareholder wealth has always been way down on the list. Yes, profit is a cornerstone of what we do—it is a measure of our contribution and a means of self-financed growth—but it has never been the point in and of itself. The point, in fact, is to win, and winning is judged in the eyes of the customer and by doing something you can be proud of. There is a symmetry of logic in this. If we provide real satisfaction to real customers—we will be profitable.*[5]

That view is contrasted by Collins and Porras with HP's comparison company, Texas Instruments (TI):

> *...we reviewed over 40 historical articles and case studies and could find not one single statement that TI exists for reasons beyond making money... TI appeared to define itself almost exclusively in terms of size, growth, and profitability. For TI, bigger was better, period—even if the products were low-quality or made no technical contribution. For HP, bigger was better only within the context of making a contribution.*[6]

Such contrasts in vision are found in pair after pair. The authors speak of the "core ideology" of a company, and they are at pains to stress that there is no "right" ideology—the key is that it consists of a vision that is "more than profits" and that it inspires and guides the company's employees. For the authors, Citicorp's value, "autonomy and entrepreneurship," is as expressive of a core ideology, as is Johnson & Johnson's, "the company exists to alleviate pain and disease."

Nevertheless, as we review each of the visionary companies' ideologies, a strong moral component is found in almost all of them. Here are some examples of moral elements in the corporate ideologies of Collins and Porras' visionaries:[7]

- **3M.** Absolute integrity.

- **General Electric.** Improving the quality of life through technology and innovation.

- **Hewlett-Packard.** Technical contribution to the fields in which we participate ("we exist as a corporation to make a contribution"); respect and opportunity for HP people, including the opportunity to share in the success of the enterprise; contribution and responsibility to the community; profit and growth as a means of achieving all the other values and objectives.

- **IBM.** Give full consideration to the individual employee; spend a lot of time making customers happy; go the last mile to make things right; seek superiority in all we undertake.

- **Johnson & Johnson.** The company exists to alleviate pain and disease; we have a hierarchy of responsibilities: customers first, employees second, society at large third, and shareholders fourth.

- **Motorola.** The company exists to honorably serve the community by providing products and services of superior quality at a fair price; continual improvement in all that the company does, in ideas, in quality, in customer satisfaction; treat each employee with dignity and as an individual; honesty, integrity, and ethics in all aspects of business.

- **Nordstrom.** Excellence in reputation, being part of something special.

- **Sony.** To experience the sheer joy that comes from the advancement, application, and innovation of technology that benefits the general public; to elevate the Japanese culture and national status; respecting and encouraging each individual's ability and creativity.

- **Walt Disney.** No cynicism allowed; fanatical attention to consistency and detail; to bring happiness to millions; to celebrate, nurture, and promulgate "wholesome American values."

Collins and Porras's data clearly support the proposition that, on the whole, a strong moral component in corporate behavior is certainly not inconsistent with long-term business success and, in fact, appears to contribute significantly to it. Other studies supporting the positive relationship between corporate citizenship and business success abound, and we cite a few here. In 1996, Waddock and Graves found positive correlations between the social performance of corporations and measures such as return on assets, return on sales, and return on equity. Social performance was defined by them as the way corporations treat not just shareholders, but other key stakeholders as well, such as customers, employees, and the community.[8] A longitudinal Harvard University study found that "stakeholder-balanced" companies showed four times the growth rate and eight times the employment growth of companies that focus only on shareholders.[9]

Besides the enthusiasm and pride that employees feel for an organization with "purpose," the research suggests a number of other reasons for the positive relationship between doing good and long-term corporate performance. One reason is the impact of broad corporate reputation, and the trust that it inspires, on purchasing decisions by consumers. Surveys consistently show that a large majority of consumers say they are likely to switch brands or retailers to ones associated with a good cause. This is not just because the consumer agrees with the cause. It is also that being "good" in one sphere—such as respecting the environment—generalizes, absent contradictory information, to other spheres, such as the quality of the organization's products. At the least, in modern marketing terms, doing good helps an organization favorably differentiate its brand from the competition.

In addition, the specific components of doing good yield tangible financial gains. High-quality products and services attract and keep customers. Beneficent personnel policies attract and keep employees. There are many instances of progressive community-relations policies generating community support for company business initiatives and protecting the company from activities that are unfriendly to it and its interests.

A particularly vivid example of the benefits of positive community relations could be seen when, in 1987, the Dart Group sought to acquire the Dayton Hudson Corporation (now the Target Corporation) of Minneapolis. A charitable giver of 5 percent of its pre-tax profit, Dayton Hudson had become an icon of good corporate citizenship. On the other hand, Dart was widely perceived as a predatory corporate raider. In defense against the hostile bid from Dart, the company enlisted the community goodwill that it had acquired over more than 100 years, and it received overwhelming support. A special meeting of the Minnesota state legislature was convened to change the law relating to the timing and organization of company takeovers in the state. That helped defeat the hostile bid for Dayton Hudson.

At the negative end of the corporate citizenship continuum are companies that engage in clearly unethical behavior. A wealth of evidence shows that behaving in egregiously socially irresponsible and illegal ways is detrimental to shareholder value. In 1997, one study investigated 27 incidents of unethical or illegal corporate behavior and concluded that such behavior resulted in significant losses of shareholder wealth.[10] And, as we have seen in the behavior of financial services companies leading up to the Great Recession beginning in 2008, the negative impact extended far beyond the companies themselves and would have resulted in their bankruptcy had the federal government not intervened.

To summarize, the research appears to show that business profitability is not simply about making money in the short term, but is also about building positive and trusting relationships with all major constituencies that promote and sustain long-term profitability. A company should want customers who are willing to go the extra mile to purchase its services, employees who give their all for the organization, suppliers who feel themselves to be genuine "partners" with the organization and therefore seek to deliver their best work to the company and in a timely manner, and a community that vigorously supports the company's legitimate business interests. The importance of these relationships might not be obvious in the short run, and they won't appear to be needed in flush times, but they are critical to sustain good performance over the long haul and especially when business conditions turn tough. A major mistake that companies make is to take their key constituencies—their stakeholders—for granted.

Short- Versus Long-Term Profit Horizon

> *"Wall Street is in the business of making money between now and next Tuesday. We're in the business of building an organization, an institution that we hope will be here 50 years from now."*

—Jim Sinegal, Cofounder and former CEO, Costco

Expecting executives not to be oriented to the bottom line is, for most companies, akin to asking them to preside over a failing company and their own professional demise. *The important distinction, as we see it, is not between a senior management that is interested in profits and one that is not but rather between having a long- versus a short-term profit perspective.* Although the correlation is by no means perfect, it is abundantly clear that "short-termism" is often a recipe for profitability now and endless problems—sometimes disaster—later, whereas a longer time horizon is part of the foundation for *sustained* success. The correlation between time horizon and success is not perfect because there are some executives who seem to flourish at the edge and are extraordinarily nimble as they get into and out of trouble and skirt disasters for themselves or their organizations. It is just the pattern of their business lives. We saw in the financial crisis of 2008 how many large banks and their executives—despite being among the primary perpetrators of the crisis—managed to survive (and even prosper!) through government bailouts and generous severance packages. Luck? Talent? Probably a combination of the two, but skin-of-your-teeth escapes—especially when so many others suffer as a consequence—are not the path one would normally recommend for the conduct of a business.

All the companies we discuss admiringly in this book because of their people-management practices have as well a strongly long-term orientation. Or, more accurately, some of them *did* have one. The marked positive impact that a long-term outlook has on company performance can be seen most sharply in companies that have significantly *changed* in that respect (because we can then compare a company to itself over time rather than to other companies that may differ from it in other ways that could affect performance). We have three important examples to discuss.

First, consider change in Toyota. From 2009–2010, quality problems in Toyota vehicles, centering on stuck accelerator pedals that caused crashes, burst into the headlines. Until that time, Toyota was arguably the most esteemed automobile manufacturer, world-renowned for the quality of its products. The problems had actually begun more than six years earlier but were not acknowledged by the company, which was now claiming that human error was responsible for the crashes. After widespread negative publicity, including Congressional hearings and actions by government regulators, the company began to take the problems seriously and made the needed corrections.

The source of the problem in Toyota, many analysts claimed, lay in the company's changed culture brought on by an excessive focus on growth. Steven Spear, of MIT, observing Toyota's drive to become the world's largest automobile company, commented on the conflict between quality and the desire for bigness, noting that the behaviors necessary to achieve each in full measure are very different: "The problem was that the 'Toyota way' was diluted by the demands of production.... People in Toyota would say, 'This is going to bite us in the behind." Jim Press, once Toyota's top U.S. executive, said: "The root cause of their problems is that the company was hijacked, some years ago, by anti-family, financially oriented pirates (who) didn't have the character to maintain a customer-first focus. Akio does."[11] And Akio Toyoda, the company's president, conceded: "The problems arose when some people just got too big-headed and focused too excessively on profit. The ultimate responsibility for mistakes...lies in me."

Since the crisis erupted, the company has sought to show it is on top of its quality problems. Quality executives have been appointed throughout the organization; an outside advisory panel has been formed chaired by Rodney Slater, the former U.S. Secretary of Transportation, to provide an independent look at the quality issues and their solutions; and it has accelerated the pace for the recall of cars. It appears too soon, as of the writing of this book, to gauge the extent to which Mr. Toyoda has engineered the restoration of his company's culture. The signs are mixed, with some commentators extolling the company's bounceback in a number of respects, including quality. On the other hand, in October 2012 Toyota had to recall 7.5 million vehicles due to a faulty door switch that could result in car fires. This was the world's largest recall in 16 years.[12]

Another example of a company changing its course has been Johnson & Johnson (one of Collins and Porras' "Gold Medalists"). The reader will learn later in this chapter about J&J's "Credo," an exemplar for decades of the positive impact of clear values and a long-term orientation on a company's practices. Basic to the Credo is this statement of J&J's purpose: "The company exists to alleviate pain and disease; we have a hierarchy of responsibilities: customers first, employees second, society at large third, and shareholders fourth."

As in Toyota, however, the beneficial corporate culture generated by this vision appears to have been seriously eroded in recent years by a short-term business focus that has triggered an array of business problems. Among the problems have been many product recalls, safety issues with J&J's artificial hips, and a number of lawsuits aimed at the way it has marketed its antipsychotic drug, Risperdal. As analyzed in *Knowledge at Wharton*, "Many say that the problems are evidence that J&J has lost its way. 'I think the credo used to be quite real there,' says Erik Gordon, a professor at the University of Michigan's Ross School of Business. 'There was a time when people really believed in it and took great pride in it. But those days are long gone.' Now, he says, 'the major function of the credo is similar to mommy's skirt—which you hid behind—or like wrapping yourself in the American flag. It is to distract people from what is going on.' Gordon argues that CEO Weldon's relentless focus on the bottom line—the company's website touts its record of 27 consecutive years of adjusted earnings increases and 49 consecutive years of dividend increases—is the reason for the current woes. 'Bill Weldon sets the priorities and the culture for the company,' says Gordon. And the problems, from overly aggressive marketing to underinvestment in safety and quality systems, reflect 'people trying to get their bonuses, hit their numbers, and keep their job.'"[13]

We come, finally, to Goldman Sachs, another corporate icon and what may be the most widely publicized recent case of a company's transformation in its operating values. We would have included Goldman as a stellar example of the principles we argue for in this book had it not been for its deep involvement in the 2008 banking crisis and the company's culture in recent years that the crisis exposed.

Our past admiration for Goldman stemmed from its renowned culture, most prominently its "partnership" view of its relationship with its clients and the extraordinarily collaborative and productive relationships among its employees. That culture changed markedly in recent years. This was dramatically revealed in a resignation letter written as a *New York Times* Op-Ed column on March 14, 2012, by Greg Smith, the former head of Goldman's U.S. equity derivatives business in Europe, the Middle East, and Africa. Speaking of the past, Smith wrote that the "secret sauce" of the success of Goldman Sachs was its culture which: "...revolved around teamwork, integrity, a spirit of humility, and always doing right by our clients." He claims that that has changed markedly and describes the current culture as "toxic and destructive," consisting of a no-holds-barred focus on making the greatest profit for the firm, no matter what the impact on the client. And, as we saw at the onset of the Great Recession, the impact on clients of this kind of culture can be severely negative. While the firm and its employees have, of course, always been interested in making money, that wasn't their only goal, Smith says. He writes of an extraordinary "pride and belief" in Goldman, which stemmed from its focus on clients' interests and a collaborative approach to serving those interests.[14]

It would be naive to claim that the past at Goldman was Utopia and that the present has been all ethical hell. Large corporations such as Goldman are complex entities with a variety of businesses, business environments, and personalities. But from what we have learned, there appears to be little question that there has been a significant shift in the basic message to employees from senior management about what's really important now—the real values of the firm, its culture—and that these revolve around short-term profits.

We spoke earlier about the naïveté of the notion that profitability can ever be a second-tier priority for senior management. The issue is whether short-term objectives override long-term considerations. Previous Goldman management thought in precisely those terms. The oft-repeated informal motto of the company, coined by Gus Levy, its senior partner until 1976, was, "Be long-term greedy, not short-term greedy." With long-term greed, money was made *with* clients, not *from* them.

Toyota, Johnson & Johnson, and Goldman Sachs were all iconic companies in their very different industries, and they have resembled each other as well in the paths they have chosen in recent years: a much more intense focus on short-term gains at the expense of their customers and their long-term core values. And, perhaps, at the expense of their shareholders, too. As compared to the S&P 500, each has underperformed markedly. While the S&P 500 has grown 13.6 percent based on full-year averages from 2009 through 2012, Toyota and J&J grew much less (5.3 percent and 2.2 percent, respectively) and Goldman Sachs declined (–7.4 percent). It comes as no surprise to Michael Krensavage, founder of investment firm Krensavage Partners, when, for example, he considers J&J's market performance. "It's been one blunder after another," he says. "It's hard to explain."

A few additional words about business ethics. Although operating for the short term is not necessarily equated with being crooked—individuals and companies can be perfectly upright in their business dealings despite a concentration on short-term earnings—that single-mindedness about profits *now* sets a climate in which unethical behavior is more likely to occur. People are complicated, and just a small percentage will do anything anytime to make a buck. But if someone has to meet this quarter's, or this month's, or even today's business goals—meet them or else!—normally honorable people can do borderline—or clearly unethical—things: deceiving customers, surreptitiously cutting corners on quality, fudging financial records, and on and on. Such behavior is usually rationalized ("Gotta feed the family!") to reduce the psychological discomfort, and we are not going to make easy and self-righteous judgments about the matter. Further, focusing on individual employees and their guilt doesn't get us very far. It is the *culture* of the organization that requires attention—a culture where misdeeds turn out to be actually, if not publicly, encouraged so that otherwise unrealistic corporate goals can be met—and this must start at *the top* of the company, not the employees. Once that is done, employees who violate the company's ethical standards can be dealt with individually.

More About Purpose

We have described doing good as consisting of purpose and principles. *Purpose* relates primarily to how an organization serves its customers, *principles* to its moral character—its behavior against legal and ethical norms in its dealings with all its constituencies.

Regarding purpose, the fact is that most organizations produce some product or service about which their employees can be proud, at least potentially. (We say "potentially" because workers might feel embarrassed by the quality with which a product or service is provided.) Not just astronauts, emergency-room personnel, or special-forces soldiers feel pride in the type of work they do. We survey all kinds of organizations and occupations—from cleaning services to research laboratories, sanitation workers to investment bankers—and an overwhelming majority of employees feel that they provide a valuable service.

A sanitation worker in a focus group tells us, "There's no job in the city more important." A packer of cookies says, "I'm doing something that makes people happy." A housekeeper in a hotel asks, "Do you know what this place would be like without us?"

We must put ourselves into other people's shoes when we think about the meaning, dignity, and purpose of work. The fact that the reader might not feel particularly proud of packing cookies is irrelevant. We want to know how *the cookie packers* feel and, for them, this is not demeaning work. Is collecting garbage demeaning? All of us might do well to consider whether our own jobs are indeed more important.

The strong desire to be proud of our jobs is the reason that the pride scores are as high as they are: the norm is 82 percent, with the least favorable company still being 55 percent. Despite this restricted range, our research shows that large gains in morale and performance can be reaped when management behaves in a way that moves the scores toward the high end of the range.

More About Principles

Some companies view business ethics only in terms of compliance with the law and contributions to charity. This chapter focuses on the impact that business ethics have on the morale of employees, and our research indicates that, in this respect, the definition of ethics needs to include much more. For one, employees are interested in the quality of the relationships the company enjoys with all its key constituencies: customers, employees, suppliers, investors, and the community. Second, genuine pride comes from more than simply obeying the law. It comes from going above and beyond that, so that *outstanding*, not just acceptable, constituency relationships are achieved.

Our discussion of an organization's purpose centered on customers and, therefore, overlaps with this discussion of principles. Customers are key stakeholders, and providing them with high-quality and useful products and services is not only the organization's purpose but also an ethical consideration. Employees certainly see it that way. At a minimum, they expect their company not to cheat or deceive customers, whether or not such actions are technically illegal. But it's more than that: they want the products and services customers buy to be exceptional—at least to provide great value for the price paid. Our survey questions relating to quality and value show strong correlations with employee morale.

When asked what they like most about their jobs, many employees talk about the customers:

> There is a great sense of satisfaction when you help someone, customer or peer, who is really in need. That person thanking you for "stepping outside of the box" and helping them is what makes my day.

> I love working with customers, knowing that I impact people's lives. Without them, I would not come to work either.

> What I like best about this company is that it stands by its word to customers, and believes in doing the right thing.

We never stop trying to out-do ourselves in regards to the services/ amenities that we provide to customers. It is little wonder that we do a great job of retaining our customers.

We strive to exceed our customers' expectations everyday and we love doing our job.

I see a real win-win atmosphere and attitude concerning the way we deal with our customers. As employees, we establish lasting relationships and partnerships with our customers and the benefits multiply as time passes.

I feel that we do put the customers first and that if the customer has a problem, we will always do the best to have the problem fixed as soon as possible.

Ethics in the Treatment of Employees

Not surprisingly, among the most strongly held employee views about the ethical treatment of stakeholders is the way employees themselves are treated. A major goal of workers is fair treatment with regard to the basic conditions of employment, such as pay, benefits, job security, and physical safety. In those respects, too, there is a continuum that ranges from practices that are clearly illegal, to those that are borderline, to those entirely within legal and ethical norms, to those that exceed what's required and expected. Job security is an example. At one extreme are companies that violate the law by, for example, providing insufficient notice to employees before a layoff or using difficult economic times as an excuse to dismiss various protected groups, such as older employees, or to dismiss employees with union sympathies. At the other end of the continuum are companies that not only operate within the law, but also do their utmost to avoid layoffs and, when layoffs are necessary, treat those being laid off with care and generosity.

Another area basic to workforce treatment is physical safety, especially in traditional blue-collar industries. We did not discuss safety in detail in the equity section of this book, having reserved it for this chapter where ethical principles are discussed.

A multitude of federal, state, and local statutes cover safety and some companies, as we see periodically in news reports, repeatedly violate the law. At the other extreme are companies such as Alcoa which, under the leadership of former CEO Paul O'Neill (who later became the U.S. Treasury Secretary), compiled an extraordinary safety record. We will soon discuss what determines the success of statements of purpose and principles and will see that CEO leadership is critical. O'Neill's role in Alcoa's safety achievements is highly instructive in that regard.

When he took over at Alcoa, O'Neill announced that he wanted a chief objective to be a marked improvement in the company's safety record:

"I said the first day that no one who works for Alcoa should ever be hurt at work... The world is so full of cynicism and disbelief about really caring about each other that the first response was predictable. The senior people came to explain to me that we were already in the top one-third of all companies in the world in our safety performance as measured by the absence of lost workday cases. At that time the lost workday average...was 5 per 100 employees per year. The 1987 number at Alcoa was 1.87, so they were very proud of themselves. They didn't say it to my face, but the hallway conversation was, "When the next tough economic time comes, he'll shut up about this. He doesn't know anything about making aluminum; how can he be here telling us what we're going to do about safety?"

And so I set out to make it reality by traveling around to Alcoa manufacturing sites. The first place I went to was a plant in Tennessee, and after lunch with 45 people that included top management and top union representatives... I said...that people should not be hurt who work for Alcoa. I told them it's not a priority, but it's a precondition. Important things are not priorities, they're preconditions. So I said to the management, "From this day forward, we will not budget things that need to be done to improve safety conditions. If you have identified something that needs to be done, you should go and do it and you should not have an excuse list that says we'll put it into next year's budget and in the meantime hope that no one gets hurt." And then I said to the hourly workers, "If the management doesn't follow up what I just said to them, here's my home phone number." A lot of the management was really horrified I would give the hourly workers my home phone number, but I did. It's interesting that I got a few phone calls. Not too many, because when people called me and they could demonstrate that the ideas were being violated, I took some action to clean up the situation."

—From a speech at the University of Minnesota's Carlson School of Management, June 2002

By 2000, when O'Neill retired, the injury rate at Alcoa was one-tenth of what it was when he arrived in 1987. George Becker, the union's president at the company, described O'Neill as "a man you can trust and believe what he says."

We see that obeying the law and adhering to commonly accepted practices and ethical standards were not sufficient for O'Neill. The companies that generate employee enthusiasm are those that go beyond that and, in effect, act as true advocates for their stakeholders' interests. Their ethical commitments are not ancillary to the conduct of the business or a constraint on it, but rather an integral part of their operational and strategic decision-making. For O'Neill, safety was important in and of itself, and he also saw it as smart business. As Leslie Wayne of the *New York Times* put it, "...he figured out how to make money—not by cutting costs or slashing the payroll, but by improving productivity and making worker safety his top goal. His relentless push on safety had bottom-line benefits—he argued that a production process that was so flawed that workers got hurt was one that could not turn out high-quality products efficiently and cost effectively."[15]

More broadly, in O'Neill's own words:

"For me, [it] is not about safety, per se; it's about leadership. And it's about a conviction I have that a truly great organization requires

*that people be aligned around important values and they under-
stand what they are. And no matter where you are in the world,
they're the same."*

—Remarks at the National Safety Summit, 2001

During O'Neill's tenure at Alcoa, the company nearly tripled in size,
with shareholder value increasing from $4 billion to $32 billion.

We recognize, of course, that what a company says and does about
its ethical commitments and social responsibility can sometimes be
deceptive and hypocritical. This often happens when a company is
particularly and visibly generous in its relationship with the community but is quite the opposite in its treatment of other constituencies
such as employees, customers, and investors. As David Vogel pointed
out in an article in *The Wall Street Journal*:

> *Enron was long regarded as an exemplary corporate citizen. The
> firm and its senior executives were generous supporters of commu-
> nity institutions in Houston, and it captured international attention
> by building a power plant in India without resorting to bribing gov-
> ernment officials... And the company pleased many environmental-
> ists with its investments in alternative energy.*[16]

Enron, in 2001, went bankrupt in a wave of accounting scandals.

The moral of the story, obviously, is that any judgment about a
firm's principles must be based on its behavior in relation to *all* its key
constituencies. A company doesn't need to be outstanding in all these
relationships, but it gets no credit—quite the opposite—from being
outstanding in one or two spheres while clearly immoral in others.

Workers usually know exactly what is happening. Consider these
examples of comments from our surveys:

> *What I am very unhappy about is the...hypocrisy under which the
> company is run. For instance, [specific example deleted]. The com-
> pany says it values its employees but acts differently. Talk is cheap!*
>
> *I think outsourcing jobs to other countries is un-American and
> hypocritical. We jumped on the 9/11 bandwagon and sent U.S. jobs
> overseas.*

There seems to be a hypocrisy that exists in our company. We need to learn lessons from other companies' mistakes. Let's not be the next Enron or WorldCom and get back to our core values and remember the greatest asset we have, our people.

The company is very hypocritical in its practices.... Treating employees with dignity and respect is a core value, yet if the company can save money by firing people (while still reporting a profit), it will do so. Loyalty should be a two-way street.

We must work to overcome the systematic maneuvers and the hypocrisy (true insincerity) of certain "leaders" who worry about showing "fake competence" to their superiors. They underreported the numbers this month so they can look better next month.

Hypocritical leadership. We hear from our leaders that they want honest feedback from us. However, if that feedback happens to be negative, we are viewed as disgruntled employees who need to go elsewhere if we aren't happy at the company. We have been TOLD by our leadership how we should give feedback. So much for honesty.

Trying to smile at the leadership when they preach loyalty to the company and they are only looking to make the most money themselves with our jobs, only to eventually outsource to other countries. This appears to be what employees will get for their loyalty to this company.

The management preaches that quality service is what they want you to give to customers. However...the...[emploees] who have bad quality but good quantity get number one ratings.

They talk ethics but their advertising is totally misleading. They advertise items we don't even have in stock.

Although workers feel positive about an organization that does good, they understand that they are not working for a charity. Samuel Gompers, the first president of the American Federation of Labor, knew that. "The worst crime against working people," he declared in 1923, "is a company which fails to operate at a profit."

The second-worst crime, Gompers would no doubt add, is a company that operates at a profit through exploiting its workforce, or, we would add, through exploiting any of its key constituencies. Workers are especially appreciative of a management that sees doing well and good as not only compatible, but mutually reinforcing: doing good contributes to a company's long-term business success, and business success enables a company to do good things.

Getting Practical: Translating Statements of Purposes and Principles into Practice

"Many mission statements are unintentionally ridiculous. We've all seen them, companies that rhapsodize about customer service when customers are routinely disdained and disregarded, enthuse about employee empowerment when employees are treated with even less respect than the customers.... In each case, thoughtful insiders might assess the date of achieving these goals as about the same as 'when pigs fly.'"

—Eileen C. Shapiro, *Fad Surfing in the Boardroom*

The great majority of companies with which we are familiar have formal statements of "purpose" or "mission" or "vision" or "values." In our surveys, however, we often uncover employee skepticism about whether these statements are ever translated into practice. This is a shame since such statements can be enormously helpful to guide and inspire a workforce. They provide employees with both an overarching purpose for their individual efforts and basic decision-making criteria. But when they are seen as empty rhetoric, they do more harm than good.

The failure to make statements credible is rarely a result of insufficient effort spent on their wording. A lot of time is usually devoted to that, with no small involvement by senior management (often at two- to three-day retreats). Indeed, employees often wonder why such high-powered, high-paid time is devoted to a matter that turns out to have little consequence for the organization.

Here are three reasons these statements are only sporadically implemented:

1. The most important reason is that, despite the resources devoted to their composition, the avowals by senior management that "this is really serious," and their widespread and repeated communication to everyone in the workforce, the statements are in truth felt by senior management to be largely peripheral to the business. It is as if the executives attended church at the retreat, but it's back to business on Monday.

2. The statements' phrasing can be so general that they seem meaningless or so concrete and detailed that they become uninspirational.

3. Other than communicating the statement to everyone, the company lacks an effective method for translating it into a daily reality that endures over time.

What is decidedly not an issue is semantics. The meetings in which these statements are formulated are often filled with endless debates about the meanings of terms such as "vision," "mission," and "purpose," and whether all or just some of these should be incorporated into the company's statement. Who cares? Any one of a variety of combinations of these categories can be used to good effect. Our preference is to limit the statement to two categories: purpose (what the organization tries to accomplish) and principles (the values that guide it). Probably the most time-consuming and unnecessary semantic debate concerns the difference between "vision" and "mission." Despite having sat through innumerable lectures and discussions on the topic, we still don't understand the difference.

Let's look in greater detail at each of the real reasons that "mission" (or whatever) statements often have little effect.

1. Lack of Senior Management Commitment

For "doing good" to be more than just subject matter for a retreat, two things are required on the part of top management: one a matter of business judgment and the other emotional:

- **Business judgment.** In line with what we said earlier about the difference between a short- and a long-term orientation, it should not be surprising that the businesses that do best translating purposes and principles into practice are those where senior management has a long-term perspective. Those are the companies which, in the normal course of doing their business, will take into account the impact of their decisions on all of their key constituencies. They don't easily scrap what they decided on in a retreat because of short-term pressures and temptations.

  But translating purposes and principles into day-to-day practice is often not simple. Companies, after all, do experience immediate business pressures such as periodic needs to cut costs. Let's say that in a company with cost pressures, analysis shows customer service to be one of the areas ripe for cost-cutting. The point of principles—serious principles—in a company is not to so constrain the organization that it suffers serious business damage. Other than prohibiting clearly unlawful behavior, the principles are rarely absolute. What a principle relating, say, to customer service does is to force attention in a business sense to the long-term impact of cutting corners on service. The question, "Can we afford to maintain this high a level of customer service?" might well become, "Can we afford *not* to?" This doesn't necessarily make the decision easier, but it more evenly balances the sides of the argument. Most frequently and beneficially, what it does is cause management to seek ways to meet *both* objectives to the extent possible: reducing costs in a way that minimizes damage to customer satisfaction with service. In fact, the Total Quality Management movement (to be discussed shortly) offers many examples where the reduction of costs (such as by eliminating bureaucratic obstacles in responding to customers) leads to *higher* customer satisfaction.

- **The emotional level.** Business judgment needs to be reinforced by the *personal* values and passions of senior executives. Purposes and principles are much more likely to be translated into practice if the company has a top management (especially the CEO) not only with a long-term business view but also as passionate about products and people as they are about profits. These kinds of executives simply would not want to be associated with an enterprise that produced shoddy products or treated its employees and other constituencies badly, whatever the business benefits. This, then, comes down to the personal makeup of executives: what makes them, at their gut level, feel good or bad about the way their organization functions. They can be highly moral people and do all kinds of good outside of work, but unless an important source of personal pride for them is their *companies'* "doing good" (in addition to well), purposes and principles will not likely have a sustained significant impact on the functioning of the business.

Doing good, therefore, should be treated as more than a collection of discrete practices or occasional gestures in parallel to the mainstream business and serving from time to time as the "conscience" of the business and helpful for public relations. Those kinds of efforts will often be found to be run by relatively uninfluential staff departments who are asked to report on their activities from time to time to senior management. Doing good should instead be viewed as a comprehensive set of policies, practices, and programs driven by senior leadership and integrated by their connection with serious business objectives and by their reflection of strongly held values aimed at building long-term, positive relationships with all major stakeholders.

2. Poor Statement Phrasing

Given a genuine commitment to "doing good," how should the statement of purpose and principles be phrased? We suggest the following guidelines for the statement of purpose:

- It should be relevant to the specific business, not so general and filled with platitudes as to be virtually meaningless.

- It should be simple and clear, getting to the heart of what the company is without a lot of detail and qualifications. Too many words can obscure the central message.

- It should be inspirational in that it appeals to values that employees hold above and beyond profits (especially the usefulness and quality of the product or service), encourages excellence in the achievement of those values, and promotes a feeling of being special—an "elite" organization that is noticeably different from others.

There are many particularly good statements of purpose. Here is one that we especially admire; it's taken from a three-person benefits department in a medium-size company:

> Benefits are about people. It's not whether you have the forms filled in or whether the checks are written. It's whether people are cared for when they're sick, helped when they're in trouble.

This statement is particularly impressive to us. After all, it was composed in a tiny organization devoid of the high-powered executive attention and professional "wordsmithing" such statements normally receive. And it was composed for the kind of department often notorious for its fixation on bureaucratic rules and procedures. It is a statement truly from the heart, with the focus in the right place: on caring for people, rather than having the right forms.

For the statement of principles (the values that guide the organization in the achievement of its purpose), the same three general guidelines described for the statement of purpose should be followed to the extent possible. A statement of principles will, of necessity, be more detailed than one of purpose, but brevity should still be a goal. Although certain ethical principles are indeed applicable to any organization (is honesty ever irrelevant?), the wording should reflect, as well as it can, the issues and conditions of the particular business for which the principles are being written.

In many companies, the statement of principles goes well beyond what might normally be considered "ethics" and depicts the major features of the company's desired internal culture. Thus, besides integrity, companies might stress the need for an internal environment that is open, empowering, collaborative, diverse, creative, and so on. These are perfectly appropriate and useful in the context of principles. In fact, these elements of internal culture often derive, in part, from ethical considerations—empowerment as an outgrowth of treating people with respect, and openness from the need for honesty and transparency.

Here are a few more particularly good examples of statements of principles from easily recognized companies:

Lands' End

1. *We do everything we can to make our products better. We improve material, and add back features and construction details that others have taken out over the years. We never reduce the quality of a product to make it cheaper.*

2. *We price our products fairly and honestly. We do not, have not, and will not participate in the common retailing practice of inflating mark-ups to set up a future phony "sale."*

3. *We accept any return for any reason, at any time. Our products are guaranteed. No fine print. No arguments. We mean exactly what we say: GUARANTEED. PERIOD.*

4. *We ship faster than anyone we know of. We ship items in stock the day after we receive the order. At the height of the last Christmas season, the longest time an order was in the house*

was 36 hours, excepting monograms which took another 12 hours.

5. *We believe that what is best for our customer is best for all of us. Everyone here understands that concept. Our sales and service people are trained to know our products, and to be friendly and helpful. They are urged to take all the time necessary to take care of you. We even pay for your call, for whatever reason you call.*

6. *We are able to sell at lower prices because we have eliminated middlemen; because we don't buy branded merchandise with high protected mark-ups; and because we have placed our contracts with manufacturers who have proven that they are cost conscious and efficient.*

7. *We are able to sell at lower prices because we operate efficiently. Our people are hard-working, intelligent, and share in the success of the company.*

8. *We are able to sell at lower prices because we support no fancy emporiums with their high overhead. Our main location is in the middle of a 40-acre cornfield in rural Wisconsin.*

Merck

1. *Our business is preserving and improving human life. All of our actions must be measured by our success in achieving this goal. We value above all our ability to serve everyone who can benefit from the appropriate use of our products and services, thereby providing lasting consumer satisfaction.*

2. *We are committed to the highest standards of ethics and integrity. We are responsible to our customers, to Merck employees and their families, to the environments we inhabit, and to the societies we serve worldwide. In discharging our responsibilities, we do not take professional or ethical shortcuts. Our interactions with all segments of society must reflect the high standards we profess.*

3. *We are dedicated to the highest level of scientific excellence and commit our research to improving human and animal health and the quality of life. We strive to identify the most critical needs of consumers and customers; we devote our resources to meeting those needs.*

4. *We expect profits, but only from work that satisfies customer needs and benefits humanity. Our ability to meet our responsibilities depends on maintaining a financial position that invites investment in leading-edge research and that makes possible effective delivery of research results.*

5. *We recognize that the ability to excel—to most competitively meet society's and customers' needs—depends on the integrity, knowledge, imagination, skill, diversity and teamwork of employees, and we value these qualities most highly. To this end, we strive to create an environment of mutual respect, encouragement, and teamwork—an environment that rewards commitment and performance and is responsive to the needs of employees and their families.*

Those statements were chosen to show that there are no rigid formulas for such things. They are all effective, yet differ from each other in significant respects. Don't be confused by the fact that these statements of principles often appear to overlap in content with statements of purpose. Merck's first principle, "Our business is preserving and improving human life..." certainly sounds like a purpose. Indeed, sometimes purpose and value statements are not distinguished from each other at all. Consider Johnson & Johnson's famous Credo, to which we referred earlier:

> *We believe our first responsibility is to the doctors, nurses and patients, to mothers and fathers and all others who use our products and services. In meeting their needs, everything we do must be of high quality. We must constantly strive to reduce our costs in order to maintain reasonable prices. Customers' orders must be serviced promptly and accurately. Our suppliers and distributors must have an opportunity to make a fair profit.*

We are responsible to our employees, the men and women who work with us throughout the world. Everyone must be considered as an individual. We must respect their dignity and recognize their merit. They must have a sense of security in their jobs. Compensation must be fair and adequate, and working conditions clean, orderly, and safe. We must be mindful of ways to help our employees fulfill their family responsibilities. Employees must feel free to make suggestions and complaints. There must be equal opportunity for employment, development, and advancement for those qualified. We must provide competent management, and their actions must be just and ethical.

We are responsible to the communities in which we live and work and to the world community as well. We must be good citizens— support good works and charities and bear our fair share of taxes. We must encourage civic improvements and better health and education. We must maintain in good order the property we are privileged to use, protecting the environment and natural resources.

Our final responsibility is to our stockholders. Business must make a sound profit. We must experiment with new ideas. Research must be carried on, innovative programs developed and mistakes paid for. New equipment must be purchased, new facilities provided and new products launched. Reserves must be created to provide for adverse times. When we operate according to these principles, the stockholders should realize a fair return.

Before recent years, the Credo's fame was well deserved: it was clear, relevant to the business, and inspirational. Since it was formulated in the mid 1940s by Robert Wood Johnson, then the CEO, it had an enormous influence on the way Johnson & Johnson operated and its employees conducted themselves. Most famously, perhaps, was how the company responded during the 1982 Tylenol crisis, when seven people died after taking Tylenol that had been laced with cyanide. The company quickly stopped production and removed all Tylenol from the market. Jim Burke, chairman at the time, remarked, "After the crisis was over, we realized that no meeting had been called to make the first critical decision. Every one of us knew what we had to do. We had the Credo to guide us."[17]

Because successful statements of principles vary greatly, let's not obsess over form. We have our own preferences, such as the distinction between purpose and principles, but other approaches serve just as well.

3. Lack of a Methodology

We come now to the third reason purpose and principles statements are often seen as executive bunkum: a lack of a methodology for translating the statement into a day-to-day reality that endures over time. Although much time and effort should be devoted to the formulation of the statement, this is but a small fraction of what will be required for it to be effectively implemented.

There is no great mystery about what is required to make noble-sounding words into a day-to-day reality:

- Strong and visible top-management support, especially the CEO's support.
- Clear, enforceable, and enforced policy.
- Internal processes that enable the policy to be carried out.
- Full communication to the workforce of the policy and its rationale.
- Training of the workforce in implementing the policy on their own jobs.
- Tools that the workforce needs to carry out the policy (including authority).
- The workforce's participation in developing the methods used to carry out the policy.
- Measurement of the results.
- A reward system geared to the results.

Two of these requirements—top-management support and workforce participation—relate to each other and deserve a bit of elaboration. Much has been written about how important it is to get the workforce involved in defining organization purpose and principles. Our view is that, in certain key respects, this cannot be a participative process because its essence—especially of an organization's purpose—*must come from the top.* The exact wording and elaboration of the statements, and certainly their methods of implementation, will profit greatly from the involvement of others, but it is more than a little ludicrous for a CEO to expect others to give her a purpose for the organization. As we argued earlier, the CEO must be the type of person who, at a gut level, takes pride in achievements in addition to those reflected in financial statements and believes that such achievements are important for long-term business performance. The CEO then *requires* that the organization behave in conformity with these values; there can be no room for debate about this. The only question is *how* they will be achieved, including how their meaning can best be captured in words; for this, broad workforce participation is extremely beneficial.

We can provide many examples of effective implementation of purposes and principles. Throughout this book, we have dealt with such implementation in the employee realm. As the primary example in this chapter, let's use the implementation of statements of purposes and principles that relate to the customer constituency.

The great majority of purposes and principles statements by America's corporations contain commitments to excellence in the products and services provided to customers. In many companies, however, surveys of both customers and employees reveal large gaps between what companies say they aim to do, what employees say they actually do, and what customers say they experience.

The companies where those gaps are smallest—in fact, where customers often say that they receive *more* than they expect—are often those in which total quality management (TQM), or some version of it, such as "Six Sigma," has been effectively introduced. TQM originated in Japanese industry in the 1950s and has become steadily more popular in the West since the early 1980s. Although TQM was originally seen by many as another management fad, it has, in our view, been an extraordinarily valuable initiative for those companies that have taken it seriously. It is responsible in significant measure, for example, for the transformation of much automobile manufacturing in this country and that industry's ability to compete on quality with Japanese imports.

TQM is an outstanding example—when taken seriously—of how purpose can be successfully translated into action.

There are many definitions of TQM, but we define it as a culture and methods that aim to provide customers with products and services that fully satisfy their needs. TQM requires continual improvement in the quality of all aspects of the company's processes so that things are done right the first time and defects and waste are eradicated from operations. Included is a focus not just on "things"—processes, products—but on people as well, such as the need to obtain workforce involvement in generating ideas for quality improvement and getting people to work collaboratively within and across departmental boundaries.

TQM is not a one-time "event," as are so many management fads. It encompasses a detailed methodology that takes considerable effort, time, and culture change to carry out well. The systematic use of TQM has been greatly enhanced in the United States—and its definition sharpened—by the federal government's Malcolm Baldrige National Quality Award. Created in 1987 by congressional mandate, this program seeks "to create an awareness of quality as an important part of organizational performance and excellence, encourage the sharing of performance excellence strategies, and recognize those organizations with particularly effective practices."[18] The Baldrige awards are given to organizations on the basis of evaluations by trained examiners on a series of criteria that include both external and internal quality performance. The criteria provide a well-reasoned, well-accepted roadmap for companies that seek to significantly improve their performance, whether or not they apply for the award.

Many organizations have "quality" programs of one kind or another, but relatively few take them seriously enough to be strong candidates for the award, even if they were to apply. Sadly, professionals in the field estimate that only about 20 to 30 percent of TQM efforts have been implemented in a truly effective way in American companies—that is, with significant and lasting quality results. For the majority, it is a fad or an isolated and staged event in one part of the business for public relations purposes.

What does taking a program such as TQM "seriously" mean? Earlier, we listed the actions that we see as necessary for turning noble objectives into reality (such as strong and visible top management support). Consider a specific case: Federal Express was a Baldrige award winner in 1990 and, Baldrige or not, is a company with an outstanding and widespread reputation for the excellence of its service to customers.

FedEx's quality policy calls for "100 percent customer satisfaction 100 percent of the time." That charge comes directly from the company's founder and CEO, Frederick Smith. How has this clear-as-a-bell policy been followed over the years?[19] Here are some of the ways:

- Two customer guarantees: if FedEx is more than 60 seconds late in delivering a package, the customer does not have to pay for it. If the customer asks to trace a package and FedEx can't do it within 30 minutes, the customer doesn't have to pay for it. Many millions of dollars have been invested in the company's tracking system. ("Customers want the security that comes from knowing we can track their packages every step of the way.")

- An executive quality board oversees the quality process; quality administrators and employee facilitators are assigned throughout the corporation.

- A Service Quality Index (SQI) measures service failures in 12 categories, such as delivery late on the right day, delivery on the wrong days, missed pickup, damaged package, and calls to the company abandoned by customers. (The focus is on failures because the company says that 99 percent is not good enough; 99 percent success in FedEx translates into millions of failures.)

- Twelve root-cause teams, one for each SQI category, seek reasons for failures in each category and act to ensure they do not recur. Each team is led by a senior executive.

- Cross-functional teams in every geographic market that meet regularly to figure out what needs to happen in their market to get those airplanes and trucks out on time every night.

- Quality-action teams work on specific projects.

- Regular surveys of customers (2,400 calls per quarter) to determine their needs, satisfactions, and dissatisfactions. Regular surveys of employees with disciplined follow-up on the issues uncovered. ("To achieve the greatest level of customer satisfaction, you need to keep your employees happy. Customers can sense if employees do not have tremendous pride in their company....")

- Empowerment of employees to do whatever it takes to satisfy customers. (Frederick Smith says of FedEx employees, "Daily, they go above and beyond to serve our customers. They are the ones who trek through all kinds of weather; deliver every package, each one critical; they persist in solving every customer's problem; they ferret out the root cause of every problem to prevent it from ever happening again. Their talent, ingenuity, and commitment drive our quality standards closer to our goal of 100 percent customer satisfaction.")

- Intensive six-week training in customer interaction for couriers and service representatives.

- Employee satisfaction, service quality, and profitability goals.
- Bonuses tied to the achievement of the goals.

FedEx's devotion to quality is a superb example of what we mean by turning an organization's purpose into a day-to-day reality.

Does serious attention to quality pay off in financial performance? In 2002, a major study analyzed 5-year returns in 600 publically traded TQM award winners. The researchers found that $100 invested in each firm one year prior to winning the award yielded 34 percentage points higher returns five years later than the same $100 invested in the S&P 500 (114 percent versus 80 percent returns, respectively). The TQM firms outperformed the S&P 500 four out of the five years. (In one year they were about even.) Performance on other financial metrics yielded similar results.[20]

Customers are an extremely important constituency of any organization, but they are just one. Detailed examples of effective implementation like FedEx's could be given for other stakeholder groups, such as suppliers, investors, and the community. In all these cases, the basic points are the same:

- Purposes and principles must emanate from strongly held convictions of senior management.
- Statements of purposes and principles will be exercises in futility unless they are accompanied by a serious implementation plan.

This chapter focused on one of the most important components of leadership—namely, providing an organization with purpose and principles of which employees can be proud and to which they will willingly and enthusiastically devote their skill and energy. The reader has learned in earlier chapters that we in no way minimize the importance to workers of equitable treatment in matters such as pay, benefits, and job security. In fact, having noble purposes—for customers, community, and so on—rings hollow if employees are treated shabbily. But conceiving of employees as working "just for a living" and the corporation as strictly an economic entity misses a vital element of human nature: the need to do something that matters and to do it well. Ironically, seeing employees strictly in economic terms is a long-term economic disadvantage for a company because it loses out on the extra performance that people who are enthusiastic about a purpose will give.

8

Job Enablement

"Most of what we call management consists of making it difficult for people to get their work done."

—Peter F. Drucker

We discussed in the previous chapter the purpose of work (doing something that matters), and in this chapter we focus on the business practices that enable workers to actually perform on their jobs and do so at a high level.

At the end of a day's work, workers want to feel that something was accomplished by virtue of their efforts. A factory employee becomes disheartened when he produces little during the day because of time spent struggling with faulty equipment and waiting for the maintenance person to arrive. An executive feels equally frustrated when she spends her day in endless departmental meetings with little discernible accomplishment. Those wasted days are depressing for most workers at all levels.

A large body of research supports these common-sense observations, but, as always, the qualitative data are compelling. There are many complaints about obstacles expressed in the write-in comments and, in our examples that follow, we highlight the various types of obstacles to make it easier to get through them. Here is a sampling of comments about what employees like least about their jobs and what can be done to improve effectiveness:

Our operations are <u>needlessly complex</u> which result in too many customer service and client-satisfaction issues.

I hate the <u>bureaucracy—we need approvals for just about everything and the number of sign-offs is ridiculous</u>.

I am constantly challenged by teams and individuals that <u>resist change</u> and have <u>silo mentalities</u>. <u>Cost control and management for technology spending is not well controlled or understood</u>. This restricts my business' ability to effectively understand costs and reengineer.

We must put an end to <u>obsolete practices</u>, with people who are afraid of change and who are an obstacle for the company. There's also the <u>lack of communication</u> about processes and policies within the company, which results in redone work and failure.

We don't talk much to each other across department lines and so there's a lot of duplication of effort and continual <u>"reinventing the wheel."</u> It is extraordinarily wasteful.

We spend too much time <u>chasing numbers</u>. We are not looking at the product; we just make sure it moves fast. It can be dirty and ugly but let's make sure it moves.

A lot of time is spent satisfying some <u>ambiguous policies</u> that everybody has a different interpretation of.

Simplification of the work processes so employees can get their work done without <u>unnecessary delays</u>.

We need to <u>slow down with all the major changes</u> we make, as an agency. We have been inundated in the field and have to endure so many changes both systematically and programmatically, it has been entirely too much to absorb. The staff believes quality must come first but they also cannot afford to <u>spend hours searching for an answer to a question</u>.

The largest obstacle here is <u>too much work</u>...which hurts quality and creates a tremendous amount of stress due to...lack of balance between work and family life.

One obstacle is the <u>lack of cooperation</u> with other departments in the organization. Everyone has an emphasis on satisfying "their" *customer, which means that if you need their cooperation in serving your customer, your customer is not their customer so you are a low priority.*

The <u>red tape</u> is an obstacle I face in getting my job done.

One obstacle is <u>company politics</u>.

There has been <u>little or no communication from our management staff as to the direction, roles, and responsibilities</u> that we will have.

We have been <u>fire-fighting</u> instead of...planning.

The <u>lack of training</u> to extend my areas of expertise is one obstacle I face in getting my job done.

There are constant <u>organizational restructuring</u> changes... I'm not even sure who my supervisor is at this point.

<u>Preventative maintenance</u> is a myth here.

Maybe I would feel better about <u>all the reports</u> we're required to fill out if I knew what they were for! They fall into a big pit never to be seen again.

However, when things go well, when workers genuinely feel accomplishment, their spirits are buoyed. Again, we highlight the key sense of the employees' comments:

The huge advantage this company enjoys in its industry is that employees like me are <u>empowered to make decisions</u> and there is very little to no red tape, unnecessary delays, no wasted time, no wasteful projects, and no unnecessary reporting. Management, keep up the good work.

The group I work with is led by a manager with a unique leadership style. <u>She allows individuals...to fully utilize their creativity, business knowledge, and talents</u>, in a <u>teamwork</u> environment to meet the challenges of our business. With each project, there is always a great sense of pride and accomplishment. My leader is <u>not the one in the spotlight</u>, she is the one leading the applause. Thanks to her for making the company the best place to work.

My immediate leaders both allow me to perform my daily duties at a high level. They have <u>confidence and trust in the decisions I make</u>. This trust and <u>their being available</u> allow for self-confidence and performance levels to be above expectations. I want to thank them for listening to and resolving our concerns when presented.

I have the <u>freedom to go above</u> and beyond for the customer and to put them first. That gives me a feeling of accomplishment.

I enjoy the <u>flexibility</u> offered by working from a <u>virtual office</u>. I like to create my own schedule in order to accomplish what I need to on a day-to-day basis.

The opportunity to <u>act independently</u> of my team when accomplishing the necessary work of my job, while at the same time knowing whenever I need my team's assistance, <u>they're always right there</u>.

I feel one of the main strengths of this company is its <u>willingness to work with their customers</u> on a one-to-one basis. This makes the customer feel more confident in the place they chose to do business and makes my job that much enjoyable.

You <u>know what you have to do</u> and (you have) the <u>tools to accomplish the task</u> with <u>teamwork</u> encouraged. We have the most <u>up-to-date equipment</u>.

The <u>empowerment</u> levels have risen in my department, and for that, I say thank you. Nothing is more encouraging than being able to say to a customer, "I can do that right now for you," or, "I can get it done by tomorrow no problem," and mean it.

We have the <u>tools and ability to really produce dynamic, cutting-edge solutions</u>. I love working for an organization...that accomplishes many great results and has great care and compassion for people.

The survey data discussed in Chapter 1, "What Workers Want—The Big Picture," which portrayed, among other attitudes, how workers feel about their ability to get their jobs done, showed variability in two ways. First, organizations differ greatly from each other. Although, on average, 67 percent of employees rate their organizations favorably on the overall effectiveness with which they are managed, the range is enormous: 32 to 93 percent. Obviously, some organizations are seen as highly effective and in others, from the employees' perspectives, it is a wonder that anything ever gets done! Workers dislike the latter intensely because they have little or no sense of accomplishment—indeed, working there embarrasses them—and because an ineffectively managed organization does not bode well for long-term job security or advancement prospects. A high degree of perceived effectiveness is a condition for worker enthusiasm.

In addition to the differences between organizations, there is great variability in the kinds of obstacles employees report encountering while doing their jobs. Over the many companies we have surveyed, one of the highest average percent favorable scores (86 percent) is obtained in response to the question, "I have a clear idea of the results expected of me on my job." One of the least favorable results (39 percent) is in response to a question about bureaucracy interfering with their jobs.

Therefore, although it is a favorite topic in the management literature, the pervasive problem for employees is not lack of information about what to do. They know what they have to do. Instead, it is getting the tasks done in the face of the barriers organizations erect, however unintentionally, to their accomplishment. The latter illustrates the law of unintended consequences: bureaucratic procedures introduced with the best of intentions can make it excruciatingly difficult for *any* task to be accomplished or decision to be made.

Where in organizations do we find the most pervasive obstacles? We established previously that employees tend to be most positive toward the two opposite poles of an organization: the immediate work environment and the total organization. Examples of the former are the clarity of the results expected from the worker, the immediate supervisor's technical competence, the skills and abilities of co-workers, and the job itself. The total organization level includes views of the company's profitability and the quality of the products or services the organization produces for its customers.

Although some organizations are viewed as dysfunctional from top to bottom, the tendency is for the major problems, as seen by employees, to be in the "middle": below senior management and the organization as a whole and above the immediate manager and immediate work environment. It is as if the products produced and the profits achieved come *despite* what goes on at those levels. Consider this comment:

> It is amazing that the (product) we deliver to the (government agency) is of such high quality considering the lousy tools we have, the politics in management, people finger-pointing and screaming at each other, and the unbelievable red tape and bureaucracy. The quality costs a bundle, of course, because of all the rework and waste, but that's what taxpayers are for.

The "middle" is where coordination and control among the parts of the organization take place. When employees complain about "bureaucracy," they don't usually see the villain as their own boss or the CEO, but rather middle management and staff departments, such as finance. When they complain about a lack of cooperation, they most often see the problem stemming from departments other than their own and not being dealt with—in fact, sometimes magnified—by the middle managers to whom their and those other departments report. A complaint about disorganization is usually directed at inefficient work processes that cut across departments, such as the way staff groups and the line don't communicate or coordinate well with each other.

This chapter is about the ability of workers to get their jobs done and, we focus largely on middle-organization issues since because that is where the most severe impediments to performance are seen to originate. It is where, on matters of performance, organizations with enthusiastic workforces most differ from their counterparts.

A further word about immediate supervision: immediate supervisors receive quite high ratings in just about all organizations. Our surveys show that 82 percent of employees are positive toward their managers' technical skills (knowing the job). Although the rating of their human-relations skills is lower (73 percent), it is still much higher than the ratings we obtain on issues such as bureaucracy. In almost all companies, only about 8 percent of managers receive truly unfavorable ratings. That 8 percent can do much harm and require attention, but, by and large, we find first-line management to be bulwarks of organizations, even of those organizations that otherwise might be dysfunctional almost to the point of collapse.

It is telling that the attitudes of first-line managers toward levels above them and toward staff groups are often identical to those of their subordinates. Managers see themselves as "buffers" who protect their workers—and their performance—from the damage that those levels and groups can inflict. A frequent theme in senior management discussions and in the management literature is the presumed weakness of first-level management: they are blamed for various employee morale and performance problems. It makes sense intuitively to target those managers because they are in direct contact with the workers and might be relatively inexperienced in management. Yes, they are a big influence, but usually for the better! Therefore, intuition fails here and improvement steps, to the extent that they target the first level, are often misplaced.

Our focus on action in the middle does not mean that what happens at the top is unimportant. The CEO is often responsible for impediments such as excessive bureaucracy because she wants the organization to operate that way and she chooses the middle-level line and staff people who will do what she wants, but her role in those respects is often invisible to the rank and file. She therefore receives unjustifiably high ratings. However, action to resolve the problems, although directed at the middle, often must begin with her.

Put another way, the key impediments to job accomplishment are almost invariably a function of the culture set by senior management—especially the CEO—that is expressed operationally in the way the organization is structured and the way people are expected to interact within that structure. Our framework for discussing these matters will be "bureaucracy" because that encompasses much of what our survey data show as problems.

Ah, Bureaucracy! The Evil That Just Won't Go Away

"I find it mind-boggling. We do not shoot paper at the enemy."

—Admiral Joseph Metcalf, U.S. Navy (Ret.), on the 20 tons of paper and file cabinets aboard the Navy's newest frigates

"The only thing that saves us from the bureaucracy is its inefficiency."

—Eugene McCarthy, former senator from Minnesota

"Bureaucracy defends the status quo long past the time when the quo has lost its status."

—Laurence J. Peter, former educator and author, and the father of the famous "Peter Principle"

What do employees mean by the bureaucracy they say they deplore? The issue is frequently mentioned in write-in comments, as shown earlier, as well as in focus groups. A number of insights emerge.

One area that workers often cite as a bureaucratic obstacle is the decision-approval process, which is seen as needlessly delaying decisions (such as decisions about resources employees need to do their jobs), detracting from the quality of decisions (often because the ultimate decision-makers are far from the action), and reflecting a distrust of employees and their ability to make the right decisions.

Another bureaucratic obstacle is the perceived obsession with rules and the enforcement of those rules. Employees see this as diverting the organization from its objectives and its ability to respond to changing conditions. It is the focus on means rather than ends that rankles workers here.

Let's not forget good old-fashioned "paperwork" (real or its digital cousin) and the endless reports produced that employees see as utterly useless at worst ("All of this data is already available to Corporate, why can't they access it themselves?") or shrouded in mystery at best ("I know they want these reports, but I have never once been asked about them; what use is made of them?").

Another facet of bureaucracy frequently mentioned is functional specialization, which is seen as narrowing the attention of units to only their own goals and creating boundaries between units that inhibit cooperation between them.

Of course, most people would prefer to operate with considerable autonomy, ignore the paperwork, and be able to rely on the cooperation of other units to effectively perform their jobs. That's not news. It seems that the term bureaucracy is rarely used in anything but a pejorative sense. Much of the disdain for bureaucracy is well earned, but before we elaborate on its dysfunctions and recommend what an organization can do about them, we must first recognize why bureaucracy is, in significant ways, simply indispensable to organizations.

Can an organization survive for long without a clearly defined authority structure? Can it survive well without executives who are unafraid to use their authority? Of course not. People who argue for the elimination of bureaucracy in organizations—much of which concerns eliminating or drastically reducing power differentials—are arguing for chaos and organizational ineptitude.[1]

Only anarchists and theorists with no practical experience advocate chaos. *Workers certainly do not.* Therefore, although the majority of comments about bureaucracy concerns its downsides, we also receive complaints in a number of organization surveys about *under-*control (that is, too little bureaucracy)! Take these comments, for example:

> *I feel that the structure is disorganized, and I don't feel as if I can get a clear answer.*

We are completely disorganized and have no real planning when we roll out new products and services!

This "matrix" structure here is very confusing—everyone seems to think they can give me orders and they conflict with each other. How do I satisfy many masters? Who am I accountable to?

This place seems completely disorganized. Every change seems to be a knee-jerk reaction, and it seems that leadership usually has to go back and change things after they see that it hasn't worked. There's no stability. This place needs an overhaul. There are too many old Band-Aids over old wounds.

Who's in charge here? Nobody seems to want to take responsibility for anything. It's a spineless management, starting at the top. No leadership, all CYA.

There's little documentation when programs change—it drives me crazy. We need at least a little paperwork! When people leave, the most elementary knowledge of what's been done leaves with them.

We are not arguing for the bureaucratic overkill that we have all come to know and hate. Chaos, however, is not the only alternative to that type of bureaucracy. In their studies of group functioning, social psychologists make a useful distinction between three types of leadership: autocratic, laissez-faire, and democratic. We call the last of these "participative" because democracy usually means that the leaders are chosen by the led and that concept has little applicability to the employee-management relationship. The key criterion is not how leaders are chosen but how they lead.

An autocratic style of management is characterized by domination of employees, inflexibility, and a belief that discipline and punishment are the most effective means to get most workers to work. This characterization can be applied to individual managers, such as compulsive, micromanaging autocrats, but also to the formal structures and processes that constitute excessive bureaucracy: approvals required for even the smallest decisions, a multitude of rules rigidly enforced, and work divided into extremely narrow tasks. Both at the individual manager and the structural levels, a fundamental assumption underlying autocratic management is a distrust of workers and their ability or willingness to do their jobs without a high degree of top-down control.

Autocratic management is not necessarily a malevolent management in the sense of unconcern for the economic well-being of workers. Some paternalistic organizations treat their workers well—in pay, benefits, and job security—but because "father knows best," their managements are normally highly autocratic. These organizations are benevolent dictatorships.

At the opposite extreme from autocratic management is a laissez-faire style, which means "to let (people) do (as they choose)." Laissez-faire managers are divorced from their employees, uninvolved in what they do (either in a directing or a helping sense). These proverbial "weak" managers can, in their way, frustrate employees as much as autocratic managers.

On a structural level, laissez-faire management is the "anti-bureaucracy," with few or no approval processes, rules, paperwork, or specialization by task. We know of no organization that is laissez-faire in its pure form, but those companies that even approximate this management style cannot endure: they soon disappear or are overhauled in order to survive. However, individual laissez-faire managers can survive for a while, especially in prosperous times when no one pays much attention to a department's mediocre performance. When times get tight, these managers can no longer be tolerated and are removed.

Unfortunately, new executives brought in "to get this place under control" usually go to the opposite extreme: the pendulum swings, and they turn what was chaos into what employees feel is a virtual prison. The assumption is not just that things need to be tightened—of course, they do—but that workers somehow enjoy chaos and must therefore be managed with an iron fist. So, the frustration of employees formerly working under laissez-faire management turns into resentment because of the severity of the controls that have been imposed and the view that employees are untrustworthy. The resistance of employees to the new management style is usually characterized as "resistance to change," which is highly misleading: it is resistance to needlessly autocratic management and the assumptions about employees that underlie autocracy.

The alternative to laissez-faire and autocratic management is participative management, whose key characteristic is mutual influence. Figure 8-1 shows the three management types depicted in terms of influence patterns.

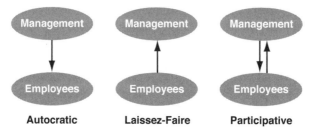

Figure 8-1 Three styles of management.

Autocratic management is top-down, laissez-faire is bottom-up ("the inmates running the asylum," as the joke goes), and in participative management, influence goes both up and down. The point of two-way influence is *not* that there is no boss or that everyone is boss. That is a laissez-faire environment, and it is not what we mean or what workers want.

In Figure 8-1, the arrow pointing down in participative management symbolizes the importance of certain traditional, top-down management principles. These principles are important to both the organization and its workers because the effectiveness of organizations and worker satisfaction require that, to the extent possible, there be clear and decisive direction from leadership; clarity of responsibilities, authorities, and accountabilities; authority that is commensurate with responsibility and accountability; unified command; and a clear approval process and rules governing acceptable employee behavior.

These principles are familiar and uncomplicated, and they encompass key aspects of what is normally termed bureaucracy. Although they are familiar, the principles deserve to be repeated because they are fundamental and, as we have said, they are seen by some influential modern theorists as largely out-of-date and dysfunctional, especially in the "new economy" or "post-industrial age" and with so-called Generation X, Y, and Millennial workers. These theorists talk about recasting traditional hierarchical organizations into all kinds of new forms, such as "spider's webs," "starbursts," "wagon wheels," and "shamrocks."

Advocating seriously for the destruction of any semblance of hierarchy shows a lack of experience with the debilitating consequences of working in a directionless organization, getting conflicting instructions from different bosses, being unable to decipher who is responsible for what, or not having the authority to carry out one's responsibilities. *These severe obstacles hinder the performance of workers, whether they work in the "new" or "old" economy and whatever their "generation."*

However, the fundamental top-down principles can be taken to the opposite extreme, and that is the nub of the problem created by the bureaucracy and the bureaucrats that we abhor. A leader being decisive can sometimes come to mean rejecting all the subordinates' input into decisions. Providing direction to an organization can turn into micro-management: instructing trained and experienced subordinates on how to do their jobs in every detail and requiring them to seek approvals for even the most minor deviations and decisions. Making responsibilities and accountabilities clear can result in rigid boundaries between departments, which makes collaboration impossible (the familiar problem of organization "silos").

These examples depict the slippage of common-sense organization principles into a rigid machine model of bureaucracy. A machine cannot function without "a place for everything and everything in its place" and without external initiation and control. That's the nature of an inanimate machine. But people are not machines or parts of machines: they can exercise judgment, have more than one job responsibility, and initiate activity. And they have emotions, such as feeling disrespected and angry when they're treated as if they cannot exercise judgment, have more than one job responsibility, or initiate activity.

Workers want, and organizations require, just as much order as is appropriate to the need, and no more. Workers in a machine shop do not pretend that they can set corporate or divisional strategies, so they want leaders who know how to do that and do it well. But they can run the machines, and they are a rich source of ideas for how to make those machines run better and how to improve many other aspects of their work environments and work processes to increase performance. Managers who obsess about how their employees do their work and about minutiae such as the exact amount of time they take for rest breaks are not only doing what they shouldn't be doing (meddling), but *not* doing what they should be doing: the planning, expediting, counseling, and coordinating that truly help employees get their jobs done.

The consequences of autocratic management—by an individual autocratic supervisor or a system that is excessively bureaucratic—are twofold in terms of worker performance. On the one hand, spurts in performance can be obtained by such top-down methods, but unless the pressure is continually applied and employees are supervised closely (and the supervisors are supervised closely), performance will soon dissipate. In other words, achieving an adequate level of performance becomes completely dependent on outside forces applied to resistant employees instead of on their internal motivation to do well and be proud of their work.

A second major consequence of autocratic management is a loss of brainpower: the ideas and ingenuity that the people who know the jobs well (the workers) can apply to improving performance. Autocratic management—whether by an individual manager or by an oppressive bureaucracy—makes the very costly mistake of assuming that wisdom is related directly and almost entirely to hierarchical level.

A Management Style That Works

Although autocratic and laissez-faire managing are different styles, both demotivate the great majority of workers, and both place severe obstacles in the way of their getting their jobs done. The research in this area strongly supports a third approach, which is participative. This approach is not simply a middle ground between the other two styles of management (a little less of this, a little more of that); it is really a fundamentally different method.

When moving away from autocratic management, some people adopt a laissez-faire approach, but this is not really leadership—it is an abandonment of leadership. Participative management is an *active* style that stimulates involvement, not a passive style that forfeits leadership. In an effective participative organization, no one is in doubt as to who is in charge. But that person expects employees to think, to exercise judgment, and not just do. Judgment is expected from workers in performing their specific tasks and in identifying and implementing ways to improve the organization's performance as a whole. That is the environment in which impediments to performance can be removed and in which employee enthusiasm can flourish.

Our advocacy of participative management is based on more than academic theory or a democratic ethic. A great deal of research evidence demonstrates the superiority of participative management for performance. The evidence comes both from laboratory experiments and from field studies in real organizations. It has been collected in systematic ways since the 1940s. Also, contrary to what is commonly assumed, its value is not limited to America or other societies with a long history of democratic traditions.[2]

Over the past two or three decades, participative management has found widespread acceptance in industry, so our arguments, which were perhaps once considered radical, might now strike some readers as unsurprising, almost truisms. Unfortunately, much of the acceptance of this management style has been superficial: we find in our studies significant gaps between what organizations and managers say—and even believe—and what they actually do, as their employees report it. Yet, some managers are consistent: they not only practice an autocratic management style, they advocate it! They reject all arguments or evidence that participative management is anything more than a naive wish or fad. These are "old school," command-and-control managers who believe that work is inherently distasteful to most people and that getting people to work and work hard requires a tough, autocratic approach.

Other skeptics employ a more sophisticated argument, asserting that the effectiveness of any approach to management depends on the conditions in which it used. Their contentions range from the obvious (for example, in case of a fire, does a manager engage his employees in a discussion of what to do?) to the less obvious, such as arguing that entire categories of work are best handled with autocratic methods.

Of course, there are specific conditions, such as many emergencies, where people don't want to be asked for their opinions; they just want to be told what to do. It is ludicrous to think otherwise, and nobody does. And, who would suggest that new and untrained employees be given latitude as to how to do their work? The workers themselves don't want that latitude—they want training and direction. Being left on their own at that time greatly frustrates them, and it is an example of laissez-faire, not participative, management. Finally, there are those few employees who simply don't want to exercise judgment or give opinions under any condition; they are most comfortable taking and following orders, and that is how they need to be managed.

These are exceptions to the usual circumstance, which is trained and experienced employees working under normal, nonemergency

conditions with a strong desire to exercise judgment while performing their jobs and to be asked for their views on how to improve performance. The exceptions do not negate the validity of the assertion
about the overall superiority of participative management; they simply point to the need to avoid unthinking, mechanical application of
this—or any—principle.

More serious and sweeping than the obvious exceptions to the
rule (such as emergencies) is the argument that *entire categories of
work* suffer if the management style and structure are participative.
It is argued that autocratic management and hierarchical bureaucracy are better suited than participation to work that is simple and
stable. "If the work is relatively simple and there is little need for
coordination and problem-solving, it is possible that the control-oriented approach [what we are calling autocratic] will produce better
results.... The control-oriented approach also works well if the type of
work is highly stable so that it can be programmed to be done in the
same way for a long period."[3]

In other words, when there is no apparent need to think, don't ask
workers to do it.

The reasoning, if correct, would make participative management inapplicable to most blue-collar manufacturing jobs and routine
white-collar work. In the most widely quoted paper employing this
reasoning, "Beyond Theory Y," the authors compare the effectiveness
of authoritarian and participative styles in two manufacturing and two
research laboratory settings. They conclude that:

> *Enterprises with highly predictable tasks [the manufacturing plants]
> perform better with organizations characterized by the highly for-
> malized procedures and management hierarchies of the classical
> approach. With highly uncertain tasks that require more extensive
> problem solving [the two research laboratories], on the other hand,
> organizations that are less formalized and emphasize self-control
> and member participation in decision making are more effective.*

They term this reasoning *contingency theory*, which is that the effectiveness of a management practice is contingent on other factors, such as the nature of the task.[4]

Contingency theory certainly makes intuitive sense, but it has a serious problem: it is contradicted by the legion of extraordinarily successful participatory initiatives in manufacturing plants throughout the world. For example, what is one to make of the extensive use by Japanese manufacturing companies of worker participation in shop-floor decision-making and the extraordinarily positive productivity and quality results that have thereby been achieved? The best-known of these applications have been with assembly-line workers in Japan's automotive industry—hardly a condition of "highly uncertain tasks."

Because of their success, the Japanese have been emulated in many countries, most frequently in manufacturing settings. That is where a change in the direction of participation has been most needed because manufacturing workers have been traditionally among the most autocratically managed. We don't pretend that manufacturing workers can ever approach the kind of autonomy that, say, research scientists or sales representatives enjoy. The nature of manufacturing work—the need for standardization and precise coordination, for example—doesn't allow for it, and workers don't expect it. But that doesn't mean that participation by workers is irrelevant or even harmful in manufacturing, as the contingency theorists appear to argue. For one, no matter how routine a job might appear, there is almost always room for worker judgment.

Second, although work may be highly standardized—to the point where a company wouldn't want individual workers to deviate from the prescribed method—improvement opportunities invariably abound that workers can spot. These potential improvements can be fully discussed and carefully planned before they're implemented. The results are encouraging and sometimes astounding.

One of this book's authors, consulting with a plastics manufacturer, heard workers in a focus group comment on the enormous amount of "trim waste" in the plant. A participant said that he had long had an idea for a device to be attached to the cutting machine that would reduce the waste by at least half. The consultant reported this to the engineering department, and after innumerable meetings, the engineering department decided to try out the idea; it was made and installed on one cutting machine, and the trim waste was reduced by 82 percent! The device was installed throughout the plant. When asked why he hadn't mentioned the idea before, the worker said, simply, "Nobody asked me."

Jeffrey Pfeffer writes of a department in the Eaton Corporation where "...workers tired of fixing equipment that broke down and suggested that they build two new automated machines themselves. They did it for less than a third of what outside vendors would have charged and doubled the output of the department in the first year."[5]

Tom Peters reports on an experience in the Tennant Company where the engineers devised a system to increase the efficiency of a welding department. The system, designed to reduce the need to store units during the welding process, would cost $100,000, which the company deemed too expensive. "A small group of welders tackled the problem. They designed an overhead monorail that could carry welded parts from one station to another so a frame could be welded together from start to finish without leaving the department... They discovered a supply of I-beams in a local junkyard and bought them for less than $2,000. In two days, they installed the monorail. In the first year of its use, the new system saved...more than $29,000 in time and storage space."[6]

Anyone who has worked with manufacturing employees and kept his eyes open would not be surprised by these and the innumerable other examples of the contributions these people can make—if only they are asked! One of the morals of our story, for the theory and practice of management, is that there is often too much emphasis on human differences and not enough on human similarities. We hear of the differences between occupations, between generations, and between nations. (We used to hear much about differences between the sexes and the races, but those views are no longer acceptable to express, at least not publicly.) Many of the presumed differences make intuitive sense because they confirm long-held prejudices. But, they usually cannot withstand empirical tests. For example, Japan and Germany were historically highly authoritarian societies, yet industrial democracy has been flourishing in both countries for decades. Isn't it so, the prejudice goes, that most blue-collar workers don't have the will or the ability to use their minds to improve work operations? We know that assumption is dead wrong, and outstanding managers have known that for a long time.

With the few exceptions we have cited, participative management to our knowledge works under all conditions and for all segments of the workforce.

We will, in Chapter 12, "The Culture of Partnership," show how participative management is an integral part of what we term, more broadly, a "partnership" culture.

Layers of Management

Central to a discussion of authoritarian and participative management is the matter of "steep" or "flat" organizations. Organizations that workers feel to be excessively bureaucratic are typically steep: there are many layers in the management hierarchy, with each level supervising relatively few employees. A flat organization is, of course, the opposite: there are few layers in the management hierarchy and, generally, a larger number of employees report to each level.

In steep organizations, workers are notably caustic and cynical about the number of management levels. The criticism does *not* indicate that workers don't want to be managed—they do. They simply see no added value—they see value *diminished*—by the many management layers. In addition to problems of over-supervision (because the boss supervises only a small number of employees, what else does the boss have to do but supervise?), their major gripes concern the large costs to the organization of so many managers (salary, expensive office space, and so on), the way these steep hierarchies inhibit timely decision making, and the way they inhibit clear communications up and down the organization. Here are some representative employee comments about management layers. They are in response to the question, "What do you like least about working here?"

> *All these levels of management and their cost! What are their jobs but to be messenger boys and work like crazy to keep their jobs? They have very few people to supervise so they're all over their employees.*

> *The unneeded multiple levels of management and the politics that exists. Managers that only care about themselves and not the process or the people are useless. I see very little value add of all these levels. If you asked me who my real manager was, I would say two levels above the one they call my immediate manager. Essentially, I don't know why they need him and his manager.*

> *There is a lack of clear communication between all these multiple levels of management, creating confusion about goals and achievements. It's like the telephone game. By the time the message gets to us, it's garbled.*

A question we often see asked, in answers to open-ended survey questions, is, simply, "What do all these people do?" It is actually a good question, and one that is occasionally asked by the people who occupy those many layers of management!

The two major reasons given by companies for their steep organization structures are control and functional specialization. It's interesting that the number of employees reporting to a supervisor is referred to as his *span of control*. The more control that is desired (in other words, the less people are trusted to control themselves), the fewer the number of people that report to managers at each level, and thus the greater the number of management levels that are required. In that sense, the steep organization consists of checkers upon checkers.

In addition, the role of managers in each layer of the hierarchy is to coordinate with other managers of interdependent departments. The finer the division of labor (specialization or "functionalization") in an organization—the more each individual or department performs just one function rather than being responsible for the "whole thing" (for example, a whole product or a whole customer)—the greater is the interdependence, and, consequently, the greater the need for coordination among the parts and for layers of management to do the coordination. In a completely functionalized organization, no one is responsible for the "whole thing" except the very top, to which all the functions report through their individual, and usually multilayered, hierarchies. We return to this matter in detail in the section "The Benefits of Self-Managed Teams," where we show how a team can within itself perform a variety of functions and thus make possible much flatter organizations.

Not much research has been done that systematically and directly tests the relationship between the number of management layers and the performance of organizations. One study, performed by A. T. Kearny in 1985 that covered 41 large companies, found a strong negative relationship between the number of management layers and long-term financial performance. The organizations with outstanding performance had an average of 7.2 layers, versus 11.1 for the others. They also had 500 fewer staff specialists per $1 billion in sales.[7] In another study, researchers found that companies with average spans of three (necessitating a steep hierarchy) spend almost four times as much to manage each payroll dollar as do firms that have average spans of eight.[8]

Many case studies reinforce the quantitative research findings: companies with records of outstanding long-term performance have extraordinarily flat structures. Nucor Corporation is a leading example of this. As F. Kenneth Iverson, the chairman of Nucor, has said, "The most important thing American industry needs to do is reduce the number of management layers....[It's] one thing we're really fanatical about. We have four management layers. We have a foreman, and the foreman goes directly to the department head, and the department head goes directly to the general manager, and he goes directly to this office."[9] Another example is the Dana Corporation, which went from 15 management layers (and barely profitable) to five layers (with greater profit).

Our discussion in the preceding chapter is relevant here, too, since many organizations with flat structures, such as Nucor, are characterized by a strong sense of purpose and principles. A powerful company culture built on a belief in the importance and value of what it does and shared norms as to what is acceptable behavior is in itself a control mechanism that lessens the need for external controls such as layer upon layer of management. And with fewer controls comes greater employee commitment and enthusiasm which, in turn and in the manner of a virtuous circle, requires fewer controls to operate effectively.

Perhaps a major reason companies with enthusiastic workforces are more successful is simply that it is so much less costly to manage them. Steep structures are especially costly, but not only because of the compensation and expenses of the occupants of the many hierarchical layers. Time and manpower spent responding to the checking and meddling of managers and their staff groups, directly or through endless report requests, is another expense source. Yet another is the inherent delays in the flow of needed information through the hierarchy and in decision making; these delays reduce the timeliness and quality of response to problems and to a changing business environment. Last, but by no means least, as we have said, is employee frustration and demotivation. There is no such thing as an enthusiastic workforce in an excessively layered organization.

The Benefits of Self-Managed Teams

A goal of every organization should be to flatten the structure as much as possible, probably to somewhere between five and seven levels for the total organization, and just three levels in any single facility.[9] Flat organizations lend themselves to decentralized decision making because managers have less time to get involved in the minutiae of day-to-day decision making. Organizations that don't take advantage of this—that simply cut managers and management levels without consciously and deliberately moving authority down the line—find that the workload of the remaining managers has increased enormously, the quality of their work has likely decreased, and their work lives have become correspondingly miserable. These organizations eventually add back managerial staff, which causes costs to balloon once again. They accomplish worse than nothing because reorganizations and re-reorganizations are expensive, and pendulum swings in structure foster (or reinforce) a cynicism in employees about their management's competence.

The decentralization that allows for effective flattening of an organization (not just head-chopping) is, by far, best accomplished by establishing self-managed teams, or SMTs. SMTs are teams of workers who, with their supervisors, have delegated to them various functions and the authority and resources needed to carry them out. Ideally, the team does the "whole thing"—builds a whole product or provides all the services for a defined customer or set of customers.

SMTs of one kind or another are required for effective flat organizations, if for no other reason than that some of the work performed by the eliminated management layers actually does need to be done!

Increasing control by, not of, employees is the essence of the SMT approach to management. This self-control is a product of less need to obtain management's approval for many decisions because these have been delegated to the team ("vertical" autonomy). There's also less need for the group to interact with other units to obtain their assent to decisions because so many functions—traditionally distributed among a number of departments—are performed within the team and, therefore, are under control of the team ("horizontal" autonomy).

Performance is further enhanced in well-run SMTs by the emergence of "group norms," in which members exert a strong influence on each other's behavior. This is especially pronounced in the case of nonproductive employees who are subjected to internal group pressure to perform, thus reducing the need for management's intervention. (Here's a reminder for those interested in improvement in the nation's schools: We referred previously—in Chapter 4, "Compensation"—to the advisability of gainsharing for the compensation of teachers and mentioned how teachers within a well-designed gainsharing system—such as one with participative teams—would be much more likely to both assist, and, if needed, put pressure on, their low-performing colleagues to improve.)

There is considerable variability in the number and kinds of management tasks delegated to the teams. Any SMT worthy of its name will have a great deal of say over work methods, work scheduling, production goals, quality assurance, and relationships with the team's customers (external or internal). But some organizations have gone considerably further and have delegated human-resources decisions, such as hiring employees, to the teams.

And there are large differences in the degree to which teams perform the "whole thing." At one end of the continuum are organizations such as Volvo, which experimented with workers building an entire car. At the other end are organizations such as Toyota, which has given teams a lot of authority, but the actual work done has remained highly fractionated.

In reviewing the research on the effectiveness of SMTs, it appears that the ideal SMT is one that:

- Produces the whole thing for an identified customer or set of customers with whom the team interacts.
- Has clear goals for which it is accountable.
- Contains within it all the skills needed to get the job done.
- Has access to the information and has control over the resources it needs to complete the job.
- Receives rewards based on team performance.

In other words, under ideal circumstances, the team operates like a small business whose members are highly involved in its management and in the sharing of its rewards.[10]

Of course, all of this can be taken to an illogical extreme. Should each small team in a company have its own computer specialists for programming, computer repair, and so on? That would be quite a luxury and only rarely appropriate. For the sake of efficiency and depth of resources, some degree of centralization (sharing) of IT services is required. Should a team of employees in an automobile-assembly plant assemble an entire car, rather than use the traditional mass-production method? The idea sounds enticing, and it has been tried in a few places, such as in the Uddevalla, Volvo, plant in Sweden. The research on this manufacturing model, such as that done by Dr. Paul Adler of USC, concludes that it can never achieve the levels of efficiency of well-run mass-production automobile-assembly plants.[11]

The Toyota paradigm is instructive because it does have teams, and it strongly encourages—in fact, is renowned for—employee participation: employees are encouraged to suggest ways to improve the manufacturing process to increase quality and reduce waste and inefficiency. Furthermore, the teams have responsibility and authority for various duties, such as quality control, scheduling shifts, maintaining and repairing equipment, record keeping, measuring performance, and ordering supplies. Workers have the authority to stop the line when they see a defect or problem. One of the principles of the Toyota production system is that people are intelligent and motivated to do a good job, and they will do that and more if they're given the right tools and adequate authority.

Nevertheless, Toyota's assembly lines are still highly fractionated and standardized. The teams in that company are responsible for a few stations on the assembly line, not the "whole thing." Volvo represents a rejection of the scientific management principles that govern the structure of the traditional mass-production assembly line. Toyota, for the sake of efficiency, accepts those principles but puts workers as a team largely in charge of the line.

Manufacturing the "whole car" is an example of taking the SMT concept too far. But the number of organizations in which the concept doesn't go far enough greatly outweighs such examples. These are the instances where SMTs and other participative mechanisms are largely antithetical to the organization's real culture and outside the mainstream of its business.

Many companies claim they have participative efforts underway but, unfortunately, those programs too often are little more than ornaments—worn by organizations to enhance their image (and even self-image), but bearing little relationship to the organization's reality. Office or plant walls display signs and slogans that preach participation and the importance of people, but the treatment of workers day-today, even when there are SMTs, makes these signs appear to be just company propaganda. In a 1997 study of the General Motors plant in Linden, New Jersey, for example, Ruth Milkman found that the company had introduced a number of participative philosophies and methods. However, despite company slogans calling for involvement and empowerment, workers at Linden "...were told they could pull a cord and stop the line to prevent defective products from proceeding, but those who did so were criticized by foremen and eventually stopped trying."[12]

The situation in Linden is reminiscent of other participative efforts, such as many formal suggestion programs that fail or just limp along because of the gap between their promise and what employees experience in practice. It has been said that suggestion programs raise morale at two times: when you put them in, and when you take them out. Who can dispute the worthiness of soliciting improvement ideas from workers and paying them for the ideas that the company adopts? Despite the promise, suggestion programs often frustrate employees.

By contrast, Toyota's suggestion system has been fabulously successful. Toyota employees, on the average, are reported to contribute 50 or more ideas per person per year, and 80 percent of those ideas are implemented. Essentially, all employees participate. In U.S. companies, however, the participation rate in suggestion programs is about 8 percent (2.4 ideas per person per year), and only about one-third of the suggestions are implemented. The difference is that Toyota has a highly participative overall culture, and its suggestion system is integral to its continuous improvement efforts.[13]

The lesson from Toyota, therefore, lies not just in the mechanics of its suggestion programs or the way it structures teams. It is that, for this company, the programs are not add-ons or symbols of the way Toyota wants the world to believe that it manages people. It is not public relations. It is the way Toyota actually treats its workers, day in and day out.

It is critical, furthermore, that participative mechanisms be at the heart of the *business* as well as the culture. Self-managing teams do best when management provides them with clear direction, high performance goals, and clear accountabilities.[14] You might recall that participative management—as contrasted with laissez-faire—contains an "arrow down," which is direction from above. That arrow ties the team to the goals and strategies of the business.

We, therefore, prefer the term "self-managed" to "self-led" teams. We have never observed an effective SMT with a weak leader or one whose top priorities did not include the priorities of the business as a business. In other words, it's not all fun and games. In fact, what is really not fun for workers is to work on things that are of little importance. In some applications of SMTs, one gets the feeling that the team, with its endless team-building exercises, becomes almost an end in itself rather than a means for the achievement of business ends. "I've seen too many groups go off on wilderness excursions or use 'structured team-building experiences' to try to turn a group into a team," says consultant Jim Clemmer. These approaches don't work because they're not focused on business and performance issues or the broader organization context and focus. They don't get any real work done."[15]

To summarize, self-managed teams and other participative mechanisms can achieve more than brief bursts of enthusiasm and performance only if they do not stand alone: they must be exemplars of—not exceptions to—the broad organization culture, and they must clearly and directly support the achievement of business objectives. Failing those, they will shrivel and, to all intents and purposes, die. But when they are integral part of the organization—not something tacked on for show—they are, by far, the most effective way to organize.

Telecommuting: Yahoo Bans Work-From-Home

In late February 2013, as we were completing the manuscript for this book, Melissa Mayer, the recently appointed CEO of Yahoo, issued an edict banning the practice of allowing Yahoo's employees to work from home. Employees would have to start showing up at their offices beginning in June. We stopped the presses on this book so that we could comment on this action in the context of the findings and point of view of the book. It is especially relevant to the arguments we presented in this chapter regarding the organization's impact on employees' ability to get the job done and work autonomously.

The announcement banning work from home, or "telecommuting," was, of course, controversial, eliciting a few supportive, but mostly negative, reactions in the blogosphere and other media. The most critical comments portrayed the edict as a huge step backward in the management of employees, with particular reference to the better work-life balance that working at home made possible for everyone who took advantage of it, but particularly for women with small children. Many of the critics spoke of their shock that a woman would take this step. There was also no shortage of reference to a new and different "generation" of worker for whom Ms. Mayer's action would be infuriating because that generation placed great emphasis on the job autonomy that working at home helped provide.

Supporters of the action tended to stress that Ms. Mayer is smart and experienced and is a CEO exercising her prerogatives, and that this was an important step in her major task: making Yahoo—universally considered to have become a laggard in a fast-moving industry—a leader again with substantial revenue and profit growth. The company had had five CEOs in the past five years, both a sign and a source of its problems.

We are by no means experts on Yahoo, but we know something about management and the steps they often take to deal with performance problems and the consequences of those steps. We mentioned a number of times in this book that cracking down on malingerers is one of the most common actions executives take—especially new executives—when they feel they have to whip an organization into shape. We will argue that that was likely one of Ms. Mayer's major reasons for her action, although that was not the reason given. Companies frequently clothe in more acceptable language policies and practices they fear will not be received well. A consultant convinced one large corporation we studied that its factory workers were doing much less work than was possible or standard. Using time-study, the corporation introduced significantly increased productivity requirements but called it a Methods Improvement Program. It had little to do with improving methods and everything to do with getting workers to work harder.

In the announcement sent to Yahoo employees, the reason given for stopping telecommuting was to increase face-to-face interaction among employees to boost innovativeness and improve worker morale:

> *To become the absolute best place to work, communication and collaboration will be important, so we need to be working side-by-side. That is why it is critical that we are all present in our offices. Some of the best decisions and insights come from hallway and cafeteria discussions, meeting new people, and impromptu team meetings.*

Interaction and Innovativeness

The research over the years on interaction has been quite clear: when people are working on interdependent tasks, interaction significantly improves innovativeness, and face-to-face interaction, despite all the improvements in communications technology, remains the gold standard. It's not that technology can't be used well for facilitating interaction in more formal, planned settings. It's that a whole lot of innovativeness is a result of unplanned, accidental encounters and discussions. Furthermore, communications are significantly improved when verbal communications are supplemented by body language, so there is no substitute for being able to size up one's colleagues face-to-face. And then there is learning, much of which is done on the job and, for almost all jobs we can think of, requires good role models—both colleagues and bosses—from whom one learns in the course of face-to-face observation and interaction.

Modern technology, of course, supplements informal interaction in very important ways, such as continuing the exchange when the participants are separated geographically. But it cannot fully replace it. Although we might like to think that technology is especially beneficial for people at a distance from each other and might otherwise not communicate, the finding, not surprisingly, is that people are much less likely to phone or email or IM for a discussion with people they haven't met face to face.[16]

Ms. Mayer, therefore, has a strong case in her argument that, for promoting innovativeness, getting her employees onsite should be of considerable help. How about the case for raising morale? Here, her position is considerably weaker.

Employee Morale, Employee Work Ethic

While some significant morale benefits can be found for onsite work—we'll get to those shortly—they are overwhelmed by the tremendous advantage to quite a few people of having the flexibility that at-home work provides. Keep in mind that when in this book we speak of the three goals of people at work, we are careful to stress that these are *work-related* goals—that is, we are not referring to the many and extremely important personal needs and desires of people. There are, for example, the needs of parents of small children; the desire to avoid the frustration and the cost of long commutes; and the possibility, because of the availability of telecommuting, of living distant from the office, in a city of one's choice.

Because these personal needs and desires are so important and can so much more easily be satisfied by working at home, they overwhelm the advantages to morale of working with one's colleagues face to face. Those morale advantages are not at all trivial; they're just of a lesser magnitude when faced with the requirement to be at the office every day. Among the other morale advantages of being onsite—in addition to the increased innovativeness that comes from such interaction (important to employees, not just the company)—are a decreased sense of isolation; quite a few people become lonely working day after day alone, missing the camaraderie that comes from the interaction with colleagues. And the isolation can be compounded by a sense of being out-of-sight-out-of-mind when it comes to selection for advancement and other desirable assignment opportunities.

Ms. Mayer's claim that her new policy would raise morale is likely broader and deeper and more transformative than portrayed by the preceding examples, and it relates to our comment about executives "cracking-down." Former and current Yahoo employees, reports the *New York Times*, portrayed a culture "...where employees were aimless and morale was low...[a company] out of competition with its more nimble rivals." In the tech world, it seemed almost an embarrassment to say you worked for Yahoo. "I've heard she wants to make Yahoo young and cool," commented one former employee.[17]

But it was clearly not simply an old and stodgy culture that Ms. Mayer wanted to change. She noticed that Yahoo parking lots and many offices were nearly empty during the work day. People were either not coming into work at all or were leaving early. Approximately 200 employees worked at home full time, and some of these were suspected of running their own-start-up businesses on the side.[18] According to media reports, Mayer, upon reviewing employees' Virtual Private Network logs, concluded that employees were connecting to the office much less frequently than they should be.[19]

So, in addition to her other reasons for the edict, Ms. Mayer's actions almost certainly reflect a distrust of the work ethic and dedication of some—perhaps many—Yahoo employees and the need, therefore, to bring them to the office where, in addition to promoting the interaction she speaks of, they could be supervised more closely. Or they will quit, which, in some cases, might not be an undesirable result. She wants, in other words, to bring discipline, as she sees it, to the organization, and this may be one of a series of steps in that direction that she is taking or contemplating.

As of this writing, we have had no direct access to the employees of Yahoo and therefore don't know firsthand what their reactions have been. Our best guess is that the reactions have been strong and mixed. Some will no doubt feel, "It's about time!" The employees seriously inconvenienced by the move—such as those who will now have to commute long distances every day and parents who will have to make other arrangements for their children—are not going to be happy. They'll probably be quite angry considering the apparent suddenness of the action, the blanket nature of the edict, and the fact that it is something being taken away and therefore seen as a promise broken.

As we have said, a major mistake managers often make is to generalize from the few to everybody. They don't see the shirkers as a small minority and may even believe that it is the genuinely committed who are few in number; therefore, they deem it important that just about everyone be watched closely. Another source of negative reaction to the edict, then, should be the resentment of hard-working employees who believe they are being treated as untrustworthy.

Telecommuting and Performance

What have we learned from research about the performance of people who work from home? We don't know what a study would reveal at Yahoo, but systematic studies of the performance of telecommuters show quite consistently that they are more productive—they produce a larger *amount*—than their counterparts in the office. Although the reverse is likely true when it comes to innovativeness, we can say with certainty that there is no evidence that allowing employees to work from home is a recipe for wholesale shirking. A major reason for the higher productivity at home appears to be that at-home workers work more hours as the boundary between their home lives and work lives blurs. A University of Texas at Austin study found that those who work from home "add five to seven hours to their workweek compared with those who work exclusively at the office."[20] Some of the additional hours are also a result of the reduction in commuting time.

A meta-analysis—a systematic "study of studies"—of 46 pieces of research on telecommuting[21] finds that "telecommuting had modest but mainly beneficial effects on employees' job satisfaction, autonomy, stress levels, manager-rated job performance, and (lower) work-family conflict. Although a number of scholars and managers have expressed fears that employee careers might suffer and workplace relationships damaged because of telecommuting, the meta-analysis finds that there are no generally detrimental effects on the quality of workplace relationships and career outcomes. Only high-intensity telecommuting—where employees work from home for more than 2.5 days a week—harmed employee relationships with coworkers, even though it did reduce work-family conflict."

Conclusions and Recommendation

On the basis of the evidence, can there be any question as to what the right answer is for companies wrestling with the issue of telecommuting? Unlike many management decisions involving people, the answer is, at least for us, clear.

Let's begin by restating a fundamental proposition of this book: there is little real conflict between the goals of the overwhelming majority of workers and those of their employers. It is in the nature of people to want to work and to do well for their companies. Very few people are inherently lazy, greedy, or dishonest. It is primarily management that, by it practices, dampens or destroys motivation, especially when those practices derive from the assumption that most people don't want to work—certainly not hard—and have little concern for their companies. Unless there has been some awful incompetence in the way people have been hired at Yahoo, it is certain that the overwhelming majority of its employees would be eager to work not only hard but probably in excess of what would normally be expected of them.

If our reasoning is accepted, we conclude that telecommuting in Yahoo will be a problem only to the extent that management makes it a problem. Otherwise, it can be a boon to both the company and its employees. Among other reasons, the company will gain because:

- It will be able to attract and keep employees for whom the ability to work at home is a major plus. And, in that respect, the company's overall reputation as a good employer will be enhanced.

- Employee morale will increase, and with it the overall performance that we have demonstrated comes from higher morale.
- Employees will work more hours, and employee productivity—the amount they do—will improve.
- The company will save on real estate and related costs.

Employees will gain in the ways we have described, which are primarily flexibility, for those who need or want it, and avoiding the frustrations and costs of commuting.

What are the downsides? Frankly, we can't think of any of any significance *if telecommuting is managed properly*. From what we read about Yahoo, it appears that, in quite a few instances, it just wasn't managed. Hence, the too-common company reaction: a swing from what appeared to senior management to be a laissez-faire environment—"Do what you like"—to the opposite extreme: a ban on all telecommuting.

What do we mean by proper management? It is, of course, neither extreme, but rather an approach that recognizes the legitimate needs and wants of employees and seeks to satisfy them in a way that not only will not damage the company but will be profitable to it. We have called this a "partnership" approach—or culture—and it will be described fully in Chapter 12. The position that Ms. Mayer has adopted on the telecommuting issue is characteristic of another approach, also to be described in that chapter, which we call "adversarial."

The policy we recommend is, essentially, a variant of "flextime." Under traditional flextime, there is typically a core period when employees are required to be at work—say, 50 percent of the working day—but they can choose which hours of the rest of the day they will be at work, as long as the total number of hours adds up to a full working day. The practice is very well received by employees because of the flexibility it gives them in their starting and stopping times. Although it's usually applied to working hours in a day and does not include working at home, the basic flextime concept can be applied to telecommuting. First, as regards core time, the application would be days in the week rather than hours in the day. And the flexible days could be worked at home. The approach would therefore provide for both workplace interaction and telecommuting for those who want it. And it would not be laissez-faire—come in whenever you want— because there would be a core set of days in the week that employees would be expected to be at work. Keep in mind that the Gajendran and Harrison (2007) study found that working relationships do suffer when employees worked from home more than 2.5 days per week. The core would be not just a number of days, but specific days, to ensure the opportunity for interaction.

How would our proposal be received by employees? With a great big hooray! Keep in mind that employees want their company to succeed. There must be no small number of Yahoo employees who believe that the previous policy—to the extent and in the places where it was laissez-faire—was nutty and they would want it changed. Further, the evidence is that it is just a very small number of employees who would choose to work from home full-time. The great majority want to interact with their colleagues, and they don't want to be forgotten for promotions and choice assignments by the powers-that-be. Even those who have to commute long distances to work consider it a blessing to be able to spend 1–2 days a week at home.

There are exceptions, of course, and these should be handled on a case-by-case basis. Among the exceptions are those who are truly lazy or who are exploiting Yahoo's beneficence to pay them while, say, they get a startup going. We'll get to these—the shirkers—in a moment. There are those for whom working at home fulltime (or nearly so) is seen as a necessity, such as some parents of young children or people who will have to move their residence. The best rule for managers in these cases is this: use your best judgment. We are personally unaware of any such situation in which a competent manager was not able to make a sound decision, such as permitting an exception, but also, in some cases, the employee having to leave the job.

What we are proposing cannot be administered in a centralized way, other than in very small companies. The policy should be handled by individual managers and their teams—hopefully SMTs as we have described them in this chapter. Tasks, individuals, and the dynamics among individuals are different across areas of a business, and specifics have to be tailored to those conditions. The tailoring is best done by people familiar with the conditions. The role of higher-level management, including the very top, is to provide ground rules and guidance to the managers and teams, such as the stipulation that core days at the office are expected. Because there are no doubt jobs and departments in which employees must be onsite, every day, and for all normal business hours, there should obviously not be a requirement that the opportunity to telecommute be made available to everybody.

What about the shirkers? Part of the guidance from top management involves how those people are to be dealt with. In a word, as we said earlier in this book, firmly. But, as we also said, the team itself will help management deal with the issue. In a self-managed team in a partnership culture, the pressures that colleagues place on each other shift from "don't do any more than you have to" to "let's do as much and as well as possible." It's hard for individuals to resist those pressures, and for those individuals who do, the company's disciplinary procedures are brought into play.

We speak of partnership as the culture where what we propose will operate best because it is congruent with, and reinforces, that culture. There is another respect in which context is extremely important: the extent to which the organization, as a whole, has a clear sense of direction with challenging goals that can be translated into clear, challenging, and credible goals for each of its subparts. We don't know that Yahoo can be described in that way, but, if not, or not in certain parts of the company, the idea of people being required to show up at the office doesn't make too much sense. If they don't have much to do at home, is it better to not have much to do in the office and fake it? We're stating the case somewhat facetiously to make this point: changes in practices, such as telecommuting, won't by themselves solve fundamental problems and may distract from them. Telecommuting, as we have proposed it be implemented, can be a terrific way to serve the company and its employees. But it also has to be seen in the context of the culture of the organization and the overall effectiveness with which the business is being run.

9

Job Challenge

"The greatest analgesic, soporific, stimulant, tranquilizer, narcotic, and to some extent even antibiotic—in short, the closest thing to a genuine panacea—known to medical science is work."

—Thomas Szasz, M.D., psychiatrist, author

The previous chapter focused on enablement, covering the type of organization that allows workers to get their jobs done and the positive impact that such enablement has on their satisfaction and pride. But efficient, even high-quality performance is not sufficient. The *work itself*—what is done—is also critical.

For example, for many workers, doing simple, repetitive work for long periods of time (no matter how well done) can be highly unsatisfying, even intolerable. Here are some comments from employees in these jobs about the work itself (in response to the question about what they like least in the company):

(I dislike) waking up in the morning to come to this boring job...my skills are being wasted daily!

Dealing with the repetitiveness. My job is always the same in my case. I don't have much of a variety of things to do, so sometimes things can be mind-numbing, frustrating, or even stressful.

The type of work we do is very tedious, and it is very hard not to get in a rut. Sometimes, the pressure of the job can get to you. You can feel the anxiety building up as soon as you enter the building.

This job is monotonous. After say, three months, there is no longer any challenge. Just being able to sit at a desk for hours at a time is the most challenge I face.

My job is mundane. It can be very boring, so it is a challenge to enjoy the actual work I do, even though I enjoy the company as a whole.

My job does not require much grey matter. I think my 12-year-old sister could do it.

Those comments are from people for whom challenging work is important and whose jobs don't provide it. The literature on work, as we have said, contains a great deal of social commentary on the presumed debilitating and dehumanizing nature of routine jobs. We are all familiar with the depiction of much work as so boring that only a trained monkey could bear it.

We would expect, therefore, a large percentage of people to be unhappy with their work. Even more broadly, it is widely believed that people are inherently averse to work anyway, no matter how it is structured. According to this view, job satisfaction is a contradiction in terms; we work because we are forced to, not because we want to. While it is a widely held, in fact ancient, notion, it is a misconception.

As reported earlier, 78 percent of millions of surveyed workers say they like their jobs. Only 7 percent report dissatisfaction. Furthermore, the range of responses from the least positive to the most positive organization on this point is from 50 percent to 92 percent. Therefore, even in the organization with employees least happy with their jobs, half are still favorable. These results, as we have pointed out, show surprisingly little variation by the type of work people do. For example, whereas 83 percent of salaried employees express satisfaction with their jobs, 78 percent of hourly employees do so.[1]

Is This an Aberration, Are Workers Delusional, or Are They Lying?

None of the above. You can gain insight into how some people view the work itself from this not atypical interchange, which is abstracted from a focus group of packers in a cookie and cracker factory. These women do routine and repetitive work.

> *FOCUS GROUP MODERATOR: What is it that you particularly like about working here?*
>
> *WORKER 1: We get good pay and this company has been here forever so I feel secure here.*
>
> *WORKER 2: Our pay has kept up with the cost of living—that's really important to me.*
>
> *WORKER 3: I like the fact that we are making a product that people really enjoy. It makes me feel good to know that what I do makes people happy.*
>
> *WORKER 4: We can have as much product as we like for free at lunch and coffee breaks but we shouldn't be eating so much. [Laughter] But the cookies really are so good.*
>
> *MODERATOR: Now, what do you particularly dislike about working here?*
>
> *WORKER 1: The equipment. It keeps breaking down. They only have two maintenance people left. It's crazy! We lose so much production waiting for maintenance to show up.*
>
> *WORKER 4: My forelady—she is always looking over my shoulder, trying to make sure I'm working and doing my work right. I've been here 27 years, for goodness sake, doing the same thing, and she wants to make sure I know how to do it?*
>
> *WORKER 3: I don't think that management thinks we're very smart. They almost never ask for our opinions and we could help. There's a lot of wastage now.*
>
> *MODERATOR: For example?*

WORKER 3: For example, we see when a machine is running so fast that it's sure to break down. And it always does. I've stopped telling them because they don't listen.

(Additional dislikes were then mentioned, such as sometimes being asked to work overtime on too short notice, heating and air conditioning that don't work well ("it's either too hot or too cold"), a co-worker who "gets away with murder," and the factory general manager who "just looks straight ahead and never says hello.")

MODERATOR: Nobody mentioned the actual work you do, packing cookies and crackers. Do you like this kind of work?

WORKER 1: It's fine; it's a job. I'm happy to have it and I do it well.

WORKER 2: Well, really, the work is boring; I'm doing the same thing over and over again. I'd rather be doing something else. Sometimes, I feel like I just can't do it anymore. I feel like a machine, but I'm too old to change jobs now.

WORKER 3: It's not very interesting, it's the same thing every day, but to tell you the truth, I don't much care. Because we don't have to think on the job, we can talk to each other. We really socialize; I love that, with all the ladies.

WORKER 4: Look, I'm lucky to have a steady job. My father was always getting laid off, always worried.

WORKER 5: Frankly, although I wouldn't say I hate the work, it does get boring. I'd like to do something more interesting. I want to do bookkeeping and I'm thinking of going to night school for it.

WORKER 6: This job is good enough for me. I couldn't be a book-keeper, numbers make my head spin.

WORKER 7: As (name) said, it's a job and a pretty good one when you consider that I don't have much education.

MODERATOR: Would any of you be interested in a promotion to a management position, such as forelady?

WORKER 2: Not interested—who needs all those headaches? When I leave work, I don't want to think about it.

WORKER 7: And we'd lose our union membership and overtime pay. It's more work for very little more pay.

WORKER 6: I couldn't stand managing people. They're a headache. And I'd lose my friends because of the things I'd have to do, like discipline them. I'd be terrible at that.

WORKER 5: Me, I think I could do it. I would certainly like to try if they would give me training. I'm a good organizer. But I've never been asked.

Notice the two different reactions to the routine nature of the work: Worker 2 said she felt like a machine sometimes, but most of the others had different reactions. Although the latter workers were not particularly positive ("it's a job"), they were certainly not particularly negative. Judging from their other comments (about equipment, the forelady, and so on), these women were not reluctant to express the negative views they did have. Their opinions about their jobs stand in contrast to the earlier ones cited, selected from employees in a number of different companies who expressed great unhappiness with the routine nature of their work.

The divergence in views supports what is obvious to us all: people differ enormously in what is attractive or unattractive to them about the content of jobs. Although there are also individual differences in the other needs we have discussed in this book, such as the importance of job security or camaraderie, these differences are small compared to the great variations in the kinds of jobs people prefer.

The variations are of two kinds. One concerns sheer preference for a type of work based on interest or personality or upbringing. Some people, for example, prefer outdoor to indoor work, office work to factory work, working near one's boss to being "on one's own" (such as a salesperson), working in the private or the public or the not-for-profit sectors, 9-to-5 jobs versus jobs with often long and uncertain working hours, and predictable to unpredictable job routines.

Given a Choice, Few People Volunteer to Fail

A second set of differences comes from people's sense of what they can do *well*. Being a professional athlete is awfully appealing to many youngsters, but they learn quickly whether they have the rare talent to be successful at it. Few without that talent continue trying for long.

As we know, workers want to be proud of what they do. If the job involves managing others, for example, and an employee doesn't feel she is good at that, she keeps away from management positions. If someone is poor in math, he keeps away from engineering studies and engineering jobs. If he is clumsy, he doesn't seek jobs requiring a lot of manual dexterity.

This is why we don't see more dissatisfaction with the work itself in our surveys, even among those who do repetitive and routine work. Many of us could not do repetitive work for long without feeling great frustration. But although we choose not to do repetitive work, others *do* choose to do it. They are not, by and large, unhappy with their choice.

Some workers feel that they're good primarily at doing the same thing over and over. In addition to the cookie and cracker factory workers, consider Melvin Reich, who's known as the buttonhole man:

> *Would you want to make buttonholes day in and day out?* The New York Times *recently ran an offbeat article on Melvin Reich, Manhattan's premier buttonhole man.* "Buttonholes are what we do. We do buttonholes and buttonholes and buttonholes. I am specialized, like the doctors," *said Reich.* "You think it's nothing. Just a buttonhole. But it's something. It's not nothing." *And the clincher:* "Zippers are a totally different field. It's a different game. A man can do so much."[2]

Note that in the group of cookie packers, only one worker expressed interest in a management position. Many workers share the view of "Who needs the headaches?" Other workers, however, thrive on those headaches. So, you might sensibly ask, "Who is the more rational (or less neurotic): workers who just want to do their jobs with minimum problems and stress and leave work without thinking any more about it, or people who appear to be unable to live without work-related stress 24/7?

We are being facetious to make the point that understanding workers requires that we put ourselves in their shoes, asking what *they* want from a job. What some workers avoid as "stressful," others seek out as "challenging." Putting ourselves in other people's shoes requires suspending evaluative judgments—such as judging to be demeaning the kinds of work that millions of people choose to do— and asserting that they must (or should) be unhappy with it.

Although a free labor market allows for the diversity of individual preferences to be matched by the diversity of jobs, it doesn't always work that way. In our surveys, an average of 7 percent say that they are dissatisfied with their jobs; so, some people obviously do find themselves doing a job they dislike. This group is a small fraction of the workforce, but the consequence of that unhappiness for their overall morale is huge. For example, 51 percent of employees who are dissatisfied with the work itself express dissatisfaction with the company overall, while only 3 percent of those satisfied with their jobs express such dissatisfaction. Table 9-1 shows the relationship between satisfaction with the work itself and overall satisfaction with an organization.

Table 9-1 Relationship Between Job Satisfaction and Overall Satisfaction

	Overall Satisfaction		
Job Satisfaction	**Satisfied**	**Neutral**	**Dissatisfied**
Satisfied	88%	9%	3%
Neutral	43%	44%	13%
Dissatisfied	22%	27%	51%

Given the importance of the work itself and the diversity of jobs available, why do some people wind up in jobs they dislike?

For one, mistakes can be made in job choices, especially in initial choices. For example, people might misjudge their abilities or be wrong about the abilities a job requires so, early in their employment, they search for other, more compatible opportunities. That is a major reason so much voluntary or mutually-agreed-upon turnover occurs within the first year or so of employment. That is healthy turnover because people should not stay in jobs they dislike, and organizations should not want them to stay.

Sometimes, however, people get "stuck" in a job that it is difficult or impossible to leave, often for financial reasons. The need to earn a living can lead people to take and keep jobs that they dislike, sometimes intensely. That is truly a sad situation—spending eight hours a day being miserable. It's most pronounced in times of economic downturn when work is scarce, and in a person's middle and later career stages when leaving an organization to search for another job can result in significant financial loss. The latter is the familiar case of the "golden handcuffs": pensions, stock options, and the like hold employees in jobs with which they are unhappy and in which they might remain for a long time just for financial reasons. Yes, man does not live by bread alone, but bread is important, especially with mortgages, college tuitions to pay, and, later in life, the need to retire with financial security.

Push and Pull

It's helpful to view job choice, retention, and satisfaction as the result of motivational *push-pull forces*. Pull forces are the factors that make a job choice (or any choice) attractive, like the interest a person has in the job, its challenge, and the promise of excitement.

On the other hand, push forces feel like coercive influences, in the sense of driving or forcing us against our will toward the choice. It might be the need to please other people ("I promised my parents

I would be a doctor!"), a choice between the lesser of two evils, or, perhaps, the need just to make a living ("I have to eat.").

When the pull forces predominate, you arise each morning and look forward to going to work. When only push forces exist, your action of choice when the sun rises is hitting the snooze button. Let's now complicate it a bit. Sometimes the type of work is desirable, but it has been structured by the organization, or managed by a manager, in a way that makes it onerous for the job occupant. Although only 7 percent express dissatisfaction with "the job itself—the kind of work you do," the results are considerably less positive on other questions regarding the job. For example, we saw how bureaucracy can affect employee attitudes. In other words, the kind of work might be desirable, but not the context in which it is performed. Consider these views, abstracted from an interview with Terry, a sales representative in a telecommunications company:

> Terry loves sales work but finds his sales job in the company to be a miserable experience.

> Terry loves the challenge of selling. He is most happy when he is with customers, either pursuing or servicing accounts. He is a salesman's salesman. He derives great pleasure from landing accounts and doing the things necessary to keep customers loyal. The money is important to him as it is to other salespeople, but Terry absolutely loves the activity itself. He believes in his product and in himself. He genuinely likes people, and people seem to like Terry. He is highly motivated to deliver on each promise to his clients, and he does not sleep well if he misses any.

> Give him a territory, a challenging quota, a clear, accurate compensation plan, and a smart leader who points him in the right direction, and he is a happy employee who will deliver the goods. What else would someone want from a salesman?

> Unfortunately for Terry and the company, Terry's day is significantly consumed by something other than selling. Paperwork is the bane of a salesperson's existence. Some of this administrative activity is seen as an unavoidable and necessary evil by salespeople and is absolutely required to keep track of important outcomes.

But, unfortunately, Terry reports to Mr. Pitz, a former top sales-
man, who also fashions himself an innovative administrator. Mr.
Pitz established an elaborate database that tracks every interaction
each salesperson has with each customer contact. He calls it TCTS
(Total Customer Tracking System). The level of detail of his data-
base grows every month and, thus, its attendant burden on his sales-
people. In fact, part of the performance evaluation of his people is
the thoroughness of their data input. Mr. Pitz presented his system
to top management, and they were impressed. The impact of the
system on Terry echoes our comments in the previous chapter about
bureaucracy.

Terry and his colleagues must track each contact they have with
customers and record the nature of the customer's business (its
gross revenue, number of employees, geography, and ten other de-
mographic characteristics); details of the conversation (whom they
talked to, what their job title is, whether they bought and, if so, how
much, what the tone of the conversation was); and the reasons of
those who didn't buy (budget issues, satisfaction with current sup-
plier, reputation of Terry's company).

Despite the fact that some of this information could be useful, Terry
feels that he has been relegated to doing the job of a clerk rather
than a salesman for a significant part of his day. It interferes with
his ability to sell. Terry would like to leave the company, but he feels
he can't because of his pay and pension, which he believes he cannot
duplicate elsewhere.

Terry loves the work itself—sales—but not his sales job in C&A. Of
course, some people just won't put up with a job in which they're
miserable, no matter what the financial impact of leaving; witness the
following write-in comment from a survey:

People are leaving this company for the competition and cannot
believe the difference in stress level and how much better they are
treated at their new job. We are constantly being pulled into inter-
nal conference calls, district calls, training, etc. Sixty percent of my
time is spent on internal non-value work. Valuable people will con-
tinue to leave the organization unless some of the non-value internal
initiatives are eliminated. This company is burning people out! I'm

going to leave even if I can't immediately find a job elsewhere. I'll
just take a little time off to recover and look for something else

When employees are unhappy in their current situation, it's fortunate when they also feel able to leave it. However, many employees are like Terry; for whatever reason (financial, lack of self-confidence), they feel stuck. Terry very much wants to be a salesman—it's his dream career—but it has become a nightmare. We will continue this discussion of job structure and what organizations should do about it later in this chapter. But first we need to return to the near-universal desire of people to feel proud of their work.

Although there are large differences in the kinds of work and occupations people prefer, almost everyone wants to be proud of what he does. Pride in the job comes from three sources: *performing well, using valued skills,* and *doing something of significance.*

Performing Well

The criteria workers use to judge their performance have both external sources (such as what the company or immediate boss wants) and internal sources (how the worker himself judges his performance, which, in turn, almost always has past external sources, especially the standards emphasized in training). The two most common criteria for evaluating job performance are quantity and quality of work, but it is quality that is the more important source of worker pride. Turning out a lot of work is just not as meaningful in terms of self-esteem as doing something well.[3] This underlies a good deal of the frequent conflict between workers and management about the amount of work expected. It is not just workers' resistance to a pace that will leave them physically exhausted or even harm their health. Those are, of course, important, but workers also fear the impact of undue production pressure on their ability to produce quality work and provide quality service to customers. That issue, in other words, is a matter of their *pride.* The following comments illustrate this point (in response to the question of what you like least about working here):

The ongoing facade that quality is so important, when in actuality, very little value is placed upon it; with the vast majority of emphasis placed on the all-important numbers, the quantity, the production, etc. My over 100 percent quality means absolutely nothing in comparison with my low numbers. Poor quality is OK, low numbers are not! But poor quality is not OK with me!

The incredible fast pace that everyone works at this company is a problem. I can't help but wonder if people at other companies work at such an incredibly fast pace. Things cannot keep speeding faster and faster, which seems to be the plan. We can't do the high-quality work we are capable of because there is not enough time to read, think, and make smart decisions and plans.

There are so many customer complaints due to layoffs and outsourcing of systems, which result in poor quality and slow response times. Supposedly it saves money, but down times are increased and clients and customers are given poorer service. I hate hearing customer complaints but there's nothing we can do. No matter what we say, we are budget driven rather than quality driven.

It is easy to interpret resistance to production pressure as proof of workers' laziness. But few workers want a lax, laissez-faire environment—there is no pride in that. They object to an emphasis on quantity when it becomes excessive and detrimental to their physical well-being, the quality of their work, and the organization's reputation with its customers.

Using Valued Skills

Self-esteem flows not just from performing well, but doing so in a way that uses skills that the employee values. In a broad sense, the importance of quality derives from this because quality is associated with traits that workers value—traits that are distinctly human, such as craftsmanship, dedication, and judgment. Sheer production, on the other hand, is most closely associated with the nonhuman world, such as robots and the proverbial "trained monkeys." In fact, for speed of output, it is rare that any human can beat a machine.

Within the human world—the world of workers—there are numerous kinds and levels of valued skill, and it is a source of great frustration when these skills are not used:

> *This organization must work on utilizing the abilities and brains of the administrative staff. It's very difficult doing exactly the same tasks over and over every month. Just because you are very good at something does not mean it's all you are capable of!*

> *My management does not have sufficient tech skills to manage me in a technical environment. They do not use my skills properly. I work more as a technician than an engineer. It's galling not to be treated as a professional.*

> *The bureaucracy is stifling. I have a management title and believe I have strong management abilities, but I'm not allowed to function as a manager. I am micro-managed every step of the way. My manager constantly goes around me directly to my employees. When he goes through me, I'm just a messenger for him.*

> *I was hired here to run Sales. The CEO was head of Sales at one time and still acts that way. I get almost no latitude. I was told when I was hired that he wanted new ideas because things were stagnant. That was just talk. I'm really his A. A. [administrative assistant]. He's not going to change and it's time to get out of here.*

> *I feel like a trained monkey on this job. It's so routine and predetermined that there is absolutely no room for using my judgment, my education. It's really debilitating.*

> *My greatest challenge is surviving the day. I feel there is way too much emphasis on administrative activities, rather than satisfying customer needs. My customer service skills are atrophying.*

On the other hand, when workers feel that their skills are being fully used, it becomes a source of joy:

> *I like the autonomy given me by my leader to use my professional skills and experience to accomplish my daily tasks. I am especially pleased about my leaders' confidence in me as a person and in my abilities. This empowers me with the motivation and pride to*

perform my job at this company with 100 percent dedication to my client and my employer.

I am really using and further developing my skills—I just love it! Who would have believed that I would have fallen into a job like this at my age—they trust me with major assignments such as managing relationships with pretty big customers.

It's very pleasurable not having a pigeon-holed job. Instead, things here are dynamic and new skills are learned every day.

I feel blessed to have the opportunity to succeed, learn, grow, and enhance my current management, HR, conflict resolution, and sales skills.

When a worker has a skill that is both important and unique or unusual in his workplace, it is a source of *great* joy. Being considered the expert in your field of work is a terrific feeling:

I hate to boast, but I don't know what they'd do here without me.

My leadership and technological skills have increased immeasurably over the last five-plus years. I am extremely grateful to the company. It is a source of great pride to me to be regularly sought out and asked by other managers what to do in particular situations.

Many workers are interested in gaining additional valued skills through training. Training, of course, has many positive consequences for a worker in addition to a heightened sense of competence and pride, such as higher potential income within and outside the organization and greater job security. The importance of training, especially in fields that rapidly change, has been demonstrated in many studies. For example, in a survey of the goals of technical employees in 25 countries, we found that receiving training—continual training—ranked at or near the top in every country in what employees say they want from their jobs.[4]

Doing Work of Significance

In addition to performing well and having their skills used, employees want to feel that what they do makes a difference, especially to their organizations and to the organization's customers. Professional employees are also often interested in having an impact on the status and progress of their professions.

We are not referring to Nobel Prize–type contributions. The workers at the cookie factory were pleased that the product they packed "made people happy." The following comments help illustrate the point:

> I like the fact that you are recognized for your contributions, and rewarded for them. I have had a really good year and made the company a lot of money. I'm proud and lucky enough to be able to go on the [destination] trip for Outstanding Contributors.

> My boss told me that I am essential to this department. That's the kind of boss he is. Compliments like that keep me going.

> The best part of my job when all is said and done is providing good service to the customers. Pleasant and satisfied customers make the work seem like fun.

> It is important to me that I feel I am contributing to my customers' success. It is especially gratifying when a customer lets me know that I have helped him or her. I feel that's why I'm here!

> In this company, they don't make you feel small. They make every employee feel important, that he or she is a key part of the company's success. That works like magic for our morale.

Employees' interest in doing high-quality work comes, in part, from their concern for customers. Customer satisfaction is mentioned frequently in employee focus groups: on the positive side when workers feel that they have served customers well, and with frustration and disappointment when they feel they have not, usually because, as they see it, their ability to provide quality service was severely hampered by workload or other obstacles.

Making a difference to customers again brings us to the matter of workers doing the "whole thing" rather than each worker being responsible for a fragment of a product or service. Although it's usually discussed in terms of products, such as producing an entire automobile engine, let's apply it here to servicing customers. Our first example is a bit far-out: the "customers" are laboratory animals.

One of this book's authors was engaged by the chief veterinarian of a pharmaceuticals company to help him understand and do something about the morale of the laboratory-animal caretakers. The veterinarian said that the caretakers were lethargic about their work, such as not cleaning the cages well, feeding the animals late, and coming to work late. In his words, "They are a really unenthusiastic crowd." His continual exhortations to them to improve did little good: things changed for a few days and then returned to their previous mediocre level.

On the basis of in-depth interviews with each of the caretakers, we concluded that the key issue for them was their highly fragmented work. They were happy with the basics of their employment (pay, benefits, and job security) and liked their supervisor, but they found their jobs dull and almost without meaning. But they also said that they enjoyed animals and saw the work done in the laboratory as important. How, then, could their work be dull and meaningless?

The heart of the problem was that each caretaker was responsible for just one function: filling the food and water dishes, or cleaning the cages, or administering medications, or keeping daily records (of food intake, weight, and so on). The work became routine: cleaning out the cages in the same way every day with little or no use of higher-order skills and little or no sense of responsibility for, or impact on, the "customer"—the *whole* customer. As one caretaker put it, "My job is not to take care of the animal; it's to shovel s...."

Unlike the cookie packers, the animal caretakers greatly disliked their fragmented jobs. The solution was obvious and was put into effect: each caretaker was given his own group of animals and almost all of the responsibility for their care. This required some training of the caretakers in their various functions, including instruction in rudimentary diagnostic techniques to help them know their animals and their condition. The training and brief learning curves on the job were about the only costs incurred in making the transition to the enriched jobs.

Follow-up interviews uncovered significantly improved job satisfaction, including the feeling that their caretaker work was now, as they put it, "more professional." The veterinarian reported that, with the exception of one caretaker who continued to be a problem and was eventually dismissed, the performance problems had pretty much evaporated.

Almost by definition, a sense of accomplishment means completing something, doing a job from beginning to end so that a worker can see the fruits of her labors. But, as previously pointed out, this is not always easy to accomplish because doing the "whole job," on an automobile assembly line, for example, can result in severe efficiency losses.

As a general principle, every effort should be made, within the constraints of maintaining efficiency, to design work so that workers have a sense of completeness to their tasks. A second principle is that it is almost invariably desirable—and especially when efficiency issues severely limit providing complete tasks for individuals—to organize by self-managing teams (SMTs) that do have beginning-to-end responsibility for significant operations. As noted in the previous chapter, SMTs are delegated responsibility for tasks such as scheduling, assigning work, improving methods, taking care of maintenance, training on the job, and performing quality control. These are a complete and enriched set of responsibilities in which individual workers participate and from which, as a team, they obtain a sense of achievement and pride.

To the extent possible, the team should also be responsible and accountable for relationships with customers. This is important because it is primarily through the customer relationship that people learn whether their work has, indeed, made a difference. Although many employees do not have contact with external customers, everyone in an organization can be said to have a customer—if not external, then internal. In a manufacturing plant, for example, those who machine parts have those who assemble them as customers. Among the customers of product development are manufacturing and sales. The customers of staff groups, such as Human Resources and Information Technology, are the line divisions.

Chapter 11, "Teamwork," details the relationships between an organization's units, and between them and the external customers. Suffice it to say for now that effectiveness and job satisfaction are greatly enhanced by organizing the teams around identified customers and setting the primary goal of the teams as meeting the needs of their customers in an efficient manner.

Organizing around the customer allows employees to focus on customers and their needs, and, if communications channels are structured properly, it permits them to know the extent to which those needs are being met. We have said that making a difference—to customers, their company, perhaps to their profession—is important for employees' job satisfaction. What we have largely omitted from the discussion thus far is how employees know that they have made a difference. They might feel that they know based on self-evaluation, but that is usually inadequate. Clear and regular feedback is absolutely vital from those the work is meant to affect. Such feedback provides both the information workers need for evaluating and improving their performance and the recognition for good performance that is so crucial for maintaining a high level of worker motivation and morale. In the following chapter, we discuss feedback, recognition, and reward.

10 ———————————

Feedback, Recognition, and Reward

"I can live for two months on a good compliment!"
—Mark Twain

The previous chapters have focused on the satisfactions and dissatisfactions that are intrinsic to the work itself. We turn now to external sources of satisfaction and dissatisfaction. We are referring to that sense of achievement and accomplishment that comes from the opinions of others, especially the opinions of those whose views we respect or can influence our careers and earnings. Feedback from others also enables us to improve how we do our work and so obtain an even greater sense of achievement.

Do Workers Get the Feedback They Need?

The majority of employees (86 percent) in our surveys say that they know what is expected of them. However, only 63 percent claim to receive sufficient feedback on how well they do their work, and 64 percent say they receive recognition for a job well done. Most interestingly, only 37 percent of surveyed workers *disagree* with the statement, "I get criticized much more quickly for poor performance than praised for good performance," which means that the performance of many employees is more likely to be "recognized" in a negative sense: when it is deemed subpar more often than when it meets or exceeds a manager's expectations. The following comments, which respond to

313

the question, "What do you like *least* about working here?" exemplify that data:

> *Having to deal on a daily basis with my manager since every time he gives feedback, it is always negative. That is the only thing I think in the mornings when going to work. Am I going to get more of his negative feedback? I leave my house with a negative feeling, drive to work with a negative feeling. When I finally get here, my motivation is sapped.*

> *I will never, never, never—I repeat never—hear anything good from my supervisor about my work. It's as if praising an employee somehow lessens him. He simply has to be the only one who matters here. But make a mistake and he's on your back immediately.*

> *My manager is a pretty good guy and certainly knows his job but has to learn that you don't only give feedback to an employee when something goes wrong. He praises very, very rarely.*

We are told that some people are entirely "inner-directed." They don't care about the opinions of others, and they don't need external impetus or feedback to be productively engaged in their work. Where these people are, we don't know! Wouldn't it be terrific if all of us were so "inner-directed" that others' reactions to our work were irrelevant? Unfortunately, that is not human nature. Aside from the usefulness of feedback in providing direction to employees and helping them improve, human beings require some degree of attention and appreciation from others to perform at their best levels. When that performance is taken for granted by management, as in, "That's what we expect; why mention it?," employees and the company lose.

Considered most broadly, performance feedback is a vehicle for the following:

- **Guidance.** The steps an employee can take to improve his performance.
- **Evaluation.** How the organization regards the employee's performance in relation to expectations and to others. Is the employee doing well, poorly, or average?

- **Recognition.** Expressing appreciation for a job well done.
- **Reward.** Recognition translated into something tangible (usually money).
- **Direction.** Communicating or reinforcing what the organization needs, values, and expects from employees.

These five aspects and outcomes of feedback are vital to employees and the organization. Although most people have a sense of responsibility and want to do their jobs well, that motivation can wane rapidly *if no one seems to care.* On the other hand, if no one seems to care except when something goes wrong, motivation can quickly turn into resentment.

Let's take a thorough look at each of these functions of feedback.

Guidance

Guidance refers to the cognitive functions of feedback. It is the process of providing employees with empirical, objective information about their performance and how to improve it. This is not the same as *affective* feedback, which relates to evaluation, recognition, and reward. In real life, of course, cognitive and affective feedback are not so easily separated: it is difficult to communicate the errors a person makes without also conveying an evaluation of her performance. That is one of the major problems in providing the kind of feedback that employees accept and use rather than resist. We will return to this problem shortly, including suggestions as to how to deal with it.

At its most basic level, nobody can function in life (much less at work) without factual feedback. We do something and want to know whether what we did had the expected or desired effect. The source of feedback does not have to be human: we learn whether we combed our hair to our liking from a mirror; whether we're speeding from a speedometer; whether we get to work on time from a clock; whether we're exercising too hard from a heart monitor. Feedback allows us to modify our behavior; for example, we can decide to take a faster method of transportation when late for an appointment, and the next time we have the same appointment, we can decide to leave home earlier.

Critical to us as humans is feedback from other humans. Some feedback requires human intervention to give it real meaning, such as a doctor interpreting the results of a medical test for a patient. Some feedback can only be from other humans, like much of the feedback people get on the appropriateness of their behavior in daily life (whether, for example, their behavior conforms to basic civility and good manners).

At work, the most crucial feedback people can receive concerns their performance. Without feedback, there can be only a limited sense of achievement and opportunity to improve performance. Almost all organizations have numerous performance measures: profitability, sales, costs, delivery time, customer defections, productivity, defective parts, absenteeism, and the like. Ideally, the measures are designed into the business or work process so that they are provided automatically and frequently—sometimes continuously—to the organization and its employees.

Even the most comprehensive and most automatic measurement systems almost invariably require human intervention. By themselves, numbers have limited meaning within organizations. What matters is how management and employees interpret those numbers. How do the numbers, for example, stack up against management's expectations? Are the changes observed in the measures—improvements or decrements—considered significant by the organization? Do other events, such as the introduction of new equipment or a change in general economic conditions, account for variations in the measures? How do the measures compare to each other (say, an increase in quality accompanied by a decrease in productivity), and what is the significance of that comparison? In general, what is the relative importance of the various measures? (They are rarely of equal importance.)

The answers to these questions are vital to making sense of the numbers and to enable both the organization and the employee to decide on a proper course of action. If, for example, the productivity of an employee declines soon after the introduction of new equipment but declines less than what was expected, it is likely that no action would be required of that employee and management might even reward him in some way. If, on the other hand, an employee's performance improves but is less than what's expected (say, months after the use of the new equipment has been fully integrated into the employee's work), that could signal the need for corrective action. The action might include greater clarity in what is expected from the employee or additional coaching on using the new equipment.

Both the employee who performs well and the employee whose performance is below expectations need feedback, not just from the "numbers," but from a manager capable of interpreting the numbers and conveying their meaning. Part of what is also being conveyed to the employee is, of course, direction: what really matters to management in the employee's performance and behavior. (We return to that function of feedback later in this chapter.)

Giving performance feedback is easier said than done. Many managers consider it among their most difficult tasks. Here is a comment about giving performance reviews from a manager's perspective:

> *The annual performance reviews I am required to conduct with my 12 direct reports is the one thing I hate about this job. I always put it off until I'm called by the HR Department and forced to do it. My employees often can't take the criticism... they argue with me. They say they're surprised at what I said and all they want to know is about the size of their salary increase. I try to make them as brief as possible, get them over with as soon as possible. Sure, I slant them toward the positive. Who needs the trouble? Yes, I'll put in something that "needs improvement" so I won't be bothered by my boss or HR; it's just a game. By the way, I haven't ever been appraised by*

> *my manager, who is the VP of Manufacturing, since I can't remem-*
> *ber when. He hates to do it, too, but HR won't get after him about it.*

This comment is not atypical: by and large, managers dislike (a few even dread) giving performance appraisals; they want to get them over with as quickly as possible and with as little trouble as possible. Some managers claim that it is a problem of time and onerous paper-work, ranking up there with organizing file cabinets.

The problem, however, is not confined to the formal performance appraisal. Providing informal day-to-day feedback throughout the year can also be difficult for managers. Comments such as this one are often heard:

> *I would like to hear from my manager now and then. You know,*
> *informally about how he feels I'm doing—might be with a few tips*
> *on how I can improve and might be a compliment from time to*
> *time. But we only speak about my performance at my annual per-*
> *formance appraisal, when I'm often surprised about what he likes*
> *and doesn't like about my performance. The only time I hear from*
> *him other than appraisal time is the rare occasion I have screwed*
> *up royally. He reads me the riot act and I probably deserve it, but*
> *it always takes me by surprise. When appraisal time rolls around, I*
> *expect the worst. It usually goes okay, but I'm always nervous before*
> *we sit down and go through my appraisal numbers.*

A Short Course on Giving Cognitive Feedback

Performance feedback is done less frequently than it should be, and when it is done, it may be poorly handled. It does not have to be so. A large amount of research has been done on the conditions that make for effective feedback.[1] From these studies, specific guidelines for managers have emerged. Adhering to these makes performance feedback less onerous for managers and more helpful to employees. Here are the key guidelines.

1. Do Not Equate Performance Feedback with the Annual Performance Appraisal

Managers often make this big mistake. Aside from the fact that many such appraisals tend to be somewhat perfunctory and, to avoid unpleasantness, are positively biased, reserving feedback for that time—even when it is comprehensive and unbiased—violates a basic principle of learning and change: namely, that feedback should be given as closely in time as possible to the actual situation. If an employee is performing unsatisfactorily in some way, it should be obvious that he needs to know about it then and there so that the behavior does not continue. (This is also true of recognition and the reinforcement of good performance; we discuss that later in this chapter.) Many of the difficulties encountered during performance appraisal sessions come from employees being surprised by what they hear.

The extent to which employees learn something entirely new about their performance during the appraisal review is a measure of the *failure* of the performance-review process. The purposes of an annual review are to summarize, in the form of ratings and commentary, the employee's performance over the year; to more fully discuss that performance and the effectiveness of the improvement steps the employee has undertaken to improve (including what the *manager* can do to help the employee); to discuss the implications of the performance for salary increases and other rewards; and to put in place plans for the next year, such as setting the employee's performance goals.

The formal annual appraisal session, then, is a mechanism for closure on one year and for planning the next. Also, it provides time away from immediate job pressures to simply talk about topics of relevance to the employee and his manager. In many organizations, this is a rare opportunity for a conversation that is more than perfunctory. Managers should be *required* to do it, and do it with the attitude and tools that these guidelines suggest.

2. Don't Assume That Employees Are Only Interested in Receiving Praise for What They Do Well and Resent Having Areas in Need of Improvement Pointed Out to Them

People enjoy being praised and prefer praise to criticism, but it is a myth that they have no interest in learning what they don't do well and what they must do to improve. This is not a hypothetical statement or wishful thinking. Take a look at some common types of write-in comments:

> *I love my supervisor. He is one of the best managers I have had since I have been here. He encourages us to do well and keeps us well informed of what we need to do, and he gives us feedback in a calm, helpful way when we do something wrong. I find what he says very helpful and I listen very carefully.*

> *My manager assists me with an actionable plan for my current job, things I can do better, as well as my career/professional development. He provides avenues for growth and development. In fact, his manager and he make up a great management team. It's a real education working for them.*

> *My supervisor is...fair and willing to listen to our feedback, but she also doesn't hold back when she feels something needs improvement. She readily tries to find solutions to any and all situations or problems and is more than willing to join us in resolving issues. I feel fortunate to have her as my supervisor. She is a good manager and friend.*

> *For the last three months, my team has a new...leader who is dedicated and honest and provides us with all the information we need to measure our success. Before, I was never given any [feedback during the year]; I was always told by my previous supervisor my job was great. The big surprise was at the end of the year when I was given what I considered a marginal rating. There were obviously improvement opportunities nobody ever made me aware of. Thank heavens this will not happen with my current team leader.*

It should not be a surprise that employees really do want feedback. Employees naturally want to know how they can do their jobs better because improvement will give them a greater sense of achievement and pride. Why, then, do managers so often assume the opposite and hesitate to point out to employees opportunities for improvement?

One reason is that a few employees are extremely thin-skinned and find even a hint of criticism intolerable. They might even see criticism where none exists, exhibiting a bit of paranoia. Such employees are difficult to deal with in this respect, but, fortunately, they comprise just a tiny percentage of any workforce. As with the small numbers of people "allergic to work" discussed earlier, do not generalize to everybody else based on just a few employees. Although many employees do seem to resist feedback and be overly sensitive to criticism, that is not primarily because of employees' psychological problems, but rather is a result of the way managers handle feedback.[2]

A second reason, therefore, for managers' hesitation in providing feedback is that many managers simply do not know how to discuss needed improvements in their employees' work without irritating or discouraging them. So they tend to avoid it entirely or deal with it through vague and indirect communications, or, most commonly, oscillate between saying little or nothing and, when that is no longer possible (as in "the last straw"), overreact in a harsh way that surprises and angers employees.

Of course, some managers neither hold back nor oscillate in their criticism; they are the managers who don't much care what employees think, and they can be unrelenting in finding fault with the performance of their employees. These managers are inclined to believe that workers don't want to work (or are careless or stupid) and that their performance will always be deficient unless they are continually reminded of what they are doing wrong and the consequences of not improving. Interestingly, we find this management style to be as common—perhaps even more so—in the way managers treat other managers who report to them (especially in the treatment meted out by high-level executives) as in the way non-managerial employees are treated by their managers. In some companies, managers are subject by their bosses to much verbal abuse, including humiliation in front of their peers. After all, senior management argues, isn't "being able to take it" one of the reasons managers are paid a high salary? "If they can't stand the heat, they should get out of the kitchen." How do these people actually react to that kind of treatment? Here are just three examples from managers:

> *My manager treats all his direct reports equally, that is, without respect and dignity. He's like a tyrant who only gives feedback when he is unhappy with something. He rants and raves, and doesn't do this in the privacy of his office. He doesn't care who is around, even the people who work for me.*

> *There is a total lack of respect and a general condescending attitude by our management. This is a daily and constant reminder of managerial incompetence and the lack of direction in which this establishment is headed. What is preached, respect, is blatantly not practiced. I and my colleagues don't behave that way with our employees. How did these upper-level managers get where they are?*

> *He [the CEO] treats the workers with kid gloves, he's like their father. With us, he's usually a first-class [expletive deleted]. He even blasts us for doing something he asked us to do because he changed his mind. Nobody dares answer back or question him; he's the king.*

Whatever the pattern, managers may not have good role models when it comes to giving feedback. As they observe employees' and their own reactions to the process, their belief is reinforced that performance feedback can be a difficult and unenviable job. But we know that there are managers who are good at it: they don't procrastinate in getting it done, and they get the performance results they want with little distress for themselves or their employees. It comes down to a matter of skill (to be discussed in detail later in this chapter) and to the fundamental assumptions that managers make about people at work. Do managers assume that their employees want to do the best job possible and would appreciate management's observations and guidance about their performance? Or do they believe that employees don't care about doing a good job and so have to be bludgeoned into doing any work at all or doing the work correctly? Or do they believe that employees care about doing good work so much and their egos are so fragile that pointing out any performance problems would be considered a mortal wound?

Our view is that besides a small minority of employees (those "allergic" to work and those inordinately sensitive to criticism), the first assumption is valid: employees want to perform well and learn how they can improve. If a manager operates on the basis of that assumption, he will succeed, provided he follows a few basic guidelines, such as those we spell out here. But, without accepting that basic premise, these guidelines become meaningless.

To summarize, feedback needs to proceed from a manager's intentions to help and guide his employees. The goal should be learning, not venting, shaming, or lambasting.

3. An Employee Whose Overall Performance Is Satisfactory and Appreciated by the Organization Needs to Be Made Aware of That

In the course of an employee doing his job, the work is usually satisfactory, and even outstanding at times, but occasionally it will not be good enough. That pattern is true of the overwhelming majority in every organization, and it is vital that an employee understands that management sees his performance that way. In other words, most everyone is good, but nobody's perfect, and it is to the employee's and organization's benefit that striving for improvement be continual and normal. (We discuss later on the case of poor performers who should never have been hired into their jobs or into the organization.)

We have seen that many employees agree with the statement, "A person here gets criticized much more quickly for poor performance than praised for good performance." That management style makes people uneasy about management's view of their *overall* performance and contribution to the organization. It is then difficult for an employee to feel anything but insecurity and resentment when criticized on any aspect of his performance, no matter how valid and needed the criticism is and how small the object of criticism is relative to the employee's total performance.

It is easier for employees to accept the need for improvement—in fact, many welcome it—when they believe that management basically likes what they do and is helping them do it even better. Believing that their contribution is genuinely appreciated requires more than being told from time to time in general terms, "We are happy with your work here." To be accepted as genuine, general comments and evaluations require a factual basis that is achieved by recognition of specific accomplishments, such as, "That report you wrote is great. I especially liked the part where you...."

Being specific in your praise diminishes the feeling that the praise is given for effect (a sort of public-relations gesture) and is helpful in pointing out the areas of performance that the employee needs to maintain. This brings us to the importance of specificity in dealing with improvement opportunities.

4. Comments About Areas That Need Improvement Should Be Specific and Factual Rather Than Evaluative, and Directed at the Situation Rather Than the Person

Positive feedback and feedback about improvement needs are similar in that both require the manager to be as specific and factual as possible. Although comments on positive aspects of performance should, indeed, convey a positive evaluation, it is better to avoid a negative tone when pointing out a need for improvement.

It is helpful to say, "You did a good job on this," but it is not helpful to say, "You did a poor job on this." Instead, you might say, "Here is something that I think needs to be done differently." Terms such as "good," "great," "excellent," and "first class," especially when accompanied by the specifics that support those evaluations, build pride in employees and reinforce the performance so that it is sustained. But is there any point to saying to an otherwise satisfactorily performing employee that she did a "poor," "shoddy," "unprofessional," or "below standard" job on something? She already knows that a problem exists because a manager has told her and is being specific about the problem. Adding an evaluative comment is likely to discourage or offend the employee and, in the long run, diminish her motivation and performance.

It gets worse when the negative evaluative comment is directed at the person rather than the person's performance. This is seen most commonly in critical comments about the supposed disposition or intention of the employee, such as, "You must not have been paying attention when you did that," "You must find it difficult to change and do it a different way," or even, "You must have gotten up on the wrong side of the bed this morning." Although the manager might feel he is being helpful with these remarks, the employee views them as attacks on his character and reacts with defensiveness. Furthermore, managers are not being paid or asked by the organization or their employees to be psychologists. Engaging in amateur psychology is often a power-play anyway (it says, "I can see into you"), and employees feel that and resent it. To summarize, stick to what the employee *does* rather than what he *is*.

There are exceptions to the recommendation to avoid negative evaluations of the employee's performance. First, the formal performance appraisal is a time when the manager needs to rate the employee on various dimensions of performance, and these might not be favorable: "You did well on this aspect of your performance, but not on this." Obviously, we all would like to receive positive rather than negative performance evaluations, but because the formal appraisal sums up the year and can be the basis for rewards such as salary increases, the manager can't, in our view, escape that responsibility.

Furthermore, employees expect and want to know how their performance over the course of the year stacks up in management's eyes. The negative effects of unfavorable ratings are greatly mitigated if, as per our guidelines, the evaluations have a factual basis and are unsurprising because they are, indeed, a summary of the feedback the employee received throughout the year.

The second exception to the recommendation regarding unfavorable evaluations is the case of the truly unsatisfactory employee; he has to know and must know early. (We discuss this situation later in this chapter.)

5. Feedback Needs to Be Limited to Those Aspects of Employee Behavior That Relate to Performance

In their performance feedback, some managers dwell on aspects of employee behavior that are personally objectionable to the manager but are unrelated, or only marginally related, to the employee's performance or to the organization's success. These aspects might be completely outside the work situation, such as the way the employee spends her leisure time, gets along with her spouse, or raises her children. On the job, some managers are overly concerned and critical about employees' dress, even when it is wholly within the bounds of appropriate work attire. One employee complained bitterly in an interview about his manager's dislike of his southern accent.

Indeed, many aspects of what an employee does on the job or the way he lives are truly none of the manager's business or are trivial and reflect little more than a manager's personal preferences and prejudices. Some managers see themselves as parental figures who provide "helpful" guidance to employees about all things, whether it's wanted or not, whether it's related to job performance or not, and whether it's important or not. The manager must try to stick to the job and those factors that significantly affect job results. Advice on other matters should be given only when the employee seeks it (assuming the manager has knowledge in those areas).

6. When Giving Performance Feedback, Encourage Two-Way Communication

When giving feedback, it is almost always sensible to involve the employee in determining what the problem is and what to do about it. Obviously, this isn't wise when the employee is so new on the job that asking his opinion adds no value. It also shouldn't be done those few times when the manager is absolutely certain she knows what needs to be done and just wants the employee to do it. Engaging the employee in a participative conversation then—other than to clarify what the manager wants—is likely to be seen as manipulative by the employee. Other than those occasions, the manager needs to ask the employee what he thinks and should genuinely listen to him. After all, the employee is on the job, and his experience and observations must be taken into account to determine how a performance problem is to be overcome, including what the manager might be doing to harm the employee's performance. A real conversation also makes the employee more of a "partner" in the improvement process rather than simply a target of criticism. It helps create an atmosphere in which the employee feels comfortable initiating questions of his manager that will help him improve his work.

7. Remember That the Goal of Feedback Is Action That Improves Performance

This guideline is obvious, but it is violated in a number of ways. The first example is when the manager assumes that the issue is the employee's will or character, in which case he simply admonishes the employee to, "Pay attention to what you're doing!," or "Get moving, we need more from you!," or "Stop talking with everyone!" Those comments are appropriate for only a few workers, the ones for whom insufficient motivation is indeed the problem. However, they are unhelpful to the great majority of employees and convey disrespect for them. What is needed is a specific, doable action plan that attacks the problem, not the person, as is shown in the following example (which is fictionalized from actual events):

> *Manager: I'd like to talk to you about meeting deadlines for reports that my boss asked you to prepare. I think you missed a couple of deadlines recently.*
>
> *Employee: I didn't realize these requests had specific deadlines. He just dropped by my desk and, in a low-key manner, asked me to obtain some information.*
>
> *Manager: That's his style. Please remember to translate any request he makes as urgent. I had the same problem early in my career. You might want to ask him when he wants this. He's likely to say as soon as possible. This usually means he wants you to start on it right away and have it to him in a day or two. I realize this puts you in a difficult situation. Feel free to come to me when he makes his next request.*

A second way this rule is violated is to require action that is not in the immediate control of the person to whom the feedback is given. Remember that the action must be doable; making it so might require resources outside of the employee's immediate control. Here's an example of a manager really "going to bat" for her employee. This is what you want to see happen (and read in your company survey):

> *My leader is... open and honest, and I am able to be the same with her. She is always available to assist me and goes out of her way to assist with my development. For example, I didn't understand the new system changes well enough. She not only provided me some materials to read and forwarded the relevant training courses available, but also put me in touch with an expert to call whenever I had a problem. I don't think I would still be here if it wasn't for her.*

The third major way in which this rule is violated is when an employee is so overwhelmed with identified problems and action steps that he simply does nothing or does things in a superficial way. A good rule of thumb is to have the employee work on no more than two or three significant action items at any time. Arriving at these requires prioritization, which is governed by what is most doable and what has the most impact on performance.

8. Follow Up and Reinforce

For most action steps following feedback, the manager needs to follow up with the employee to assess progress: whether action has been taken, what the results were, and what, if anything, still needs to be done. Follow-up also gives the manager an opportunity to compliment the employee on the changes made, which positively reinforces the behavior. Furthermore, the act of following up—and the employee knowing that it will occur—emphasizes to the employee the importance of taking action.

9. Provide Feedback Only in Areas in Which You Are Competent

We leave the most obvious guideline for last: know what you are talking about. Our guidelines, as focused as they have been on how feedback should be conveyed, cannot substitute for inaccuracies and gaps in what is conveyed to an employee. Only under duress will employees pay attention to feedback from managers who know little or nothing about the workers' jobs. We see this problem frequently when the organization hires recent college graduates into supervisory jobs. These new supervisors find themselves managing workers who have been on those jobs for years and who, in many respects, are more knowledgeable than their managers. We often see comments such as this from frustrated workers:

> This company must stop hiring these young hotshots into front-line supervisory positions just because they have college diplomas. They come on the job and tell us what to do, but they know diddly squat. They think they can learn the job in a day or a week, but it takes years to know what's really going on with the machinery, by working with those who really know what's what. In the old days, the

*foremen rose through the ranks. We respected them because they
knew the job at least as well as we did.*

Be modest and honest about what you know, and get the right kind of
help for the worker. When we discuss advancement later in this chapter, we question the wisdom of most of the hiring that is done directly
into managerial positions.

We conclude our discussion of cognitive feedback with a brief
mention of a technique increasingly being used—namely, "360"
feedback. Thus far, our focus has been primarily on feedback from
managers to employees. Through the 360 process, ratings on various aspects of performance are gathered from a variety of sources in
addition to the manager, especially subordinates (if the employee is
a manager), peers, and internal and external customers (hence "360"
for 360 degrees, or feedback from a number of angles). 360 feedback
is valuable precisely because it provides data from multiple sources
and perspectives. (Other terms for the technique are multi-source
and multi-rater feedback.) A manager may be personally biased in his
evaluations of employees, but even if not biased may be unaware of
crucial aspects of employees' behavior, such as the way they interact
with their peers. There is quite a bit of research data supporting the
effectiveness of 360 feedback in changing behavior, particularly when
the process is facilitated and supported by follow-up counseling.[3]

Evaluation, Recognition, and Reward

We come now to the affective or evaluative side of feedback, which
is the manager's and the organization's judgment of *how well* the
employee is doing and what the implications are of that judgment.

In our previous discussion of cognitive feedback, it was impossible to ignore entirely the affective side. Although it is desirable to
avoid evaluative comments when the feedback concerns improvement needs, we don't want to separate facts from evaluation when the

employee does something well. In that case, evaluation and facts are inseparable because nothing needs to change in the employee's performance, so there's no reason for any feedback other than to praise and thank the employee for a job well done.

How important is employee recognition for generating enthusiasm and maintaining good performance? On the surface, it might not seem to be terribly important. From the organization's perspective, isn't the company already *paying* the employee for good performance? But providing such recognition is vital: *receiving recognition for one's achievements is among the most fundamental of human needs,* from early in life—think of young children eagerly awaiting their parents' praise for their accomplishments in school—to and through adulthood, even though it may not be as visible then. Just as parents do well by their children when they express admiration for their children's "work," so do managers when they praise their employees' contributions. In our interviews and the write-in questions on our surveys, workers tell us with deep feeling how much they appreciate a compliment.

When managers do not bother to acknowledge high levels of employee performance, the effect is discouraging to most employees and devastating to some.

The desire for recognition of one's achievements is neither childish nor neurotic. Freud, the pre-eminent student of both childhood and neuroses (and the relationship between the two), is said to have quipped at his 80th birthday party that, "An individual can tolerate infinite helpings of praise." We sometimes hear people deny that recognition is important to them; a worker might say "forget the praise; just give me the money," but their behavior belies this assertion. We did a study once at a media organization in which a tough chief executive scoffed at high-priced employees craving professional recognition. However, those employees reported that when the CEO was passed over for a prestigious industry award, there was much fulminating and stomping around his office.

Of course, the desire for recognition can also be extreme and dysfunctional. We see this in some people in the way their need for praise is insatiable: they require it continuously, often for achievements not particularly noteworthy, and become depressed or agitated when it is not forthcoming. Furthermore, they are not too discriminating about the sources of the recognition: they want it from everyone, from people they respect and from those they disdain, from those with power and from those with no influence over their careers. Often, they are the employees we see vying for the spotlight and grabbing credit for achievements that are either not theirs or not solely theirs. They tend to be noisy and visible (often whiny), but as with the other needs we have discussed, this extreme constitutes a tiny percentage of the workforce.

Psychologically healthy people want to be recognized for their genuine achievements and are concerned primarily with the opinions of those whom they admire and, because they are realistic, with the opinions of those who can help or hurt their careers.

Before continuing this discussion, let's reiterate the difference between recognition for performance and respectful treatment of workers (the latter was the subject of Chapter 6, "Respect.") As we use the term, respect is a matter of equity that's owed to employees simply by virtue of their employment, just as they are owed a living wage as long as they are employed. Respect, in other words, is a function of who they are—employees and human beings. On the other hand, recognition is for what they *do*: how they are performing for and contributing to the organization. Respect and recognition are not entirely independent, of course. The term recognition has two meanings: to acknowledge someone's performance, and to acknowledge someone's existence. The latter is a mark of respect in the workplace, such as managers being sure to say hello to employees and referring to them by name. That is important to a worker but is not the kind of recognition that is the subject of this chapter. For recognition, the parallel comment is, "Thank you!" Whether, how much, and how a worker is thanked varies with the worker's performance. That differs from respect, which dictates that everyone deserves a hello. The importance of recognition is evident in the panoply of awards (both financial and nonfinancial) dispensed by public, private, and nonprofit organizations throughout America and, indeed, the world. The range is enormous, from Nobel Prizes, Oscars, and building and street names for the famous (or soon-to-be famous) to company pins, plaques, gold watches, and various cash awards for the obscure (and now less obscure). These are the formal means of recognition, and organizations understand that they meet deeply felt needs. Unfortunately, these formal means might be administered in a way that severely dilutes their impact or even boomerangs to the detriment of the employees and the organization. It is also unfortunate that when executives think of employee recognition in their organizations, they usually equate that with formal recognition programs and give not nearly as much attention to informal recognition, such as managers acknowledging good performance day-to-day on the shop or office floor. Or, they equate recognition with the compensation system—pay, pay increases, bonuses, stock awards, and so on. In that view, recognition programs, if they exist, are seen as "icing on the cake"—nice to have, but not really at the heart of what employees want, which is money.

What Makes for Effective Recognition of Workers?

There are four major means to recognize employees. No one vehicle, such as money, suffices to provide the recognition to employees that is most important to them and beneficial for the organization:

- **Compensation.** Providing differential compensation to employees based on their performance.

- **Informal recognition.** Day-to-day recognition of performance, most importantly by the immediate manager.

- **Honorifics.** Special awards given as part of formal awards programs and that may be accompanied by cash for an employee's performance.

- **Promotion.** Advancement to higher-level positions for performance.

First, we will consider compensation, informal recognition, and honorifics, all of which involve just the current job of the employee and require no criteria for their exercise other than performance. We will then discuss the role of advancement to higher-level jobs.

Management can use compensation, informal recognition, and honorifics to recognize employees either individually or in groups. The three methods are independent of each other in certain respects and interdependent in other ways. They are independent because each is important in its own right and cannot be substituted for each other. In previous chapters, we took strong exception to the view that satisfaction with the work itself can be substituted for money, and the corollary proposition that when workers complain about pay, they are really complaining about unsatisfying work. We argued that workers want *both* (and more), and to neglect either will significantly diminish employee satisfaction and motivation.

Similarly, we take issue with those who argue that only money serves to give workers genuine recognition, or, at the opposite extreme, that all they "really" crave is "attention" or "esteem" (and that a focus on money is a displacement brought on by their frustration in not getting what they really want). And so, some suggest that the basic human need to feel appreciated can be satisfied by recognition programs and no-cost job-recognition devices.[4] This advice might comfort managements trying to economize, but it is unhelpful—and even dangerous—because it ignores money's importance to people and can cause managers to believe that they can manipulate and "psychologize" people and save on labor costs. They can't—not for long, anyway. It doesn't matter that part of the power of money is its symbolic or psychological significance. Whether symbolic or practical, it is of great importance to most people and cannot be satisfied with nonfinancial rewards.

Psychological rewards are not a substitute for money, but managers should not make the opposite error, which is believing that money can be a substitute for psychological recognition. Both are important. For example, a high-level executive in an investment bank told one of the authors, in the late 1980s, about an experience he had with the bank's chairman. It was the end of the year and bonuses were being distributed. The chairman came into the executive's office, gave him an envelope with his bonus check, and said, "This is for you," and walked out. The check was for $500,000. The executive was discouraged and angry. "Why didn't he say anything to me?" he asked. "I have no idea what he really thinks of my performance and whether he cares whether I stay or leave. He never tells me."

This sounds nutty. Shouldn't $500,000 be enough? Doesn't the amount of money speak for itself? No, it doesn't. It is terribly important that employees also *hear* from their management directly and personally that their performance is appreciated. Employees in that company describe the chairman as keeping employees on a "slippery slope," perpetually anxious about his evaluation of them. When he meets employees in the hallways, he almost invariably "greets" them by mentioning something that *hasn't* gone well in their area of responsibility or something they haven't done. The chairman has a difficult time expressing appreciation to others, even when giving them large bonuses; that, of course, would be an ideal time to do so. The executive left the company about six months later because, as he put it in a private conversation, it was "an opportunity I couldn't refuse," and "I could no longer take [chairman's name]."

The needs for both money and nonfinancial rewards are important. Neither can replace the other. There are also, however, two senses in which they are interdependent. First, they are multiplicative—not just additive—in their effects. Put negatively, if one form of recognition is absent, not only is the total effect reduced, it is reduced by more than would be expected simply by its absence. This is because it also diminishes the impact of the other form of recognition. We saw this clearly in the previous example in which not getting a "thank you" reduced the positive impact of a substantial bonus. By the same logic, *adding* one form of recognition to another increases the value of the latter. Consider honorifics, which are the formal awards programs of organizations. The lesson of our argument for those programs is that their impact on employees is usually increased when money accompanies them. As in the investment bank case, adding words of appreciation to the bonus would have increased its value for the executive, so adding money to an award conveys to an employee that the organization really means it because it is putting its money where its mouth is. To be most effective, then, most formal awards programs require both mouth and money. Although the money involved is no substitute for basic kinds of compensation (salary increases, bonuses, and so on), it should be substantial enough to be seen as more than just a token.

Our argument does not, of course, imply that day-to-day informal recognition be accompanied by money. But what is said informally loses its impact if it is not reflected at the appropriate time in the employee's compensation.

The three means of recognition are also interdependent in that they need to be consistent with each other in the criteria used for recognition. For example, if a company has embarked on a quality improvement effort—at least in its public statements—it is likely to use its formal awards programs to recognize employees for quality contributions and to do so in a public way. In day-to-day informal communications and recognition and in compensation (such as pay increases), the message might be different: if it is then really quantity that counts, the messages are inconsistent and counterproductive. It's the kind of contradiction that creates confusion among employees as to what management wants and skepticism about management's integrity; those severely compromise the impact of an organization's recognition efforts. The criteria must be aligned, and this should be achieved by aligning each with the organization's real goals and values. In that way, employees are rewarded, and the goals of the organization are advanced and its values reinforced.

To be most effective, therefore, organizations must think of recognition as a *cluster* of components integrated with each other and with the organization's goals and values.

How is recognition best implemented? There are a number of basic principles here, some of which we touched on earlier:

- **Be specific about what is being recognized.** The employee needs to be praised for concrete achievements. This both reinforces the particular behaviors that the manager wants to see repeated and, in the eyes of the employee, increases the credibility of the praise.

- **Do it in person.** Although this might sound obvious, recognition by long distance or proxy is not nearly as effective as face-to-face recognition.

- **Be timely.** Give recognition as soon as possible after the desired behavior. By and large, the greater the interval between the completion of a behavior and the delivery of a reinforcing consequence, the less effective is the reinforcement. This advice is wonderfully summarized in the phrase "catch them at being good." Catching people in the act, as it were, is usually reserved for misdeeds, but applying the same principle to good performance is exactly what managers should do.

  The guidance regarding timeliness is applicable primarily to informal feedback. The other forms of recognition—compensation and honorifics—cannot normally be done at the moment and on the spot. However, they are important to formally "reinforce the reinforcement" and to demonstrate to the workforce that the organization backs its words with money and public recognition. Taken together, as we have said, the three means of recognition constitute a powerful package.

- **Be sincere.** This is an odd piece of advice; after all, a manager either means praise sincerely or he doesn't. We can do nothing to help a manager who does not genuinely appreciate her employees' performance. Some managers never do—they truly believe that only their efforts count—and this book is not an instruction manual in acting sincerely. Other managers, however, are sincere in their praise, yet it doesn't come across that way to their employees. They might be so general in what they say or so tardy in when they say it that expressing appreciation seems to employees like something a manager feels he has to do rather than something he genuinely wants to do. Or, he might give mixed messages about an employee's performance, such as, "You did well on that, but...," or "Thank goodness you finally got that right." Perhaps because of their own discomfort, managers might undermine the effect with "humor," saying something like, "You've done such a good job, you would never know that you had an MBA," or "He's so loyal to the company, he hasn't seen his family in months." Managers can overdo it, exaggerating the achievement with meaningless flattery, such as, "The most wonderful...," "the greatest...," "never in the history of the company...." Although much of the advice about how to give recognition—and perhaps recognition itself—might seem trite and even corny, be assured that recognition is vitally important to employees and that employees listen carefully to every word that is said when it is given. The simpler and more direct the compliment, the better, such as, "You did a great job on... and I want you to know that. I especially liked... Thank you very much." If the praise is exaggerated or too flowery, it won't be believable. If it is a mixed message, the employee most remembers the negative comment or implication, even if the manager finishes on a positive note. Simply stated, people want honest and deserved acknowledgment of their contributions and, when received, it is greatly appreciated. Don't spoil it.

- **Recognition should be given for both group and individual performance.** In our chapter on compensation, we suggested that, for most employees, pay for performance should be based on group accomplishments. We argued that individual reward schemes (such as piecework and merit pay) can be administrative and employee-relations nightmares that result in many employees feeling no sense of reward, and that they tend to diminish teamwork. But we must still deal with the fact that in a group some individuals contribute more than others (perhaps much more). Should—and how do—these people get recognized? In part, recognition is obtained from co-workers, especially when the pay or bonus is group based. An outstanding contributor is valued by the group under that condition because his work is financially beneficial to all (which is in contrast to the "rate buster" within individual pay systems who is ostracized because his high performance is detrimental to his co-workers).

Fully employing the three means of recognition allows both individuals and groups to receive due acknowledgment for their efforts. Although we suggest that for most workers compensation for performance be based on group performance, informal recognition by the manager will usually be given to individuals. And, as the occasion warrants, the manager will also bring the entire group together for a collective thank-you.

Honorifics, which are the formal awards, also need to be distributed to both individuals and groups. However, these should, in our view, be reserved largely for truly outstanding achievements: the organization's "Nobel Prizes." We suggest dispensing with the multitude of recognition awards distributed by some organizations, such as gift certificates, reserved parking spaces, dinner-for-two, and employee-of-the-month. After they are in place for a period of time, our attitude surveys never show anything better than a lukewarm response to these programs. Indeed, they generate numerous complaints, especially about who is selected for the awards and the mystery that normally surrounds the selection process. The workforce should greet programs of this type with enthusiasm—after all, they are designed to provide recognition—but they seem to have the opposite effect on most employees. Upon hearing of the complaints, management often revises the programs to distribute the awards more widely so people don't feel excluded. As recognition for performance, most of these programs then become increasingly meaningless.

Our suggestion, then, is to have just one program (or very few) and to limit these to truly outstanding contributions. The awards should be for both individuals and groups, and the choice of awardees needs to be made by a panel that includes the employees' peers. Including peers goes a long way toward reducing the mystery and enhances the perceived fairness of the selection process.

Advancement

We have discussed recognition and rewards within the context of the employee's current job. However, one of the most powerful rewards for many employees is the opportunity for a promotion to a higher-level position within the organization. It is powerful because it delivers a number of rewards simultaneously: more money; more status; often, a more challenging, interesting, and influential job; and public recognition.

A major issue for employees is the degree to which their companies are committed to promoting from within. To be a bit facetious, companies can be categorized into two kinds: those that do their utmost to promote from within, and those for whom current employees are, in effect, "soiled goods." As one manager in a client company described his organization's philosophy when searching for a new executive,"I guess we feel that anyone who works here can't be too smart, so we'd better get someone from the outside." This frustration is found often in write-in comments:

> *Current opportunities for personal growth through promotion... are severely limited... this company brings in many people from the outside to fill critical managerial and professional positions. I don't believe mechanisms are in place here to identify the best candidates within the company for positions when they come open.*

> *My biggest problems with this company are recognition, growth, and promotion from within as opposed to bringing so many people into leadership roles from outside the company.*

> *Despite messages to the contrary, I see no evidence that senior management in my business unit here are interested in promoting from within. Do they really think all the talent is on the outside? How about experience with our company and our products—doesn't that count?*

Organizations that do not adhere to a promote-from-within philosophy lose out in a number of ways:

- They send a message that they don't have much respect for their own employees' competence, so they lose out on the commitment and enthusiasm that respect for people generates.

- They lose out on the motivational impact of promotions and promotion prospects, which causes ambitious employees to feel stagnant and frustrated.

- They lose out on the edge that an experienced workforce—experienced in *that* business and industry—gives to an organization.

- They lose out on the stability of organizational goals and culture.

- They lose out on the recruitment and training costs that hiring entails.

Companies give three main reasons for not promoting from within to higher-level job openings. The most common reason is that the right persons for the positions cannot be found within the organization or significantly better persons are available on the outside. Another reason is that the organization is in such trouble—or is so stagnant—that "new blood" must be brought in. Lastly, it is argued that "high potential" people need to be hired for whom open positions—usually first-level management—provide "developmental" opportunities. These arguments make sense theoretically and are certainly valid in specific instances. If, for example, there is a need for a particular type of specialist that cannot be found within the company, that specialist will have to be hired.

However, the research that has been done supports overwhelmingly the proposition that, on the average, organizations that adhere to a promote-from-within policy perform much better than those that do not. For example, in *Built to Last*,[5] Collins and Porras conclude from their research on higher- versus lower-performing companies that the former "... develop, promote, and carefully select managerial talent from inside the company to a greater degree than the comparison (lower-performing) companies...." In fact, the CEOs of the higher-performing companies were six times more likely to be insiders promoted from within.[6]

Some executives talk interminably about the flaws of the people who work for them. But when describing someone they are about to hire, that person has no imperfections; it seems that "hope springs eternal." This is largely a pipe dream because the perfect executive does not exist, and this is discovered—sometimes with shock and dismay—after the new person is on board. The right—not the perfect—person for the job is usually under management's noses, if only they had looked. If that person is not there, it was probably not for lack of raw material, but because that material was not developed as it would have been if an effective management succession and development program had been in place. Or, the right person was not found because qualified people left the organization, having become frustrated with the lack of opportunity for them.

It is imperative that the company first seek all possible internal candidates for an opening. To be fully effective, this policy obviously must be accompanied by programs for the identification and development of the organization's talent.

Should companies promote only the best performers? This is an interesting and troublesome question, mostly because of the perceived danger of promoting workers to levels above their competence. The best engineer might not be the best engineering manager, or the best salesperson the best sales manager. But if the best-performing people are not promoted, wouldn't that impair their motivation and enthusiasm? Yes, it would, and although it would be ludicrous to suggest that a promotion always go to the best performer (that employee might really be unsuited for the job), it needs to be always offered to someone from among the best-performing people. Selecting a "satisfactory" employee is a serious mistake when higher-performing employees are qualified for the job. The satisfactory employee might have all kinds of other attributes that would appear to make him more suitable for the promotion, but he has not earned the right to it. Put negatively, the high-performing employees—with the exception of the clearly unqualified—have earned the right to fail, and it is most unlikely that a reasonable candidate would not be found among those employees.

The Other Side of the Equation: Dealing with Unsatisfactory Performance

From time to time in this book, we have referred to employees whose performance is clearly and continually unsatisfactory. Most of these people should not remain in the organization, at least not in their current jobs. Such employees constitute a small percentage of any workforce (rarely more than 5 percent), but they consume an inordinate amount of management's time.

Employees who are clearly and continually unsatisfactory come in three general varieties:

- Those who, with competent guidance, clear goals, and considerable encouragement can improve to a satisfactory level in their current positions.
- Those who are in the wrong job and will not improve until they are correctly placed.
- Those who do poorly no matter how much guidance they receive or in what job they are placed.

Not dealing with poor performers has morale consequences for their co-workers. In fact, among the largest and most consistently negative employee survey findings are those about the organization's approach to poor performance. When asked, "How do you feel about the extent to which (the organization) faces up to poor performance?" the percentages obtained, on the average, are revealing (see Table 10-1).

Table 10-1 Response to the Question "To What Extent Does Your Company Face Up to Poor Performers?"

Answer	Percentage of Respondents
Much too much	2%
Too much	5%
About right	52%
Too little	29%
Much too little	12%

It is not that 41 percent of employees (29 percent plus 12 percent) are seen as poor performers. The poor performers are typically a small percentage of any employee population, usually just one or two people in an individual department. However, they aggravate many employees. What is especially discouraging is management's perceived unwillingness to confront this problem and do something about it. The problem is clear to everyone, and there is usually no disagreement among the workers as to who the culprit is. In focus groups, they almost always point to the same person—sometimes literally!

In a focus group we conducted in a government agency, the group consisted of all ten employees in a particular section. A major complaint expressed by many of the participants was that one employee in the section "loafed all day." The discussion about this employee went on and on even though that person must have been present because everyone in the section was there. The discussion finally shifted to another topic, and a worker who had been quiet up until then began to participate. The rest of the group in seeming unison nodded at the moderator; they had subtly let him know who the loafer was.

The consensus among co-workers is not just about the culprit, but about the reason for the poor performance and the solution. Employees are insightful when it comes to diagnosing the problems their co-workers are having, such as a lack of training or a mismatch between employee and job. ("He's just not a salesman.") About others, they say simply that, "Nothing can be done about him." They want help given to those they feel can be helped and, understandably, have mixed feelings about what to do with employees they consider incorrigible. Employees typically do not want their colleagues fired, but they become reconciled to it and supportive if they believe that management has done whatever is reasonable to help the employee improve and has otherwise treated him fairly.

Whatever the reason for poor performance, it is critical that it be dealt with quickly, squarely, and fairly. The first step is to provide guidance in a way that conforms to our previous suggestions, including the opportunity for the employee to express what he believes the problem to be and what the solution might be. Improvement goals should be set and follow-up done to assess whether satisfactory performance—or at least sufficient progress—has been achieved. If not, and enough time has elapsed, the manager (in consultation with his management and usually with Human Resources) needs to decide whether the appropriate solution is to transfer the employee to another job in the organization or to fire him. Transfers should not be sought for two kinds of employees: those unlikely to have the ability for any job in the organization (why continue the torture?), and those who have the ability but whose personality (overly rebellious, overly passive, totally disorganized, just plain lazy, and so on) would make them a poor risk as an employee anywhere.

We won't review the legal and administrative requirements that govern the firing of employees, such as providing sufficient notice to them of impending action and having adequate documentation. Suffice it to say that those requirements need to be followed, and not just to avoid lawsuits and penalties. Although it is time-consuming and costly to abide by the rules, they are there to provide necessary protection to employees against arbitrary actions by management, and abiding by them reinforces confidence throughout the workforce in management's fairness.

Management frequently blames unions or civil-service regulations or Human Resources departments for the delays in dealing with poor performers. To the extent we have been able to study this, our data do not bear this out. The problem of management's unwillingness to face up to poor performers appears unrelated to those variables. For example, our data show little difference between the way workers in unionized and nonunionized companies respond to the question about the company facing up to poor performers (see Table 10-2). The problem, therefore, appears to lie largely in *management,* not in the constraints that unions impose.

Table 10-2 Response to the Question "To What Extent Does Your Company Face Up to Poor Performers?" by Union and Nonunion Workers

	Percentage of Respondents	
Answer	**Unionized Companies**	**Nonunionized Companies**
Much too much	2%	3%
Too much	6%	4%
About right	48%	52%
Too little	31%	29%
Much too little	13%	12%

Feedback Sets Priorities

An extremely important function of feedback, both cognitive and affective, is to convey messages to the workforce as to what the organization's priorities are. Employees quickly learn that what companies say in their formal pronouncements—such as in their vision and values statements—is less important than what they hear from their managers day-to-day at work and how their financial and other rewards are determined. If, for example, a company preaches customer service, but employees in a customer call center hear from their managers only when the *quantity* of the calls they process is insufficient, they learn that it is quantity—not quality—that really counts. If the company talks about ethics but winks at employees cutting corners as long as the numbers come out "right" (in fact, may *reward* them for those numbers), the message about ethics to employees is clear: don't take them too seriously. If the company talks about "excellence in everything we do" and does nothing about poor performance, "excellence" becomes a high-sounding word with little relevance for how the organization actually runs.

An explicit vision and values statement is beneficial only if the company takes it seriously, which means bringing the messages conveyed by performance feedback and recognition into line with that statement. That is the reason why, in Chapter 7, "Organization Purpose and Principles," we emphasized the importance of implementation. It is only through the implementation of overarching goals and values that employees learn what the organization really cares about. Having serious gaps between words and deeds is worse than having no words at all because the gaps breed employee cynicism about management's competence or motives.

Part IV

Enthusiastic Workforces, Motivated by Camaraderie

11

Teamwork

"We must indeed all hang together, or, most assuredly, we shall all hang separately."

—Benjamin Franklin

"When he took time to help the man up the mountain, lo, he scaled it himself."

—Tibetan Proverb

Human beings are profoundly social animals. Characterized by a need for membership and getting pleasure from giving and getting help, it is natural that emotionally healthy people cluster into groups, spending most of their lives in association with others, especially family members, friends, and work associates.

This book is about the workplace, not about relationships per se. Yet, the quality of social relationships in the workplace—its "social capital"—is of great importance, not only because of the general need people have for camaraderie, but because cooperative relationships are critical for effective performance and, therefore, for a sense of achievement in one's work.[1]

A Look Back

In a sense, it is almost comical to consider a time when the great majority of businesses deliberately and forcefully discouraged social interaction among workers, fearing that it would lead to wasted time and be nothing more than an opportunity to "goof off." Once, in a survey we did in an industrial setting, we received the following comment:

> *If you try to talk, the forelady comes running over with a lot more work to do, or she yells, "Why aren't you finished yet?"*

It sounds like something out of a comedy routine, but it nonetheless represents in very large measure the state of human relations at work not all that long ago.

The field of industrial and organization psychology emerged in the 1920s and 1930s, largely in reaction to these jaundiced views of worker motivation and behavior. On the basis of the famous Hawthorne studies, Elton Mayo, widely considered the founder of the "human relations" movement in industry, made the social needs of workers central to his theory:

> *Man's desire to be continuously associated in work with his fellows is a strong, if not the strongest, human characteristic. Any disregard of it by management or any ill-advised attempt to defeat this human impulse leads instantly to some form of defeat for management itself.*[2]

What did Mayo mean by a "defeat for management?" He refers to two manifestations: the negative impact on employee morale and the lessening of the cooperation required for the effective performance of almost every job.

The field has come a long way since the "human relations" movement. Although its theories and prescriptions have been broadened to include other human needs, such as those addressed in this book, the importance of social relationships is undeniable for both the satisfaction and the performance of people at work.

Are We Doing Better Now?

Having been schooled in human relations, many of today's managers do not readily and publicly admit to concerns about workers who socialize on the job. But the unease persists, even at the highest levels. For example, in the course of an in-depth interview with the CEO of a large computer-services corporation, the executive shared these views regarding his top managers:

> *There is one thing that bugs me, not so much my immediate team but some of the people who work for them. It's their lunch habits—I'm told they can take two hours or more for lunch. I know sometimes it's with customers, but they also take each other to lunch and, believe it or not, they charge the company, they put it on their expense accounts. That can happen a few times a month. They say they're talking company business but I don't know....*

The interviews with those managers showed a sharply different picture. They said that they didn't just socialize over lunch and that they usually got an enormous amount done (by being "away from the phone," "away from the boss," and so on). These lunches were mostly work sessions, they said, and claimed that the company was getting more than its money's worth. Besides, considering their 60-plus hour work weeks and their level, they wondered why anyone would worry about the time they took for lunch.

Would a CEO of a major corporation fret over a matter as apparently trivial as whether senior executives took unduly long lunch breaks? You bet! When it comes to human relationships, the fundamental issues are amazingly consistent from level to level. Pettiness is as prevalent in the executive suite as it is on the shop floor, as any senior manager can tell you.

Do employees want to waste time? Some surely do; those few would spend the whole day socializing if they were allowed. But the overwhelming majority of employees are *frustrated* when time is wasted. They don't like to waste time on the job (such as in unproductive meetings) or in excessive work breaks. Of course, they don't want to and cannot work every minute of every day. Work breaks are no more a waste of time than are vacations.

We are not referring to situations where the work or work environment is so onerous that socializing is an escape from it or a way for employees to express resentment of the company. That is, when workers are apathetic or angry, breaks are more than simply needed pauses in the workday. They are then also likely to be excessive, which causes managers to crack down on the "malingerers," which further alienates the workforce. This vicious circle harms the organization and its employees.

In organizations that incorporate the practices we describe and recommend in this book, employees are motivated to work hard. Taking time to rest and socialize is nothing to worry about; in fact, it should be encouraged. Such breaks are needed because they add to overall employee performance and provide a sign of management's concern for employees' well being, including their health.

Socializing While Working

Although people at work derive pleasure from associating with others, such as during breaks, *their greatest satisfaction comes from interacting as a team on the job in the service of common business goals.* That is a tremendous source of morale for employees. And, as we said in our discussion of telecommuting in Chapter 8, "Job Enablement," it is a prime source of innovative ideas.

In fact, a good deal of the interaction while socializing is work-related. In organizations with good teamwork, the boundary between work and breaks becomes blurred, and even when the conversation is about matters unrelated to the work, socializing helps cement relationships among team members. In effect, through teamwork and simple and repeated social interaction, a *work community* is established:

people who enjoy each other's company and have a shared commitment to each other and pride in the group's achievements.

It is fortunate that social relationships are as important as they are to people because practically all work requires a high degree of cooperation. This seems too obvious to mention, but some managers and management theorists still maintain that there are numerous jobs where teamwork is simply unnecessary. The example most frequently cited is that of assembly-line workers performing highly fractionated jobs. What would teamwork add to performance on jobs so simplified, standardized, and segregated into individual tasks? It would just be time wasted in chit-chatting and in useless meetings. We discussed previously the similarly skeptical view about the value of participation in decision making by workers on routine jobs. We showed that that skepticism is belied by the many successful participative experiments that have been conducted in precisely those environments.

In fact, the participative experiments have, to our knowledge, always involved a team approach, such as self-managed teams. The technique requires that people work collaboratively (within and between units) to solve problems and make decisions. This, as has been repeatedly demonstrated, is an enormously effective approach to management and organization.

Why should this be true for work that has been standardized and structured—like that of a machine—into minute and individually performed tasks? It is true because the reality of such work situations is different from the theoretical conditions suggested by the machine model. The fact is that when work is highly fractionated, the interdependence among the parts is actually greater than when a job consists of doing the "whole thing." The performance of a worker assigned to just one step of an operation depends on receiving work product from the previous worker on time and with the quality required to perform the task. Workers in a multiple-shift organization depend on their co-workers doing the same job on other shifts for a smooth hand-off of the work. There is great dependence on various support departments to provide the resources that enable workers to do their jobs (such as machine maintenance). Changes (in specifications, procedures, equipment) are likely to be frequent, and workers need others to inform them of the changes clearly and on time and provide any training that might be required.

There is, therefore, a great deal of interdependence among workers doing even the most highly fractionated work. In fact, teamwork is needed for just about every job at every level. Things don't happen automatically; they require cooperation. *Cooperation—not job descriptions, not organization charts, not formal procedures—is the glue that binds the parts of the organization.*

Uncooperative Co-Workers Have an Exponentially Negative Effect

When a co-worker doesn't cooperate, the effect is not simply a reduction in effectiveness in proportion to the degree of that person's noncooperation. The impairment is exponential because it almost always results in a reduction in the cooperation from others. Furthermore, lack of cooperation can lead to serious conflicts fueled by paranoia, such as, "You're not helping me because you'd like to see me fail, so I'd better defend myself, and the best defense is a good offense."

If senior management ignores these battles, they escalate as a matter of course and can be costly. The costs are not just the time spent in battle but also in not being able to exploit opportunities collaboratively.

Just as a lack of cooperation can escalate into a large-scale problem, good cooperation can have a significant and positive synergistic effect. When organizations are managed as more than a collection of individuals, the resulting whole is typically greater than the sum of its parts. Although groups are often derided as promoting dull conformity ("groupthink") or, conversely, bizarre solutions ("a camel is a horse put together by a committee"), the research evidence shows that the quality of group performance, such as in problem solving, is by and large superior to that of an individual working alone. In addition to the esprit de corps they generate, groups, when structured and managed correctly, allow for the emergence and consideration of different perspectives, which are vital to solve problems and make good decisions. Further, they generate greater acceptance by the members of the outcome.[3] Our own analyses almost invariably show strong positive correlations between teamwork in organizations (as perceived by employees) and organization performance.

At the obvious extreme, there is absolutely no way the Manhattan or Apollo projects and thousands like them could have succeeded without high-functioning teams. For those cynical about doing work "by committee," keep in mind such well-known products of committees as the U.S. Constitution and the King James Version of the Bible. Committees or teams fail when they are not structured and managed properly (more on that later), or when they are devices put in place to avoid, rather than make, decisions. Those are not the committees or teams we have in mind.

Contentious Workgroups Are Drags on the Organization

As we said in Chapter 1, "What Workers Want—The Big Picture," teamwork tends to be good within work units (80 percent satisfied), but less so between units (66 percent satisfied). It's favorable within units because there is a natural inclination to cooperate and, unless management acts in a way that disrupts those relationships, people find ways to work together. Take this example, which is from an executive interview in a retail corporation, of a senior manager disrupting naturally forming cooperative relationships:

He (the manager) keeps telling us that we don't work well together. He's right, we're always arguing, but it's mostly his fault. For example, someone gets an assignment in a meeting and then, after the meeting, he gives someone else the same assignment without telling the other person. We're all running around—and our people are running around—trying to get it done and we find out others are doing it, too. So we assume that the others are invading our turf and we're p.o.'d at each other. And it's a great waste of high-priced time. Another thing: he's always bad-mouthing us to each other.

When it occurs, conflict within units is often the result of a manager's particular style or the quirks of one or two individual employees. Conflict between units is more frequent because, in addition to individual factors, broad organizational forces at work can create discord. Organizations are divided, by necessity, into business or functional units, and the members of the units focus primarily or exclusively on the achievement of their own goals. They are convinced that achieving their own goals is beneficial not only for them, but for the organization as a whole and for the units with which they interact. In practice, however, they are often at odds with those units.

For example, many organizations are beset by serious and continuing disputes between "line" and "staff" functions. Line functions, such as product development, production, and sales, are directly responsible for accomplishing the end purposes of the organization, whereas staff groups, such as information technology, human resources, finance, and legal, exist primarily to assist the line in its work. (The term "staff" derives from the rod or stick that assists walking, and it comes from a Sanskrit root meaning "support.") Although staff personnel firmly believe that they are dedicated to supporting the line and should therefore be welcomed by the line, the opposite is often the case. As the saying goes, "With such friends, we don't need enemies."

The most frequent example of this kind of conflict may be the one between information technology and the line. We detail that relationship later in this chapter. Perhaps the second most common type of conflict is the relationship between the Human Resources department and employees—yes, employees! Shouldn't the Human Resources department *help* employees? Well, take a look at some of these comments:

> *After choosing (a benefits package), I found there was misinformation from HR, which caused much stress. I found that our Human Resources department was useless. It feels as if we are left out to dry when it comes to benefit issues.*

> *I am never able to find the right people to talk to when we have questions related to human resources. I go in circles being transferred to multiple people who know less than the next one.*

> *I am completely frustrated talking with Human Resources about payroll issues, changing benefits, and getting reimbursement for time or business expenses.*

> *I hate dealing with Human Resources regarding a range of issues. Either I can't reach the proper person or the person gives me wrong advice and answers. I think each division of this company should have a qualified representative on site that can assist with your needs and that really wants to assist.*

> *It is difficult adjusting to Human Resources and compensation policy changes that are enacted by the leaders of the company without a true warning, such as the elimination of overtime/compensatory time right at the beginning of the busy season. HR is not an advocate of the employee but nothing more than the mouthpiece of higher management.*

> *They [the Human Resources department] are just a bunch of bureaucrats—everything is forms, forms, forms and the answers are no, no, no. We call them Inhuman Resources.*

Inter-unit conflict is not limited to line-staff relationships. Consider the tensions between production and sales, which are two line organizations.

From the sales side:

I am in a position of selling to willing customers but our production organization doesn't handle my orders in the time the customers want them. Not a few of my sales opportunities are therefore lost. How can we get them to respond in a timely manner? They seem completely resistant to trying out new ways that will speed things up. Also, it often takes days for them to return my calls. It's much easier dealing with other companies.

From the production side:

Our salespeople should understand what we can produce and how fast we can do it. Promising the customer something in a time we can't deliver it frankly drives us crazy. Before making a commitment, it would be great if they checked with us first. By not doing this, escalations are the norm rather than the exception. We are not working as a team.

Working together is a natural human instinct, yet much internal discord exists. The work community we spoke of earlier seems not to extend, in many cases, to the organization as a whole. Ironically, the problem is magnified by the need for camaraderie. Here's the downside of the desire for strong relationships with others: it might be satisfied at the expense of relationships with those not in the immediate group. Whoever's not in the immediate group can be viewed as competitors and even as the "enemy camp." Employees frequently refer to a "we-they" atmosphere within their organizations: "they" might be the people in another department on the other side of the hall or a group in corporate headquarters on the other side of the country or world.

Conflict, of course, is not inherently detrimental. On the broadest level, conflict and its corollary, competition, are at the heart of our economic and political systems, and they yield great rewards. Companies in the same industry, for example, need to compete aggressively with each other. But such aggressive competition among entities *within* a company does serious harm to the organization's effectiveness.

The damage has three major elements: the resources that need to be expended to pursue the battle, the loss of collaborative opportunities, and the negative impact on employee morale. Regarding morale, although the "we-they" phenomenon can temporarily boost in-group identification in relation to the "enemy," few employees enjoy such conflict over the long term. It inhibits their performance and the organization's performance, and it is tiring. Most employees want to battle the competition—that can be exhilarating—not each other.

Besides being wasteful and debilitating, much of the conflict in organizations is needless and irrational. It is needless because it's resolvable: the parties can be brought together in a collaborative or win-win relationship. It is irrational because it's driven by misperceptions of the inevitability of conflict between them. Yes, inherent conflicts of interest exist where one party's gain equates to the other party's loss. Numerous issues in labor-management relations are of this kind. No one should expect workers to participate gladly and collaboratively in being downsized, outsourced, or offshored. Incompatible interests of that kind can usually be settled only through the traditional adversarial process, which is basically a matter of the relative power of the two sides, their skill in employing that power, and an appreciation of the costs of not settling the dispute.

Much of the discord between groups in organizations, however, does not stem from an inherent incompatibility of interests, but from a perception that such incompatibility exists. For example, does an inherent conflict of interests exist between an IT function and its "user" divisions? The parties might *act* that way, but doesn't IT exist primarily to help its users do their work, and don't both groups exist to further the organization's success? The parties don't act that way because that's not how they see it: each group sees the other as acting solely in its own selfish or myopic interests and often in ways that are detrimental to the other party. Therefore, each group protects itself and, as the conflict continues, it generates intensifying perceptions of malice in each other's intentions. In fact, the perceptions then *do* become grounded in reality because each party, because of its assumptions, *does* begin to act in ways that seek to undermine the other. It is no longer a distortion for each side to see the other as untrustworthy and dangerous: the conflict process has made the perceptions a reality. In other words, if the parties believe a conflict exists, it does—or soon will.

Building Partnership

Other than those few managers who believe that conflict between individuals and groups within an organization is beneficial (as in "good old American competition"), most managers understand that conflict of that kind is extraordinarily and needlessly costly. In fact, they detest it, as do almost all of their employees; people don't want to come to work to fight! *It is important to understand this fundamental desire to work collaboratively—this fundamental goodwill—because that is the basis on which teamwork is built after the layers of suspicion and resentment are removed.*

As we have said, conflicts differ in how real or psychologically based they are. Approaches to reduce conflict must take this into account, and there are two basic strategies:

- **Conflict management.** The parties agree not to fight and to establish mechanisms to help avoid and settle disagreements.
- **Partnership building.** The parties agree to collaborate actively in the achievement of mutual goals—that is, to establish a relationship aimed at adding value and not just minimizing discord and its costs.

Conflict management is most appropriate when the conflict stems from a real divergence of interests; partnership building is appropriate when the root cause is misperceptions. The labor-relations arena provides good examples of the two approaches. An antagonistic and costly relationship between labor and management can be converted, through conflict management, into one where workers and the company agree on mechanisms to prevent and handle disputes, such as an orderly and relatively noncontentious grievance procedure and, to prevent strikes, commencing bargaining well in advance of contract expiration. That happens when the parties, despite their different specific financial interests, recognize that the mutual interest of the parties is served by containing or reducing the costs of conflict that can only shrink the economic pie that's available to both groups.

The parties can, however, agree to go beyond this truce-like result to consider how they can work together to increase the economic pie that they share, by improving quality, efficiency, and the like. That is the difference between a relationship of respectful adversaries and one of active allies.

Getting management and labor to cooperate in areas such as improving quality first requires successful conflict management. Antagonism between the parties on basic equity issues makes a collaborative relationship on other matters difficult. But managing such conflict well does not guarantee that the parties will move to the next level. Another hurdle must be overcome: the misperceptions the parties usually have of each other regarding their interest in matters such as quality improvement and their interest in establishing a truly collaborative relationship to achieve those ends. With regard to quality, for example, management tends to assume that workers don't really care about quality, whereas workers tend to assume that all that management wants is production, no matter what the quality. These beliefs are rarely accurate or, at least, are distorted significantly. Unless misperceptions are clearly identified and acknowledged, the parties have no chance of becoming allies in a sustained way to improve quality. The foundation for success (like that of the self-managed teams described in Chapter 8) is that both parties trust that they share common goals.

How Can the Misperceptions Be Uncovered, Confronted, and Corrected?

The first step toward resolving organizational conflicts is simply to get the perceptions of the various sides "on the table." This is best done through survey methods, whether through interviews or a combination of interviews and questionnaires. This phase of the process is one of the most helpful because it usually shows in no uncertain terms just how *similar* the two parties actually are: in many of their fundamental interests, in their positive assumptions about themselves, and in their negative assumptions about each other. Such data, if analyzed well and reported candidly, can be an immensely powerful catalyst for change.

To illustrate, let's thoroughly examine the relationship we uncovered between the IT function and its "user" divisions in a large financial-services company. The reason for the study was expressed strong user dissatisfaction with internal IT functions. Complaints included errors, excessive costs, and, especially, "attitude," a sense that many IT personnel were indifferent to providing genuinely good service to users. The senior management of the company, which was largely sympathetic to the users, asked us to determine, in essence, what was wrong with IT and how it could be fixed.

In-depth interviews were conducted with all the managers in those units and with samples of nonmanagerial personnel. What we found was more complex than was thought: the villain was neither party individually, but the *relationship* between them.

To start, each group considered itself to be competent, committed to serving the interests of the company, and highly dedicated to doing its job well. Contrary to how they were viewed, IT employees felt themselves to be dedicated to providing users with high-quality, timely, and cost-effective work. Each side, however, saw the other as committed only to its own success (that is, unconcerned with either the company or the other party). The IT employees typically considered users to be unreasonably demanding, continually chang-ing their minds about what they wanted (disregarding the impact such mid-course changes had on IT and its ability to do the job), and oblivious to costs (unless the costs were billed to them, in which case they felt they had been overcharged). This was compounded by IT's view that many users' ignorance of technology was matched only by their ignorance of their ignorance. It was further compounded by IT's conviction that users were unconcerned about IT's frustrations, espe-cially the way that function was bombarded with "the highest priority" projects, all of which required timely and error-free completion that IT just didn't have the resources to provide.

The user divisions had an equally jaundiced opinion of IT person-nel's characteristics. The IT department was typically seen as having little sense of urgency in doing the work (hence, the frequent late-ness in delivery), failing to understand the users' objectives (even though, according to the users, these objectives were clearly spelled out), being resistant to user ideas and suggestions, being frequently careless in the quality of their work, being unresponsive to the users' daily needs (including not returning phone calls, which was a tremen-dous frustration), and grossly overcharging for their work. In parallel with the IT function's view, the users saw IT as ignorant of (and quite unconcerned with) the company's mainline business and its changing demands.

In essence, the views were mirror images of each other: each party saw itself as dedicated and competent and the other as largely self-absorbed and ignorant.

Although these perceptions might have had some degree of validity (for example, the users typically did not fully appreciate the pressures on the IT function), they were, in essence, misperceptions because of their assumptions of a basic incompatibility of interests and the other party's incompetence. There was an assumption of con-flict, for example, in the users' views that IT made mistakes because it didn't care about serving users well rather than because of inordinate pressures on them or misunderstandings as to what the users want. Also, there was an assumption of incompetence in the view that users change the project specifications continually because they really don't know what they want rather than because of changing demands on them or new insights.

The reader might be tempted to ask, "Why don't these people grow up? They're acting like children, 'You did this to me,' 'No, I didn't—you did that to me.' Why don't they just get down to business and stop the incessant bickering and blaming?"

If only getting down to business was that simple. Childish or not, we know that emotion is rarely absent in people's relationships, including the relationships between mature businesspeople, and that misperceptions and misunderstandings frequently arise. These feed on themselves, which causes increasing, needless, and serious damage to everyone's interests and morale. Although at times these problems can be resolved by the parties themselves, they usually need help from a third party, a skilled diagnostician and facilitator.

We now describe in detail an approach to partnership building that has been used successfully in numerous settings. It assists the parties to achieve mutually beneficial and collaborative relationships. The approach has been applied to a variety of relationships, such as between business units, home country and overseas units, acquirer and acquired company employees, and the members of senior-management teams. It has also been applied to a company and its key external constituencies, such as suppliers.

A facilitator manages the process, and its centerpiece is an intensive partnership-building workshop that uses survey data as its springboard. Although the approach must be tailored to the objectives and conditions of the organization in which the work is being done, the following sections describe a fairly typical set of basic steps.

Lay the Foundation Prior to the Workshop

Orientation and Assessment of Readiness. The facilitator meets with senior leaders of the organizations to gain an understanding of the situation from their perspective; understand their goals in a partnership-building effort; review with them the method to be used and its perceived appropriateness for the problem, the personalities involved, and the organizations' culture; and determine whether they are prepared to devote the required resources and time (including their own) to achieve genuine and lasting collaboration.

Planning. Having determined that the approach is appropriate and the organization is ready for it, the objectives, procedure, schedule, and specific expected outcomes of the process are finalized.

Communication. The partnership-building objectives and plan are fully communicated to all employees in the organization who will be affected by them.

Diagnosis. Through interviews, or a combination of interviews and questionnaires, the organization's members are surveyed. The surveys yield in-depth profiles of the views the members hold of themselves and the other party; what they see as the key components, causes, and consequences of the lack of collaboration; the suggestions they might have to increase collaboration; and, what they deem to be the potential benefits of increased collaboration in terms of specific business problems and opportunities.

Establish Workshop Ground Rules

Following the diagnosis, a workshop is conducted that aims to establish the basis for a productive and lasting partnership between the parties. The workshop normally lasts about three days, and the participants are those whose work will significantly benefit from improvements in collaboration. As long as the participants follow a number of ground rules, the workshops almost invariably succeed. They succeed, basically, because the participants want them to succeed: they want to collaborate, and they want the high levels of performance that teamwork can produce. The key workshop ground rules, which are sustained throughout the workshop by the facilitator, are as follows:

- **Business orientation.** Unlike some team-building efforts, the process employed is clearly and directly business-related. The goal is not to build relationships per se, but to build relationships that promote business objectives. This type of workshop rarely uses simulated exercises to get people to work together; instead, they work collaboratively on business issues and opportunities that are real, significant, and best dealt with as a team. The human-relationship issues are identified and resolved within this business context and, as appropriate, the workshop takes the time needed to assess, discuss, and resolve those issues.

- **Open atmosphere.** It is important that the workshop participants feel free to express their views. This is aided immeasurably by the diagnostic attitude data collected prior to the workshop that assess the viewpoints people hold of themselves and the other party. At the beginning of the workshop, the facilitator presents these data and initiates a discussion to bring those issues into the open that, at least initially, the workshop participants might be reluctant to bring up themselves. The issues then become "safe" topics for discussion and help set an open atmosphere for the remainder of the workshop.

- **Constructive atmosphere.** The open exchange of views should take place in an atmosphere of mutual respect. Mutual respect is demonstrated by a visible effort to appreciate the situation of the other party, showing an intention to work collaboratively on the issues and demonstrating trust in the other party's intention to do so, and avoiding rude, insulting language.

- **Action orientation with follow-up.** The outcome of the workshop is a jointly developed action plan that involves close and continued collaboration between the parties and will contribute significantly to achieving their mutual business objectives. The plan includes mechanisms for following up to ensure that the agreed-upon actions are being taken, including structural changes, such as changes in the reward system of the total organization that reinforce inter-unit collaboration.

- **Flexible approach.** Although certain general principles govern the partnership-building efforts, the specifics are often modified as the workshop proceeds. The interactions in the workshop are dynamic and unpredictable in many respects, so it is vital that adjustments be made on the spot.

In summary, the keys to a productive workshop are timely preparation of the participants, an open and respectful expression of views, an unyielding focus on the business objective of what is transpiring, disciplined action planning, and a willingness to make adaptations to the agenda as the situation warrants.

A Typical Workshop Agenda

1. Senior management and the facilitator review the objectives, agenda, and ground rules of the workshop.

2. The participants present their views of the relationship between the parties, covering key strengths and improvement needs and the specific business activities that could benefit from increased collaboration.

3. The facilitator presents the findings from the diagnostic survey. These normally tend to be more focused than the participant presentations on sensitive relationship issues.

4. The participant presentations and the diagnostic findings are discussed, starting with the human relationship concerns (for example, the misperceptions that cause friction in the relationship) and concluding with the substantive business issues.

5. The participants reach agreement on a limited number of priority business issues that will benefit from collaboration. They then decide how best to tackle the key issues in the workshop (for example, those that need to be dealt with by the group as a whole and those best handled in subgroups).

6. The participants carefully define the priority issues and develop action plans to deal with those issues.

7. The workshop concludes by establishing mechanisms for the following:

   • Reviewing, finalizing, and implementing the action plans.

   • Determining how the collaborative relationship between the parties can best be sustained. Unless this is addressed, it is almost inevitable that, over time, the teamwork the workshop produced will largely dissipate as the participants resume their normal routines and are subjected to pressures that generate friction and discord.

In addition to the business sessions of the workshop, various social activities are scheduled (usually in the evenings) to provide an opportunity for relaxed and informal interaction.

Action Example: IT and Its Users

We described previously the contentious relationship between the IT function and its users in a financial-services company. Here is a summary of what they accomplished in their team-building workshop and in follow-up meetings.

The workshop participants decided on the following basic objective for their work:

> *To help IT become a truly user-focused organization, every user must feel that IT is doing its best to help him or her do the job; every user must feel that IT is concerned about him or her individually; every user must be satisfied with the services he or she receives from IT. This will be accomplished both by changing attitudes and processes within IT and by changes among the users to help them become more involved and informed consumers of IT services so that IT can assist them more effectively.*

Here, in the participants' own words, are excerpts from their actions plans:

1. Establishment of a company-wide IT-User Partnership Council to assure smooth working relationships; will meet monthly with an agenda consisting of:
   - Specific problems that have been encountered; Council will decide how to resolve them.
   - Consideration of basic changes that still need to be made to assure a good working relationship.
   - Opportunities for additional collaborative undertakings between IT and the users.
   - Review of the results, as they are available, from regular measurements of attitudes and performance of IT and user employees.

   Individual user organizations may set up their own Partnership Councils to assure adequate attention to their specific issues.

2. Individuals will be appointed by IT to serve as the interfaces with each user organization. These persons will be the primary—but not sole—points of contact between IT and the user organizations. Through communications and coordination, these persons will work to assure that the users' expectations of IT are satisfied, including helping set realistic user expectations.

3. Communication and involvement:

- Within each user organization, communication sessions will be held with IT in which:
  - The relevant aspects of the user's business will be fully described for IT.
  - The relevant IT processes will be fully described for the user.
  - Guidelines will be presented for the kinds of behavior—on both sides—that constitute a cooperative working relationship.

  Enough time will be allowed for questions and discussion, with time for socializing and interaction. Each session's agenda will be developed jointly by IT and user representatives to assure clarity and relevance.

- All projects will now begin with a full discussion between IT and the users of the project's objectives and requirements; requirements will be recorded, but as a working document that will likely change (versus a legalistic and static document); will be followed up with regular meetings reviewing project status, changes, etc.; also, electronic notification will be provided to users regarding project status; "no surprises" billing: costs fully detailed and explained at beginning of project; when modified, detailed explanation will be given to user with opportunity to question and negotiate.

- IT projects which are not initiated by a user but will affect that user will be discussed in detail with the user to assure understanding and to obtain user input.

- Telephone inquiries from users will be answered within two hours.

- Monthly newsletter will be published (electronic) for both IT and user personnel (accomplishments, new developments, etc).

4. Training to be scheduled:

- For IT personnel (including help-desk personnel) in basic communication and customer-relationship skills
- For IT personnel in new technologies (both on- and off-site training)
- For user personnel in systems that have been developed for them

5. IT internal structure and processes:

- Will reduce needless bureaucracy: A lengthy approval process to be shortened considerably by reducing the number of approvals required, especially in the applications development process; a "destroyer" task force will review all paperwork and eliminate paperwork that is no longer useful.
- Cross-functional communication mechanisms (meetings, etc.) will be strengthened within IT.
- New and transparent prioritization process will be developed (combination of time of request, urgency, and amount and availability of resources).

Action implementation began. A follow-up interview survey, conducted eight months after the workshop, revealed sharp gains in most respects in collaboration-related attitudes. Here's a typical comment from an interview with a user:

Things have changed for the better here. Most of them (IT employees) have a different attitude now. They actually return my phone calls and right away. Most seem to want to help. A big change is how we now plan development projects together and we don't have to worry about dotting every "i" and crossing every "t" because we know that things will change anyway, and we'll have to keep communicating and working together. Also, if things will be late, they tell us; if they don't understand what we want, they ask us. The only real problem is with one small group of programmers who are stuck in the past. It's their manager—he's still the same arrogant (expletive deleted). Also, I think their internal approval process is still a little too bureaucratic and time-wasting.

This comment is taken from an IT employee's interview:

> *I enjoy my work more now—the haggling is much less now. We understand each other much better now. I used to think they were not so smart—that's the way I always thought about bankers: expensive suits, not much else. They're still not really up on technology but I see now a lot of dedication and business sense on the part of most of them. It's great working together to solve their problems and I've gotten more interested in the business. We still have problems with them wanting too much too soon, and they get frustrated with us. But, the anger isn't there like before and they now almost never go around us to top management to force us to give in to their demands. One guy still does. We talk more face-to-face about the problems and we work most of them out. We understand more the pressures on each of us.*

The partnership-building process does not result in Utopia. Certain issues remain and must be dealt with and, given the forces in an organization that pull people and units apart, attention must be paid continually to the relationship or serious problems will certainly recur. It is, therefore, a good idea for the parties to meet periodically offsite for a day or so to examine fully and candidly the state of their relationship. This examination usually leads to further changes to reinforce and enhance collaboration; some changes might be quite basic and some might be painful to individuals.

For example, the parties might decide that structural modifications are in order, such as decentralizing segments of a staff function into the line organization. Certain relationships might lend themselves to modifications in compensation to make pay more reflective of teamwork and not just individual effort. Personnel changes might be needed, such as moving an employee to another job, or even firing those individuals who, despite counseling and time to change their behavior, simply will not or cannot conform to the new collaborative norms. These measures make partnership-building more than a passing fad or a temporary fix for a problem. They serve to institutionalize and sustain a genuinely collaborative culture.

Part V

Bringing It All Together:
The Culture of Partnership

We have recommended many specific management policies and practices throughout this book, ranging from broad company policy to relationships between organization units to the conduct of day-to-day interactions between employees and their bosses. These may seem disparate, but they are all representative of and reinforce a particular, and particularly powerful, organization culture: the culture of "partnership." In Part V, we discuss what we mean by partnership, including a case study of Mayo Clinic, an exemplar of partnership culture; we describe the essentials of genuine leadership, especially as these pertain to the leadership of partnership cultures; and, we provide guidance for organizations seeking seriously to change in the direction of partnership.

12

The Culture of Partnership

"As they say on my own Cape Cod, a rising tide lifts all the boats. And a partnership, by definition, serves both partners, without domination or unfair advantage. Together, we have been partners in adversity—let us also be partners in prosperity."

—John F. Kennedy, June 25, 1963, West Germany

"I have found no greater satisfaction than achieving success through honest dealing and strict adherence to the view that, for you to gain, those you deal with should gain as well."

—Alan Greenspan

In this book, we have enumerated the specific components of management behavior that produce employee enthusiasm and high performance. Our aim is to provide guidance to managers and executives who seek to change themselves or their organizations. We hope that individual managers find our suggestions helpful in dealing with their own people and other units in the organization. But to bring about truly significant and lasting organization change, we must think of the components not just individually, but together as a *system*, one that is governed by an organization *culture*.

By a system, we mean that the parts interact so that changing one element without changing others significantly reduces the impact of the first. In fact, changing just one element might negatively affect the other elements, as when a company seeks to create a "participative" environment for a workforce that feels seriously underpaid.

377

Management is then viewed not only as miserly, but as hypocritical. It's better to be seen as a genuinely miserly boss than one who is also a phony.

By culture, we mean the standards and values that define how people in an organization are expected to behave, especially in their relationships: with each other and with external stakeholders, such as customers. It is not sufficient to put in place good practices, such as an effective compensation system. To have maximum impact and be sustained in their fundamentals as conditions change, business practices must be supported by deeply felt and explicitly stated values ("We do this because...," "We will change this, but not that, because...." A good illustration of this was the Johnson & Johnson Credo, discussed in Chapter 7, "Organization Purpose and Principles," which had guided the company in its policies and practices for more than 60 years.

In other words, the multitude of practices must be sustained by a strong and coherent organizational culture.

The essence of the system and culture we describe in this book is a "partnership" relationship. We explained in Chapter 1, "What Workers Want—The Big Picture," that partnership is a business relationship *plus.* The plus is the human dimension—the trust and goodwill that allows people to go beyond what is required by strictly monetary calculations, formal contracts, and short-term interests. We have offered considerable evidence to demonstrate that a partnership relationship generates, on the average, the highest level of long-term performance for organizations. Partnership has both a vertical dimension, which consists of the relationships between workers and management, and a horizontal dimension, which is the relationships between individuals, between work units, and with other constituencies. *It is people working together—up, down, and across—toward common goals.*

Partnership has both psychological and economic components, such as employees' confidence that they are making significant contributions to the organization's success and that they are sharing in the financial gains of that contribution. It is a high-involvement model: involvement in what the workers give to an organization and in what they receive from it. Both parties' interests are being served.

More specifically, here are the hallmarks of a successful partnership:

- **Win-win.** The parties recognize that they have key business goals in common and that the success of one party depends on the success of the other.
- **Basic trust.** The parties trust each other's intentions.
- **Long-term perspective.** The parties are committed to a long-term relationship, one that can survive the short-term vicissitudes of business.
- **Excellence.** The parties set high performance standards for themselves and for each other.
- **Competence.** The parties have confidence in each other's competence.
- **Joint decision making.** The parties make key decisions jointly on matters that affect them both.
- **Open communications.** The parties communicate fully with each other.
- **Mutual influence.** The parties listen to and are influenced by each other.
- **Mutual assistance.** The parties help each other perform.
- **Recognition.** The parties recognize each other for their contributions.
- **Day-to-day treatment.** The parties routinely treat each other with consideration and respect.
- **Financial sharing.** To the extent that the collaboration is designed to generate improved financial results, the parties share equitably in those gains. In tougher times, they share equitably in the required sacrifices.

These criteria can be applied to any business relationship: between employees and management, between work units, and to relationships with other business entities or individuals, such as customers and suppliers.

Some might argue that the term "partnership" does not fit the employee-management relationship. For these people, the term implies a fundamental equality between the parties that is rarely present in any practical sense in the employee-management relationship. Applying it to that relationship therefore might seem dishonest and manipulative—an attempt to subtly convince employees that their power is more than what it is.

However, that is neither the objective nor the point. Power inequalities exist in every organization: almost everyone has a boss, even CEOs who answer to boards of directors. But bosses vary greatly in what they *do* with their authority, and those differences lead to hugely diverse outcomes. In that sense, the use of power is a central concern of this book. So, although it is true that there is a large discrepancy in power between workers and management, it is also true that workers accept the legitimacy and the necessity of this. They are, in fact, disturbed when leaders don't lead, such as when they are unduly hesitant about making decisions or have an unclear business strategy. But workers do not accept the legitimacy of being treated by their bosses as lazy or dumb—that is, unwilling or unable to contribute significantly to the success of the enterprise. It is not authority that is at issue here—it is the *proper exercise* of authority. Analogously, workers do not bridle at pay differentials. To some people, partnership might imply pay equality, but in our formulation, it is pay *equity*. We have never heard workers objecting to senior management being paid more than them. They complain about senior management pay primarily when the gap with their pay is enormous, it appears to be unjustified by the performance of the organization, and that performance has caused the workers' pay to suffer. Otherwise, they think, "Let the brass make as much as they can—I'm doing well."

The partnership organization stands in contrast to three other major organization types. As with all typologies, no organization fits any type perfectly and all are, to one extent or another, mixtures. They are mixtures because, for one, the individual criteria that define a culture—such as those listed for partnership—while correlated, do not necessarily come as a package. A company that lays off people quite readily, can, in its day-to-day management practices, be quite respectful of workers' talents and ideas and provide them with considerable autonomy on the jobs. This is not uncommon because the impact of modern management theory and research—which tends to focus on autonomy and other aspects of "human relations" on the job—has been quite considerable. They just don't feel that their employees are particularly "entitled," say, to a measure of job security, which is a fundamental feature of partnership organizations. Also, mixtures of styles are evident when organizations are in the midst of change because of changing business conditions or the advent of a new top management bent on revamping the organization's operations and culture. And different strata of a workforce, such as salaried compared to hourly employees, might be treated differently, and individual managers and managements might act differently depending on the circumstances of the moment. Although we therefore never find complete consistency, strong tendencies allow us to identify most organizations, and the major units within them, as closer to one type or another (or, at least as moving from one type to another).

In addition to partnership, the major organization types are *transactional*, *paternalistic*, and *adversarial*.

Transactional. We have seen in the past few decades the emergence of an explicit philosophy and set of management practices wherein employees are treated essentially as commodities that have a "price" and are owed little or nothing but that price (that is, little or nothing beyond their paychecks). We discussed this management style earlier, especially in Chapter 3, "Job Security," and depicted it both as a response to a more competitive world and as a reaction to the costs and inflexibility of company paternalism. Its most visible manifestations have been the downsizings, restructurings, re-engineerings, rightsizings, outsourcings, and offshorings of the past two or three decades—all terms usually signifying getting rid of workers. These have occurred most visibly in companies that had previously been well-known bulwarks of employment security, such as IBM, Kodak, Xerox, and GE. The transactional approach also manifests itself in the greatly increased use of temporary employees, independent contractors, and subcontractors who can be hired and fired at will.

Personal responsibility and personal accountability are among the catch phrases used to describe and ideologically justify a transactional approach to management. These terms are contrasted with an entitlement mentality assumedly bred in employees by organizations that operate paternalistically.

As we have pointed out, being treated as a faceless commodity—an interchangeable part to be disposed of at the first whiff of less-than-sterling profitability—has consequences for employee morale and performance. The employee response is not so much anger as it is resignation and an indifferent attitude toward work and the company, such as, "This is the way it is these days; company loyalty is dead, so why should I care?" Transactional management should not be confused with a "cruel" management that seeks to squeeze every last dime and ounce of sweat from its workers. Transactional organizations generally pay at or near the going wage rate and, as far as workload is concerned, are not, by and large, throwbacks to the infamous era of sweatshops. Essentially, it is an *indifferent* management—indifferent to the value of people other than to follow orders and perform the specific tasks for which they are being paid. They don't expect more than that from a worker and, if they get less, the worker can be fired. There is, in the purest form of transactional management, no other connection or obligation to the worker, not even a negative connection. Why get aggravated and pressure the worker when he is not performing or is often absent or late? A manager might talk with him once or twice, and if the worker doesn't improve, the manager just fires him.

A transactional orientation is not limited to the shop or factory floor; in our experience, it occurs as frequently in the executive suite. In Chapter 10, "Feedback, Recognition, and Reward," we related an anecdote about a corporation whose executives felt themselves continually on a "slippery slope," their past performance seemingly irrelevant to the CEO; it was, "What have you done for me today?" In interviews conducted with senior management of a Midwest manufacturing company, the attitude of their CEO was described this way by an interviewee:

> *Let me tell you something: he does not give a damn whether we stay or leave. He thinks he is the reason for any success the company has had and he can buy anybody to carry out his orders. Sure, when you're hired, you get a big sales job, you're a big hero then, "we really need you," but you go "from hero to zero" in just a few months. He just can't stand the competition from anyone who works for him. We're like a commodity. He's the only one with value.*

All the other members of senior management expressed similar views. The turnover rate in this group was 80 percent, with only one executive having been with the company more than 18 months. They had all left voluntarily and were, by all reports, highly competent executives.

Paternalism. As the term connotes, this is a relationship between a company and its employees similar to that between caring parents and their children. In the United States, it dates largely from the late nineteenth and early twentieth centuries, the period that saw a great upsurge of industrial growth in the country, accompanied by a tide of labor-union activity but had for the most part died out by the last decade of the twentieth century. It has been replaced, in large measure, by companies with a transactional orientation.

Above all else, paternalistic organizations provided security for their employees in the form of protection against job loss and the provision of benefits that freed employees from medical and retirement financial worries. Additional amenities often included educational programs, recreational facilities, subsidized cafeterias, company loans, and, in its earliest days in "company towns," low-cost housing. The great majority of employees joined such companies with the prospect of lifetime careers for themselves.

Companies that were labeled paternalistic were not all alike, not by a long shot. Most important was the difference between companies that indeed treated their workers well and those in which paternalism was a façade to conceal exploitative, even inhumane, management practices. The latter were especially characteristic of many "company towns," where the company owned just about everything—housing, stores, schools—and employees had little alternative but to rent lodging, buy goods, and so on from their employer. Pay was low, and the company, in all its beneficence, would allow employees to draw a portion of their wages before payday in the form of scrip. The scrip coupons, however, were redeemable only in company-owned stores, and once an employee began using scrip, it was difficult for him to get out of debt to the company. A worker might owe 95 percent of his check to the company.

That kind of management must be distinguished from the paternalism of other corporations whose practices were truly benevolent and made these companies employers of choice for their workers, such as IBM, Eastman Kodak, Sears Roebuck, Corning, and Johnson & Johnson. These companies provided their workers with above-average wages, excellent fringe benefits, employee stock ownership or purchase plans, good working conditions, and, of course, job security. But despite, or rather because of, their benevolence, these companies were also subject to sharp criticism from a number of sources.

We mentioned one line of attack—namely, that paternalism is too costly and too inflexible in a highly competitive and rapidly changing business environment. This criticism came most strongly from those who bemoaned almost any worker "entitlement" and any constraint on management's ability to manage for the highest efficiency.

The other attack came from the opposite end of the ideological spectrum—the left, especially labor leaders, who argued that paternalism was but a ploy, an insidious instrument for fighting unions and maintaining control over workers.

There is no question but that a major goal of paternalistic companies was control, in two senses. Through paternalism, employers attempted to prevent the unionization of their workers, but they also sought, to an astounding degree, to govern their personal and social lives in line with the employers' conception of moral behavior.

Regarding unionization, paternalistic companies tried to provide for their employees financially at least as much as—and often more than—they could obtain by joining a union. That was the basic economic reckoning, but the economics gave birth to strong emotions as well: great trust in, and loyalty to, the organization by workers, further reinforcing their reluctance to organize a union. David Sirota, the lead author of this book, worked for IBM—a nonunion company— toward the end of its paternalistic era and can attest to the enormous loyalty that company was able to engender among the great majority of its employees.

It could be argued that, on economic grounds alone, it made no sense for these paternalistic organizations to fight unions. After all, the things they did for employees to avoid unionization might have cost more than a union could have obtained for them. Cases can be made on both sides of that argument, and we won't get into that here. But the fact that the economic benefits to a company of benevolent paternalism are not that clear brings us to the noneconomic motivations for paternalism. Many of the people who founded and ran these paternalistic organizations also genuinely believed they had a mission: not only to care for their workers financially, but also to *morally elevate* them. In other words, they really did see themselves as parents.

To today's students of management, the degree to which business leaders of an earlier era were driven by moral and religious impulses is truly amazing. These employers saw it as their duty to regulate workers' activities both inside and outside the workplace.

> *David Humphrey, founder of Humphreysville, Connecticut, made his "mill girls" go to bed early and eat plenty of fresh vegetables. The Merrimac Mills in Massachusetts invented a boarding-house system, with girls living in supervised boarding houses run by housekeepers. The company also made the girls sign a contract that demanded everything from "propriety at all times" to regular church attendance.*[1]

Parental control evidenced itself as well in the way the firm was managed. When "papa knows best," his control is rarely limited to employee relations. Paternalistic companies tended to be highly centralized in all manner of decision making, just as are paternalistic families. The independent exercise of judgment by employees was not particularly valued: all major, and often the most trivial, of decisions normally went to the boss for his approval. This centralization of power and authority—epitomized, too, by large central staff groups serving the boss ("the king and his court")—added to the rigidity of paternalistic organizations.

The importance placed in paternalistic organizations on the carrying out of the wishes of "papa" resulted as well in an emphasis on loyalty as a criterion for advancement and other rewards. It would be a mistake to say that performance was not valued, but the "court" of the "king" had a large proportion of what can best be called retainers—persons who achieved their positions by showing absolute fidelity to the CEO and his wishes and views. Although high performers could also obtain high-level positions, their chances were limited if they were viewed in any way as too independent. These organizations, therefore, tended to be less attractive places to join and stay for persons with talent, ambition, and independent dispositions. Family members of employees often were given preference in hiring.

Another factor diluting the average ability levels in these organizations was their hesitation to face up to poor employee performance.

In part, this was a result of the fear of unionization, but it also stemmed from the emphasis on loyalty rather than performance. There was much less hesitation firing—or otherwise penalizing—an employee who violated one of the organization's moral codes.

Despite the performance issues inherent in paternalistic organizations, they survived well—some even thrived—when they faced little significant competition in their industries or regions. Many were virtual monopolies. The onset of international and domestic competition made this management style largely unsustainable.

Adversarial. The paternalistic pattern arose to a significant degree to avoid unionization, and most of them did. Say what you will about dependency, conformity, and the manipulation of workers, but the workers in these companies—the benevolently paternalistic companies—thought they were getting a terrific deal. Although they often had complaints about matters such as excruciatingly slow decision-making by management, their own lack of involvement in decision-making, and the criteria used to select employees for advancement, lifetime employment, excellent fringe benefits, and other amenities were powerful inducements not to make too many waves and to stay with the company until retirement and to encourage their children to do the same.

Other companies had employees who did make waves—big ones. These were companies whose employees fought to organize into unions to improve what they considered to be deplorable employment conditions. Once organized, they felt they had to continue battling to maintain what they had achieved and to further improve their conditions. This is the adversarial organization where workers believe that their company's management gives them nothing unless they're forced to and, if conditions are right, they organize into unions to get what they feel workers need and deserve. Among workers in these organizations, there is a sense that they and management share no common objectives; they are destined to be implacable and perpetual foes.

The "win-lose" view of workers in adversarial organizations almost invariably has its genesis in the beliefs and behavior of *management*. Workers work to earn a living and derive a sense of achievement from their jobs and satisfaction from their association with their co-workers. They certainly don't come to work to fight. The few who do are quickly marginalized by their co-workers if there's nothing to fight about. However, if a strong sense of unjust treatment exists, those workers can become the leaders of an incensed workforce.

Management also doesn't come to work wanting to fight, but in adversarial organizations many do come with an extremely jaundiced view of workers, and they act as if a battle is inevitable. Workers must be fought, they believe, if their outrageous economic demands, desire to do as little work as possible, and wish to "run the place" are to be restrained. It's necessary to be tough—very tough—with workers or "they'll run all over management." Workers usually respond with their own toughness; in their views and behavior in these companies, they are a mirror image of management.

Adversarial organizations differ from each other in how much conflict and travail they generate. These differences mirror the extent to which workers feel ill treated. At one extreme are the reactions of workers to employment conditions in the company towns previously described (the malevolent form of paternalistic management) or in the sweatshops of cities. These were the scenes of some of the most bitter and violent labor conflicts in American history.

At the other end of the adversarial scale are companies where labor relations can be described as tense, but not explosive. There is no love lost between the parties, but they learn to coexist and contain the costs of conflict. This relationship is more characteristic of today's adversarial organizations than the bitter confrontations of the past.

In fact, over the past five decades or so, there has been a remarkable decline in the Unites States in the manifestations of conflict between labor and management. For one, there has been a huge reduction in work stoppages. Thirty-five years ago, more than one million workers were involved in 298 stoppages. Twenty years ago, there were 35 work stoppages involving 364,000 workers. And in 2012, there were just 19 major work stoppages involving only 148,000 workers.[2] The decline comes as no surprise to those familiar with what has been happening to the labor movement in general in recent decades. Today's workers are much less prone than in the past to join unions: the total labor force in unions in 2012 was 11.3 percent, as compared to approximately 35 percent in the 1950s.

What accounts for this extraordinary quiescence on the labor front, this near-disappearance of visible adversarial behavior? Many reasons have been proposed for the decline in union membership, such as the shrinking percentage of the workforce engaged in manufacturing, which historically has been more heavily unionized than the service sector; the greater ability of companies to move operations to other parts of the country and overseas, thus heightening the dangers to workers of joining a union or engaging in militant union activities; the increased participation of women in the labor force, many of whom hold part-time or temporary positions and are more difficult to organize; and weaker enforcement in recent years of the laws governing the rights of workers to organize.

But one systematically conducted study attributes the decline in union membership almost entirely and simply to the waning interest of workers in unions. Reviewing attitude surveys conducted from 1977 to 1991, the researchers find that the percentage of workers responding affirmatively to questions about their interest in joining a union dropped significantly in that period. This was paralleled by an increase in their satisfaction with their conditions of employment. Because interest in union membership and dissatisfaction correlate highly both with each other and with actual union membership, and because union membership has been declining in the United States since the 1950s, it is probably safe to assume that interest in unions has also been declining since then and that satisfaction has been increasing.[3]

What accounts for these trends in union interest and satisfaction? First, basic employment conditions for workers are, on the average, much better than they were in past decades. Other than conditions in benignly paternalistic companies (always a relatively small percentage of the economy), there really is no comparison between then and now. American labor has won a lot through their unions, such as higher pay, better benefits, more time off, better and safer physical working conditions, and other employers, in part to avoid unionization, have had to improve the conditions they provide their own workers.

Further, government at the federal, state, and local levels protects workers in the form of wage and hour, occupational safety and health, and antidiscrimination laws. Workers also receive financial support in the form of unemployment insurance and welfare benefits. Unions have fought long, hard, and successfully for government to take these measures but, ironically, that very success has reduced the need for unions in the eyes of its potential members.

Few of today's transaction-oriented companies are unionized—even those that aroused some anger in employees as they shed paternalistic practices. The loss of labor's clout has allowed them to move to a transactional mode without too much worry about being organized.

These companies are still pretty good places to work. There is an important difference between adversarial and transactional management as these modes play themselves out day-to-day in the workplace. The sins of adversarial management in the workplace can be described as largely sins of commission—what they do in their relationship with workers—while those of transactional management are those of omission—what they don't do. In a transactional organization, in its purest form, managers don't pay enough attention to workers as human beings; in adversarial organizations, they pay all too much attention, and of the wrong kind, because they are told that there is no way to get high levels of production from workers other than to drive them through close supervision and punitive measures for not performing. Employees of a transactional manager may complain, in frustration,

"He doesn't know I exist," but those of an adversarial manager want the manager off their backs. Workers don't join unions to get more attention from management; they join for protection from behavior that they consider abusive, and there is much less of that in American industry today. And keep in mind that in some companies today where "entitlement mentality" is a pejorative (referring, say, to the expectation for job security), workers' day-to-day treatment—such as the amount of autonomy they have in doing their jobs—can be exemplary, approximating that of partnership organizations.

In a word, in the current environment, union representation is, by and large, no longer perceived to be as valuable as it once was.

Much of American industry has therefore reached the point where neither the confrontational pattern of adversarial relationships nor paternalism appears to suit current conditions. Today, the choice facing organizations in managing their workers is between an arm's length transactional relationship and an arm-in-arm partnership relationship. Or, rather, it is a decision about the degree to which they will move in either or both directions, because a blending of the two, although not ideal, is possible.

It is tempting to choose the transactional path. Why assume so many of the commitments that partnership requires if management doesn't have to?

Well, management doesn't have to, but our basic proposition throughout this book is that committing to employees in fundamental respects pays off big time over the long term. In considering our argument, we ask that the reader keep in mind that our reference is to the commitment that partners have to each other, not to that of parents to children. A major difference between partnership and paternalism is that partnership is a business relationship, so a high level of performance by both partners is a condition for its sustainability. If one party can't or chooses not to perform as expected over a period of time, the partnership dissolves or significantly changes to reflect the performance difference. Thus, performance matters tremendously in partnership, but it's not defined by the question, "What have you done for me today?," as in a transactional relationship.

If a partnership or collaborative approach is so clearly preferable, why is it, in its comprehensive or near-comprehensive form, characteristic of such a small minority of companies? (One estimate is about 10 percent.) Why has the dominant tendency in the United States been toward transactional relationships? The answer lies, first, in the attractiveness to American executives of avoiding commitment to workers because this allows management to shed workers with minimum cost and travail (to the company). And other aspects of commitment might seem to be more trouble than what they are worth, such as the need to communicate and listen in meaningful ways to workers.

The need to listen brings us to a second reason that partnership is often unattractive: many senior executives' strong belief in the need for control through top-down management. (Transactional management more often than not includes a top-down structure and style.) Partnership differs from all three other models of management in its willing—in fact, deliberate—distribution of authority to the workforce. Although it is naïve to speak of equality of power, in a collaborative setting, the worker's influence on the way the job is performed and on the decisions made in the immediate work environment is much greater than within any of the other three models. For some executives, distributing authority to the non-management workforce is, at best, silly—after all, what can workers contribute?—and to others, it's frightening because they equate such decentralization with organizational anarchy (the unstable laissez-faire management described earlier). There is, of course, no evidence that most workers want authority outside of their work areas; they want a leader steering the ship, but a leader who recognizes that the day-to-day workings of the units of the ship are best left to those most knowledgeable of the work in those units.

A third impediment to the acceptance of the partnership approach is the short-term orientation of many senior managers as they seek rapid gains in profits and in the company's stock price. Obtaining collaboration takes time and thus requires a longer-term perspective. The research evidence we present in this book about the positive impact of collaboration on business performance is about *long-term* results. We made a similar point earlier in relation to a company's purposes and principles (which, by the way, often contain a commitment to collaboration): if the purposes and principles are not to be mere window-dressing, a long-term orientation is almost invariably required.

Fourth, the attractiveness of transactional management is enhanced by its compatibility with an anti-entitlement ideology. As we have pointed out, collaboration is often confused with paternalism where performance is, indeed, often secondary to entitlement as a criterion for rewards.

Therefore, strong forces militate against a partnership approach and these have, over the years, been reinforced by the viewpoints of some union leaders who deeply distrust any approach that is not adversarial. Unions are still a force to be reckoned with in certain industries and companies.

A number of unions and companies, however, have chosen a collaborative path and have achieved impressive results. In these cases, the parties recognize their common interests, such as improving product quality, and they establish mechanisms that enable them to work together on those while reserving areas of contention for the collective bargaining process. Research suggests that positive union-management relations are, in general, associated with higher organization performance.[4] Bringing that relationship to yet a higher level—actively working together to identify and solve performance problems—can yield truly dramatic results.[5]

Labor-management collaboration, which began in earnest in the United States in the late 1970s and early 1980s, is particularly relevant to our broad argument because it underscores the growing inappropriateness of highly adversarial relationships in a fiercely competitive business environment. There is no inherent contradiction between being unionized and establishing a worker-management partnership. A good example of this is Southwest Airlines. Southwest is not only unionized, but—and this comes as a surprise to just about everyone— it has the highest percentage of unionized workers of any airline in the United States! President and chief operating officer of Southwest Colleen Barrett says the following:

> We treat all as family, including outside union representatives. We walk into the room not as adversaries but as working on something together. Our attitude is that we should both do what's good for the company.... [Unions] have their constituency, their customer base. We respect that. We have a great relationship with the Teamsters and they have a reputation for being tough negotiators. We try to stress with everybody that we really like partnerships.[6]

Marcie Means, a customer service agent and union activist at Southwest, offers a worker's point of view:

> Southwest has helped me make a wonderful contribution in my world. I am not looking to abuse the company or take advantage. I just want the right thing. There are things we need to have represented. But there is no need to threaten the company.... It's fine to strike if you can't settle your differences any other way. But we don't need to strike.... We don't want to fight. We belong to this company. It's a system that works, that's been working for years.[7]

The spirit suggested by these comments contrasts starkly with most U.S. airlines, where the relationship between management and unions has frequently been highly adversarial. Any objective analysis of this history reveals that the quality of labor-management relations has largely been a consequence of the attitudes and behavior of management. When management treats workers and their organization as enemies, they are treated as enemies in return. It's as simple as that.

Partnership does not require a complete identity of interests between the parties. There can be differences, but what partnership does—what an atmosphere of trust and mutual respect does—is allow these differences to be settled in more realistic, constructive, and often innovative ways that serve the interests of both parties.

Application to Other Constituencies

The partnership concept is powerful and can be applied to the relationships of an organization with all its key constituencies. For example, consider suppliers. Suppliers can be treated as untrustworthy adversaries who must be continually and closely monitored and from whom every last nickel needs to be squeezed. Or, they can be treated as "transactions," that is, not poorly, but as business entities to whom the company owes nothing but payment for their goods, and who need to continually rebid for work with the company. Or they can be treated as genuine partners. Studies of supplier relations reveal substantial benefits from a partnership relationship, especially in the quality of the products or services the supplier provides to the customer and in the timeliness of delivery. This heightened performance is a result, in part, of increased supplier capability because of better two-way communications with the customer and the experience gained from a long-term relationship. It stems also from the extra effort the supplier applies to its work for a customer that treats it as a partner.

Let's return to Southwest Airlines. How does Southwest Airlines see its relationship with its suppliers? Here is a comment from a director of an airport; airports, of course, comprise a key group of suppliers of services to airlines:

> [Southwest] makes the airport part of their team. We make a presentation to them, and then they turn around and make one to us, saying here's how we see us working together.... It gives you the impression that this is a group I really want to work with, as opposed to [other airlines] where you wonder if you can get them to call you back. With Southwest, you want to see what you can do for them. I think it pays huge dividends. My reaction to how I'm handled by Southwest is that it makes me want to bend over backwards.

—Kevin Dillon, Director of Manchester (NH) Airport[8]

The spirit of this remark is not much different from what we hear from enthusiastic employees whose companies treat them as partners. People, especially employees and suppliers, don't expect that kind of treatment from a company. When it happens, the positive effects—the willingness of people to go all out in their performance—are profound.

A Cultural Case Study of Mayo Clinic

The practices of Mayo Clinic—as they exemplify a partnership organization—have been mentioned a number of times in this book. Based on our in-depth knowledge of Mayo, we now provide a more detailed description of how its specific practices combine into a coherent and powerful culture that works to the benefit of those it serves and those it employs.

This description should make clear why we consider Mayo Clinic an exemplar of partnership organizations. No, it's not a Utopia, as we remarked earlier in reference to outstanding companies. It is composed of human beings with all their many frailties. Our goal is not to change people in any basic sense but rather to change their work *environment* so that what is good and decent about the great majority of workers—their better angels—naturally emerge and become predominant in the conduct of their work lives.

Mayo Clinic is a world-renowned leader in medical care, research, and education. Providing its services to more than a million patients annually in three locations, the clinic is recognized by a greater number of well-known national assessment organizations than any other major U.S. hospital or clinic. It is consistently ranked at or near the top, for example, in *US News* Best Honor Hospital Roll. Further, Mayo Clinic has been on the list of *Fortune Magazine*'s "America's 100 Best Companies to Work For" ten years in a row.

The Clinic has been studied extensively by Sirota. On the basis of our research there, we can say that Mayo Clinic exemplifies as few other organizations do what we mean by a genuine partnership culture. It is this culture that is fundamental to understanding Mayo's renowned accomplishments and the extraordinarily high morale of its employees. (In the 2011 employee survey at that institution, 89 percent expressed satisfaction with working at Mayo. The norm for that question for that year was 73 percent.)

The senior author of this book, Dr. David Sirota, published a paper in 2010 about the Clinic.[9] He wrote it because that time was the beginning of the intense debate in this country about healthcare reform, and the achievements of Mayo Clinic had direct relevance for a number of provisions of Obamacare (the Patient Protection and Affordable Care Act). In addition to providing affordable healthcare insurance for millions of Americans, the major aims of Obamacare were to improve healthcare quality and reduce the rate of increase in healthcare costs. Mayo was frequently touted, a number of times by President Obama himself, as a model for both high-quality and cost-effective care.

Dr. Sirota's paper, amplified and updated for this book and presented next, does not comment directly on the pluses and minuses of Obamacare. Rather, it seeks to demonstrate how critical the culture of an organization is—yes, it takes more than legislation—for true organizational excellence.

What's So Special About Mayo Clinic?
Core Values Are What Count
By David Sirota

Amid the cornfields of south central Minnesota, in the small city of Rochester, stands, improbably, the largest and founding location of Mayo Clinic, one of America's premier healthcare institutions. Established in 1889 by two physicians, brothers Charles and William Mayo, the Rochester location employs 33,000 and each year provides services to hundreds of thousands of patients from throughout the world. It would not be surprising to find an institution of this size and renown bordering the East River in New York City. But Rochester, Minnesota? That's just the beginning of the anomalies. (The other two Mayo facilities are in Jacksonville, Florida, and Scottsdale, Arizona, and were established in 1986 and 1987, respectively.)

Mayo Clinic received a lot of attention, including frequent accolades from President Obama, in the course of the debate over the Patient Protection and Affordable Care Act ("Obamacare"). The care Mayo provides is demonstrably among the highest in the nation but, anomalously, the cost of that care is among the lowest. The outcomes at Mayo belie the conventional wisdom that quality is necessarily expensive and the Clinic's methods have therefore been of considerable interest to those seeking to reform the nation's healthcare system. The goals of Obamacare include a significant reduction in the rate of increase of healthcare costs and an improvement in healthcare quality.

Skeptics argue that the challenges Mayo faces are very different than those of healthcare institutions elsewhere, especially those in large urban centers where patients are poorer, sicker, and less-well educated. Mayo, however, is but one of a number of health care institutions with outstanding performance and they are in quite diverse settings. Cleveland, Ohio, for example, hardly resembles Rochester, Minnesota, but that is the home of Cleveland Clinic, an institution that closely resembles Mayo in its practices and results. Other similarly successful institutions frequently cited are

Geisinger HealthSystem in Danville, Pennsylvania; Intermountain Healthcare in Salt Lake City; and Kaiser Permanente in Northern California. Finally, the other two Mayo facilities, in locations different in many ways from Rochester, achieve results very similar to it.

The anecdotal evidence about individual high-performing healthcare organizations is strongly supported by systematic research across thousands of such organizations. For example, the Dartmouth Atlas of Healthcare finds wide variations in per capita healthcare spending across the U.S. but concludes that "... just 30% of excess spending... could be attributable to (patients') income and health." What accounts for most of the rest? It is wasted spending: the Dartmouth group and others estimate that an astounding $600–700 billion of the Nation's health bill is wasted on unnecessary tests, procedures, hospital stays, doctors' visits, and the like, and there are large differences between healthcare institutions in this respect.[10]

Many experts identify the fee-for-service reimbursement system as the major culprit when medical services are overused because it rewards healthcare providers for the amount, rather than the quality, of the care they provide. George Bernard Shaw put it well nearly a century ago: "That any sane nation, having observed that you could provide for the supply of bread by giving bakers a pecuniary interest in baking for you, should go on to give a surgeon a pecuniary interest in cutting off your leg, is enough to make one despair...."

Contrary to accepted wisdom about the relationship between quality and costs, the Dartmouth researchers find a tendency for areas of the country with the highest quality to have *lower* costs. There are many reasons for this. As Shaw reminds us, unnecessary procedures can be unhealthy as well as costly. Excessive hospital stays can be dangerous as well as expensive because of errors and negligence there. And, poor quality often requires "rework," thus inflating costs. From the perspective of U.S. health care as a whole, therefore, quality pays! But, from the perspective of the healthcare provider, quality can depress earnings.

And so, the key question is: How is it that in the face of such perverse incentives, some institutions have managed to swim against the tide and provide such high levels of quality and do so efficiently? The same question can be asked about many industries. Automobile manufacturers, for example, are for-profit entities whose revenues come from the volume of cars they sell, a parallel to the fee-for-service system. Why did some companies, such as those from Japan, perform so much better than others over decades in the quality of the products they produced?

When accounting for an organization's success, observers tend to emphasize highly visible, distinguishing practices, such as formal quality programs in Japanese companies. In healthcare, there is much written about how doctors in many high-quality, low-cost healthcare institutions—such as Mayo—are full-time, salaried employees. There are therefore no financial rewards for them for excessive tests, procedures, or visits.

Employee compensation is important, but focus on it distracts attention from the cultures of these institutions—their "invisible architecture"—of which the salary system is but a part and from which it, indeed, derives. After all, when pay is unrelated to performance, the effect might be a reduction not just in unnecessary treatment but also a general decline in the care and effort physicians devote to their jobs. Further, while the doctors are paid salaries, their employers' revenues depend largely on fees for services. Why would they not pressure the doctors to increase volume and suffer the usual deleterious quality and cost consequences?

The answer lies indisputably in an institution's culture, defined here as what the institution's leadership genuinely values and, therefore, what it expects from its employees. In every industry we have studied, differences between organizations in their quality and efficiency can be explained largely by differences in their values and the skill with which the values are executed. Let's see how this plays out at Mayo Clinic.

Mayo's culture, remarkably pervasive throughout the organization, has its source in its simple, seven-word mission: "The needs of the patient come first." While this sounds like innumerable other well-worn and hollow slogans, it is absolutely clear from our studies that in Mayo, the mission is genuine and drives the day-to-day behavior of employees at all levels. In a recent employee survey, 90% of the Clinic's employees agreed that, "At Mayo, the needs of the patient come first."

In discussions with physicians, they repeatedly mention the mission and its genuineness as a primary reason they came to and remain with Mayo. Surveys of patients show just how impressively the mission is realized in practice. Mayo employees are frequently reported in these surveys to go to extraordinary lengths in their attention to patients' needs. "Two nurses gave up their day off to be with us for my peace of mind," comments a former patient. "They brought me smoothies. They hemmed the pajamas my mother sent. They were so wonderful." "The phone rang," says another. "It was a Mayo heart surgeon. I couldn't believe it. He personally called to say come see him." A third commented: "My oncologist is...the kindest man I ever met. He related some of his personal life to me. I was more than my problem to him. He related to me as a person." These representative experiences may seem trivial at first glance but they have a tremendous impact on patients and their confidence in their care.

The mission impels daily behavior and is the basis as well of Mayo's formal policies and practices. These range from an obsession with compliance with legal and ethical standards to an investment in unusually attractive and comfortable physical facilities for the physical and emotional well-being of patients. The straight salary system flows directly from the mission: the institution wants its physicians focused entirely on the needs of the patient and not on what might increase their own compensation.

A hallmark of the Clinic's practices has been its collaborative approach to the delivery of care. Physicians and other health professionals work in multispecialty teams whose composition is dictated by the medical problems in a case. Working in teams helps to assure quality care and decreased repetitive testing, procedures, and appointments, and is fostered by a broadly egalitarian environment where mutual respect is an explicit standard of behavior.

In support of its team methods, Mayo studiously avoids the "star" system in the recruitment of physicians. It seeks those who are top-notch in their abilities but it wants their primary attention to be on patient care rather than building their individual external reputations. Straight salaries reinforce teamwork in that there is no incentive for doctors to hoard patients for the sake of financial gain. The most important criteria in the evaluation of physicians' performance are the quality with which clinical care is delivered and the ability to work cooperatively with colleagues in delivering that care.

Collaboration in Mayo involves not just the doctors. It is expected of all employees and this requires an environment of mutual trust across levels as well as across specialties. In addition to technical competence, the major source of mutual trust in the work situation at Mayo is egalitarianism, where status and other needless barriers are at a minimum. Egalitarianism is characteristic of the Mayo culture to a degree rarely realized in healthcare institutions. As one example, status distinctions between doctors and others, while not entirely absent in the institution, are greatly diminished. On the Mayo employee survey, 76% agreed with the statement, "Based on my personal experience over the last year, there is mutual respect between physicians/scientists and allied health staff." We have no normative data on that question, but we do know that disrespectful treatment of the non-physician staff by physicians is a well-known and serious issue in many healthcare organizations. Verbal reiteration of the need for mutual respect is reinforced in Mayo by required formal training for all in human relations.

Teamwork among employees is paralleled by a strong bond between employees and the institution as a whole. People want to work for an organization of which they can be proud and for an organization that has a genuine concern for them. 94% of Mayo employees say in their survey that they are proud to work for Mayo and 75% agree that "Mayo takes a genuine interest in the well-being of employees." (The Sirota norm on the former question is 81% and on the latter 65%.) One way the Clinic exemplifies its interest in employee well-being is a policy that layoffs will be a last resort in times of financial difficulty—and this played out in 2009, as the

Great Recession took hold, when physicians and senior administrators in Rochester forwent salary increases in order to prevent layoffs and provide salary increases for the rest of the staff. There is a large investment in employee education and development that prepares employees to transfer many times across different functions in the course of their careers at the Clinic and undergirds their job security.

The result of all of this is a dedicated workforce allied with Mayo and with each other in the service of patients. It is a culture of partners in which people go above and beyond in the performance of their jobs and in which most want to—and do—spend their careers. Mayo's attrition rate was 4.1% in 2012. The attrition rate nationally in healthcare institutions was 13.5%.

Mayo values may appear anachronistic, a throwback to an era when loyalty—to customers, employees, and employees to each other—was considered vital for business success. But this model—we call it "partnership"—has worked for Mayo since its founding more than a century ago, a period in which the practice of medicine has changed enormously in just about every other respect. In 1910, co-founder William Mayo wrote, "The best interest of the patient is the only interest to be considered, and in order that the sick may have the benefit of advancing knowledge, union of forces is necessary....It has become necessary to develop medicine as a cooperative science...." Little needs to be added to describe Mayo's core mission and values a century later.

How has the Mayo partnership culture been sustained for so long? For one, the Clinic *works at it*. Considerable effort is required if a culture is to survive periodic and sometimes severe financial pressures, varying personalities of executives, and the allure of management fads. The mission is kept front and center by continual reiteration, celebrations of the Mayo brothers' legacy and values, employee recognition for their achievements in line with the values, and conscious vetting of relevant policy and practice changes against the values.

Further, Mayo is a physician-led institution and, with rare exceptions, these physician-executives are promoted into their jobs from within Mayo, helping to assure cultural continuity. It is truly an institutional culture, not dependent on the outlooks or whims of one or a few individuals.

All of this effort at continuity would, of course, be for naught if the result was insolvency! While the institution has faced significant financial challenges over the years, its ability to survive and thrive is, ironically, due in no small part to a core mission devoid of financial goals. The focus on patients has resulted in a reputation for excellence—one of the best-known and most-highly-respected healthcare brands—that helps assure a continuing flow of patients from throughout the world. A large cadre of former patients contributes generously to Mayo in appreciation of the care they received there.

Sustaining a genuine institutional culture requires a lot more than slogans or borrowing the practices of admired organizations. American automobile manufacturers diligently copied Japanese quality techniques (after finally acknowledging that Japanese products were, indeed, superior) but had difficulty for decades closing the quality gap. Why the difficulty? Here is what an American automobile worker told me in the mid-1980s in a plant whose walls were emblazoned with quality slogans: "Let me tell you what really counts here—it's what my boss tells me: 'Get the pieces out the door'."

Skeptics seek coincidental reasons for an organization's success, reasons other than skilled and farsighted management. We see this in the way the successes of Mayo Clinic and similar institutions have been attributed to the characteristics of their patient populations. When the Japanese automobile manufacturers began shipping high-quality cars to the U.S. and capturing a significant share of the market, the reason often given for their success was the discipline and dedication of Japanese workers. The Japanese then opened plants in the U.S. and continued to produce high-quality automobiles with American workers. Among the reasons then given for their success were the newness of their plants and the fact that the workers were non-union. These were excuses, not reasons. The primary reason for the achievements of these Japanese companies was their culture which, among other things, put quality first, treated workers as partners, and organized the work by teams. Sound familiar?

It is the values of an organization that count, values in healthcare institutions such as Mayo Clinic that dictate that patients' needs come first and are satisfied in an environment of trust and collaboration among partners. Managements seeking to transform their organizations need to focus initially not on practices, no matter has easily copied, but rather on core values and determine whether these can be enthusiastically embraced. The task then is to bring the values to life through practices that reinforce them, are best suited to an institution's particular conditions (such as whether physicians are full-time employees), and can be adapted to changing conditions. Leaders at Mayo Clinic say that everything is up for change except their core values. The substance and constancy of those values paralleled by a willingness to adapt how they are realized in a changing world are what account for the institution's amazing longevity and success.

Partnership in These Times

An important lesson from the Mayo example is how a partnership culture helps a company cope effectively with change. The essence of the case is that strong core values—an inspiring purpose coupled with genuine cohesiveness as partners—generates a resilience that is immeasurably important as an organization's conditions change. What could be very threatening, confusing, and disheartening can be turned into a challenge that people want to overcome and believe they will overcome. "We're all in this together for something we believe in," becomes the guiding motto. This is very different from the situation in which the first—and second and third—impulse in a time of change is to fiercely fight fellow employees for one's own piece of what is feared could be a shrinking pie or to prepare to get out of the company altogether.

Although, historically, there have been periods of great national, social, and economic upheaval, it can reasonably be argued that there are few if any periods since the Industrial Revolution in which the velocity of change has been as great or the changes as large and numerous and long-lasting as what we see today. Think of information technology and the changes in hundreds of directions that it has wrought in just a few short decades, and with no end in sight. Or globalization and the way it has facilitated worldwide competition, innovation, and low-cost production and the international flow of capital at light-speed. Or global warming and the immense impact it—and mitigating it—will have on the way we will lead our lives and how institutions, including businesses, will function.

Adaptation of organizations to changes in the business environment happen in two contexts: the needs of the human beings that are affected by the changes and the organizational culture. As we will point out in our final chapter when discussing resistance to change, it is inaccurate to assume that people instinctively fear and resist change. There are many positive changes that are eagerly welcomed, such as the success of a new product or business strategy that will bring business expansion and enhanced job security and opportunity for employees. But there are changes that are threatening—they can be deeply threatening—such as the emergence of a competitor with dramatically lower-cost products or new and innovative products that better meet customer needs. In today's fluid, highly competitive world, those types of challenges are inevitable for the great majority of companies.

Organizations need to change to cope with a changing environment and, in this endeavor, culture counts tremendously. The organizations that have done this best are, ironically, those which, like Mayo, have core values that are *un*changeable. Those values include, as Collins and Poras have demonstrated (see our discussion in Chapter 7), a "more-than-profits" purpose and, from our point of view, they also include a set of principles that make it clear that "we are all partners in this endeavor." Being partners has, as we have shown in this chapter, a number of different attributes, including open communications up, down, and across the organization, joint decision making, mutual assistance, and respectful interaction. There is no way most external threats can be handled by one person or a small group of people, and it is only partnership that allows a company to draw on talents, ideas, and enthusiasm from throughout the organization. And unchangeable core values provide the partners with a steady and shared compass for navigating the inevitable storms of business life.

Essential as well to genuine partnership is financial sharing. This means sharing in the sacrifices that need to be made to meet external challenges and sharing as well in the gains that an effective response will bring. When people do not feel they will be in jeopardy as a result of change (not "thrown under the bus," as it were), resistance is obviously greatly reduced, and their contribution to the change process commensurately enhanced. Just as obviously, we understand that among the outcomes of a change effort may be actions that are harmful to groups of employees, such as a downsizing to cut unsustainable costs. We have shown, however (in Chapter 3), that, although not an ideal circumstance, these measures can be undertaken with good planning, care, and generosity, thus greatly mitigating the damage.

We are, in essence, asking management: do you want your employees working with you or against you in responding to change in the business environment? This might seem like a rhetorical question—isn't the answer obviously "with you"?—but there are many executives who would answer, "it doesn't matter."

These executives are normally brought in to "save" a poorly performing company "from itself," especially when its business environment has changed. They quickly and radically centralize authority, assume that the organization's people are the problem, certainly not the solution, and ram change down their throats, with no consideration either for the talents they can bring to help or their needs. And why involve them in the change process because "people inevitably are going to resist change"? This mode has had a number of well-known practitioners, Albert J. Dunlop probably being the most famous—or infamous—of them. Mr. Dunlop's most widely publicized feat was at Scott Paper. After stints at several other companies, he was brought into Scott in 1994, as the company's first outside CEO, with the expectation of quick action to restore the company to health. Scott's revenues and profits had been disappointing for years. Like many old-line American companies, Scott was slow to react to aggressive competition from rivals such as Procter & Gamble.

And quick action they got. Dunlop came to Scott with a reputation as a turnaround specialist that endeared him to many on Wall Street. The reputation was quite extreme, even for his specialty, earning him the nickname "Chainsaw Al" for his tactics of rapidly slashing workforces and ditching assets. In less than a year at Scott, Dunlap eliminated almost one-third of the company's 34,000 hourly and salaried employees, through layoffs and asset sales. And, eighteen months after he joined the company, the company was sold to Kimberly-Clark; by that time, the market value of the company's common stock had increased more than 200 percent (more than $3 billion), and Dunlap's personal wealth had increased by nearly $100 million, reflecting his compensation and Scott stock holdings and options.

We will not here debate or make moral judgments about Dunlap's actions or results. Suffice it to say that they are highly controversial, and on business—not just humanistic or ethical—grounds. For example, Peter Cappelli, the George W. Taylor professor of management at The Wharton School and director of Wharton's Center for Human Resources, argues that, "[Dunlap]... is persuading others that shareholder value is the be-all and end-all. But Dunlap didn't create value. He redistributed income from the employees and the community to the shareholders."[11] (In addition to his other actions, Dunlap ended Scott's decades-long practice of contributing $3 to $4 million a year to community organizations and matching employee contributions to United Way.) Despite his assertion that his goal was the rebuilding of

Scott for the long term, others speak of Dunlop's intention from the very beginning to prepare the company for a quick sale.

Our point is that there are strikingly different ways of dealing with the need for change. We said at the outset that this book will not be of much interest to people whose goal is short-term, even if not as extreme as Dunlap's restructuring and sale of a large corporation in eighteen months. *This book, instead, is written for those interested in building an enduring institution with enduring value.* The Mayo brothers are an obvious example of what we mean by that, but so are private-sector executives and companies that have been discussed throughout this book, such as Ken Iverson at Nucor, Herb Kelleher at Southwest Airlines, and Jim Sinegal at Costco. Central to their ability to meet and overcome serious short- and long-term business challenges is their culture, in two senses. For one, in times of change they all maintain—indeed, often intensify—their already strong focus on understanding and meeting the needs of their customers. So they don't cut there. Second, rather than treating employees as the problem, they enlist them as strong, knowledgeable, and natural allies in the battle. Among their prime assets, then, for dealing successfully with change are their unchangeable core values.

13 ——————————————————

Leadership and the Partnership Culture

"It is a terrible thing to look over your shoulder when you are trying to lead and find no one there."

—Franklin D. Roosevelt

What are the implications for leadership of a partnership culture? We have made reference to leadership—or "the CEO" or "senior management" or "executives"—many times in this book. It will come up again in some detail in the next chapter, where we discuss the implementation of a partnership organization, because without strong and continuing support from the top, no genuine culture change can be sustained. In this chapter, we explore in some detail leadership itself—including the evidence-based conclusions about the specific characteristics of great leadership—and the intimate relationship between great leadership and culture. More often than not, great leaders—those who build organizations with *sustained* high performance—do so through cultures of partnership.

Our conclusions about leadership are based on our own many systematic studies of leadership, our observations of the great and not-so-great (and some downright miserable) leaders we have worked with and otherwise observed throughout the years, and the research of others. Leadership has been one of the most extensively researched topics in the field of organizational behavior.

The Critical Importance of Effective Leadership

Despite all the talk about "new generations" of workers who seek autonomy and the need for radically new, fluid—even anarchic—organizational forms to combat the dysfunctions of hierarchy, companies cannot function without leadership and cannot function well without strong leadership. Leadership is the organization's rudder, that which gives it its direction and defines how its goals will be achieved. Without leadership, a company falls apart or just slogs along. One of the first questions asked of any organization—by employees and others dealing with it—is, "Who's in charge here?" When the answer to who's in charge is ambiguous, that is a serious deterrent to effectiveness. When there is no answer, that is a disaster. When the ambiguity or absence of leadership is an issue, employees register strong complaints about it on our surveys—whether the problem is at a company-wide level or in their own part of the business.

Here are some positive comments from employees about leadership:

> *All levels of leadership are very approachable, set a clear vision, display and expect high levels of ethical behavior, and expect excellent results.*

> *Our CEO and leadership team has a strong and clear vision.*

> *We have great leaders in top management, who can drive the company successfully.*

> *I enjoy the fast-paced nature of the company and the goals that we're working toward.... I greatly respect our CEO and Sr. Leadership team.*

> *The executive team has intelligence, vision, passion, and openness. It makes me feel 100% confident in the product and future of our company. Though we have our growing pains, I could not imagine working anywhere else.*

I like the stability that comes from strong upper management vision & leadership.

I appreciate the overall goal and focus of upper management. Through everything, the end result has remained constant.

Visionary leadership allows employees to trust the senior leadership and the direction the company is heading.

And now, here are some unfavorable comments from employees about leadership:

There is a lack of clear leadership—no one and everyone seems to be in charge, which results in factionalism, waste, and inefficiency.

Continual changes in Senior Management makes for a very unsettled feeling.

Decision making is so fragmented and unclear that when it comes down to crunch time, people are still weighing in on what to do... but when you're supposed to launch a product the next day, we need clear leadership to break stalemates.

Everyone is on a power trip about who's in charge.

Having three powerful leaders has led to disconnection in our strategies and will lead to poorer outcomes for [the company] overall. The CEO should lead us toward developing one strategy that we all execute off of, not a series of unrelated strategies to help disparate leaders meet their own individual goals.

Our leadership team is scared and uncertain in this time of change. They act young and inexperienced rather than as a beacon of confidence for the rest of us.

The loudest voice in the meeting room seems to win. Someone with real authority needs to step in with a real overall vision.

The organization is run bottom up and not top down. Too many levels, too many groups, and no clear leadership. Focus is constantly changing; what's important this month is not important next month.

There is a desperate need for clear leadership and vision.

There is also not a clear leader that we have been able to rally behind.

In an abstract sense, leadership would not be required in a company that is completely steady-state—that is, where nothing changes, everything is routine and has been preprogrammed. But nothing in human endeavor is ever steady-state—only death is. External conditions change (in the economy, in competition, in customer preferences), and there are never-ending internal changes that require vigilance and constant adaptation (employees enter and leave the organization, new technology is introduced, things don't work as they were supposed to, and on and on).

It's not just a matter of organization functioning in the pure business sense. Leadership also sets the internal culture, the values that determine how things get done and how employees and other stakeholders are treated. A culture can require ethical behavior or wink at (or even encourage) misconduct. It can be dedicated to providing value and service to customers or tolerate indifferent treatment of customers. It can place value on employees as assets rather than as interchangeable "hands" to get the work done. It can be highly bureaucratic and rigid or encouraging of employee autonomy and creativity. The culture of an organization flows directly from the real values and the observable behavior of the company's leadership. It is striking how greatly the cultures of companies differ and how, in company after company, the culture is virtually a direct reflection of what the CEO wants, and, indeed, of the type of person the CEO *is* (open or secretive, oriented to the short term or the long term, collaborative or competitive, ethical or unethical).

Trust

Organizations have many "leaders"—that is, those in positions of formal authority with others reporting to them. We use quotes because power does not a leader make. There is no leader without followers and, for our purposes, leadership implies *willingness*—eagerness, in the best case—of followers to follow.

Followers follow for one of four reasons: they can be *forced* to follow; they can be *paid* to follow; they can be *made dependent* so they will follow; or, they can be *inspired* so that they *want* to follow. When someone is given formal authority over others in an organization, that authority includes the first three of these—that is, the power to apply negative and positive sanctions to influence behavior. When, however, organizations say they seek and want to develop "leaders," they almost invariably mean the ability to inspire employees. The importance of that kind of leadership is universal, applying even to what on the surface appears to be the most top-down and force-reliant of organizations: the military.

> *"The first thing a young army officer must do is to fight a battle, and that battle is for the hearts of his men. If he wins that battle and subsequent similar ones, his men will follow him anywhere. If he loses it, he will never do any real good."*
>
> —Bernard Law Montgomery, British Field Marshal

> *"You do not lead by hitting people over the head—that's assault, not leadership."*
>
> —Dwight D. Eisenhower

When discussing leadership, we and others tend to focus on the top of an organization—especially the CEO—but leadership applies at all levels, and it emerges even when not accompanied by formal authority. Think of informal groups—whether at work or not—and how leaders materialize spontaneously, those persons to whom others willingly look to for direction and approval. This is true even in children's play groups. Within departments at work, individual employees will often be invested by their peers with leadership mantles that can work to reinforce or circumvent the formal supervisor. In other words, leadership is not simply about a position or title. An individual can have a high-sounding title such as CEO and not be considered a leader. And that, as we have said, is an enormous problem.

Who emerges spontaneously as a leader or acts or develops as a genuine leader when appointed to a formal position of leadership? We will soon describe what research and informed observation have taught us are the key elements of leadership. One way of comprehending the importance of these elements is that they are the foundation for *trust* in a leader. Voluntarily following a leader is, after all, making a bet on the future, relinquishing some degree of control over one's fortune to someone else in the expectation that benefits will accrue from it. This soon becomes more than a rational calculation as an emotional bond develops—even in economic, supposedly rational, entities such as companies—between followers and trusted leaders.

Leadership, then, is not a solo act: it is a *relationship* between the parties with obligations on both sides. It is not simply the leader determining direction and telling his followers what he expects of them. Genuine leadership requires an understanding of what the followers want and how the leader can help them get it. This is not a matter of selfishness of followers as selfishness is normally conceived. Companies have needs and their employees have needs, and a fundamental premise of this book is that the right approach to management assumes the compatibility of most of these needs most of the time and, therefore, the possibility of a commonality of purpose. It is not, further, simply a question of employees' financial needs. As we said, people are complex, and although a company ignores its workers' financial needs at its peril, they are a part of a larger array of worker goals that great companies and great leaders understand and work to satisfy. Included in this array of goals, it will be recalled, is the need to be proud of your work and of the company for which you do it. In some companies, we can add to those sources of employee pride the accomplishments and character of the company's leader.

It should be clear that genuine leadership, as we understand it and whose elements we will soon describe in detail, is congruent in all its aspects only with a Partnership culture. The primary control mechanism of a Transactional culture is money: we pay you to follow. An Adversarial culture relies on force (often stimulating counterforce as workers seek protection). Paternalism depends on dependency, like the trust a child has in its parent to lead the way. Partnership, too, depends on trust, but it is the trust between mature adults who, with mutual respect and admiration, have voluntarily joined together to achieve their long-term goals. This is not to say that a boss and his subordinates are equal in power in a partnership relationship—that is a fantasy, and it is dysfunctional when attempted. It is the *use* of the boss's power that is dramatically different, most especially as it derives from the confidence the boss has in the intelligence and integrity of his subordinates. That confidence leads him to see his subordinates as much more than "hands" with little to contribute beyond what they are ordered to do and driven by a desire to do as little work as possible while demanding as much money as possible. The leader-as-partner, having trust in his subordinates, is comfortable distributing his power to them, which helps ensure both higher-than-average levels of per- formance from them and higher-than-average levels of financial and psychological return to them.

When we speak of the performance of a company in relation to great leadership, we mean, as we have said, *sustained* performance— sustained even after the leader retires or otherwise leaves. Many clever CEOs know how to achieve outstanding short-term results, such as by sharply and quickly reducing the workforce and otherwise cutting costs. We described in our chapter on job security the often negligible long-term gains of such measures. A key question for us, therefore, is whether the company's leaders are building for the future—that is, even after they are no longer on the scene. That brings us to the topic of charismatic leadership and the indispensible leader.

Charisma

"The graveyards are full of indispensible men," said Charles de Gaulle. Many of those leaders, typically described as "charismatic," were believed while they lived to have been set aside from ordinary men, seen even as superhuman with "a divine gift of grace," and the reference was mostly to political, military, and religious figures. Over recent years in the United States, a number of business leaders have evoked intense admiration—people such as Lee Iacocca, Jack Welch, and Steve Jobs—and although we haven't heard any of them described as possessing "divine gifts," the regard for these charismatic CEOs has been such that when they left their companies there was more than a hint of despair that those companies would be on the way to mediocrity, even ruin. Charisma, in other words, is believed by many to be vital to truly great leadership.

Charisma is typically thought of as something mysterious, even magical. We propose to demystify it, at least in the business arena. In our view, when someone in business is described as having leadership charisma, it means, simply, that people sense strongly that following that person will take them in the direction they want to go. They sense that because that person possesses more than others a combination of the basic leadership characteristics we will shortly describe, such as being smart, visionary, decisive, energetic, and having a genuine concern for the well-being of his followers. Further, business leaders seen as possessing charisma have almost invariably been known to have achieved outstanding business results.

In other words, in our terms and simply, *there is no difference between the qualities that are important for truly effective business leadership and the qualities that are typically used to describe a charismatic leader.*

With one major exception.

You surely know by now that we will argue that a concern for the needs and interests of followers is a core characteristic of effective leadership. The term charismatic, however, is often applied to people for whom the needs and interests of their followers are irrelevant. They are the narcissists whose focus is entirely on what makes them compelling personally rather than on what makes the organization as a whole compelling and satisfying to its employees and other stakeholders. Indeed, some of these "leaders" are incredibly destructive—of their organizations, the people in them, and sometimes, ultimately, of themselves.

Everything has to be centered on these grandiose types: attention, prestige, decision-making power. They want the success of the company to be associated entirely with them and usually fail to prepare for the day they will leave. What good would it do, because they are indispensible? They are the flames around which the moths flitter.

Although those outside the organization may describe these persons as charismatic, most of those inside—those who have come to know them best—are not fooled for long. Rather than charismatic, these leaders are "egomaniacs," "Napoleons," "blowhards," "manipulators," and other terms not to be mentioned in a family book.

Some writers have therefore made a useful distinction between two types of charismatic leadership: Self-centered (or "personalized" or "unethical") charisma and organization-centered (or "socialized" or "ethical") charisma. The former is the type of leader who:

> *Uses power only for personal gain or impact; promotes own personal vision; censures critical or opposing views; demands that own decisions be accepted without question; one-way communication; insensitive to followers' needs; relies on convenient external moral standards to satisfy self-interests.*

> *On the other hand, the organization-centered leader uses power to serve others; aligns vision with followers' needs and aspirations; considers and learns from criticism; stimulates followers to think independently and to question the leader's view; uses open, two-way communication; coaches, develops, and supports followers; shares recognition with others; relies on internal moral standards to satisfy organizational and societal interests.*[1]

Jim Collins, in his widely read and influential book *Good to Great*, goes even further with his argument that the "great" leaders (he calls these leaders "Level 5") tend to be persons of "deep personal humility." "A company's long-term health requires a leader who can infuse the company with its own sense of purpose instead of his or hers,"

Collins argues. He has "ambition first and foremost for the company and concern for *its* success rather than for one's own riches and personal renown."[2]

The real world of people and organizations is, of course, more complex than the black-and-white portrayals encountered in the business press or management literature. Although there is no shortage of leaders at or near the extreme of self-centeredness, it is folly to think of the organization-centered leader as devoid of self-interest and ego. We are not dealing with self-effacing saints at the higher reaches of organizations, at least not in the experience of the authors of this book. The organization-centered leader understands his value full well and wants an equitable reward for it. He also understands the value of others—and wants them rewarded for that. Of great importance, he understands that *his value is multiplied many times over because of the contributions of others.* That is the essential difference between him and the narcissists.

We add that the organization-centered leader may not always act in the interest of others, and he doesn't always appreciate how much they contribute to his own achievements. These leaders are, after all, human, so it is probably best to talk about *degrees* of organization-centeredness, rather than *the* organization-centered leader.

The situation is made even more complicated by the fact that the same person can act differently under different circumstances. For example, there is no dearth of political leaders who achieve a great deal for their constituencies but, in aspects of their private lives and simultaneously with their achievements, act recklessly with apparent contempt for others. In another context, our case study of former mayor Rudy Giuliani shows how key facets of leadership can change markedly with changing circumstances, in his case with the 9/11 attacks on New York City when he was transformed from the largely self-centered, indispensible man of his mayoralty to the community-centered, compassionate but still-strong mayor providing leadership and solace to a traumatized city.[3]

The Nine Key Leadership Attributes

We come now to our summary of what research and informed observation have taught us are the key attributes of highly effective leadership. With an understanding that no single leader has all of these in full measure—and certainly not all of the time—we find the following nine attributes to be the foundation of truly effective leadership.

Sheer Competence

Organizational psychologists, fond as they are of factors such as human relationships and personality, often forget the cognitive side of organizational leadership—that is, the need for intelligence and business competence. Or, to put it colloquially, soldiers don't want to be led into battle by a jerk. A jerk is not to be trusted to lead. For employees, the evidence for competence comes in part from what the leader says and how he thinks, but the primary source is what the leader has *done*—his past and present record of results. Steve Jobs was arguably the most charismatic business leader of his generation, with an almost cult-like following. Was his charisma a function of his communications skills (especially his flair for the dramatic) and his personality? Those played a role, of course, but he would have been another somewhat odd IT guy had it not been for his extraordinary track record of successful products and profits.

Forward-Looking and Acting

A leader can be defined in a number of ways, some dynamic—such as someone who moves people in a new or better direction, and some static—such as, simply, the decision maker or organizer. Traditionally, the latter has been associated with the term "management" rather than leadership. There is no need to debate definitions; suffice it to say that when we ask people why they regard a particular senior executive as a leader, they almost invariably talk about the matter in dynamic terms: someone who is deliberately taking the organization to a significantly better place than where it is. They will also, therefore, often describe him as a "visionary." They may or may not see him as being a particularly good manager. In some cases, he may be a pretty awful manager, which can be a serious impediment to his ability to lead, or to translate his vision into concrete changes and business results. In the best of circumstances, a leader recognizes that weakness and makes up for it by bringing into senior management executives with strong management skills.

When does a leader's vision for an organization generate enthusiasm in its members? We have written about this in other parts of the book (especially in Chapter 7, "Organization Purpose and Principles") and need not revisit the subject in detail. In essence and for our purposes here, a vision should be *credible*—not platitudes or fantasies or academic theory; it should be *inspiring*, embodying goals and values with which followers can identify, including goals and values above and beyond profits; it should be *long term*: what we aspire this company to be like over a matter of years, not the next quarter or two; and, it should contain a conception of the aspired-to *corporate culture,* most desirably a partnership culture, through which the vision is to be achieved.

Deserving of some elaboration and emphasis is that the vision of an outstanding leader is truly long term. That leader wants to build an *enduring* organization, indeed—one that will outlast him.

> *"The final test of a leader is that he leaves behind him in other men the conviction and the will to carry on."*

—Walter Lippmann, journalist and philosopher

Of the organizations we have studied, Mayo Clinic probably comes closest to attaining this ideal. We described in the previous chapter how the Clinic, founded by the Mayo brothers more than a century ago, stands today dramatically altered except in its basic values—especially "the needs of the patients come first" and "uniting for the good of the patient"—and the basic structures and processes that flow from those values, such as the team approach to delivering care. The genius of the Clinic's founders was to promulgate a vision of excellence in medicine and establish an institution that would fulfill that vision and far outlast the founders. This has meant for Mayo, as we noted, that leadership is not defined in heroic terms: the "star," brought in from the outside and bent on remaking the institution and its culture in his own image, and often for short-term gain. A long-term perspective, even when faced with short-term challenges, is paramount in Mayo.

Mayo's leaders are proud of the services their organization provides. Often associated with leaders with a long-term vision is a keen interest in—even a love for—the organization's products and services. And so for that reason also they see the business as more than a financial undertaking and frequently display an intimate knowledge not just of the company's profit-and-loss statements, but also of its offerings, its operations, and its customers. Of course, this can be a two-edged sword because in their ardor, they may be tempted to interfere with the work of others down the line. But we find that, by and large, workers down the line are immensely appreciative of such interest as a sign of a boss whose values and pride match theirs and who has a long-term view of what it takes to make a business successful.

Integrity

In our survey research, we see time and again how important it is to workers to work for someone with integrity. In business, the integrity of a leader has two basic components:

- **Basic ethics.** He does not act unlawfully or otherwise unethically in his business dealings, such as falsifying financial records, misleading customers, or selling unsafe products.
- **Credibility.** He does what he says he will do. There is a reason terms such as "walks the talk" and "puts his money where his

mouth is"—and their opposites—are heard so often in companies: the credibility of a boss is enormously important to employees.

It is almost oxymoronic to think of people willingly choosing to follow someone they see as dishonest: blatantly dishonest in his behavior (a cheat, a crook) or dishonest in the gap between his words and his deeds. They may remain in the company for a time—sometimes a long time—because of a lack of employment alternatives, but the relationship will likely be no more than transactional (you pay; I work). A lack of integrity—even from someone highly competent in his field—is toxic to the trust that is the foundation of the leader-follower relationship.

Strength

It is not enough to have an impressive vision for the future. Leadership requires as well *fortitude*—weak-willed leadership being another oxymoron. It is essential that followers sense in their leader determination, drive, courage, self-confidence, decisiveness, resilience—all of those attributes that we associate with strength and what we mean when we say someone is a "strong leader." Employees want a doer—someone who ensures that the organization moves ahead on its goals and strategies—not merely an interesting thinker or a good orator. They want someone who is not wishy-washy and is willing to be held accountable for his decisions. You often hear in companies about executives whose opinions are those of the last person they spoke to. That is said with disdain, and sometimes alarm, not admiration.

There is a positive relationship between strength and the attributes of a long-term perspective and integrity. Essential to integrity is having the backbone to say "no" when an action, which may produce a short-term profit, is clearly or even borderline unethical and would likely do harm to the long-term health of the business.

Modesty and Open-Mindedness

Don't confuse strength with bluster. And don't confuse it with arrogance, such as the unwillingness to listen to others' views. The truly strong, self-confident person doesn't have to bluster, doesn't have to be a know-it-all, and doesn't have to be the center of attention and regard.

But don't confuse modesty in these respects with shyness, or, as we have said, with a disinterest in financial reward. There is no shortage of eminent chief executives—people who built great, long-lasting companies—who, in the process, became rich. That has not been accidental, a by-product of loftier goals; the ones we have studied and have known personally have been clearly interested in building their wealth.

The essential differences between these great executives and others are that, first, they aren't focused exclusively on wealth: other goals—building an enduring company, having great products—are also essential to them. Second, in line with their long-term term view of the business, they tend to have a long-term view of their personal wealth accumulation—they are not greedy to grab every penny they can and do so now.

The third difference relates to how they see their goals being achieved: do they see the realization of their ambitions to be a function solely of their intelligence and efforts, or have they come to understand that their success is in very large measure dependent on the intelligence and efforts of others? Central to the wisdom of great leaders is modesty in the sense of an understanding of their reliance—no matter how bright and strong and energetic they are—on others.

Great leaders, then, are open-minded in that they are aware that for many of their decisions, they have just a fraction of the information and the experience needed.

Unafraid to Face Facts

The same modesty and open-mindedness that permit a leader to listen to—indeed seek out—the views of others allows him as well to face unpleasant facts that may for a time reflect poorly on him and the company. Unpleasant facts are, well, unpleasant, and human beings expend a lot of effort avoiding or denying facts that run contrary to what they believe or would like to believe.

Failures and mistakes in the course of running a business are inevitable. An open-minded leader understands the human tendency—likely including his own—to look away from weaknesses, and he deliberately and consciously disciplines himself to face reality. And he ensures that the appropriate processes are in place to unearth the facts in the first place so that a steady stream of reliable, relevant information is available to him and other decision-makers. This cannot be done mechanically. For it to work, the proper climate has to be established—one where problem identification and problem solving are rewarded and problem avoidance and blame-placing are strongly discouraged. In the best of cases, this becomes the natural and normal mode of operation of the business—its mind-set, as it were. An example, applied to business processes, is the methods and mentality of "continuous improvement," developed originally with great success by Japanese manufacturing companies. The underlying premises of continuous improvement are that improvement is always possible, that the problems identified are a result of the system in place and not the workers, and that the remedies, using a disciplined problem-solving approach, will come largely from the workers.[4] The right culture—open, nonblame placing—is essential if continuous improvement is not to become just "another program." And the establishment of such a culture depends, first and foremost, on the attitudes and actions of senior management.

Concern for Employee Well-Being

It follows that modest leaders—those who understand that their success depends to a large degree on the intelligence and efforts of others—will have a strong interest in the well-being of those others, and that interest is a fundamental attribute of genuine leadership. We said that no one wants to be led into battle by a jerk, but few will voluntarily follow a leader who they believe will sacrifice them on the altar of his own ego or greed. The followers must have a sense that *the leader is with them,* that he adheres to the old Army maxim, "First feed the troops."

As reiterated throughout this book, concern for employees has both economic and psychological facets. The economic side consists, in essence, of the degree to which the financial gains of success are shared equitably with employees and the sacrifices required in hard times also shared equitably. If it is a matter of executives raking it all in when times are good and suffering hardly at all during downturns (perhaps raking it in even then!), don't expect much willing follow-ership. Decisions need to be seen as motivated by mutually-serving rather than self-serving motives. On the psychological side, it's difficult to follow a leader who, aside from job security and pay (which may be satisfactory because of a tight labor market or an aggressive labor union), treats employees as children or criminals. A leadership that doesn't trust won't be trusted.

> "It used to be a business conundrum: 'Who comes first? The employees, customers, or shareholders?' That's never been an issue to me. The employees come first. If they're happy, satisfied, dedicated, and energetic, they'll take real good care of the customers. When the customers are happy, they come back. And that makes the shareholders happy."

—Herb Kelleher, former CEO, Southwest Airlines

"The greatest source of power available to a leader is the trust that derives from faithfully serving followers."

—James O'Toole, professor of Leadership Studies, University of Southern California

Facilitator of Workers' Performance

Strongly associated with concern for the well-being of employees is providing them with what they need to get their jobs done and done well. A leader who trusts the intentions of workers will not only be respectful of them in the ways we have described but will see his responsibilities to include setting the right conditions for their maximum performance. In that respect, he "serves" them, and to best serve them, he needs not only professional expert advice—say, from efficiency experts—but alertness to workers' frustrations and their own ideas for improvement. This is, of course, a very different way of understanding and improving worker performance than the usual command-and-control, carrot-and-stick model. The idea is not simply to exert authority to get what a leader wants but, more importantly, to *help* workers do what they are asked to do and, we trust we have demonstrated, *want* to do. The resources that workers need range from the macro—such as a proper organization structure as it affects them—to the mundane but vital needs, such as adequate and adequately maintained equipment and accurate and timely communications to them. It is not the executive who turns out the pieces or provides the services for customers: it is the workers, and serving them in their work is a fundamental responsibility of leadership up and down the line.

Fosterer of Collaboration

As a corollary to the proposition that no leader stands alone is the equally obvious one that no worker stands alone. Leaders have a major responsibility to ensure that a collaborative culture is initiated and fostered; otherwise, cooperation can quickly degenerate into competition and conflict as the pressures for performance of *my* unit (department, division, function) and of me as an individual overwhelm workers' natural cooperative instincts and do severe damage to the performance of the whole.

A senior leader has three important responsibilities in this respect:

- To structure the organization to minimize conflict—for example, the team structure described in Chapter 11, "Teamwork"

- To gear rewards and penalties to reinforce cooperation—through both the formal reward system (for example, pay increases and promotions tied in a significant way to cooperative behavior) and informally (what the leader, through his day-to-day actions, indicates are the behaviors of which he approves and those of which he disapproves, in fact, will not tolerate)

- To model cooperation in his own behavior, especially with his senior management team

"The leaders who work most effectively, it seems to me, never say 'I.' And that's not because they have trained themselves not to say 'I.' They don't think 'I.' They think 'we'; they think 'team.' They understand their job to be to make the team function. They accept responsibility and don't sidestep it, but 'we' gets the credit.... This is what creates trust, what enables you to get the task done."

—Peter Drucker

Again, we don't have to take this to the extreme of ego-free sainthood to recognize how important teamwork is to performance and how it can be damaged by the need of the leader to be a one-man show, maintaining that status through a pattern of one-on-one relationships with his subordinates and encouraging competition among them and their organizations for his favor.

That is our summary of the key attributes of leadership, abstracted from a voluminous amount of leadership research, by ourselves and others. We did not, however, mention one attribute because it applies to every job, not just that of a leader: YaGottaWanna! We often assume that everybody in a company is interested in a leadership position, in being a boss. Not true. There are workers who see being a boss as a headache, and for some it is even a terrifying prospect. Think of the cookie and cracker packers described in Chapter 9, "Job Challenge," most of whom liked their routine work and had very little interest in moving into a supervisory or management position. This is true of some people in all kinds of work, from low- to high-skilled.

What, at its heart, is the job of a boss? It is getting work done through others and accepting accountability for their performance. As with any job, its attraction for people is to a significant degree a function of whether a potential job occupant feels that he can do it well. One of the last things some people feel able to do well is manage others. They are especially wary of having to tell their subordinates things they don't want to hear: about their performance, about changes in their hours, about an impending layoff, and so on. Perhaps underneath a lot of the discomfort about obtaining a position of power is, ironically, a sense of powerlessness: having to get things done through others represents some loss of control over outcomes because the boss is dependent for results on the performance of others. "I'd rather just do it myself," say more than a few workers.

Many others, of course, can't wait to be a boss. They not only like the extra money and status, they feel they can do it well, and they enjoy power. Enjoying the exercise of power is not necessarily a negative. To evaluate the desire for power, we need to ask: power for what and is power being monopolized. If it's power just for power's sake, there will almost surely be a problem. But if it is also power for a purpose—say, to build a department or total organization that gets admirable things done—then that is exactly the right drive. And, if the power, rather than being hoarded, is distributed to subordinates as "partners," that is exactly the right allocation of power. A wise leader soon learns that that approach, rather than diluting his influence, significantly enhances it.

14

Translating Partnership Theory into Partnership Practice

We advocate a partnership culture as the surest path to a high-performance organization. Partnership works because it harnesses the natural motivation and enthusiasm that is characteristic of the overwhelming majority of workers. Other management modes dampen that motivation and enthusiasm. (Some come close to destroying them.) The partnership organization is effective precisely because it is based on the assumption that most workers are, by nature, motivated. Rather than a vicious circle (assume and expect the worst and you get the worst), a partnership philosophy generates a virtuous circle (assume and expect the best, and that's what you get).

Does partnership always work? Nothing that we know of *always* works, and some conditions make partnership inappropriate.

First, there is the matter of individual differences. We have said throughout this book that there are some individual workers who cannot be treated as partners. They are naturally too lazy, hostile, or dishonest to participate in collaborative endeavors. It is self-defeating for management to try to do so because they will not respond positively; these workers, who are almost always a small number of individuals, must be dealt with separately: by dismissal from the company or by placing them in jobs that minimize their impact on co-workers and the organization.

It is an unfortunate reality that there are workers with whom it is impossible to establish a collaborative relationship. And, there are managers with whom this is impossible. In that case, the problem tends to be more one of philosophy: managers who simply do not accept the notions underlying partnership, the assumption, for example, that workers want to work or that they are reasonable in what they expect in their employment conditions. This problem can sometimes be overcome by training and counseling from experienced managers with a partnership approach, but sometimes it cannot. Organizations that have moved to a partnership culture have always had to deal with managers who could not (or would not) change, and they have usually had to remove them from managerial positions. Otherwise, they create cross-currents damaging to the establishment of a new culture.

We come now to senior management. The issue here is not whether senior management expresses agreement with the partnership concept and methods—if they don't, it won't happen—but whether they genuinely believe what they say. In many companies, senior management has initiated (or, more precisely, allowed to be initiated) programs that sound good but have little substantial follow-through. Genuinely believing in partnership means more than just words; it means taking the kinds of actions we have described throughout this book and sticking with them. Changing an organization's culture in the direction of partnership should never be attempted in a superficial way, as with slogans instead of deeds or with isolated deeds that are unconnected to each other or the reality of what goes on in the daily lives of employees. These efforts, which usually soon disappear (called, derisively, "programs of the month"), do nothing but generate or reinforce workers' skepticism about management and its intentions. If senior management, especially the CEO, does not genuinely commit to partnership by demonstrating its willingness to take serious action, forget it! (We return to this crucial matter of senior management commitment later in this chapter.)

We have not qualified the use of partnership by occupation or by national culture. There is no evidence that the approach does not work when it's applied to certain types of work or in certain nations or ethnicities. Obviously, adaptations must be made, but the fundamental concepts are, to our knowledge, applicable everywhere. Is there an occupation where collaboration for the achievement of common ends is not desired? Is there a country where collaboration is not called for? We think not. It's time to shelve the stereotypical portrayals that we apply to large groups of workers, stereotypes that can function, in part, to allow blame for problems to be placed on the "character" of workers or the cultures of countries instead of on the way workers are managed. As we have said, individual employees might have character issues, but for the majority, whatever they do and wherever they are, the proper injunction is, "Management, first heal thyself."

Throughout this book, we have suggested specific best practices that can translate key partnership concepts into action, such as "rings of defense" to help avoid or minimize layoffs and group rewards that promote teamwork and share performance gains with workers. We didn't make these up; they come from organizations that took serious action based on partnership ideas and researchers that carefully assessed these efforts. These are what the best organizations (in our terms) and research studies have taught us. In describing these actions, we also paid some attention to the methods by which ideas can be converted into action, especially in our discussion of the translation of "purposes and principles" into practices such as total quality management (TQM, discussed in Chapter 7, "Organization Purpose and Principles") and the building of teamwork between interdependent units of a company (see Chapter 11, "Teamwork"). The current chapter gathers these strands into a more comprehensive statement of a process for advancing an organization toward a partnership culture.

It Starts at the Top

Many partnership organizations didn't have to change to that form; they started that way with a visionary founder and CEO who strongly believed that this is the way people should be managed. Frederick

Smith of Federal Express and Herb Kelleher of Southwest Airlines are good examples of this. But other organizations that have long operated with an entirely different management mode have consciously and deliberately undergone profound culture change to a partnership pattern. Good examples of these are Gordon Bethune's massive culture change and turnaround of Continental Airlines and F. Kenneth Iverson's similarly highly successful efforts at Nucor.

A major lesson from these examples of partnership organizations is that *action must begin with, and be sustained by, senior management.* This chapter's goal is to help interested senior managements implement partnership concepts and practices.

There are executives who, without reading this book or perhaps anything like it, naturally operate in a partnership mode. That's the way they *are*. Take the following excerpt from an interview with Gordon Bethune in *Human Capital: Strategies and News* about the way he engineered the turnaround of Continental Airlines:

> *Continental Airlines was just three weeks away from failing to meet its payroll in 1994, losing about $55 million per month. After churning through 10 CEOs in 10 years, the airline only occasionally got passengers to the right place at the right time—maybe with their luggage.*
>
> *This was a crummy place to work. The culture at Continental, after years of layoffs and wage freezes and wage cuts and broken promises, was one of backbiting, mistrust, fear, and loathing," says Bethune. "People, to put it mildly, were not happy to come to work. They were surly to customers, surly to each other, and ashamed of their company. And you can't have a good product without people who like coming to work. It just can't be done.*
>
> *HCSN: How important is company culture and morale to the turnaround of Continental Airlines?*
>
> *Bethune: It's everything. You can't quantify it. I mean, how important is your liver? There isn't going to be any success if you don't have the right culture and morale. It just doesn't work.*

HCSN: When you came to Continental, you concluded the employees were basically a good group of people despite all the messes. Why?

Bethune: All you had to do was walk around. If you've been in this business, you could see there was nothing wrong with these people's thinking; their tools were fine, we had our stuff. But if you're running an airline, why would you run a late one? You can't figure out what time of day it is? You don't know how fast the planes fly? I mean, this is sixth-grade arithmetic we're talking about here. The fact is, everybody kind of knew what to do, but nobody cared about doing it. If every time, for the last 10 years, no matter what you did you lost, then you quit trying.

HCSN: How were you able to gain employees' trust?

Bethune: You have to earn and develop trust. It's like dealing with abused children. They kind of like the way you talk and act, but every adult they ever met screwed them over—so they're going to be a little hesitant until you just patiently, with consistent behavior, show them that you're not just a new deal from the same old deck. It took time and some concrete changes around here for them to believe things really were different.

HCSN: In your book, From Worst to First, you talk about the importance of dealing with employees honestly, of communicating with them, of clarifying expectations and of removing a lot of rules and policies. What else?

Bethune: Most importantly, we showed them concrete examples of positive change for them. We became a no-smoking company the first week. We took the locks off the executive suite doors. We went casual on Fridays just to change our dress behavior. We started rewarding extra if we did our job better. When we did our job better quickly, their lives got better because when we were on time, they were on time. They started getting home to pick up their kids from school or whatever mattered to them.[1]

Bethune goes on to describe the other changes he introduced, such as a focus on customer satisfaction, monthly bonuses for on-time performance, and replacing the "authoritarian" employee manual with a set of guidelines that didn't "box them into ridiculous procedures for every element of their work." He also felt that he had to replace a number of middle managers.

Here's Bethune's comment on the source of his ideas: "Someone asked me... how come I know so much about people? I said, 'I used to be one.' So I think understanding your co-workers is kind of a prerequisite to success. You're not going to make it without their help, so you have to learn how to talk to them and how to appreciate them."

The Action Process

We discussed what partnership is and we come now to how it can be introduced and sustained. We don't have a cookbook recipe; you can bring about culture change in many ways, and it is never a neat and entirely predictable process. Nevertheless, certain approaches seem to work better than others (a series of steps is described later in this chapter), and knowing what they are should help an organization take significant steps forward with minimum downside risks (when adapted to individual circumstances).

You might have one of four broad kinds of reactions to this book: this is nonsense; this is what we already do; this sounds interesting, let's explore further; or this is exactly on the mark, let's go! There can, of course, be all sorts of intermediate responses, such as, "We do some of this and the rest is nonsense or too radical."

You probably don't believe that what we've been saying is nonsense because if you do, you wouldn't have gotten this far in the book. If you feel that this is what your organization already does, we ask you to hold on for a moment. You might be right, but you might not, or you might be only partially right. Some executives believe that they run their organizations as a collaborative endeavor with employees because they communicate frequently to them, they have suggestion programs, they have an "open door" policy, they call their employees "associates" or "team members," and so on. But by using the diagnostic methods we suggest in this chapter, these executives might learn that the reality is different. The only reality that counts here is the *employee's* reality, not senior management's.

If you feel that the ideas and practices we have been espousing can be useful to your organization, you might be inclined to start implementing them right away. We suggest, however, that the first step is not implementation, but assessing just how ready the organization—especially senior management and, most especially, the CEO—is for partnership. This is greatly aided by *data* at the senior level that help those executives confront how they really feel about partnership concepts and policies. Later in this chapter, we explain how a "readiness" questionnaire can assist executives in getting their views "on the table" so that the basic decision—is this really for us?—can be made.

Here, then, is a process by which partnership can be considered and introduced into an organization. The recommended steps are largely designed to be applied to an organization that wants to change itself in its entirety (whether the organization is a total company or a relatively self-contained business unit). The process can be usefully applied to segments of organizations, such as individual departments, but often with less marked results because what goes on in those units is usually heavily influenced by the culture of the entire organization in which it exists and by its relationships with other units.

The recommended steps for introducing partnership are defined by these questions that each step addresses:

Step 1. What is our business goal?

Step 2. Are we ready for this?

Step 3. What, exactly, do we want?

Step 4. Where are we now?

Step 5. What are the major aspects of the organization that need to be changed to get us from where we are to where we want to be?

Step 6. How should the plan be communicated to the workforce?

Step 7. How do we decide on the specific changes that need to be made and how they should be implemented?

Step 8. How should managers be trained for the implementation of partnership?

Step 9. How do we assess how well we have done?

These steps are abstracted from our own experience and that of many other practitioners as to how this kind of culture change can most effectively be introduced. Although the steps appear neat and sequential, in practice considerable overlap will exist among them, and you might move back and forth as the situation dictates. Before we describe the steps, here are four principles that should govern their application:

- **Don't lose sight of the business goal.** This chapter is largely devoted to process, in two senses: partnership itself is a process because it defines *how* people can best work together in a business organization; we now describe *how* that process can best be introduced and sustained (in other words, another process). In all this discussion about how things should be done, we might lose sight of *why* they are being done. The effort can disintegrate into "collaboration for the sake of collaboration," which is a parody of the concept. Such process-infatuation is not too different from the way a bureaucrat overfocuses on the means (the procedures and rules) rather than the ends that the means are designed to accomplish.

  Although having a clear business goal for the effort does not guarantee the success of partnership, neglecting this certainly ensures its failure. In a short time, the organization turns its attention to its business objectives, and the means familiar to it for achieving those, which will almost definitely not be partnership. Partnership then atrophies into a sideshow. The business goal must be an integral part of the way an organization defines partnership for itself and the way it will assess its value once introduced.

- **Where partnership has worked best, the primary business goal has most frequently been improved products or services for the customer.** Collaboration—up, down, and across—is fostered to better meet the needs of the customer and usually to delight the customer. This goal works wonders because it is in the direct service of the business, and employees can get really enthusiastic about achieving it.

- **Introduce change using partnership principles.** The use of the principles of partnership should not be limited to the goal of the effort (the partnership organization), but should also govern *how* that goal is reached. Inconsistency in ends and means opens the credibility of the entire effort to question: "Does management really believe this stuff?" Furthermore, change that is essentially positive and that affects many people is best achieved by working collaboratively. Just as people welcome partnership, they welcome the opportunity to participate in its development and implementation as long as they feel it is serious business and not just another exercise. The basic structure of the process that we will suggest is that senior management be primarily responsible for setting the overall objectives and rationale of the effort. That is a requirement of leadership, and employees want to know that the basic objectives come from the top. But the translation of that statement into detailed policies and practices and their implementation is the responsibility of task forces composed of individuals from throughout the organization. For most issues, "diagonal slices"—people selected across levels and functions—are the best way to form the task forces. To help ensure that they continue to receive the support and attention they need, members of senior management should chair most task forces.

If the organization is unionized, the union's active participation should be sought. Labor-management cooperative efforts have almost always been run by a joint labor-management steering committee.

- **Avoid assuming that people naturally resist change.** This assumption about resistance to change is another in a pessimistic outlook about people at work that we discuss throughout this book (such as the view that people are naturally lazy). People resist changes that they see as harmful to them or the organization, and they gladly welcome changes that they see as helpful. When was the last time anyone saw a worker turn down a salary increase? Or be upset because his new manager treated him more respectfully than his previous manager? Or complain about management adjusting the work pace to allow workers to turn out higher quality work? Those *are* changes, and if workers naturally resisted change, they would resist those changes, too. The notion that people have a difficult time with change is often a way to explain "psychologically" why workers don't want to do something that management wants them to. They don't want to do those things because they consider them harmful! Does a worker resist a new technology that will replace him because he "resists change?" Is he upset about a transfer to a less interesting job because he resists change? He resists getting hurt.

  The belief that people naturally resist change causes managers to act in counterproductive ways, such as developing plans secretly and springing them on workers at the last minute; not listening to the genuine and specific concerns that people have about changes (after all, why listen, if they're "just resisting change"?); needlessly overselling changes to workers; and, not doing the necessary planning to buffer the ill effects that change might bring ("they'll complain whatever we do"). Because of these behaviors, people do, indeed, act as if they resist change. It's the self-fulfilling prophecy at work again: employees' behavior reflects the way they are treated. Therefore, our advice is to largely ignore the assumption of "natural resistance" and, as we have said, assume that most employees will welcome the changes that partnership will bring. Proceed with its development and introduction in ways consistent with that belief.

- **Maintain continual senior management attention and involvement.** We cannot emphasize enough the importance of visible senior management commitment to the change process. The change must emanate from the top and be continually sustained by it. Everyone in an organization wants to know what the top wants, especially in an effort as untraditional and innovative as the introduction of a culture of genuine partnership. The forces that tend to militate against partnership—the inevitable frustrations of the workplace and the tendencies of organizations to pull people and units apart as they focus on their own objectives—make essential reinforcement of the importance of partnership from those in power. That support must be communicated in word, but especially in deed, including the way rewards and recognition are distributed. If recognition is given irrespective of people's performance as partners, the partnership values will begin to appear hollow.

Here are the suggested key steps to begin and sustain the transformation of a company to a partnership culture.

Step 1. What Is Our Business Goal?

The primary reason that partnership is introduced in an organization must be the achievement of specific business objectives. It can't be just that "things will be better this way" or "employees will be happier" or "we should emulate those successful Japanese companies." As we mentioned earlier, among the most successful partnership efforts that we have observed have been those where improved products and services for the customer has been the primary goal. But whatever it is, the business objective must be an integral part of the way the organization thinks about partnership and the way it will evaluate its effects.

Step 2. Are We Ready for This?

The decision to move to a partnership culture to achieve business objectives should be deliberate and thoughtful, with full understanding that culture change is a long and demanding process; the biggest pitfall is the temptation to do it superficially—that is, avoid grappling with basic issues and changes and transform the effort instead into a "program" with catchy slogans, slick communications, and committees upon committees. All those are quite unrelated to the mainstream of the business and what goes on in the daily work lives of employees.

In this early step, senior management requires two things: a good understanding of what partnership is and what it does, and a good understanding of themselves. The former is achieved through reading, discussions with experts in the field, and visits with managers and employees in organizations that operate with a partnership culture. Visits to those organizations to see partnership in action—including its performance impacts—are especially useful because the greatest effect on executives' thinking comes from observable facts—seeing something actually working—and those facts explained and verified by other executives they respect and trust.

Self-diagnosis should follow immediately; for this, we suggest using a diagnostic questionnaire to assess readiness (such as "The Readiness Questionnaire" provided free of charge on our website at www.sirota.com/enthusiastic-employee). The questionnaire should be completed by all top management personnel, usually the chairman, the president, and their direct reports. It is critical, of course, that these people be asked to complete the questionnaires as they *genuinely* feel, not what they believe is the socially acceptable answer or what their bosses want them to say. Individual answers must be kept completely confidential, so it is best that the completed questionnaires be sent to an outside party or some other trusted source for scoring. The method for scoring the Readiness Questionnaire can also be found on our website at www.sirota.com/enthusiastic-employee.

Senior management needs to thoroughly and critically review the results of this self-diagnosis. This is best done in an offsite setting where full and frank discussion is possible and encouraged. The questionnaire results are not precise measures of readiness but stimulate the discussion required to make a thoughtful decision about whether and in what respects to go forward.

Step 3. What, Exactly, Do We Want?

Assuming the decision is made to proceed, the next step, preferably at the same offsite meeting, is to formulate an initial draft of a statement as to what the organization wants to do and why, providing specific examples of the action steps that might be undertaken. It is best to integrate this with the organization's "purposes and principles" or vision statement (see Chapter 7), if one exists, and it should include the business rationale for partnership. Tying it publicly to business goals will make the statement—in fact, the entire process—more credible in employees' eyes, and credibility is further enhanced by being specific and avoiding platitudes. Being specific is also a good discipline for executives planning a cultural transformation of this scope: it makes the effort real—that is, this is what we are going to be living with. The statement, for example, might include items such as, "We will pay a wage and provide benefits that are fully competitive" and, "We will organize into self-managing teams that will be delegated the authority they require to get the jobs done effectively." Credibility is further enhanced by including limits on what the organization is prepared to do, such as, "We cannot guarantee lifetime employment" (but stating what it will do, such as handling workforce surpluses, to the extent possible, with normal attrition and with the retraining and redeployment of workers).

It is critical that the statement be developed by senior management and, when eventually made final and released, be identified to the workforce as the product of senior management's thinking and intentions.

At this stage, the statement will be in draft form and will be finalized in Step 5 and distributed in Step 6.

Step 4. Where Are We Now?

Having decided on the basic direction, it is now necessary to get a good reading on the condition of the organization in relation to the partnership goals set forth in the statement. It is not sufficient to depend on senior management's views of this. Senior managers might think that they know where an organization stands, but they are often incorrect and the bias can be either positive or negative.

The best way to find out where an organization stands is a combination of subjective measures, such as an attitude survey, and objective measures. Regarding compensation, for example, you would learn from the survey how employees see their pay and from objective measures how their salaries actually compare to those in other relevant companies. On certain issues, it is impossible to obtain data other than through an attitude survey, for example, how employees feel about the respect with which they are treated. It could be argued that the employee survey measures are the most important; if, for example, the salary survey shows that the company pays competitively, but large percentages of employees disagree, does it really matter what the salary survey data show? Recall that our surveys do not confirm the widely held view that workers will always be unhappy with their pay. When they are unhappy but the salary survey data say they shouldn't be, it is likely that the criteria employees are using to judge the fairness of their pay differ from those used in the salary survey. Employees might be comparing their pay to that of workers in a different set of companies (perhaps nationwide instead of locally). At the least, a discrepancy should cause management to investigate why it exists rather than, as is usually the case, rely solely on the objective information to measure where the organization stands and then "educate" employees as to why they are wrong.

We have been referring to organization-wide results. But a survey should be conducted so that information is generated not just on employee views overall, but for various units, occupations, and levels as well. This provides a veritable X-ray of the organization: not only what the views are but where they reside. This enables greater precision in the development and application of action. It may be, for example, that blue-collar workers feel much less respect is shown them than is true of professional workers; or employees in particular departments might report much less cooperation with other departments than is true elsewhere in the company. Thus divided, the data at a later stage of the process can provide individual managers with an assessment of how their own employees score on the various dimensions of partnership, which is extremely useful information for self-analysis and for the training and coaching of managers. The use of the survey questionnaire for individual manager feedback is discussed more fully later in this chapter.

The survey instrument, developed to provide direction at the beginning of the process, is also a means—in conjunction with objective data—to assess later on the impact of the actions taken.

Step 5. What Are the Major Aspects of the Organization That Need to Be Changed to Get It from Where It Is to Where It Wants to Be?

Having at least tentatively determined the kind of partnership the company wants and where the organization stands now, senior managers are ready to be much more definitive about the major changes they believe need to be introduced and the ordering of their introduction. These four principles can help guide those decisions:

- **View partnership as a total system.** As we have said, many elements of a partnership culture are interdependent: changing one element without considering the others can reduce the impact of a change and even have negative consequences. Management must be especially cautious about changing the non-financial aspects of its relationship with workers without first attending to equity deficiencies, if found (such as pay and job security), or at least declaring its serious intention of so doing. There is no way that the value of, say, informal recognition or greater job authority can be substantial or long-lasting if people feel mistreated on the basic equity issues. And don't expect increased collaboration if one of its consequences is increased productivity that results in surplus workers and the danger of layoffs. Order of implementation, then, is not simply a matter of which elements are more important, but also which are more basic—that is, which, when implemented, are more likely to facilitate the resolution of other issues.

- **Do something visible fairly quickly.** Despite management's best intentions, the early stages of the change process are probably going to be met with some skepticism by many employees because they will probably have had prior experience with programs that sounded terrific but went nowhere. It is therefore helpful if, after proper consideration of the way the different elements of partnership relate to each other, one or two significant and highly visible actions be decided upon and introduced. These are, in effect, expressions of management's good faith. The diagnostic survey data can provide important clues as to what these steps might be. For example, one company learned from its survey that the "executive floor" was a major obstacle to performance and timely decision making because it made interaction between employees and the senior leaders of their units difficult. (In truth, management didn't need the survey to uncover this complaint; they had heard it for years. The survey brought it to the surface and made it difficult to avoid.) It was decided to relocate the managers to offices near their employees, which was a heartily welcomed change by most of the managers themselves. It is a good illustration of an action that is important, visible, consistent with the partnership concept, and relatively easy to quickly implement.

Another category of important changes where implementation can be started fairly quickly are those concerned with inter-unit relationships. Most surveys reveal damaging conflicts between specific units that lend themselves to the type of partnership-building intervention described in Chapter 11.

- **Give the development and introduction of most of the changes the time they deserve.** Some changes can be introduced quickly, but most require considerable time to investigate and implement. Take self-managed work teams, for example. That is a fundamental structural change that must be thought through carefully and that involves not just creating the teams themselves but also supporting actions, such as the training of managers and employees to prepare them for it. Self-managed teams, and other such major initiatives, are often best introduced on an experimental basis in one or two areas of an organization; that way, they can be carefully observed and modified as needed to get them right for the business and the people in it. Although the introduction of a new culture is an undertaking that never really ends, a large organization should consider three to four years as the approximate amount of time it needs to achieve what most everyone will come to see as a genuinely participative culture.

- **Modify the action plan over time.** The initial plan of action is just that: initial. It is meant to be a dynamic plan that will be added to, subtracted from, and otherwise modified as the effort proceeds. Some changes will be a result of oversights during the planning phase, but others will be caused by changing business conditions or new, creative insights that are gained with experience. The evolutionary nature of the plan needs to be communicated early to employees with encouragement, and mechanisms, for their participation in suggesting how the plan can continually improve.

Working with these principles, the initial statement of purpose, business goals and possible actions, and the measures of where the organization currently stands, senior management identifies the changes it wants to see undertaken or, at least, investigated for feasibility. At this stage, the individual actions should not be too detailed. Here are verbatim excerpts of this kind of action plan from one company. The major business goal of the effort in this company, which is a large financial-services company with many clerical employees, was "to dramatically improve customer service."

Actions to Achieve Partnership—Initial Plan

1. **Job security.** Assure employees that no layoffs will occur as a result of actions taken through this program; develop a system to minimize layoffs for any reason (explore rings of defense).

2. **Compensation.** Investigate and correct pay inequities where they exist in specific departments; study the impact of placing all employees on salary.

3. **Start organizing by customer.** Investigate setting up teams, where feasible and on an experimental basis, to service specific groups of customers (by product and by industry); organize measurements around these teams; consider team-based bonuses (but prevent inequities to rest of company); train managers in team and participative management and team members in working cooperatively with each other; learn from the teams the obstacles in the way of providing the best possible service to customers.

4. **Team building.** Initiate team-building program between staff and line departments, especially between (departments named).

5. **Formal communication.** Initiate regular communication of business results (including customer service and satisfaction measurements) to entire workforce.

6. **Operating committee [senior management] visits with employees.** Develop schedule and method for all O.C. members to visit and interact informally with employees at all of the company's facilities.

7. **Dress code.** Institute informal dress code (with exceptions, as appropriate, such as for customer meetings).

8. **Status distinctions.** Eliminate reserved parking spaces for executives—make it first come, first served for all employees; eliminate separate dining facilities for officers.

9. **Physical working conditions.** Correct problems in departments (department names).

10. **Recognition.** Investigate means for giving special recognition for outstanding individual and team performance.

The two changes that senior management wanted started immediately were the elimination of status distinctions and the introduction of an informal dress code. These were what they felt would be important and visible changes that would build early credibility with the workforce.

It is our experience that Steps 1 through 5 of the action process we have recommended can be accomplished in about three offsite senior management meetings of two to three days each. Obviously, a lot of supporting staff work is required, such as preparing educational materials, obtaining speakers, preparing visits to other companies, and conducting and analyzing the survey.

To this point, the program has pretty much been the province of the senior management group. It is now appropriate to vet the ideas in meetings with other management levels, usually the next one or two levels down. The products of senior management's thinking are presented to the managers—the action steps tentatively decided upon and the process by which the effort will be introduced—and their reactions are obtained. At this time, it's especially important to address how the effort is likely to affect *the managers themselves* (for example, the nature of their jobs under a team approach and the training they will receive for it). Some might feel some resentment at some of the changes, such as the loss of the status symbols that, as a manager in one of the meetings put it, "I've worked all these years to achieve." Their role in the process, such as serving on the task forces that will turn the broad partnership plan into specific actions, also needs to be described.

It is essential that the strong commitment to partnership of senior management be affirmed in these meetings. Equally important is that, at that time, the managers have an opportunity to voice their concerns, suggestions, and what they foresee their needs will be to make the program work in their areas. Senior management needs to listen and, as appropriate, act on what they hear. They will not act on suggestions that would significantly weaken the effort (such as maintaining status distinctions), but the bulk of what will be suggested will be useful, and the plan should be modified accordingly.

Step 6. How Should the Plan Be Communicated?

The plan should be fully communicated to all employees and, in that communication, a balance must be struck between management's high hopes for the partnership approach and realism about the time and hard work that will be required for its success. In their eagerness to get employees "on board," organizations tend to overplay in their communications the benefits of this kind of effort; they treat it as a sort of miracle drug and understate what is required over an extended period of time to make it happen and the possible snags along the way. There is no need to convince most employees that partnership is a good idea; the convincing they need is of management's sincerity, and that will be accomplished only through *action*. The purposes of the communication are to let people know the rationale for a culture of partnership, especially the impact expected on the success of the business and the job satisfaction of employees; what its major components are; the involvement that will be required from employees throughout the organization to make it work; and its limitations and potential pitfalls. That is, management must convey its excitement for the partnership approach, but do so in a way that is informative and realistic. Conviction and credibility—not salesmanship—are the keys. After employees are informed, they don't have to be sold on anything except that management means it.

The plan should be communicated both through the organization's formal media as a message from the CEO and in small group meetings of managers with their employees. To accomplish the latter, it is first necessary to meet with managers up and down the line to fully brief them on what is being planned and why, to answer their questions and concerns, and to prepare them for their meetings with employees.

Step 7. How Do We Decide on the Specific Changes That Need to Be Made and How They Should Be Implemented?

After senior management develops the basic plan, its translation into specific implementable action steps should, as we have said, in most cases be the province of task forces composed of representatives from throughout the organization. The "diagonal slice" method is useful for selecting taskforce members: the members are chosen from across levels and across functions. We strongly suggest that a senior management member lead each of the task forces. Employees will not resent that type of leadership structure; on the contrary, it is an additional signal of the seriousness with which the organization is undertaking the effort. If a senior management member does not have a management style or point of view that's appropriate for this kind of leadership role, he should not, of course, be chosen for it.

The major exceptions to the taskforce approach are those instances in which the issues are best discussed and decided upon by management, usually senior management. Pay is a good example of that. Unless there is a union and a formal bargaining process, it is inappropriate and awkward for employees to be involved in decisions about the company's salary structure. They might be queried about their views of pay—for example, why they believe their pay is not competitive when a salary survey indicates that it is, or how they might view group-based variable pay—but the recommendation about what to do should reside with management. The benefits package is another example. Here, too, however, useful information can be gained from employees regarding benefit preferences and trade-offs.

After being fully oriented about its mission, each task force is responsible for the following:

- Defining the assigned issue thoroughly
- Learning all it needs to know about the issue, including the way other organizations deal with it
- Developing a recommended action plan
- Delineating responsibilities, resources needed, timetables, and so on for implementing the plan
- Suggesting how the effectiveness of what is being proposed can be assessed

The task force and implementation effort should be coordinated by an organization-wide steering committee that, on average, will probably meet about once a month and to which the task forces will regularly report their progress. The committee will suggest modifications in the individual taskforce plans and will approve, or seek approval for, the actions that are finally decided upon. The steering committee also serves as the mechanism for airing and doing something about the concerns and suggestions emanating from the workforce as the change process proceeds. A senior executive should chair the steering committee.

By this point, you might feel that we demand a lot of senior management's time. You're right; a lot *is* required of them. If this was "just another program," little of their time would be taken—probably just to approve the overall objectives and plan; hear an occasional, formal progress report; and give an occasional speech. In other words, it wouldn't be serious business. Here, we are talking about a fundamental change in the culture of an organization. If that level of seriousness is not present, the organization should reconsider whether it wants to go forward.

Step 8. How Should Managers Be Trained for the Implementation of Partnership?

In addition to the preparation managers receive in the basic tenets of partnership and how to communicate the implementation plan to their employees (in Step 6), they require training in the implications of a partnership culture for their own behavior. In this book, we have recommended policies and practices at the broad organization level, such as policies concerning job security and formal recognition programs. But we have also discussed in detail matters relating to individual managers, such as how to treat employees respectfully and provide day-to-day recognition for good performance. These should help any manager that seeks to improve the morale and performance of his employees, but they are especially useful for managers working in a partnership organization or an organization seeking to become one. Because the culture and policies of an organization have a profound impact on employees, it is often difficult for individual managers to have as much positive effect as they would like when working in a non-partnership environment. However, the reverse is also true: a partnership culture will obviously not have nearly the desired impact on employees whose managers do not behave in conformity with partnership principles.

A number of manager-training methods are available. One that is particularly relevant and effective for our purposes is *behavior modeling*, where managers learn in part by observing and then emulating models of good managerial behavior.[2] Training must, of course, be adapted to the circumstances and objectives of the organizations in which it is applied and to the needs of individual managers. The adaptation can be governed in large measure by what the attitude survey results reveal about the strengths and weaknesses of the organization's managers and their readiness for partnership. Broad issues might pertain to all managers, but there are invariably differences between managers that are revealed by dividing the survey data into an organization's units. The survey data thus provide direction for the training that is needed and, when employee attitudes are reported to a manager, they can be a powerful driver of change because they confront the manager with a mirror image of his behavior—the mirror being the views of his employees. The combination of individual survey data feedback with behavior modeling training therefore offers a particularly useful tool for bringing managerial behavior into line with an organization's partnership culture.[3]

Step 9. How Do We Assess How Well We Have Done?

In addition to its complexity, culture change is a long journey because it is never done perfectly, even after a careful experimental introduction. We are dealing with human beings, and they never fail to surprise. A manager of a self-managing team might, under pressure from his boss who is concerned about serious and immediate business issues, revert to his prior autocratic style. A crucial support function can turn out to be uncooperative with the team. A new pay system introduced to reward team performance might provoke questions about the validity of the measurements being used. These kinds of things happen in the real world, and the organization must regularly ask, "How are we doing?" and be prepared to act on what it has learned. Regular meetings need to be scheduled with employees—meetings that are devoted to surfacing and dealing with these issues. We also advise that employees be surveyed periodically to obtain a quantitative measure of their views that can be tracked over time and reviewed in conjunction with performance results. After all, a major purpose of partnership is to enhance the employee morale that underlies performance; that should be measured as systematically as the performance. If the company has indeed made significant changes and has made them well, the impact will readily be seen in well-designed surveys. Poorly conceived or implemented changes show up as no change, or a decrement, in attitudes. This is true both at the organization-wide and individual-manager levels.

It's ironic that among the most satisfying aspects of organization life—as of life in general—are those where improvements can be achieved only by hard work. This is especially true of attempts to change relationships: how people treat one another in their pursuit of earning a living. We refer both to the way differential power is used, which are the "vertical" relationships, and the "lateral" relationships among individuals and groups of relatively equal power. A key theme of this book is that the overwhelming majority of people in organizations act in simple pursuit of equitable treatment, a sense of achievement (for themselves and their organization), and camaraderie. They don't want to do either the organization or their colleagues harm, but it often appears that way or, at the least, it appears that they don't care whether the organization or their colleagues succeed or the organization improves. That occurs because of what happens to people when they join organizations, a combination of the daily on-the-job frustrations that cause them to act in ways not in their better nature, the way management treats them as sources of problems, costs, and resistance rather than as assets, and the behavior of the tiny, often highly visible minority of employees that really don't care, or even do harm, and so reinforce management's pessimistic view of people at work.

Partnership organizations emerge when senior leadership—in most cases, it has been the CEO—has the foresight to see what should and can be and not just what is. This requires not only insight into human nature (especially that people want to do good for a good organization) and not just eloquence in communicating the partnership philosophy, but also perseverance, hard work and consistency over a period of years to translate the philosophy into specific policies and daily management practices—the kinds that we have described throughout this book. And, it requires seeing and treating employees as genuine allies in achieving change.

Endnotes

Introduction

1. Some anecdotal material is derived from our recollection of comments made in focus groups, interviews, and observations over the years; some write-in comments have been modified to protect the confidentiality of the respondents.

2. We try to present quantitative information in a way that will make sense to readers unfamiliar with, or not particularly interested in, complicated statistical analyses. The latter are primarily "multivariate" analyses through which a number of variables are manipulated simultaneously. We employ such analyses in most of our work—especially multiple regression analysis and structural equation modeling—but reserve reporting and discussing them for other researchers. A major benefit of those analyses is to test the conclusions we reach with simpler methods, such as whether the correlation between two variables holds up when other variables are added. Most of the statistical results shown in this book have been subjected to these tests. We have been unable to do this when the data did not lend themselves to it, such as a number of the relationships with objective performance measures. In those instances, the quantity of units for which measures were available for all of the variables was insufficient.

3. Likert, R. *The Human Organization*, New York: McGraw Hill, 1967; Maslow, A. H., *Motivation and Personality*. New York: Harper and Row, 1954; Mayo, E. *The Human Problems of an Industrial Civilization*, New York: Macmillan, 1933; McClelland, D.C., *Personality*, New York: Dryden Press, 1951; McGregor, D., *The Human Side of Enterprise*, New York: McGraw-Hill, 1960.

Part I

Chapter 1

1. Munk, N. "The New Organization Man." *Fortune*. January 31, 2002.

2. Gross and Scott. "Proceeding with Caution." *Time*. July 16, 1990.

3. O'Toole. J., et al. "Work in America: Report of a Special Task Force to the Secretary of Health, Education, and Welfare." MIT Press. Cambridge, USA. 1973.

4. Herzberg, F., Mausner, B., and Snyderman, B. *The Motivation to Work*. Wiley. New York. 1959.

5. Rothschild, E. "GM in More Trouble." *New York Review of Books*. March 23, 1972.

6. AARP. 2007. "Leading a Multigenerational Workforce." AARP Report.

7. Krywulak, T. and Roberts, M. November 2009. "Making the Most of Generational Differences and Similarities in the Workplace." The Conference Board of Canada.

8. Jennifer J. Deal. 2007. "Retiring the Generation Gap: How Employees Young and Old Can Find Common Ground." Jossey-Bass and CCL.

9. Ibid.

10. Krywulak, T. and Roberts, M. November 2009. "Making the Most of Generational Differences and Similarities in the Workplace." The Conference Board of Canada. Page 8.

11. Ibid., page 54.

12. Ibid., page 27.

13. Ibid., page 50.

14. Jennifer J. Deal. 2007. "Retiring the Generation Gap: How Employees Young and Old Can Find Common Ground." Jossey-Bass and CCL. Page 212.

15. Ibid., page 213.

16. Equity has been studied by one group of organization psychologists under the designation "organization justice." The researchers make a host of fine distinctions between different forms of justice—much more than we feel important for our argument or managers' practical use—but their basic conclusions are the same as ours: a feeling of being treated fairly is extremely important for workers and for their contribution to the organization. For an overview of the research, see Colquitt, J. A., Conlon, D.E., Wesson, M. J., Porter, C., Yee Ng, K. (2001). See also: "Justice at the Millennium: A Meta-Analytic Review of 25 Years of Organizational Justice Research." *Journal of Applied Psychology*, 86, 425–445.

17. The correlations with camaraderie tend to be lower than that with achievement largely because of a technical reason—namely, the significantly smaller variance in response to the camaraderie question.

18. Sara Hottman. 2008. "Rethinking Minority Business." Inc.com website.

Chapter 2

1. Pfeffer, J. and Sutton, R. "The Knowing-Doing Gap." Harvard Business School Press. 2000.

2. Coleman, D. (1998). *Working with Emotional Intelligence.* New York: Bantam Books.

3. Achstatter. G. As quoted in "Honesty." *Investor's Business Daily*, found at www.mta.net/other_info/ethics/perspectives/ perspectives_stories/honesty.htm.

4. Kruse, K. May 22, 2012. "What Is Employee Engagement?" Forbes.com.

5. Pfeffer, J. (1998). *The Human Equation: Building Profits by Putting People First*. Boston, Massachusetts: Harvard Business School Press.

6. Moore, T. 2011. "Investing in the '100 Best' Beats the Market, Hands Down." CNN/Money Online.

7. Sirota Consulting, LLC. (2003). Unpublished analysis of the relationship between employee satisfaction and defect rates of the Credit and Risk Group of a large financial institution.

8. See, for example, Rucci, A. J., Kirn, S. P., and Quinn, R. T. (1998). "The Employee-Customer-Profit Chain at Sears." *Harvard Business Review*, *(76)*, 82–97.

9. Smith, S. B., Del Duco, S. M., and Mischkind. L. A. "The Impact of Social/Cultural Factors on Tornado Warning Performance." Presented at the Society for Industrial and Organizational Psychology 18th Annual Conference, Orlando, Florida (April 12, 2003).

10. Boehm, J. K., Lyubomirsky, S. (2008). "Does Happiness Promote Career Success?" *Journal of Career Assessment*. 16, 101.

11. Crowley, M. C. February 22, 2013. "The Proof Is in the Profits: America's Happiest Companies Make More Money." Fast Company website.

12. For example, see Simon, D., Gomez, M. I., McLaughlin, E. W., and Wittink, D. R. (2009). "Employee Attitudes, Customer Satisfaction, and Sales Performance: Assessing the Linkages in US Grocery Stores." *Managerial & Decision Economics, 30,* 27–41; Eskildsen, J. J., and Dahlgaard, J. J. (2000). A causal model for employee satisfaction. *Total Quality Management, 11,* 1081–1094; Maister, D. H. (2001). *Practice What You Preach.* The Free Press: New York; Oliver, J. (1998, March 1). "Invest in People and Improve Profitability and Productivity." Retrieved from www.managementtoday.co.uk/news/411393/; Ostroff, C. (1992). "The Relationship Between Satisfaction, Attitudes, and Performance: An Organizational Level Analysis." *Journal of Applied Psychology, 77,* 963–974; Schneider, B., Hanges, P. J., Smith, D. B., and Salvaggio, A. N. (2003). "Which Comes First: Employee Attitudes or Organizational Financial and Market Performance?" *Journal of Applied Psychology, 88,* 836–851. Black and Scherbaum. April 2007. "Exploring Financial and Managerial Determinants of Employee Engagement." Accepted and presented at the 2007 Society for Industrial and Organizational Psychology Annual Conference.

13. For example, see Reichheld, F. F. (2001). *Loyalty Rules! How Today's Leaders Build Lasting Relationships.* Boston, Massachusetts: Harvard Business School Press; Reichheld, F. F. (1996). *The Loyalty Effect.* Boston, Massachusetts: Harvard Business School Press.

Part II

Chapter 3

1. Sloan, A. (1996, February 26). "Jobs—The Hit Men." *Newsweek,* page 44.

2. Reichheld, F. F. (1996). *The Loyalty Effect*. Boston, Massachusetts: Harvard Business School Press.

3. Pfeffer, J. (1998). *The Human Equation: Building Profits by Putting People First*. Boston, Massachusetts: Harvard Business School Press.

4. Cascio, W. (1993). "Downsizing: What Do We Know? What Lessons Have We Learned?" *Academy of Management Executive*. 7(1), 95–104; Lehrer, S. (1997). "Effectively Coping with Downsizing." *The Government Accountants Journal*. p. 12–13; Cascio, W. F., Young, C. E., and Morris, J. R. (1997). "Financial Consequences of Employment-Change Decisions in Major U.S. Corporations." *Academy of Management Journal*, 40(5), 1175–1189; Hitt, M., Keats, B., Harback, H., and Nixon, R. (1994). "Rightsizing: Building and Maintaining Strategic Leadership and Long-Term Competitiveness." *Organizational Dynamics, 23(2)*, 18–32.

5. Thurow, L (2001, March 21). "Worst News on Layoffs Lies Ahead." *USA Today*, p. 15A.

6. Sharplin, A. D. "The Lincoln Electric Company. Case Study," in: G. A. Steiner, J. B. Miner, and E. R. Gray. *Management Policy and Strategy: Text, Readings, and Cases*. Macmillan, New York, 1982, pp. 958–980.

7. Iverson, K. "How Nucor Works." *New Steel*. November 1997. As cited in *Plain Talk: Lessons from a Business Maverick*, by Nucor Chairman Ken Iverson, with Tom Varian. John Wiley & Sons, Inc. New York.

8. Kiger, J., Hansel, J., March 12, 2009. "Mayo Says No Layoffs Are Planned." PostBulletin.com.

9. *Fortune*. 2002. "100 Best Companies to Work For" report.

10. Ibid.

11. Business for Social Responsibility (2001). *Downsizing: Layoffs/Closings*. Retrieved from www.bsr.org.

12. As reported on WKPRC. See Click2Houston.com. "Thousands Furloughed at Continental Airlines—International Layoffs Still to Come." Posted: 1:13 P.M. CDT, September 21, 2001.

Chapter 4

1. Levine, D. I. (1992). "Can Wage Increases Pay for Themselves? Tests with a Production Function." *Economic Journal, 102,* 1102–1115. Royal Economic Society.

2. Pfeffer, J. *The Human Equation.* Boston: Harvard Business School Press. 1998, p. 200.

3. Harbour Report, 2006.

4. Abowd, Kramarz and Moreau. "Product Quality and Worker Quality," NBER Working Paper # w5077, 4/95; "Policy Brief—Prevailing Wage Laws." January 7, 2000; found at www.lbo.state.oh.us.

5. Clark, Kenneth and Miriam (1996). Choosing to Lead. Center for Creative Leadership, pages 58-59.

6. Zimmerman, Ann. May 18, 2011. "Costco's Dilemma: Be Kind to Its Workers, or Wall Street?" In HireCentrix.

7. Shapiro, N. December 15, 2004. "Company for the People." SeattleWeekly.com.

8. Coleman-Lochner, Lauren. August 2006. "Wal-Mart Stores to Increase Starting Pay Rates (Update3)." Bloomberg.

9. ADP Research Institute. 2012. 2012 Study of Large Employer Health Benefits Benchmarks for Companies with 1,000+ Employees. APD.com/Research.

10. Greenhouse and Barbaro. October, 2005. Wal-Mart Memo Suggests Ways to Cut Employee Benefit Costs. New York Times online.

11. Carmichael, Evan. "Respect Can Reel in Greater Returns." Evancarmichael.com.

12. Hellriegel and Slocum, 2010. "Organizational Behavior," South-Western Cengage Learning, p. 389.

13. Kagarise, Warren. 2011. "Jim Sinegal to Retire as Costco CEO." Issaquahpress.com.

14. Lawler III, E. E (1998). "Lawler in Strategic Pay." *The Journal of the Minerals, Metals and Materials Society, 50, 11*, pages 57, 80.

15. Whyte, W. F. *Money and Motivation: An Analysis of Incentives in Industry*. New York: Harper and Row. 1955, pp. 41–44.

16. Our norm for attitudes on the fairness and accuracy of appraisals is 70 percent.

17. Lawler III, E. E. (1992). *The Ultimate Advantage*. San Francisco, CA: Jossey-Bass, page 177.

18. Lawler III, E. E (1998). "Lawler in Strategic Pay." *The Journal of the Minerals, Metals and Materials Society, 50,11*, page 125.

19. Protsik, J. (1996). History of Teacher Pay and Incentive Reforms." *Journal of School Leadership, 6*, 285–286.

20. Springer, Matthew G., Ballou, Dale, Hamilton, Laura, Le, Vi-Nhuan, Lockwood, J. R., McCaffrey, Daniel F., Pepper, Matthew, and Stecher, Brian M. 2010. "Teacher Pay for Performance: Experimental Evidence from the Project on Incentives in Teaching." RAND Corporation.

21. Odden, A. (2000). "New and Better Forms of Teacher Compensation Are Possible." Phi Delta Kappan. January: p. 1.

Chapter 5

1. The S&P/Case-Shiller National Home Price Index.

2. PWC Report. 2010. Health and Well-Being Touchstone Survey.

3. PBS Newsmaker Interview Air Date: October 26, 2011. Between Jerry Brown (host) and Bob King (UAW president).

4. Thomas Kaplan. August 16, 2011. "State Employees' Union Accepts Wage and Benefits Concessions." *The New York Times* online.

5. Towers Watson. 2010. Global Workforce Study.

6. Gallup Consulting Report. 2010. State of the American Workplace: 2008–2010.

7. Aon Hewitt. 2012. Trends in Global Employee Engagement Study.

8. Deal, Stawiski, and Gentry. 2010. "Employee Engagement: Has It Been a Bull Market?" Center for Creative Leadership. Greensboro, North Carolina.

9. Robert Half. 2010. "Workplace Redefined: Shifting Generational Attitudes During Economic Change."

10. Some studies did find a morale improvement, but we found in a review of their research that they were not comparable to the research we have cited. For example, Boston Consulting Group in a 2010 report said that "employee engagement suffered during the past two years because of layoffs and other cutbacks." But, as far as we can tell, this was from a survey of executives, not employees. What executives believe employees feel does not normally tell us very much about what employees actually feel. [Boston Consulting Group, Creating People Advantage (2010).]

11. Ross Douthat's column. 10/1/2010. *The New York Times* online.

12. Brownstein, R. September 28, 2012. "Struggling to Advance." *National* Journal.

13. Towers Watson. 2010. Global Workforce Study. For additional research data supporting the flight to preservation hypothesis, see:MetLife. 2011. 9th Annual Survey Study of Employee Benefits Trends a Blueprint for the New Benefits Economy; Randstad Workmonitor. May–June 2012. Global Press Report. Trade Job Security.

14. Steve Nyce. February 2012. "American Workers Seek More Security in Retirement and Health Plans." *Towers Watson Insider*, Volume 22, Number 2.

15. *Towers Watson*. 2011. Retirement Attitudes Survey.

Chapter 6

1. Kilborn, P. T. "Strikers at American Airlines Say the Objective Is Respect." *New York Times* (November 22, 1993): A1, A8.

2. Witness, for example, the characterization of Kathryn Jones in her March 2001 *Texas Monthly* "Biz" column, *American Flyer*: "Crandall was the hot-tempered, cutthroat CEO who built Fort Worth–based American into an industry juggernaut by the sheer force of his competitive thirst for blood. Nicknames like Fang and Darth Vader stuck for good reason."

3. American Airlines was reported to have begun, after Robert Crandall left the company, a major initiative in its relationship with its employees, seeking a true "partnership"—rather than adversarial—relationship with them. "A Profile: American Airlines changes its business operation to move on workers' ideas." National Public Radio, *All Things Considered*, September 13, 2004.

4. See *The Nordstrom Way: The Inside Story of America's #1 Customer Service Company* by Robert Spector and Patrick D. McCarthy. Also see Peters, Tom. *Thriving on Chaos*. Knopf, 1987, pp. 378–379.

5. Peters, T. J. and Austin, N.A. *A Passion for Excellence*. New York: Warner Books, 1985, p. 207.

6. Caudron, S. "The New Status Symbols." *Industry Week*. 248, no. 12, June 21, 1999, p.44.

7. Peters, Tom. *Thriving on Chaos*. New York: Knopf, 1987, p. 381.

8. We say "typically," because there are numerous variations on these practices for salaried employees. For example, in some organizations, a salaried employee can lose pay if he is absent beyond an allotted number of "sick" or "personal" days. Also, certain salaried employees—those whose work resembles that of hourly workers—are not exempted from the legal requirement to be paid overtime. Furthermore, we do not address the legal distinction between exempt and non-exempt workers. Although the U.S. fair labor laws tend to speak to the same kind of status distinction that we describe, the law's purpose is to protect workers from owners who might otherwise impose harsh compensation rules based on arbitrary time restrictions and definitions. Here, we are concerned with the effect of maintaining wage status distinctions on the culture of the employment environment and, hence, on worker enthusiasm.

9. President's message (Roger E. Benson). November 1999 (PEF web page).

10. Taken from the *Sirota Consulting* handbook.

11. Muoio, A. "The Truth Is, The Truth Hurts." *Fast Company Magazine*. April 1998, Issue 14, p. 98.

12. A full treatment of Stack's philosophy can be found in: Stack, J. and Burlingham, B. *The Great Game of Business*. New York: Doubleday and Company. 1994.

13. Peters, T. J., Waterman, R. H. Jr. (1982), *In Search of Excellence*. New York: Harper Row.

14. Sherman, Scott. "Stability: Donald Graham's Washington Post." *Columbia Journalism Review*. May/June 2002.

Part III

Chapter 7

1. The correlations range from .389 (pride in efficiency) to as much as .644 (pride in products and services).

2. Collins, J. C., and Porras, J. I. (1994). *Built to Last*. New York: Harper Collins.

3. In their calculation, all dividends were reinvested and appropriate adjustments were made when the companies became available on the stock exchange.

4. Collins, J. C., and Porras, J. I. (1994). *Built to Last*. New York: Harper Collins.

5. Ibid, p. 57.

6. Ibid, p. 57.

7. Collins, J. C., and Porras, J. I. (1994). *Built to Last*. New York: Harper Collins. Chapter 3.

8. Waddock, S. A. and Graves, S. B. "The Corporate Social Performance-Financial Performance Link." Strategic Management Journal. Vol. 18, No. 4, 1997 (p. 303–19).

9. Cited in Business for Social Responsibility Web site, White Paper, "Introduction to Corporate Social Responsibility."

10. Jeff Frooman. "Socially Irresponsible and Illegal Behavior and Shareholder Wealth." *Business and Society*. Vol. 36, No. 3, September 1997 (p. 221–249).

11. Ohnsman, A., Green, J., and Inoue, K. February 26, 2010. "Toyota Recall Crisis Said to Lie in Cost Cuts, Growth Ambitions." Bloomberg.com.

12. LeBeau, Phil. November 26, 2012. "Toyota Is Back. Can It Stay on Top." GlobalPost.com.

13. *Knowledge at Wharton*. 2/15/2012. "Patients Versus Profits at Johnson & Johnson: Has the Company Lost Its Way?" http://knowledge.wharton.upenn.edu/article.cfm?articleid=2943.

14. Smith, G., March 14, 2012, Op-Ed. *The New York Times*.

15. "O'Neill Looks to Repeat Alcoa Success at Treasury," Leslie Wayne, *New York Times Service*, January 17, 2001.

16. Vogel, David. "Recycling Corporate Responsibility." *The Wall Street Journal*. August 29, 2002 (in *Manager's Journal*).

17. Kahaner, Larry. "How Their Mission Statement Helped Johnson & Johnson Survive the Tylenol Crisis." www.kahaner.com, excerpted from Jones and Kahaner, *Say It & Live It: 50 Corporate Mission Statements That Hit the Mark*, First Edition. Currency Books, May 1, 1995.

18. The Malcolm Baldrige National Quality Award was created by Public Law 100–107, signed into law on August 20, 1987. The Award Program, which is responsive to the purposes of Public Law 100–107, led to the creation of a new public-private partnership. Principal support for the program comes from the Foundation for the Malcolm Baldrige National Quality Award, which was established in 1988.

19. Hude, Hal. "Quality in the Service Sector, Proceedings of the 1991 Making Statistics More Effective in Schools of Business (MSMESB)," The Wharton School, Univ. of Penn., 1991; See also Frederick Smith. "Customer Satisfaction: A Job That's Never Really Done." J.D. Power & Associates Customer Service Conference, November 13, 2003, Santa Monica, California.

20. Singhal, V. R. May 10, 2002. "TQM Significantly Boosts Bottom Line." *EFQM Excellence One Magazine*.

Chapter 8

1. For a sophisticated defense of hierarchy, see Jacques, Elliott. (1990). "In Praise of Hierarchy," *Harvard Business Review*, January 1990, 127–133.

2. One of the best known and instructive investigations of the effects of different leadership styles was conducted in the 1930s by Lippitt and White. Known as "Leadership and Group Life," the study was conducted under the leadership of Kurt Lewin. The study involved directing groups of school children in the production of arts and crafts artifacts in four different clubs. They had three types of leaders assigned to them: 1) autocratic: aloof, used orders, no consultation with group; 2) democratic: offered guidance, encouraged group participation; 3) laissez-faire: gave knowledge but did not do much else. The results were that 1) authoritarian: two kinds of behavior: aggressive and apathetic. The aggressive kids were rebellious, demanding attention from the leader, and blaming each other when anything went wrong. Others were submissive. The group's productivity overall was higher than the democratic group, but the quality was much poorer. 2) democratic: morale high; group members friendly; good relationship with leader; when leader left room, operated independently; fair amount of originality; and, although they produced less than the authoritarian group, the quality of production was much higher; 3) laissez-faire: was worst group with poorest productivity and quality; lowest morale; most demands placed on leader; least independent work; and, least cooperation. See Lewin, K., Lippit, R., and White, R. K. "Pattern of Aggressive Behavior in Experimentally Created Social Climate." *Journal of Social Psychology*, 10 (1939): 271–299.

3. Lawler. *The Ultimate Advantage* (p. 33).

4. Morse, John J., and Lorsch, Jay W. *Harvard Business Review*. May 1970.

5. Pfeffer, J. (1994). "Competitive Advantage Through People." Harvard Business School, 43.

6. Peters, T. (1987). *Thriving on Chaos*. New York: Alfred A. Knopf. 291.

7. Excerpted from Tom Peters Company website.

8. Tomasko, Robert M. *Downsizing: Reshaping the Corporation for the Future*. Amacom. 1987.

9. Derived from Drucker. *The Practice of Management*; Peters. *Thriving on Chaos* (p. 359); and Lawler. *The Ultimate Advantage* (p. 62).

10. For research evidence on SMTs, see Manz and Sims. *Business Without Bosses: How Self-Managing Teams Are Building High- Performing Companies*; Orsburn, J. D., Moran, L., Musselwhite, E., and Zenger, J. H. Self-Directed Work Teams. Homewood, Illinois: Business One Irwin, 1990; Katzenbach and Smith's (1992); Katzenbach, J. R. and D. K. Smith. *The Wisdom of Teams: Creating a High Performance Organization*. Boston: Harvard Business School Press, 1992; Yeatts and Hyton, C. *High-Performing Self-Managed Work Teams: A Comparison of Theory to Practice*. Sage Publications Inc. 1998.

11. "I'd be the first to agree that if the performance level of (these) self-directed work teams were close to that of Toyota, then it would be worth sacrificing a little performance to have more fun at work—but it's not close; it's not even in the ballpark." Interview with Dr. Paul Adler, Prof. at USC, by David Creeman, on HR.com, May 14, 2001.

12. Milkman, R. (1997). *Farewell to the Factory: Auto Workers in the Late Twentieth Century*. Berkeley, California: University of California Press.

13. The Profit Professionals of Business Solutions—The Positive Way. www.profitpro.us/profit__ideas.htm; see also the federal government's *User's Guide to Successful Suggestion Programs, the Interagency Advisory Group Committee on Performance Management and Recognition, Suggestion Program Working Group, Office of Personnel Management* (1995 Edition).

14. Katzenbach, J. R., and Smith, D. K. (1992). *The Wisdom of Teams: Creating a High Performance Organization.* Boston: Harvard Business School Press; Fandt, P. (1991). "The Relationship of Accountability and Interdependent Behavior to Enhancing Team Consequences." *Group and Organization Studies*, 16(3), 300–312.

15. Clemmer, J. (1995). *Pathways to Performance: A Guide to Transforming Yourself, Your Team, and Your Organization.* Toronto: Macmillan Canada.

16. Allen, Thomas J. (1995). *Information Technology and the Corporation of the 1990s: Research Studies.* Oxford University Press, New York; Allen, Thomas J. (1984). Managing the Flow of Technology: Technology Transfer and the Dissemination of Technological Information Within the R&D Organization. Cambridge, MA: MIT Press. A Literature Review on Challenges of Virtual Team's Leadership. *HosseinGazor Journal of Sociological Research* ISSN 1948-5468 2012, Vol. 3, No. 2.

17. Miller, C. C., and Perlroth, R. March 5, 2013. "Yahoo Says New Policy Is Meant to Raise Morale." *The New York Times* online.

18. Miller, C. C., and Rampell, C. February 26, 2013. "Yahoo Orders Home Workers Back to the Office." *The New York Times* online.

19. *Business Insider.* "How Marissa Mayer Figured Out Work-At-Home Yahoos Were Slacking Off." Nicholas Carlson. March 2, 2013.

20. Noonan, M. C., and Glass, J. L. (2012). "The Hard Truth About Telecommuting." MonthlyLaborReview, 2012(6), 38–45.

21. Gajendran, R., and Harrison, D. A. (2007). "The Good, The Bad, and the Unknown About Telecommuting: Meta-Analysis of Psychological Mediators and Individual Consequences." *Journal of Applied Psychology*, Vol. 92, No. 6.

Chapter 9

1. Keep in mind that we are discussing *job* satisfaction, not *overall* satisfaction. These two terms are easily confused. The latter is the global concept: how, *in general*, people feel about their employment situation—their "morale," as it were. Overall satisfaction is the product of a number of specific factors, such as attitudes toward job security, pay, leadership, ability to get the job done, and the work itself. The last of these—attitudes toward the work itself—is "job satisfaction," and it is just one of the specific factors that go into overall satisfaction. It is distinguishable from those factors, as in, "I wish I could stay here because I really love the kind of work I do, but I can't live on what they pay me."

2. As described in Peters, T. J. *On the Nature of Work*. May 7, 1993; found at www.tompeters.com.

3. Employees also prefer managers who stress quality. The correlations between managers being seen as stressing quality and satisfaction with those managers are in the .70s. The correlations between managers stressing quantity and satisfaction with them are slightly negative.

4. Sirota, D. and Greenwood, J. M. "Understand Your Overseas Work Force." *Harvard Business Review*. 1971, pp. 53–60.

Chapter 10

1. For an overview of the research, see Hellervik, L. W., Hazucha, J. F., and Schneider, R. J. (1990). "Behavior Change: Models, Methods, and Review of Evidence. In M. D. Dunnette and L. M. Hough (2nd ed.), *Handbook of Industrial and Organizational Psychology* (pp. 823–895). Palo Alto, California: Consulting Psychologists Press.

2. Employees who are inordinately sensitive to criticism need a lot of attention, praise, and reassurance. The guidelines we propose should be followed quite literally with them to keep a difficult situation psychologically from getting even worse.

3. Lepsinger, R., and Lucia, A. D. (1997). *The Art and Science of 360° Feedback*. San Francisco, California: Jossey-Bass; Sederburg, M. E., and Rogelberg, S. G. (1998). "Informed Decisions: Research-Based Practice Notes 360 Degree Feedback: Methodological Advice from Multiple Sources." *The Industrial-Organizational Psychologist, 36,* 67–76.

4. See, for example, Smith, G. P. (November 2001). *Here Today, Here Tomorrow: Transforming Your Workforce from High-Turnover to High-Retention*. Chicago, Illinois: Dearborn Publishing. Smith prescribes praise over cash when it comes to retaining "the best and brightest." "People have a basic human need to feel appreciated, and recognition programs help meet that need," notes Smith. "Money might attract people to the front door, but something else has to keep them from going out the back." Also, see Bob Nelson, writing in the *Quality Digest*: "Salary raises and bonuses are nice, but they seldom motivate people to do their best on the job on an ongoing basis.... Having learned that employees are motivated by intangible rewards, companies would be wise to consider the power and possibilities of no-cost job recognition when trying to motivate employees to do their best." Nelson, B. (2004). "Secrets of Successful

Employee Recognition." *Quality Digest, QCI International.* Retrieved from www.qualitydigest.com.

5. Collins, J. C. and Porras, J. I. *Built to Last.* New York: Harper Business Books. 1997.

6. *Built to Last.* supra (p. 173).

Part IV

Chapter 11

1. Among the more interesting explorations of "social capital" and its importance is Don Cohen's and Laurence Prusak's *In Good Company: How Social Capital Makes Organizations Work* (Harvard Business School Press, 2001).

2. Elton Mayo. *The Social Problems of an Industrial Civilization.* New Hampshire: Ayer. 1945 (p. 111).

3. See Hill, G.W. "Group Versus Individual Performance: Are N+1 Heads Better Than One?" *Psychological Bulletin.* May 1982 (p. 535). See also Morgan, John, and Blinder, Alan. "Are Two Heads Better Than One: An Experimental Analysis of Individual Versus Group Decision Making." National Bureau of Economic Research. September 2000, No. 7909.

Part V

Chapter 12

1. Alice Ross, "Boarding Houses," *Journal of Antiques and Collectibles*, March 2003.

2. U.S. Department of Labor, Bureau of Labor Statistics, Mass Layoff Statistics (MLS), www.bls.gov/mls/home.htm.

3. Farber, H., and Krueger. A. "Union Membership in the United States: The Decline Continues." Working Paper No. 4216, National Bureau of Economic Research, 1992. These conclusions were reached on the basis of an analysis that controlled for the effects of structural changes in the economy, such as the increasing proportion of service workers.

4. Katz, Harry C., Kochan, Thomas A., and Weber, Mark A. "Assessing the Effects of Industrial Relations Systems and Effort to Improve the Quality of Working Life on Organizational Effectiveness." *Academy of Management Journal* 28 (1085): 519; Ichniowski, Casey. "The Effects of Grievance Activity on Productivity." *Industrial Relations Review* 40, 1986: (p. 75–89).

5. See, for example, Adler, Paul S. "The 'Learning Bureaucracy': New United Motor Manufacturing, Inc." *Research in Organizational Behavior* 15, 1992: 120; George W. Bohlander and Marshall H. Campbell. "Problem-Solving Bargaining and Work Redesign: Magma Copper's Labor-Management Partnership." *National Productivity Review* 12; Russell Eckel, Paula Falzon Eckel, and Andrew Herman. "Lean Manufacturing, Worker Empowerment and Labor-Management Collaboration at Ford Cleveland Engine Plant #2."

6. Gittell, Jody Hoffer. *The Southwest Airlines Way: Using the Power of Relationships to Achieve High Performance*. McGraw-Hill, 2003.

7. Ibid.

8. Gittell, Jody Hoffer. *The Southwest Airlines Way: Using the Power of Relationships to Achieve High Performance*. McGraw-Hill, 2003, p. 183.

9. *Sirota Monthly*, 2010.

10. The Dartmouth Atlas of Healthcare.

11. As quoted in: Byrne, John A. and Weber, Joseph. (1997) "Did CEO Dunlap save Scott Paper—or just pretty it up?" Business-Week Archives, copyright Bloomberg LP.

Chapter 13

1. Excerpted from *The Ethics of Charismatic Leadership* by Jane M. Howell and Bruce J. Avolio, Academy of Management Executives, 1992, Vol. 6, No. 2; *The Charismatic Leader as Narcissist* by Daniel Sankowsky, *Organizational Dynamics*, Spring 1995, Vol. 23, No. 4; "Why Charismatic Leaders Are Not Always the Answer." Dr. Mike Rugg-Gunn. On Human Development International website, 2011.

2. Collins, J.C. (2001) *Good to Great*. New York: Harper Business Books. Chapter 2, p. 26–27.

3. David Sirota (2001). "Observations on Mayor Giuliani's Leadership in the Wake of 9/11." Sirota Survey Intelligence.

4. Crosby, Philip B. *Quality Is Free*. New York: New American Library, 1979; Juran, Joseph M. *Quality Control Handbook*. 4th ed. New York: McGraw-Hill, 1988.

Chapter 14

1. "At Continental, Morale Is Everything." *Human Capital: Strategies and News* (no date found, after 1998).

2. Goldstein, A. P., and Sorcher, M. *Changing Supervisory Behavior*. Pergamon Press, New York, 1974.

3. The "360" technique described in Chapter 10 is also an effective way to provide feedback to managers on their own behavior. Here managers receive data from a number of sources, not just their employees.

Index